Atlantic Ocean

San Juan
PUERTO RICO
DOMINICAN REPUBLIC
HAITI
FEDERATION
TRINIDAD
Paramaribo
Cayenne
George-town
GUIANAS
BR.
DU.
FR.
EQUATOR
Caracas
VENEZUELA
Belém
Recife
Cartagena
Santarém
Salvador (Bahia)
Medellín
Bogotá
COLOMBIA
Manaus
Amazon R.
BRAZIL
Porto Velho
Anapolis
Brasilias
Belo Horizonte
Quito
ECUADOR
Iquitos
Rio de Janeiro
Beni R.
Riberalta
São Paulo
BOLIVIA
Campo Grande
PERU
Lima
Cuzco
Lake Titicaca
La Paz
Puno
Cochabamba
Arequipa
Santa Cruz
Sucre
PARAGUAY
Asunción
Iquique
Salta
URUGUAY
Montevideo
Córdoba
Buenos Aires
CHILE
ARGENTINA
Valparaiso
Santiago
Temuco
Pacific Ocean
N

NEW HORIZONS IN LATIN AMERICA

Other books by John J. Considine

AFRICA, WORLD OF NEW MEN

ACROSS A WORLD

CALL FOR FORTY THOUSAND

WHEN THE SORGHUM WAS HIGH

NEW HORIZONS IN LATIN AMERICA

By JOHN J. CONSIDINE

ILLUSTRATED WITH PHOTOGRAPHS

DODD, MEAD & COMPANY
NEW YORK
1958

Library of Congress Catalog Card Number: 58-13081

Printed in the United States of America
by The Cornwall Press, Inc., Cornwall, N. Y.

The author acknowledges valuable assistance from several score of collaborators in the accumulation of the material in this book. He desires to recognize in particular the data received from Reverend Prudencio Damboriena, S.J., of the Department of Missiology of the Pontifical Gregorian University, Rome.

Introduction

The Road to the Real Latin America

Not so long ago—remember?—Latin American crowds threw rocks at Vice-President Nixon. What relation, if any, have these pages to those events?

They have no direct relation. Yet in a modest way this book may contribute toward reaching the understanding that is the key to the unhappy incidents. The flying rocks were but the end product of a long process of slow deterioration that had gone on for years in Latin America, unknown to U.S. citizens.

Riding one afternoon with a Peruvian friend through Lima we passed the United States Embassy. "There," he commented with a sly twinkle in his eye, "is the present seat of the Peruvian government."

"I suppose a lot of joking of that sort goes on here," I observed.

"Unfortunately it has become more than joking," my friend replied. "The men from Washington here are merely dutifully carrying out control provisions in the lend-lease act or in other fiscal relations with us voted by your Congress. But this is all seen locally as interference. You hear comments such as, 'Just because they've loaned us their confounded money they think they can tell us how to run our country.' "

This is the first of half a dozen factors that contribute to the bad relations between the United States and Latin American peoples. This first one we might call *the busybody Uncle Sam factor,* that accumulation of mild irritants that have entered on the scene as the unfortunate backwash from our very commendable desire to lend a helping hand to less affluent nations everywhere including Latin America.

We have no desire to be busybodies. But can we discover the secret for avoiding the charge? Everyone who has carried responsibility anywhere in the world, whether in a government, or a university, or a business enterprise, or in a religious organization, understands how difficult it is to take initiative in any complex situation in which the human equation looms large without being accused of being a busybody.

A second factor in the U.S. unpopularity picture may be called *the dictator factor.* This is two-pronged; we accuse the Latin American of being soft on dictators; the Latin American accuses the U.S. of being soft on dictators.

Many a U.S. citizen is disdainful of one or other Latin American nation because it possesses such a notoriously bad government. The superficial view is that the people deserve bad government if they are stupid enough to put it in power. We haven't realized how much the Latin peoples hate dictators.

"Why don't you get rid of your dictators?" I heard an unwise young American say to a group of university students.

"Get rid of them!" cried one of the students, "If you North Americans would stop maintaining them in power we might have a chance."

The fact is, all Latin America today seethes with hostility toward dictatorial governments though this does not remove them from the scene. In every walk of life, including ecclesiastical circles, anger and indignation prevails against dictators.

An Argentinian priest visiting in Mexico during the days of peace between Peron and the Church remarked to a clerical confrere, "Here in Mexico you enjoy the blessed aftermath of a persecution; in Argentina we suffer the disgrace of peace." It was an open secret that large numbers of clerics and lay people in Argentina were unhappy because the Church accepted favors arbitrarily granted by President Peron. When finally Peron, angered by the coolness of Churchmen, launched a persecution in November 1954, an Argentinian remarked to me, "Wonderful! Nothing else matters now so far as the Church in Argentina is concerned. What a stain it would have been on the pages of history if Peron had come and gone and the Church was recorded as having bowed in subjection to the blandishments of the dictator."

"The Latin American peoples are ripe for democracy," states former President Jose Figueres of Costa Rica, "They have heard so much for such a long time about representative government, free elections, respect for the dignity of man, division of governmental powers, and all that goes with the democratic creed, that you could no more erase those political aspirations than you could eradicate the Christian faith."

The hostility against the United States in several Latin American countries but particularly in Venezuela stems from the charge that we have coddled the dictators. While the rebellion was forming against President Perez Jimenez in Venezuela, Washington went out of its way to decorate Perez with the U.S. Legion of Merit and to show him other favors. In Argentina, Colombia and Cuba and other lands to the south the feeling is, regardless of the practical impossibility of U.S. intervention, that the American government helped maintain dictators in power against the people.

A third factor creating hostility to the United States is born of the strange turn of events in Latin America that gives our land the label of *Uncle Sam the wealth destroyer.* Astounding as it may seem, our country is currently regarded not as the great benefactor to Latin American production enterprises but as the major source of economic harm. Latin America is a producer of basic commodities of metals, of coffee, of sugar and similar products that are the football of world trade.

As in Asia and Africa, Latin American mines and plantations may turn in a splendid operational job only to have their year's output made worthless by a chill breeze in the world market that destroys the crop or metal prices.

Uncle Sam to many a Latin American is Mr. World Market. It is Uncle Sam, therefore, who lately has visited so much misery on Latin America's owners and workers by the slump in the commodity market which results in two things—first, we buy less, secondly, we pay a lower price for what we buy. True, this second point is but the application of the inexorable law of supply and demand. But, the Latin American says, the U.S. overcomes this law at home by fixed prices that save the American farmer. The Latin Americans, rightly or wrongly (and indeed the Asians and Africans) call for fixed world prices in commodities.

In friendly fashion but quite emphatically, our spokesmen, including Dr. Milton Eisenhower, have made it clear that any hope of workable fixed world commodity prices is very dim. Well-wishers of Latin

America urge the area to employ an economic federation in some form that will render as much protection as possible in this field.

Another lament of Latinos is that the United States government tries to force L.A. nations to let U.S. oil interests work the local oil though in Argentina, Brazil and other lands there is an almost fanatical hostility to permitting the nation's natural wealth to get into the hands of foreigners. Oil-possessing nations feel that we should permit the local governments to borrow our money to develop their oil. "You make loans for railroads, for docks, for industry," writes the Brazilian editor Hernane Tavares de Sà, "Why can't you make a loan to our government oil company? Can't you understand we want to exploit our oil ourselves? To everybody in Brazil, it looks like oil companies are dictating your Government policy."

Mr. John Foster Dulles during his cordial conversation with President Kubitschek in the summer of 1958 made it clear that the U.S. would continue to support Brazil's fine development plans with public and private loans for power, transport and communications but could not help set up a government-operated oil company. This was a job, he said, for private enterprise.

A fourth factor in the anti-U.S. picture is the *human want factor*. The gaunt truth is, the great mass of Latin Americans live in abject poverty. "Half of us Latin Americans have never slept in a bed," comments a Latino, "have never had enough to eat, have never seen the inside of a school room." Conditions are improving but not fast enough and Latin Americans feel that we provide very little help. Only \$1. out of every \$36. voted by Congress in 1958 for foreign aid went to Latin America. Here is where the Communists come in. Poverty is a ready sauce for every Communist pudding. The Reds are few in Latin America but they have had a field day because it is their clever manipulating that has stirred mobs of thousands to action against the U.S., principally with the cry that we callously leave the L.A. masses in rags and hunger and support the local despots who grind down the poor.

The fifth factor grows out of this fourth. We may call it *the disdained-poor-relation factor*. For twenty years, so the argument goes, the U.S. has taken Latin Americans for granted. "As Christians they can't go over to the Reds even if they don't like us," we are charged with saying, "Don't waste money or attentions on them." Lately this our reputed attitude toward them—borne out by a great deal of evidence—has prompted the Latins to whip themselves into a frenzy of resentment.

Our government is convinced that much more can be done to provide a meeting of minds through frequent consultation among high officials of North and Latin America. "If we take Latin American opinion into account fully," says a State Department spokesman, "we will be on the way to a happier relationship with the other American republics."

The sixth factor applies to the Catholic sector in the United States population. It may be called *the U.S. Catholic indifference factor.* Hardly another single factor would contribute more to assuaging the current irritation than the removal of this incomprehension of Latin American Catholics by North American Catholics. I have encountered strong disappointment with North American Catholics among Latin American clergymen who have visited the United States.

An Argentinian Passionist remarked to me, "At times in U.S. rectories I found myself in a fury at the bleakly ignorant statements levelled at me regarding my homeland and the Church in Argentina and regarding life in other parts of Latin America."

A Colombian Jesuit friend who had studied in a U.S. college said to me one day in Bogota, "What is there in the U.S. Catholic that makes him, despite his lamentable ignorance of South American ways and religious traditions, assume the role of the Eternal Father himself in tendering us unsolicited advice as to what we must do to lift ourselves out of our shame? Heaven knows we need help but why not offer it to us not as our masters but as our brothers?"

Frankly, I, for one was shocked to learn of such irritation against U.S. Catholics and particularly the U.S. clergy. Certainly we know very little about Latin America but so far as dispositions are concerned we are more than ready to stand shoulder to shoulder with our harassed co-religionists south of the border. Perhaps there is need for a better coordinated and more ably directed plan to achieve such cooperation.

Contents

SECTION FIVE: ***Vignettes of Middle America***

Illustrations

Following page 78

Forward March!—Joaquin Blanquero walks six miles along the railroad track every morning from his father's farm in the country and is never late for class at Santo Tomas Parochial School in Temuco, Central Chile.

A better world—Among Brazil's laity are thousands keenly aware of their country's social problems. A Grail team nurse in São Paulo makes a house to house visitation aimed at serving the great city's needy families.

Blessed milk—Fathers Keenan and Callahan of the American Redemptorists in Paraguay bless UNICEF milk served to their 2,000 school children.

Chilean boys drink U. S. surplus milk from Catholic Relief Service.

Schools—San Marcos University, Lima, is the oldest in the hemisphere. The young men in the picture aim to be paleontologists.

Maryknoll Sisters teach at Lima's first parochial school, named after Lima's beloved St. Rose.

The Andean Corridor—This wild plateau country is beautiful in a harsh, desolate way. Hardy cattle, horses, donkeys and sheep are part of every landscape. The llama, alpaca and vicuña belong to the upper mountains.

House with windows—The Christ Schools in Bolivia hold a better homes contest in Coipasi. Windows are introduced into the adobe walls of an Indian home.

Indian housewives try out the modern flatiron.

Wild rubber—Father Joseph Flynn of Cleveland examines a shipment of 300 pound balls of wild rubber, the latex gathered drop by drop

from jungle trees, ready to journey from Bolivia down the Amazon to New York.

Holiday in the country—Fiesta time in Panama calls for happy excursions to rural villas where placid oxen substitute for the modern automobile. The women folk wear the beautiful Panamanian costume, the pollera, of white cambric richly ornamented with brightly embroidered flowers, birds and garlands.

Sick call—Bishop Charles Brown, a native New Yorker, journeying as a Maryknoll Missioner into the Bolivian mountains to a dying Indian.

Indian teachers—Expressionless but deeply earnest, these men train in Azangaro as religion teachers for the villages of Peru's altiplano.

Perfect poise—The Guatemalan market woman carries her basket on her head with the same aplomb that the American housewife carries her bag on her arm. Guatemalan dress is notable for its lovely color combinations.

Younger set—Natty looking Ecuadorian student nurses get a lesson in nutrition at their Quito training school.

A lively chat between the girls at Colegio Monte Maria of the Maryknoll Sisters in Guatemala.

Cardinal's theatre—The cultural theatre of Monsignor Salcedo's radio schools in Colombia is named after Cardinal Crisanto Luque of Bogota. Over 6500 radio schools bring learning and religion to the mountaineers.

Benignity—The Mayans dwell today in Yucatan (southern Mexico) and in Guatemala. Many a Mayan grandmother is the guide and mentor of a houseful of hacienda children who love her for her kindly warmth and devotion.

Young Christians—A Havana matron is sponsor for an infant receiving baptism from Father John McKniff of the Augustinians.

Father George Hogan of Maryknoll gives First Communion to a youngster in Peto, Yucatan.

Mary had a little lamb—as cute as it could be. She brought it to school with her one day. Tommy didn't approve. Thus boys in the Bolivian Pando have the same problems with girls as everywhere else in the world.

NEW HORIZONS IN LATIN AMERICA

SECTION ONE

Brazil, the Colossus

• • ● • •

Chapter 1

Dona Salette and Her People

A LARGE BUSH of vivid poinsettias flourished in the yard of the vacant property next door. Beside the flowers stood a mango tree heavy with fruit. As Father Miles and I gazed out the window of the friary of the American Conventuals on the outskirts of Rio a small boy climbed over the iron fence in front of the next-door property and threw stones at the mangoes. Then, his arms full of his green burden, he dexterously worked himself back to the street.

"He's probably from one of the favelas," observed Father Miles. "Those mangoes will figure in the next meal."

"I'd like to run along with him and see how he lives," I remarked to Father Miles.

High above us on the cliff-like hills that rose behind the friary stood several favelas, the notorious shack towns of squatters that harbor a fifth of the three million people who live in the capital city of Brazil. There are one hundred and twenty favelas in all, and five of these are within St. Francis of Assisi Parish with its teeming thousands of lower class *cariocas,* the nickname for the citizens of Rio de Janeiro.

Recently Cardinal Camara, the lovable and affable spiritual father of Rio, preached a mission in St. Francis of Assisi Church and told its people that they belonged to the model parish of the city. Surely the Conventuals have succeeded extraordinarily well in maintaining in its life all the warmth and devotion that the Brazilian loves so much, at the same time introducing here the characteristics of North American Catholic life that serve so well to provide a framework of discipline and a foundation of strong instruction for modern living.

"Our parochial grade school and high school are the first such schools of their kind in Rio," a parishioner told me with great pride. "For long we were the talk of the city."

I celebrated the seven o'clock Mass on Sunday morning and was struck by the well cadenced responses of the congregation as it participated in the *Missa Recitata.* Silvio Dias, who holds a responsible post in the Banco do Brasil, was the able leader of the congregational prayer. Silvio and his wife were among the several hundred who went to Communion.

"The Cardinal has a great love for simple people such as live in this quarter," explained Father Sixtus, "I remember a sick call he insisted on taking while here. It was to a crowded building of one-room apartments where people in some ways are worse off than in the favelas. These desperately poor folk merely stared glumly at His Eminence; it meant nothing to them that he was in their building, though they knew the role of the priest in the presence of death. But for the zealous Cardinal it was a soul-warming experience because it brought him into touch once again with the hidden core of crude poverty that lies at the heart of this seemingly brilliant city."

One afternoon Fathers Sixtus and Miles took me in a rickety automobile up the steep road to the San Carlos Favela. The view of the city and of the harbor far below was breathtaking. Rio de Janeiro is one of the most strikingly beautiful cities in the world. It was established originally on the knobby ribs of the coastal mountains that all but rise out of the Atlantic Ocean. The old, unhealthful, unimproved Portuguese city that reminded one of an overgrown rural village is today a superb modern metropolis. Rows of fine docks border the bay and now, far below us, extended like fingers into the gleaming waters. Along the margin of the water a stone seawall has been built, with a wide tree-lined avenue between it and the first row of buildings. People who live along the waterfront can on almost any day of the year run down from their apartments in their bathing suits and plunge into the surf. All that the world offers in luxury residences is to be had in the Copacabana District and similar areas. At one end of the famous Avenida Rio Branco is the downtown business section with its mounting pile of skyscrapers.

Not all of Rio is beautiful, however. A periphery of some thirty hills forms an edging between the city proper and the background of green forest-clad mountains and bare rocky cliffs. On these hills cling the favelas. San Carlos, where we now were, is typical. Sardonically, it is built about a huge tower that furnishes much of the water supply for the lavish homes of Copacabana.

We stopped at the Catholic Social Center, one of eight operated in the favelas of the city, the San Carlos center serving not one but three favelas, a total of more than 21,000 people.

A vital young lady with sparkling eyes and evidently possessed of tremendous energy came out to greet us.

"This is Dona Salette, the directress of the Center," announced Father Sixtus in Portuguese as he introduced me. "She is one of our hopefuls," he continued to me in English. "She is twenty-seven years old, the third to occupy the post but the first to make an outstanding success of it. She was born and brought up here in the San Carlos Favela; her family occupied a shack on land just a few yards from where the Center now stands. She is one of our best arguments that lots of wonderful people are hidden away in these places."

"How did you discover her?" I asked.

"When the Center was about to open she applied for a job as teacher. She was then nineteen. She later became secretary and now she is directress. She is married to a man named Boa Vista and they have a child and live in the better neighborhood at the foot of the small mountain on which San Carlos is perched. Her husband does not like her to work here in this wretchedness."

"How does Dona Salette feel about it?" I asked.

"Father asks how you feel about continuing to work here in San Carlos," repeated the priest to her with a smile.

"These are my people, Padre," she replied, turning to me. "I have always been here. I love to help the young and the old, the sick and the well. And I think they all like me very much. I am very happy here."

Dona Salette, I soon recognized, possessed a natural ability to be a leader. Under her worked a staff of twenty-five—sixteen teachers, five social visitors and four nurses.

"We are in the course of taking a census," she explained. "Results thus far show that a thousand families are legally married either religiously or civilly and two thousand are without legal wedlock, either religious or civil."

"How much real poverty do you find here?" I asked.

"Less than ten per cent have what they need in food and clothing. Most houses are one room plus a cubbyhole for a kitchen. They are made of matchwood with tin roofs. Sometimes as many as four families, as many as twenty people, live in a single house. For water there are a dozen spigots at various spots through the settlement to take care of 20,000 people. Drawing the water is a major operation in a place like this."

"Take a look at the spigot here at the corner," Father Miles suggested.

It was not drawing time and therefore no one was carrying off water when we approached. Instead, there was a huge line-up of over sixty empty oil tins with handles, the standard equipment for the water carrying operation.

"By thus placing their tin in line these people establish their turn for getting to the spigot during the hours when the water is turned on," explained Father Miles. "Position is important because sometimes the water runs dry and the tail-enders lose out. Touching another man's water can is as serious as moving a man's stakes used to be during the gold rush days in the American West. There's been many a knife fight over the place in that line. Men have been killed in squabbles about a can of water."

There is nothing but open sewage throughout the favela, giving off strong and sickening odors.

"Some half of the houses have a properly constructed latrine," explained Father Miles. "The rest serve nature as best they can. Someone in every neighborhood has a hook-up for electricity and barters with those about him for the right to an outlet. Cooking fuel is charcoal for those who can buy it, while collected bits of wood serve the rest. Beans and rice are the standard diet."

Dona Salette showed us the schools. They work in shifts, as indeed many a school in the United States is now forced to operate.

"Attendance at school is not compulsory," Dona explained. "Hence only the rare parents with ambition see to it that their youngsters report. There are four years of school and we have also a weaving class."

At the Catholic Center I met the four women teachers. The first was a wan and worn lady whose whole appearance seemed to cry out, "I am very old." The second was a haggard lady, likewise well along. The third and fourth possessed a bloom and bespoke youth and energy. The teacher of the weaving class was an Austrian lady who knew a little English and bore herself in a manner that bespoke a past of better days. "The children do wonderfully well," she said. "Stores in Rio take the products of our looms; Sears Roebuck has bought from us."

The classes this particular afternoon counted from twelve to twenty each, boys and girls who, if I judged rightly from our few fleeting minutes with them, were not exactly delighted to be confined within school walls but who showed intelligence and, I ventured to guess, would be among the minority who would burst the bars of their childhood prison of poverty and rise to something better than life in a favela.

"I want you to visit the homes of some of my friends," said Dona Salette.

First we passed the police station, a fortress-like unit with the police embattled on the second floor. About it are a cluster of shops. We took an untidy lane and as we trudged along Dona Salette saluted everybody with easy familiarity.

She met a youngster. "Antonio, you weren't at school this morning. You have an exam next Monday."

A moment later we passed a housewife working in her yard. "Dona Lucia, Joaquin has an exam next Monday."

"Thank you, Dona Salette; I'll make him prepare."

We wound down past some ugly shacks and picked our way into one. Three boys sat in the single room that was thoroughly filthy, a crude bed in a corner, a very dirty stove in another, everything grim and repulsive.

"Where's mother?"

"She's out working."

We crossed the yard to another hut. A tiny dog barked shrilly at us but a Negro boy grabbed him and made a vice over his mouth with his fingers.

"Where's mama?" asked Dona.

The youngster called and his mother appeared, pale and coughing. Evidently her damp-ridden house, that got none of the glorious sun that showers the hillside, was getting the better of her. The house was unkempt. She had four children; the boy in the yard was the eldest, while second and third formed equal steps down to the fourth, a wispy mite in a cradle.

"Sometimes my man comes home, sometimes he doesn't," the mother remarked laconically.

"These are the typical houses," explained Dona Salette, "Now we'll see some of the exceptions."

We turned sharply to the right and went down some long winding steps lined with banana plants. I sensed immediately a new atmosphere. Everything was neatly in place. Dona picked the wooden lock on a gate and we entered a very neat yard. A tall man of very erect carriage walked toward us, a quiet, kindly smile on his face.

"Good afternoon, Don Ribeira," greeted Dona Salette and, introducing me, Dona explained, "Padre, one of Don Ribeira's daughters married my brother."

"Don Ribeira," added Father Miles, "is a Spaniard from Galicia who came here with his wife penniless and has raised up a family of three sons and three daughters, all very presentable persons. We are going to visit Julia Ribeira who is married to Dona Salette's brother, Wilson Mathias."

To my astonishment, the home, a new three-room cottage, was immaculate, with parquet floors, plastered walls, painted trim in tasteful hues, and pictures ornamenting each room. One was a good print of the Agony in the Garden. There was a neat dining room table while a sideboard contained a quantity of sparkling cut glass. Off the dining room was an attractively arranged bedroom.

The young couple was on hand to greet us. They were married but eight months and it was clear that they were still under the glow of the wonderful experience of possessing this lovely home. Julia was a fair-skinned Spaniard with shy haunting eyes, a sweet person hardly meant for a tough neighborhood. Wilson was four years younger than Dona Salette, a tall, mannerly boy who evidently has dreams. She was with child. Why, I puzzled to myself, are they content to stay in a favela?

"You must meet my two sisters, Agnes and Sonya," Julia proposed after the animated talk-fest about her dining room table.

We journeyed further along the pathway to another attractive house and met Dona Agnes. Here we were made to sit. Dona Agnes brought in a carafe of ice water and poured each of us a sparkling tumbler full.

"Is it filtered water?" I whispered to Father Miles with the instinct of a traveler. To my embarrassment he passed on the question to Dona Agnes.

"No," she replied with a deeply injured look, "Perhaps he is afraid it is not clean."

"Not at all," I rejoined in distress and took a long quaff from the glass. Imagine spoiling these few precious moments with these wonderful people by hurting their feelings!

"Dona Agnes," announced Dona Salette at this juncture, "is to be the president of the Sodality of the Apostleship of Prayer that we are organizing in San Carlos. We already have forty-four members."

Dona Agnes beamed brightly and forgot my slur about the water.

We visited another attractive household in this elite neighborhood of San Carlos. This last family was Portuguese. One of the daughters was nursing a darling babe but ten days old.

"What is its name?" asked Father Miles.

"Sandra."

"A pretty name," he observed. "Is she baptized?"

Immediately all became vague. Indeed, as it developed, the references to the father likewise were vague.

"The real difficulty regarding baptism," Father Miles explained later, "is the money for the feast that these people by local custom feel they must give for all the friends and neighbors on such an occasion."

Sandra's proud grandma served us a delicious Portuguese wine in tiny liqueur glasses and Sandra's mother stood at the door and waved us a fond farewell as we moved up the path. The odors in the open gutters were quite as strong and unpleasant as before but now they seemed to be much less important. Crude as a favela may be, I decided, many real people live within its confines.

"Marijuana gangs and other lawless groups are found in these slum areas," commented Father Sixtus as if reading my thoughts, "but the people as a whole are not a criminal class. Rather, they are simple folk, many just new from the country districts and not given to violence in any extreme form."

"Why doesn't Brazil clean up its favelas?" I asked.

Because, I found, the favela problem at the moment is too big for Brazil. The land occupied by these people is either governmental or private. Brazil can't afford the tens of millions of cruzeiros needed to build 100,000 homes. It hasn't the power to force these people into legally established neighborhoods.

At the outbreak of World War II a piece of ground owned by a German company was expropriated by Brazil. Squatters were permitted to settle on it. By the time postwar negotiations were completed for the return of the land to the German owners, 15,000 people had established themselves on it in a favela. The government posted a notice that the fifteen thousand should move in two weeks. The fifteen thousand read the signs and quietly went on as usual, probably exchanging a sly wink or two among themselves. What Brazilian government would dare throw fifteen thousand people out of their homes? They are still on the land.

Dona Salette, the hardy little lady, smiled happily when I told her how proud she could feel about the fine work she was doing for her people. The two priests had to stay for work at the Center so Dona called Fabriano, a quiet little twelve-year-old, to lead me through the wilderness of swirling, dipping paths and precipitous steps back to the outside world.

Fabriano was very attentive. He picked the course with care, pointing out every pipe that I might trip over, every broken pavement, every sudden gully that I must step around. Only the youngsters shrilling for a *santo* (a holy card) tried to distract me. True, I did find moments for brief glimpses out over the glorious waters of the bay, beyond which the sun was setting.

We dropped quickly down among the encrustments of shabby

houses. Finally a wide thoroughfare appeared. We had reached the borders of another world, the world of the accepted.

"Goodbye, Fabriano! Many thanks, my boy," was my salute as I pressed some cruzeiros into his hand.

"Goodbye, Padre," Fabriano replied, his face as expressionless as an Indian brave's. He turned immediately and with alacrity started back up the cliff-like hillside. Why should he hesitate? For him the favela was home.

That evening on the porch of the friary I gazed at the huge Christ of Corcovado, thrillingly bright in the flood of electric light that pours upon the celebrated statue high above Rio. I thought of my new acquaintances on the hills behind me, shrouded in darkness. The many fine people who dwelt in favelas were included, I now knew, in the embrace of the gentle Jesus whose arms I could see extended in the night over the city.

Chapter 2

From Cabral to Tomorrow

LUIS COSTA, one of Brazil's leading architects, was called upon to design the High Altar for the International Eucharistic Congress held in Rio de Janeiro in 1955. It was a mammoth structure, 450 feet in width, elevated 40 feet on an artificial mound of earth that permitted all the ceremonies to be clearly visible to the quarter of a million and more who gathered in the vast Congress Plaza in downtown Rio.

Most distinctive, however, were the covering and side wings of the altar which the architect designed to represent an ancient caravel sailing into the harbor. The effect was marvelous. A great mast with full rigging towered skyward, and the lofty unfurled sail, billowed by Atlantic breezes, carried the coat of arms in gold of the Holy See.

"It could well have been one of the pioneer ships out of Portugal captained by Pedro Alvarez Cabral," explained a Brazilian friend.

Cabral is very much in the mind of many Brazilians, even though he made history over 450 years ago. And then it was not by sailing into the harbor of Rio de Janeiro.

On March 9, 1500, ten proud caravels and three transport ships put to sea from the Tagus River, the harbor of Lisbon, under the captaincy of Pedro Alvarez Cabral. The expedition aimed to establish Portuguese settlements in the newly entered land of India, far to the east of Africa on the recently opened ocean route to South Asia. Accidentally, it was also to link Portugal with the New World.

By the treaty of Tordesillas, entered into in 1494 by Spain and Portugal with the Holy See acting as umpire, the eastern portion of South America was to be colonized by Portugal. Cabral, however, was to have had nothing to do with that continent. After stopping at the

Canary Islands he set sail for India, but in order to avoid the dreadful calms—or doldrums off the African coast, he turned far out into the Atlantic.

So far out that five weeks later Cabral saw plants and seaweed floating on the ocean. Soon the fleet found a harbor on what is now the Brazilian coast near Bahia, a harbor that Cabral named Porto Seguro. There were sixteen missionaries in the expedition and their leader, Father Henry of Coimbra, a Franciscan, on April 26, 1500, celebrated the first Mass on South American soil. A superb painting in the national gallery in Rio commemorates the event and an imposing monument on a piazza in Rio gives Father Henry of Coimbra a place among the great in Brazil though he stayed but eight days on Brazilian soil and then sailed off with Pedro Alvarez Cabral to far-away India.

Today only the Soviet Union, China and Canada possess more territory than Brazil. The country is the size of the United States plus an extra Texas, the size of Europe minus the Scandinavian Peninsula. Its population of 55,000,000 represents more than a third of the inhabitants of Latin America, much more than half of the inhabitants of South America. While even today no political division on earth contains so much unused employable land, yet it is one of the faster growing areas of the globe. It is not among the wealthier nations of the earth or among the more powerful but it is certainly among the major nations of the Western world. Since in the 1950 census some fifty million of its population declared themselves Catholic, it can properly describe itself as the largest Catholic nation in the world.

The eighteenth century brought the flood of gold and diamonds in Brazil's Minas Gerais Province and in the nineteenth century came coffee. Coffee planting began around Rio but soon São Paulo State held the primacy. After 1850 most of the European immigrants went to the new coffee lands of São Paulo with a resulting distinctive population in this area. Coffee brought wealth to São Paulo and Paulista enterprise turned São Paulo and its environs into the leading center of manufacturing in all Latin America.

Brazil, completely separated from Spanish America, was not involved in the joint struggle for independence that rocked the Spanish world during the half century from the late 1700s through the early 1800s. Nevertheless, under the strangest of all circumstances it became free. Prince John of Portugal fled to Brazil when Napoleon conquered the Iberian Peninsula. In 1821 when he returned to Lisbon he left his son Pedro as Governor of Brazil but advised him to throw in his lot with the colonists if the independence movement grew; thus he would keep Brazil in the family. Pedro did just that.

We have the spectacle of a revolutionary meeting in São Paulo, before which the royal successor to the Portuguese crown appears. To the astonishment of the crowd the prince royal tears the Portuguese colors from his uniform and shouts, "The time is here—independence or death!" Pedro was declared Emperor Pedro I of Brazil. He was not popular and did not rule long but his son, born in Brazil, succeeded him and ruled as Pedro II until he was overthrown in 1889 and royalty was abandoned for a republic. Thus Brazil is one of the youngest republics in the Western Hemisphere.

The rule of Pedro II was marked by grave setbacks for the Catholic Church in Brazil, reverses that explain in part the handicaps from which the religion of Brazil's majority of citizens is only now freeing itself.

Padre Serafim Leite, one of Brazil's historians, tells us that Brazil was born Christian. Certainly there was a Christian impress on the events that unfolded through the several centuries of Brazil's development as a nation. Father Jose de Anchieta, S.J., who reached Brazil in 1553, became known as the Apostle of America and headed a line of outstanding missionary leaders whose influence reached deeply into the cultural as well as the spiritual life of the nation. The priest was the first schoolmaster of Brazil and the Indian, insofar as he was reached for good, was approached through that amazingly relentless penetration that Euclides da Cunha describes as "the slow tread of the missionary." The priest promoted as well the mass conversion of the Negro millions, that dishonored race brought in shackles from Africa.

"For almost three centuries," explains Fernando de Azevedo, "the history of culture in Brazil was intimately bound to the history of missions. The church and the school had a place so close together in colonial life that no Indian village, no town or city within the sphere of missionary action was without not only its place of worship but its classroom where boys could learn to read and write."[1] As early as 1578 the Jesuits were examining young men at their college in Bahia for master of arts degrees.

Throughout the seventeenth and eighteenth centuries laymen with keen interest in religion, and clergy with strong interest in everything that had to do with the life of Brazil mingled in common concerns to constitute the social elite of the country. Azevedo cites thirty-two representatives of the clergy who were prominent participants in the Revolution of 1817. There was a natural union of Church and state that was strongly social and that eventually led to the undoing of the Church.

Brazilian historians trace this to the rise of Freemasonry. Freemasonry, which had its start in London in 1717, reached France in 1725 and Portugal in 1735. It was well established in Brazil by the end of the eighteenth century. Various Popes from Clement XII, in 1738, to Leo XIII, in 1884, condemned its secret nature and its improper penetration of the spiritual; nevertheless it attracted many Catholics of Brazil who were impressed by the dignity and sumptuousness of its ritual, by the social and humanitarian doctrines it professed and principally by the political goals it set for itself in the new world.

"Its religious tolerance and its political aims—the independence of Brazil, the destruction of the monarchy, the republican ideas," states Azevedo, "permitted Freemasonry to win over to its secret societies, along with civilian and military leaders, Churchmen and friars as well. . . . Prominent figures of the diocesan and regular clergy . . . some of the greatest sacred orators at the time of the Empire, enlisted in Masonic lodges, all thirty-third degree Masons. There was no Masonic lodge in which there did not figure, side by side with civilians, some liberal wearers of the cassock, fighting for the same ideals and participating in their rites and activities."[2]

This was the setting for the nineteenth century struggle between religious and political forces that Azevedo describes as "the major conflict of our history." The critical years of the struggle were from 1872 to 1875. The Bishop of Rio de Janeiro in 1872 suspended a priest for refusing to abjure Masonry. The Bishops of Olinda and Para supported the Bishop of Rio. The lodges of Brazil were called upon to undertake an offensive against the episcopacy. The growing preeminence of the civil authority over the ecclesiastical became the nub of the controversy from the Church's point of view. The Bishops of Olinda and Para issued an interdict against religious communities which refused to punish priestly members who continued as Masons. The Freemasons appealed to Pedro II who declared the interdict lifted. The two Bishops refused to obey the government's order against the interdict, were tried and convicted as rebellious and were sent to prison.

This struggle shook public opinion to the depths and separated as they had never been separated before in Brazil the secular elements from all those genuinely interested in a healthy spiritual life in the nation.

Freedom of the Church from control of the secular arm finally came with the establishment of the republic in 1889. The legislation, however, resulted not wholly from a desire to befriend the Church. New currents of thought—Auguste Comte's Positivism and the secularist movement—advocated indifference to religion and the neutrality of the state (which often meant the hostility of the state) in religious matters. "Let's wash our hands of the whole idea of religion," was the sentiment of these groups. Nonetheless the Bishops of Brazil in their pastoral of March 19, 1890, noted that the Church had secured "a certain sum of liberties which she had never succeeded in obtaining during the time of the monarchy."

Despite this gain, the Church had lost heavily by the end of the nineteenth century. The spirit of the clergy had suffered, vocations had dropped to a trickle, the life of devotion of the Catholic masses had been sadly neglected.

But, as in all Latin America, the twentieth century has witnessed an upward swing for the Church in Brazil. Beginning in the 1920s a renewal of vitality began that Azevedo characterizes as "the most vigorous Catholic movement of our history." This does not mean that this eminent sociologist wishes to classify the religious life of Brazil's Catholic millions as strong in every respect. Rather, it has experienced a marked advance from its previous position of weakness.

Here are five points of improvement in the Church's position in Brazil:

New penetration of the living forces of Brazilian society

In the colonial period Christianity "belonged" so far as Brazilian life was concerned. After the strife of the nineteenth century the Church was completely disassociated from great currents in the life of the nation. Recent decades have witnessed a moderate swing of the pendulum back toward concern for Christian thinking and respect for Christian thinkers. An eminent intellectual, Jackson de Figueiredo, began the Catholic spiritual movement and gained it prestige through the fact that he was one of Brazil's major essayists. On his death in 1928, Alceu Amoroso Lima became the most notable Catholic in the literary field.

Lima was converted from indifferentism in 1932 and, in addition to his unquestioned greatness as a writer, possesses genuine religious zeal. He is professor at the Catholic University of Rio and a follower of Maritain. The power of such a man lies in his influence on other men of action. Lima is credited with bringing back to religious practice Carlos Lacerda, the fearless crusader who uncovered the corruption in the Vargas regime. Lacerda is currently a very popular radio commentator and presents himself to the public as a declared Catholic.

Brazil's literature now counts a measure of fine works that are Catholic in spirit, some the product of ecclesiastics such as Father Leonel Franca, S.J. A great deal more is from the pens of laymen who no longer hesitate to dwell on spiritual themes in a Christian way.

Catholic schools in Brazil today number 2,900 and have an enrollment of 450,000. The Catholic Education Association is headed by Padre Artur Alonso, S.J., a clear-eyed, level-headed administrator who has done an excellent job in strengthening the Catholic educational institutions of the nation. A major aim is better teachers. Catholic normal schools total 252 in the country and have trained 65 per cent of the teachers of Brazil. In the single government teaching union, 85 per cent of the membership is Catholic. Protestant teachers for the most part combine with the Catholic and thus the antireligious extremists are a tiny minority.

Over 80 per cent of the secondary school students in Brazil are in private schools, with almost half this enrollment in Catholic establishments. The Jesuits, Benedictines and Marists are the largest educators of young men.

"Brazil's greatest need is a greater number of teachers thoroughly grounded in educational principles," Padre Alonso explained to me. "The teacher must understand the role of cultural subjects in making men and the role of sociology and economics in making modern men."

Catholic women's colleges in Brazil in many respects dominate their field. An awareness of the need to train women leaders is abroad in these schools. The readiness to be self-critical is refreshing. "Brazilian girls are even more generous hearted than are those of my native France," explained Mother Marie de l'Eucharistie of the Santa Ursula College of Philosophy in Rio, "but they often lack conviction through want of spiritual training and discipline. Too often we accept them for their heart and neglect to put religious principles in their heads and thus we are to a degree responsible for their inadequate religious concepts. However, we've made tremendous progress in the past twenty years."

American Holy Cross Sisters from Notre Dame have a college outside São Paulo. "The Brazilian girl is a very lovable person," one of them explained, "though sometimes she lacks the drive that we find in the U.S. girl. When a youngster is soft it comes from too much coddling by overfond parents. Most São Paulo parents, though, want their children to be thoroughly educated young ladies."

Father Corbeil, the Canadian head of Holy Cross College in São Paulo, testifies to this desire of many parents for thoroughgoing educational standards. "There is a certain Catholic elite in Brazil," explains Father Corbeil, "that is superior in culture, religious and otherwise, to our Catholic elite in the United States and Canada. They rank with the best in the Catholic world. Though educational advances have been great in the past quarter of a century, much of it has been merely quantitative. I greatly admire this minority that insists on the very best in quality."

What of the parochial school? "To our pleas for parochial schools," observes Father John Baptist of St. Francis of Assisi Preparatory College in Anapolis, "the Brazilians reply that they are too costly and quite unnecessary since religion may be taught in the state schools. Greatest problem, perhaps, is lack of appreciation of Catholic grade school education by a clergy that has never experienced its benefits."

In the state of Rio Grande do Sul, in the far south of Brazil, the now prosperous offspring of European immigrants have organized the best system of parochial schools in all Latin America. Brazil as a whole, however, is without such a system.

"Government grade school life without religious instruction is our greatest single weakness in Brazil," declares Father Corbeil. "The fault rests entirely with us Catholics. The law permits religious instruction for the majority religion of every school but the opportunity goes unemployed through our inability to provide religion teachers."

A broad Catholic social program

A recent writer in *America* made the observation, "The influence of the Church in Brazil has never in recent years been as widespread as it is today and much of this influence must be ascribed to the present activity in social welfare measures." Catholic strength in this field stems from the old Portuguese institution, the Santa Casa de Misericordia, a Catholic charities activity for the aged, the orphans and similar needy groups. The contemporary social welfare movement generally is Catholic in its thinking, thanks in great part to the fact that twelve out of eighteen social welfare schools in Brazil are Catholic.

The Archdiocese of Rio de Janeiro has a contract with the government to handle its local social action program. Professional personnel provides for the major operations but many of the parishes play their role. The Church of the Sacred Heart in the Gloria district of downtown Rio offers an example of a well organized social center. In a large stone building it has a movie and conference hall. A dispensary is attended by four doctors, each of whom donates one afternoon a week, while medical specialists in the parish have an agreement with the pastor to receive from him one free patient per day. A trained social service worker coordinates her work with the doctors. The parish Boy Scouts (called in Brazil the Bandeirantes) and the parish Girl Scouts each have quarters. In addition, the national headquarters of the Girl Scouts of Brazil is on this parish property.

Not everywhere are Catholics so well equipped for the task but priests, Sisters and dedicated lay folk throughout Brazil have made a crusade of traditional Catholic charity and modern social welfare. The country possesses over 1,100 Catholic social and charitable institutions.

Frequently one encounters Catholic enterprises that are entirely lay in operation. At the headquarters of the Federation of Christian Families in São Paulo, an organization counting over 3,000 families in the São Paulo area alone, the young lady secretary explained to Father Sheehan and me, "Our group has no priest connected with it. We are all Catholics but the Federation is not a religious association. As our prospectus states, it is a social and civil institution directed by Christian principles." The Federation's program well represents Christian principles in action: (1) legal assistance to families, for which the Federation retains lawyers; (2) economic cooperation, particularly through cooperatives; (3) social and recreational activities—family reunions, excursions, entertainments, music and arts, sports, operation of choral and dramatic groups.

Aggressive Christian campaigning

Since World War I, Azevedo explains, a new spirit has prevailed among Brazilian Catholics. "They came out of the churches and convents to take positions in the trenches, and the trench was everywhere, in parliament, in the government bureaus, in the press and radio, in the schools and youth associations."

Campaigns, partially successful, have had to do with religious education in the state schools. Others have been directed against divorce and in favor of current moral programs. JOC, the Young Catholic Workers' Movement, had its South American start in São Paulo in 1948 and now has nine full-time staff leaders in that area, eight in Rio, and more in other parts of the country. Often in the labor unions, for want of other organized Catholic groups, it is zealous JOC members who attempt to offset Communist operators.

"It is like David facing Goliath," explains Father Melancon. "The Red leaders are superior in age and experience. But our boys have become game fighters, sturdy and sure of themselves. Formation for action is our motto; we prepare well. The Reds would like very much to steal some of our men, and have offered them trips to Moscow."

Primacy of spiritual values in life, private and public, is the goal of the forward-looking elements in the Church who are behind this Christian campaigning.

A systematized apostolic movement

The International Eucharistic Congress in Rio in 1955 brought into new focus the movement in progress for years in Brazil to conquer spiritual ignorance and to promote organized Catholic devotion. Large-scale Christian instruction was one of the four key proposals of the Latin American hierarchy after its Rio meeting.

"Brazil would need a quarter of a million religion teachers to do a proper job of instruction among its fifty millions," exclaimed a prelate during a discussion of the subject.

"Don't forget," came the reply, "that we already have tens of thousands of zealous teachers, some of whom are doing magnificent work. Have courage; call for thousands more and soon we'll have enough."

This optimistic approach is getting results. Everywhere I went priests pointed out excellent lay cooperators, some of whom were quite extraordinary.

In Campo Grande I met Angela Giordani, the railroad catechist. She goes up the railroad to pueblo after pueblo teaching religion in towns that have no priest. As each class is ready she calls the pastor from Campo Grande, he holds the examination and the community has its First Communion festival. Angela's work grows more effective every year.

At Anapolis, in Goiás, I met Leander the shoemaker. He is the leader of six men in Padre Benedito's parish who give slide lectures on Christian doctrine to groups throughout the city. "These men are so good that people would listen to them every night of the year if they could," explained the Padre.

Everywhere the emphasis is on long-term, systematic conquest of the general state of ignorance.

"Strong impact on the Catholics of each given community is the secret of the revival of Christian fervor," explains Father Maerz, Provincial of the American Redemptorists in Mato Grosso. "The priest or missionary cannot afford to spread his effort too thin no matter how many the calls. We have watched it work here in Mato Grosso for 25 years and are enthusiastic about the results. The Brazilians are good spiritual stock. Millions of them are like plants without water; they are dried up from neglect. They respond marvelously when organized Catholic life is put within their reach."

A more numerous clergy

Brazil increased its clergy from 6,500 in 1946 to 8,000 in 1954. This is at the rate of less than 200 new priests a year, but, again, in view of its traditional parlous condition this improvement of 20 per cent in the total clergy is noteworthy.

Much more important is the new phenomenon in Brazilian life, the growing reappraisal of the priesthood by the Catholic body. "Twenty years ago when I was professed," explained a teaching Sister in Rio, "the average family in Brazil experienced a distinct sense of dread at the thought of having a son a priest. The nineteenth century disrepute into which the priesthood had fallen is now in great part dissipated."

"The factor still lacking in many parts of Brazil," explained Father Andrew, rector of the new Franciscan seminary in Goiás, "is the widespread, systematic presentation of the priesthood to Brazilian youth as a high vocation that challenges the ideals of the finest of the nation's young manhood. Brazil can have as many vocations as we have in the United States. In the U.S. we have 44,000 priests from among thirty million Catholics. This is nine times the ratio of Brazil. The fault lies in the lack of the priestly ideal among Brazil's youngsters."

"How are the Franciscans faring here in Goiás?"

"Remarkably well; after only eleven years we already have twenty candidates. Three are from the town of Catalão where a very apostolic schoolteacher, Dona Yolanda, has a great capacity for awakening fine ideals among the young men she teaches. Eighteen out of the twenty boys attribute their vocation to the influence of our Franciscan parochial schools. The Salesians in Brazil never lack vocations because they show great devotion to the youth in every neighborhood where they work."

One quiet evening in Campo Grande among the American Redemptorists of Mato Grosso we talked of vocations.

"In the very promising tomorrow that lies ahead for Brazil," one of the circle remarked, "the strongest single influence for vocations will be the admiration which the young Brazilian will conceive for the priest who sacrifices himself for his people. This influence is already at work in the country."

"Why do you feel so sure?" someone asked.

"Because I have a good example in Mario de Souza."

Then we heard the story of Mario. Mario's uncle was a cowboy who worked away from home and one evening while visiting his brother's family regaled Mario with tales of life on the cattle fazenda. Among other things the uncle told of the Fathers who rode horseback many days through the cattle country attending to the religious needs of the fazenda people, chatting with the cowboys, doing them many little good turns.

"They are wonderful men, Mario," remarked the uncle. "Some day when you grow up I hope you will be very good to other people the way they are."

The remark was unusual in view of local traditions about the priesthood, but it hit the target. Mario was inspired by the story and after a while wrote a letter to the nearest Redemptorist mission a hundred and fifty miles away saying that he wanted to meet a Redemptorist, that he wanted to be a priest.

One of the Fathers was making a tour of the back country and would touch a settlement some seventy-five miles from Mario's home. He wrote to the boy and told him to meet him if he could. The priest reached the settlement, handled his duties and was about to move on when a very weary but much excited teen-ager riding an old nag that was more bone than flesh pulled up at the door.

"Mario and the Father talked," the speaker explained. "It is now four years since they met and the youngster has put in four years as an exemplary student in our preparatory school."

"As I see it," the Padre concluded, "there's many another Mario in Brazil, waiting to be inspired by an example of fine accomplishment. There must be many bearers of the message like Mario's uncle and a great deal of effort by everybody to create a clean, healthy climate in which young fellows will be stirred by high ideals."

Chapter 3

Three Men in São Paulo

SUDDENLY ALL SEEMED as still as a pool in the woods. On every side in this quiet spot in the heart of the city was a potpourri of rather well-worn dwellings, Syrian and Turkish houses with quaint grilled windows, Swiss chalets, English Tudor houses, Spanish casas, Italian villas, an occasional old Portuguese colonial house.

And as suddenly we were back again in the mad vortex of modern São Paulo.

"That was a tiny bit of the São Paulo that was," remarked Father Sheehan, my American Oblate friend with whom I was riding. "Few cities in all South America have had immigrants from so many countries. The more prosperous ones in years gone by built homes to remind them of their homelands. But no more. Everyone today is decidedly Brazilian."

We were now in the famous Triangle district in downtown São Paulo. About us rose great business structures that suggested New York's Park Avenue. On the ridgetops of the city's high hills beyond stood plush apartment blocks. Then mile on mile of private homes. Finally the sprawling colonies that housed the factory workers. This was the Paulista metropolis with its two and a half million citizens, the urban miracle that is far in the lead of any other city in Brazil, stronger in commerce and industry than the slightly larger city of Rio.

Father Sheehan and I entered one of the modern buildings, a great department store, and went up by elevator to the offices of the president of the company with whom we were soon chatting.

"A wonderful place, São Paulo," I remarked to Senhor Isnard, as we were introduced.

"Tremendous!" he replied with the enthusiasm of a Texan. "We are growing at the rate of ten thousand a month—not enough light, not enough water, not enough roads, buses, policemen, firemen, not enough of the spiritual. But we are growing!"

"Are you a native Paulista, Senhor?" I asked.

"Decidedly so. Our family has conducted our department store here in São Paulo for a hundred years. In 1885, when the boom in coffee was launched in this area, São Paulo had but 35,000 inhabitants. We were in business before the boom and have grown with it from the beginning."

We had but to look about us to see the evidences of growth. The Isnard department store is a modern multifloored structure with hundreds of employees operating a multimillion dollar enterprise.

John Baptist Isnard was tall and well built, quietly dressed, easy in his manner. He is typical of the alert, aggressive men of the business world of São Paulo who remind North Americans so forcefully of similar circles in our own cities.

"The great migration to this part of Brazil began in the last quarter of the nineteenth century," explained Senhor Isnard. "Today São Paulo accounts for over forty per cent of the industrial output of all Brazil. During the nineteenth century our country moved away from the so-called gold-and-slave team of the colonial era and worked toward the coal-and-machine team of the modern world. In this type of operation, our São Paulo area has since 1910 run ahead of all the cities of all Latin America. We don't have coal but we have instead an abundance of electricity through water power."

"And everything started with coffee, did it not?" I suggested.

"Yes, coffee brought the first immigrants here and coffee profits gave us our first substantial capital. Too much coffee, curiously, gave us the manpower for our industrial plants; when the coffee market became glutted thousands of families left the plantations and moved to the city where they provided the plentiful labor force for our factories."

"Paulistas are famed for their readiness to adopt the very latest in new ideas," I commented.

"That's our reputation," replied Senhor Isnard. "We are quite deeply absorbed in the game of getting ahead. We are frequently compared with North Americans on this score and, I must confess, not always with the intention of paying us a compliment. Many of our fellow countrymen like to say that we are grossly material-minded."

"That is not what I have heard as regards your own activities, Senhor Isnard," I observed. The Isnard family is outstanding in São Paulo for solid Christian living; John Baptist is himself a daily communicant.

"Sometimes the exaggerations of our friends play tricks on us," Isnard replied.

"I think you deserve all that men say about you as regards your work for the laymen's retreat movement," I rejoined.

"Thank you!" this merchant prince answered with evident pleasure. "It is true that the retreat work gives me great satisfaction. Brazilians have religion in their hearts but not always very much in their heads. I know well the better class men and women of São Paulo and I appreciate them highly. I have long felt that as a group we have within us the capacity for many fine accomplishments if some way could be found to prepare stronger spiritual leaders. Hence my interest in the retreat movement.

"At first I felt very hesitant to mention the idea. I began bringing it up to companions at lunch and at social affairs. Many shied away from it of course, but a number took to it quite enthusiastically.

"We bought a piece of property at Barueri about thirty kilometers outside the city. It is charmingly located along the River Tiete but the original residence was poorly equipped. Among ourselves we raised some five million cruzeiros—about a hundred thousand dollars—and built a modern structure that we call the Pius XII Pavilion. This provides private rooms with individual toilet accommodations for forty retreatants and now everybody is delighted with the set-up."

"Who handles the operation?" I asked.

"It is all done right here in our offices," Isnard explained. "Let me show you."

We left the reception room where we had been chatting and went along the corridor to a small office. It was furnished very simply, a large chart on one of the walls catching our particular attention.

"This is the headquarters of the retreat movement," explained Isnard. "São Paulo's wonderfully zealous religious community dedicated to social service, the Missionary Sisters of Jesus Crucified, supplies one of its members as secretary and she comes to this office for several hours each day. This chart tells the story of how each year's activities are organized. As you will gather immediately, we plan something over forty week-end retreats each year and Sister handles all the arrangements."

I found myself absorbed with the entries that were fast claiming all the available facilities of the year. One week-end in the autumn was for married couples. A week-end in August was for bankers. Various groups of Isnard employees were listed for a total of six week-ends. Officers of Pirelli, the rubber goods manufacturer, had reserved a week-end.

"What type of schedule does the retreat master require of the participants?" I asked.

"It is passingly severe," Isnard replied. "Complete silence must be maintained during the entire period until Sunday evening. Each room contains only a bed, one chair and a *prie-dieu* and, while the retreatant may consult with the priest in charge, idle chatting in the rooms is not encouraged."

"Do you get any evidences of the after-effects?"

"Decidedly; they are a source of never-ending satisfaction. Characteristically, some men who accepted grudgingly the invitation to participate in a retreat have been so deeply impressed that they have insisted on rising at the last session to express their enthusiastic appreciation. Of greater importance is the quite complete conversion of life some people have experienced."

Father Sheehan and I let Senhor Isnard get back to his desk and shouldered our way through the shoppers with their bundles who crowded the store and the busy streets.

"That was an interesting experience," I commented, "a dry goods merchant whose greatest pleasure comes from his work for the laymen's retreat movement."

"I've got another fine gentleman for you," replied Father Sheehan, "a druggist who has built up a great pharmaceutical laboratory with 1,400 employees that is one of the model establishments in all Latin America for its Christian social welfare organization."

"Lead me to him," I cried.

São Paulo has 40,000 industrial plants. Most of these are small but a central core of 2,000 employ 350,000 people. Father Sheehan took me away from the center of the city out to the industrial suburb of Santo Amaro. A little searching brought us to a huge, modern block-long plant with an imposing façade, across which was spelled out the trade name of the corporation—"Laborterapica." "We are to be the guests here of Senhor Pires," Father Sheehan explained, "the creator of this very successful pharmaceutical establishment."

Senhor Jose Pires de Oliveira Dias was born in Campinas, a city a short distance north of São Paulo that at one time in the nineteenth century was larger than its now famous neighbor. Senhor Pires began as a pharmacist in Campinas but soon moved to São Paulo and operated a large retail drugstore. Next he became a wholesale distributor for drug manufacturers. Finally in 1934 he began his own manufacturing business and now operates this sizable plant that is among the largest in South America.

We were met by an earnest gentleman who introduced himself as Luis Lopes.

"I am the president of the Employees Association," Lopes explained. "Senhor Pires suggests that I show you through the plant until he can join us."

"Tell us something about what you do here," I suggested.

"Good!" said Lopes. "We make some eighty pharmaceutical products that are distributed by fourteen affiliates in Brazil and by twenty-two affiliates in other countries. Our products go to every part of Latin America."

"What are your specialties?"

"Our plant is new and thus we have come to specialize in the new drugs. We are strong in the production of insulin, vitamins and penicillin. I am going to show you first our penicillin laboratory."

We were not to enter this laboratory. Instead, we stood at a special window through which we could see a score of young women working inside. To protect them from the burning rays of the lamps that guarantee absolute asepsis, each woman wore a ghost-like white habit that covered her from head to foot and included a mask with fitted-in goggles.

"This is one of the Grade A penicillin units in the world," Luis explained with pride. "But we feel that every operation here is Grade A. The secret of Pires' success, as of course it is in all production of drugs, is thorough testing. Each month the plant manufactures 700,000 units of prepared pharmaceuticals and everything is carefully tested before it goes to the public."

Lopes opened a door and we found ourselves among cages containing hundreds of rabbits and white mice. Several young women were inoculating a meek little cluster of the latter.

"Today the staff is testing a deadly poison," noted Luis. "These little fellows will serve science by turning up their toes to prove that the drug has been properly made."

Rabbits nibbled blissfully at delicious-looking lettuce, awaiting their turn at the needle. Cute little fellows, I reflected as I watched them, whose glory goes unsung as they do guard duty that protects millions of Latin American lives.

"The young women who work in this entire section have special ratings," Luis observed. "They get extra lunches and shorter hours and particularly good salaries. They represent one of Senhor Pires' special triumphs in precision."

It was interesting to hear Lopes reiterate in various ways the working principles of the builder of this business in terms of the high qualities that the staff, the great majority of whom are women, are required to bring to its work to insure success. My curiosity was heightened to meet the man himself.

It was with keen satisfaction, therefore, that we finally sat down with him. He proved to be a quiet, thoughtful person, undramatic in his ways. Father Sheehan had told me previously that he was a pious man who, with his wife, went each morning to Mass and daily Communion.

"You seem to have a very fine body of helpers," I remarked.

"Yes," he replied in a low voice. He possessed a certain shy reticence. "They interest me very much. I worked for a living a long time myself. As a young man I used to think considerably of the human dignity that we should recognize in others."

Unusual words, I thought to myself.

"Evidently you've been very generous in dealing with your employees," I commented.

"The fact is, I used to give them a great deal. Then I found out how wrong I was."

"Wrong?"

"Yes. In 1951 I went to a series of lectures on Christian social principles. They changed my whole philosophy. I found out how wrong it was merely to hand out charity."

"What did you decide you should do?"

"I decided that paternalism is old-fashioned and unhealthy. I decided that at least in principle people should be allowed to pay for what they get, to feel that they are on their own and not beholden to anybody, certainly not to their employer."

"Just how did you do this?"

"I abolished all my practices of giving gifts. I instituted an Employees Association with officers chosen by the personnel as of right and approved by the company, likewise on the basis not of privilege but of right. These officers now are answerable to the personnel and to the company for eighteen divisions of individual or family assistance which is paid for jointly by the personnel and the company."

"In other words, you are no longer paying for various assistances as a charity to the employees but as a recognized condition of their employment."

"Correct."

"What are some of these assistances?"

"Let us go to lunch and I'll demonstrate one of them to you," answered Pires with a smile.

We entered a large dining hall simple in its furnishings but with attractively set tables, white tablecloths and napkins. Hired waitresses served everybody alike. The table at which we sat was identical with all the others and the food we ate, a substantial and tastily cooked meal, was the same served to the entire staff of 1,400 that day.

At table Senhor Pires was joined in the conversation by his eldest son and by a doctor who sat near us. The senior Pires sat quietly as his son explained the operations which, while now a couple of years in function, were still new and still somewhat experimental.

"The dining hall, you understand," said the younger Pires, "is operated not by the company but by the Employees Association. Last month, as the published financial statement shows, 250,000 cruzeiros were expended. Of this, the personnel paid 55,000 cruzeiros, a little more than twenty per cent. The company paid 195,000 cruzeiros."

"It seems a very fine arrangement," I observed.

"Yes, but there are still problems to solve," continued the son. "My father is an idealist. He wants the restaurant to do more than merely feed the staff. He wants a full meal served in a way that all may eat as family men and women should eat. Hence he is opposed to a catch-as-catch-can cafeteria style. The cafeteria would spare him a great deal of grumbling."

"What do you mean by that?"

"Well, a portion of the personnel, particularly the skilled staff, is accustomed to eating a meal fixed by a menu. But the poorer elements complain. Some who have no tablecloths at home think tablecloths are wasteful. Some who never have salad at home remark, 'Salad is for rabbits.' "

"The predicament puzzles me somewhat," the elder Pires observed with a laugh. "I don't want to impose anything that makes people uneasy. Yet I hesitate to agree to letting people take their food and bolt it down off in a corner as some might be inclined to do."

"I take it you are one of the company doctors," I remarked to the gentleman across the table from me.

"No," he replied with a smile, "I am engaged by the employees as well as by the company. Senhor Pires doesn't like the term 'company doctor.' There is a medical service in the home when the staff or their families are ill. There is as well a clinical service in the plant that provides prophylactic care to prevent tuberculosis and other diseases. Current medical practice, you know, emphasizes preventive medicine. The officers of the Employees Association are enthusiastic for this form of care but some among the personnel are impatient at our regime of periodical examinations."

"There are two full-time dentists who likewise provide periodical dental checks during working hours," explained the younger Pires. "The Employees Association has voted this but, again, many shy away from the requirement of facing the traditional horrors of a dental chair."

"People must have their freedom," remarked the elder Pires.

After lunch we visited the social welfare services and saw some darling little tots in the so-called *casa cuna,* the cradle house.

"Mothers bring their babes here each morning when they come to work," explained one of the welfare workers. "The Employees Association pays a bonus of a thousand cruzeiros to a couple each time a child is born. The company has a family wage plan which is graduated according to the number of children."

The Employees Association has the services of three full-time titled social assistants as supervisors of its three service departments, the Department of Health, the Department of Financial Assistance, and the Department of Recreation and Culture.

While "Laborterapica" is an unusually good example of the employment of social welfare techniques in industrial plants about São Paulo, the practice is quite widespread in other plants.

"Of the three hundred young women graduates of the Catholic Social Service School of São Paulo," explained Senhorita Colombo de Bartolo, assistant director of this largest social service school in the city, "a third are engaged by private organizations and some fifty of these are in industrial plants."

"Our problem," added one social assistant to whom I talked, "is the philosophy of the proprietors of these plants. Some of my companions have felt it best to give up their jobs in places where they are not sufficiently free to carry on for the workers. There are several semi-official organizations that tend toward a paternalistic approach to social welfare. Such organizations are the SESI, representing industry, the SESC, representing commerce, the SENAI for social training in the industrial field, and the SENAC for training in the commercial field."

One morning we spoke of these currents of thought with Senhorita Helena Jonqueira, an experienced professional in government social service work. "North Americans will probably be surprised to know how mature the social welfare thinking is in Brazil," she remarked. "So far as Catholics are concerned, our aim must be to establish a program that avoids the extremes of the right and the left. Rightist thinking gives greater trouble than leftist since often Catholic conservative elements among the proprietors stand in the way of Catholic social thinking as required by the Papal encyclicals."

I was to hear this judgment passed on Catholic conservatives in many countries of Latin America. Businessmen and landed proprietors of generally high ideals suffer through lack of social education. They cling to outmoded concepts as regards their relations with their employees. Several times in Latin America I sat in on discussions of thoughtful people well versed in Catholic social principles who in most decisive fashion have exposed the social errors of Catholic proprietors who are otherwise good men. Catholic social justice represents neither the right nor the left but the philosophical center in social thinking. It represents the refined balance of the papal social pronouncements.

"One fine feature of the program of the Employees Association is the interest of the officers in the practice of religion," explained Senhor Pires. "Years ago I used to go through the plant and speak of religion but this had its delicate side. I did not want to seem to be using my position to influence my workers unduly. Now it is not I or the company officers but the staff itself that takes the initiative."

"Behind their activities, however," I commented, "is the knowledge that you are very anxious for the personnel to make a fine record in this regard."

"True, it gives me sincere pleasure," replied this interesting man. "Twice a year, at Easter time and on the local town feast of Santo Amaro in August, the Employees Association officers urge the Catholics to participate in a public Communion. We arrange for confessions and the Mass here in the plant. This year's Mass in Easter week was particularly well organized. It was preceded by a three-day plant retreat. Over twenty bad marriages were rectified with the cooperation of the local priests. The Employees Association now operates special eight-week premarriage courses to help couples get their ideas straight. The company gives time out for these courses."

"Do you strike any radicals who are hostile to religion?"

"The percentage is low but we get our share. Protestants do not participate in Catholic services and of course we respect their wishes. As a body our people want religion."

Senhor Pires' last comment fitted in with a verdict I heard many times expressed. The American Oblates who conduct a huge parish of 40,000 in the neglected Vila Alpina area on the periphery of São Paulo bore this out.

"Our problem with these people is one of past habits," remarked Father Lyons. "They have gotten away from systematic religious practice. Many in the Vila Alpina neighborhood are from Bahia. Others are from Minas Gerais, or from regions of the sertão where there is neither priest nor organized parish."

"This does not mean that they are not interested in religion," added

Father McCann, Father Lyons' assistant. "Father Lyons is worn to a frazzle from their calls for help that begin with knocks on the door at daybreak and continue late into the night. They are factory workers, most of them unlettered and ignorant, most of them very confused about many things but all good at heart, on the whole not rebellious people."

Here was another side to the life of the hordes of newcomers who make up the growing cities of Brazil, the homes that supply most of the workers in Laborterapica and its thousands of companion plants. The Oblates were struggling to build a church and operated a school in motley buildings that looked like a collection of chicken coops.

"We get two hundred youngsters into these buildings," explained Father Lyons, "and we operate not two but three shifts daily. The first youngsters arrive at eight and study till eleven; the second shift is here from eleven until two, and the third from two until five. Thus we are giving some schooling to six hundred children. We have a dispensary to handle some of the sickness in the neighborhood. Some 1,500 out of the 40,000 people in the parish get to Mass either at our small center church or in the out-chapels. The number is steadily growing."

"In the case of most of the people," continued Father McCann, "the habit of going to Sunday Mass has never been acquired. If it ever existed in their families it was lost generations ago. Many of them have worked out a way to get along in religion almost entirely without the priest."

"How, for instance?" I asked.

"Let's get in this jeep of ours and I'll show you one of the current ways."

We left the only paved street in this part of the city and slithered along the mud roads for a considerable distance.

"Every few blocks in this area is a separate neighborhood," explained Father McCann. "Most people begin out here at the newer end of town. They live in a wooden shack of one room. Given a few years and a certain minimum of ambition, their houses become more livable. Sections such as this we are now passing through are some fifteen years old. These people have stuccoed brick homes that are quite nice."

"And I suppose they build them themselves."

"That's right. They are called Sunday homes since the owners build them on their days off, which are the Sundays. The owners, often brick layers, buy the bricks at 800 cruzeiros per thousand and use mud for mortar. There is no sewage yet in this part of town; each house has a locally constructed latrine. The hills help the drainage. There are no water mains yet. There are wells. Even we Fathers have to get water by pail from our more fortunate neighbors."

Father McCann stopped suddenly and called to a flaxen-haired Russian girl. "Lucia, where is the Pilgrim Virgin today?"

"I don't know, Padre; better ask Narciso."

We drove on a block or so.

"Sandra," Father called to a woman in a yard, "where is the Pilgrim Virgin today?"

"I don't know, Padre; Narciso will know."

So we unlocked the gate at Narciso's and entered his worn wooden house. There at the table in the sitting room sat a tall, kindly man with sparkling eyes.

"Narciso!" cried Father McCann. "I'm surprised to find you at home."

"Dona Geralda is ill, Padre, so I'm tending her."

"And the work?"

"It will wait," replied Narciso with an easy laugh. "Say a word to Dona Geralda; she's not terribly sick, you know."

The priest had a pleasant exchange with the mother of Narciso's brood, four boys, a couple of whom were likewise in the house. Narciso's mother completed the family group. On the table was a family Bible, old and well thumbed but in good condition. "We brought it with us from Minas Gerais," explained Narciso's mother.

"We wish to visit the Pilgrim Virgin, Narciso," explained Father.

"It's a couple of blocks down the street. I'll bring you to it."

"Meanwhile tell this American Father the story of the Pilgrim Virgin here in Vila Alpina."

"It is all Dona Geralda's doings," began Narciso. "She is the pious one in this house. Some two years ago she decided that we should have the Virgin here to help us. She collected the offerings and got the statue which Father Lyons blessed."

"How is the devotion conducted?" Father McCann prompted.

"The Virgin is carried in procession by the neighbors to each house it is to visit and enthroned in the best room in the house. It stays in each house for nine days and then is carried to the next. Every other evening the people of the neighborhood gather and say the rosary before the Virgin."

"Who makes the arrangements?" asked the Padre.

"You know very well, Padre," expostulated Narciso. "Dona Geralda takes care of everything. I help her. I keep the records."

With this Narciso reached in a drawer and took out a notebook. I looked at its pages and then took a new look at Narciso. He was a bland, quiet man and probably did not have much push. But it was evident that he was unusually methodical and conscientious because here before me was a meticulous record of the two years and more of peregrinations of the Virgin in Vila Alpina. There was the name, address and attendance with the dates of nine days' stay in the home of each of the folk who had received Our Lady.

One finds interesting people in a city like São Paulo, I thought to myself. There was John Baptist Isnard, the merchant who enthused about laymen's retreats. There was Jose Pires de Oliveira Dias, the millionaire maker of drugs who doted over his Employees Association. And now there was Narciso Leite do Silva, an unskilled employee of a shipping company who devotedly recorded the journeys of the Pilgrim Virgin in the shack town of Vila Alpina.

"I'll take you to Dona Maria's," suggested Narciso.

We crowded into the jeep and churned through the mud to a house down the street. A little throne was set up on the table in the front room of the humble dwelling that we entered and on the throne stood a twelve-inch statue of the Black Virgin of Aparacida. Long ago off the Brazilian shore some fishermen found the original statue floating in the sea. Believing that it had been sent to them miraculously they built a temple for it. Today at a spot between São Paulo and Rio the Redemptorists tend this greatest shrine of Our Lady in Brazil and thousands make pilgrimages there every year.

"A pretty shrine you've made, Senhora," remarked Father McCann to the woman of the family who appeared. The statue was almost smothered in a volume of filmy curtaining. The throne was covered with silver tinsel and decorated with a quantity of artificial daisies.

"It is wonderful to have it in the house," exclaimed the excited Senhora.

"The house is full every night we pray," explained one of the boys of the family. "We have more than twenty. We've never had so many people in here before."

"Do you say the prayers, Senhora?" asked Father McCann.

"No, we could not say the beads ourselves," replied the woman. "Narciso prays. Narciso is the rezedor in this neighborhood."

"A rezedor is the reciter of prayers among these people," Father McCann explained to me. "It is a species of neighborhood catechist, a local institution in the villages of Brazil. It is another outcome of the scarcity of priests."

"But by ourselves we all pray here in this house," the Senhora continued earnestly. "I pray often, many times a day now that the Virgin is here. The children pray. And my husband is a religious man; he prays often too."

"Do you come to Sunday Mass at the church, Senhora?" Father McCann asked.

"No," replied the woman, "it is too far. And besides we never went to Sunday Mass before coming here."

"Some day soon you must begin, Senhora," Father McCann said gently.

The simple housewife did not reply but a new light lit her eyes as she stared sharply at the priest. Perhaps it was only my lively imagination; yet I saw new-born resolution in that look. Thus the unchurched millions of Latin America are slowly moving back toward the practice of the Faith that is so deeply entrenched within them.

Chapter 4

Tribal Gods in Catholic Bahia

AN OCEAN LINER, standing high and proud above the waves, moved majestically through the indigo blue of Bahia harbor. Several small coastal steamers—stumpy, dirty boats, heavy with cargo—wallowed low in the water. Scores of little fishing craft with their white or red sails, scampered about in the smart wind. Many of these were *jangadas,* sea-going rafts of peeled logs held together by pegs. A centerboard, a sail and a steering oar complete the primitive structure, a distinctly Brazilian product inherited from the Tupi Indians.

I watched all this from a lovely home perched high above the bay and the upper and lower cities of Bahia. The entire city of 400,000, fourth largest in Brazil, extended before me. Bright-colored houses with red-tiled roofs piled and overlapped one another up toward the highest placed of the towers of the hundred churches that dot the metropolis. A white-hot sun poured down on the rose-colored walls, the myriad, narrow cobbled streets and the magnificent boulevards along the bay and the ocean.

Out beyond the city in centuries gone by a florid, luxurious plantation life grew up that Gilberto Freyre describes in his classic work, *Casa Grande e Senzala,* which, translated, means "Big House and Slave Quarters." Relations between master and slave were, as in the old American South, cordial and intimate. When by the eighteenth century competition in the Caribbean took the profit out of Brazilian sugar, this gracious living was curtailed but the traditions to a degree continue to this day. The past aids us to understand the present. Brazil possesses a triracial society—European, African, American Indian—which is remarkable in its freedom from racial injustices but which is strongly marked by class distinctions. Fernando de Azevedo does not hesitate to admit the presence of prejudices. "The three races, white, red and black, are distributed in ethnic stratification. . . . Racial prejudices, even though they never reached the point of creating conflicts and opposition, have always existed among us, too, as principles of social classification."[1]

Bahia State has five million inhabitants of whom a million and a half are whites. Full-blooded Negroes are approximately a million and the remainder of the population, two and a half million, are mestizos. Seven out of ten in the city of Bahia are colored and they enjoy absolute equality before the law. No one because of his skin is barred from trams, trains, hotels or schools, much less from the churches. Seven of the eleven judges in the Court of Justice are of Negro descent. Negro doctors and lawyers are in many instances outstandingly successful and have white as well as colored clients. Colored priests minister alike to parishioners of white, Indian and Negro ancestry.

Harry W. Hutchinson, writing in a UNESCO publication, *Race and Class in Rural Brazil,* describes the racial distinctions in the Reconcavo, a typical area outside the city of Bahia. "In the Reconcavo," says Hutchinson, "three race stocks are recognized: the white, the Negro and the Indian. A white is called a *branco.* The term *negro* is rarely used to denote a person of African descent. Rather such a person is called a *homem de cor* (man of color). Negro is used abstractly to denote the Negro race, but is almost never used to single out an individual. . . . When the *bahiano* speaks of *indio,* he usually thinks of the wild Indian of the interior of Mato Grosso or of the Amazon. When he wishes to indicate people of American Indian physical type in the Reconcavo, he generally says *caboclo.*"[2]

"In Bahia," explained Antonio Lobo on whose porch I was sitting, "Negroes and mulattoes find themselves for the most part in positions of inferiority. They belong to the lowest social class. Most of the illiterates are colored. They find employment generally as domestics, waiters, soldiers, peddlers, dockworkers, laborers, farm workers and fishermen. Their families are large, their homes are poor, with much confusion and often little cleanliness."

"Why are they so consistently in this condition?" I asked.

"In looking for the causes, we must admit that easy-going indolence is one of the explanations. Only the exceptional ones have much enterprise. Most of them love best a life of music, feasts, fireworks displays, entertainments. Many feel no incentive to methodical day by day work that strengthens the spirit, encourages saving and builds up strong families."

With Mrs. Lobo I went down to the huge markets in the lower city where everything is for sale. On the way we passed through the plaza before the Church of Our Lady of Carmel.

"Here the new slaves from Africa used to be sold," Senhora Lobo explained. "When a man completed his purchase, we are told, he brought his fresh workers into the church and they were baptized. Here in the plaza, also, slaves who committed crimes were punished, sometimes executed."

"And to this day," I commented, "people continue to recall, I suppose, that it is under these circumstances that the Negro reached Brazil."

"But people here have none of the prejudices against them that we hear you have in the United States," Mrs. Lobo replied. "As you'll see in the markets, they brighten up every scene. They are the liveliest sellers and the noisiest buyers. They perk up life for everybody."

Physically the Negro market women presented a vivid picture. Their dress is a combination of African and Empire styles. How queenly that sweets vendor is, I remarked to myself as she passed us, carrying her tray on her head above a bright yellow turban. Big golden hoops hung from her ears. Her blouse was pale green, her skirt a brilliant red, so heavily starched it would have stood by itself had she stepped out of it. Her bosom was entirely covered with beads and necklaces and her arms were heavy with bracelets; she wore literally pounds of costume jewelry.

Thoughtful students of Catholic life in Bahia have long felt concern over the deficiencies in the local religious practices caused principally by the severe shortage of clergy in the region. In 1954 there were but 354 priests to serve the five million inhabitants of the state. Since there were 1,607 churches in the state, there were almost five churches for every priest.

"The Cardinal of Bahia heads a wonderfully loyal body of faithful," observed Father Machado, a Jesuit in the city, "but His Eminence is desperately short of hands to give elementary training to these people.

Men like Father Guido del Toro are enthusiastically rallying the Negro children into instruction groups but the numerical inadequacy of the clergy only highlights the impossibility of getting anywhere without new recruits."

Scholars like Azevedo see the situation as something much deeper than a current shortage of clergy. He would lead us to believe that a great portion of the lower classes in Brazil were never at any time in the history of the nation supplied with a sufficiently adequate body of clergy. Thus they were never satisfactorily trained in the Faith and directed in its systematic practice.

The manner in which great numbers of the American Indians and African Negroes were melded into the Catholic ranks, says Azevedo, "could not help but create the risk of exposing Catholic beliefs and rendering them vulnerable to the cultures of the aborigines and the Africans, to their beliefs, rites and superstitions. The Christian religion, inherited from Portugal, was contaminated with all these Afro-Indian impurities, above all in the lower social strata of colonial society."[3]

Today the better classes in Bahia possess a faith that in no respect is contaminated. At such swank schools as the Colegio do Merced, conducted by the Ursulines, hundreds of the young ladies are daily communicants.

"They bring their religious convictions with them into the good Catholic homes that they establish at marriage," said Mother Marie Xavier, the superior, in speaking of her graduates.

"Among the upper classes, Mother, is there ever a trace of interest in the Brazilian varieties of voodoo, the *candomblés,* or in other popular cults such as spiritualism?"

"Very little," replied Mother. "In the course of years there have been few instances of such penetration into higher society. The husband of one of our graduates was dying and his family argued for bringing in a spiritualist medium. The girl opposed the idea and pleaded with her mate to remain faithful to his Christian tenets. He did. Every once in a while we hear of a man of good family who gets mixed up in the *candomblés* but this is rare."

Thales de Azevedo, a social anthropologist of Bahia who is a devout Catholic, corroborated this in the course of our conversation one morning. "Bahia State probably represents the lowest level of Catholic religious life in all Brazil," he remarked. "Yet there is little conscious revolt against Catholicism as such. The increase in spiritualism and in the Afro-Brazilian sects occurs among the lower classes who have the idea that one can be a Catholic and follow these cults as well. The upper classes are not involved though every now and then an individual struggling with a problem will turn in desperation to one of these cults."

Among the poorer classes this is not the case. Lobo and I stopped one day to chat with some fishermen unloading their catch along the shore.

"You made a big haul today," Antonio remarked to a strapping big Negro.

"Why not?" the man replied exultantly. "Anselmo knows how, Anselmo has the secret," and with this he pointed mysteriously to his companion, likewise a burly Negro, who was dragging a netful of fish across the sand.

"How's that?" Antonio pressed.

"Yesterday," said our informer coming closer, "we paid Janaina. Anselmo knows how to call her. We brought her out two fine jugs of rum. Anselmo called her and threw her the rum. And today, see our wonderful catch! Anselmo knows how, Senhor!"

"What is he talking about?" I asked Antonio.

"Janaina is the goddess of the sea. For many of these fishermen, the cult of Janaina is their principal devotion. Every so often they put a load of rum or other gifts into their boats, go out to the fishing grounds, call Janaina and throw her the gifts. Then Janaina sends them the fish."

My mind jumped immediately to another seashore far across the Atlantic on the coast of Africa. Some years ago while visiting in Luanda, the capital of Portuguese Angola, I rode down by the ocean to the fishing parish of a grand old African priest, Padre Felip, and he brought me to see his people.

"They are fine people," explained the kindly patriarch after we had visited with a number of families, "but of course I have a time with them with their superstitions. No matter what I say they insist on paying Kianda. Kianda is the god of the sea. Every little while when the catch becomes poor they put a load of meat and port wine in their boat and bring it out to Kianda."

I mentioned this experience to Antonio.

"Most interesting, Padre!" he exclaimed. "In Angola it was Kianda; in Bahia it is Janaina. This Bahian folk cult undoubtedly came from Africa. But much more than Janaina comes from Africa, Padre. So much of our popular magic and other forms of superstition were brought to us by the slaves. The Bahian *candomblé* comes from Africa."

"Are you familiar with the *candomblé,* Antonio?"

"Padre, I have been interested in it for years. As you know, it is a mixture of Catholic religious practices and African pagan rites that was compounded by the African slaves. It is not peculiar to Brazil; it has existed in much the same form in many parts of the African slave world of Latin America but particularly in Haiti and Bahia. I'd like to show you how it operates here."

"It's a bargain, Antonio," I replied.

Years ago in Ouidah, the chief city of Dahomey, during a visit to West Africa, Bishop Steinmetz brought me one morning to the snake temple across the street from his cathedral. Catholic prelate though he was, he dropped into this pagan center with the nonchalance of a housewife going to the grocery store. Besides displaying his snakes, the temple priest obligingly showed us the crude mud altar and explained in West African French his complicated temple duties.

"The voodoo cult in Haiti got its snake rites from Ouidah," Bishop Steinmetz remarked as we walked away. "Many Dahomeans were sold as slaves in Haiti and remembered the honor paid to the snakes in Ouidah. The snake, they tell us here, is our mythical animal ancestor."

A little later I was in Ibadan in Southern Nigeria, described as the largest Negro city in the world. It is the great center of the Yoruba people, of whom thousands were shipped as slaves to the Americas. Thanks to missionary confreres, I saw many of the god temples, or *orisha,* in Ibadan and picked up fragments of the lore of Yoruba polytheism. The Yoruba supreme being, I learned, was Olorun, for whom there was no cult. Lesser divinities were Shango, god of rain and thunder, and Ogun, god of the chase and of war.

"Eshu, guardian of houses and villages," explained one of the Irish missionaries, "is a mischievous minx who makes out very well for himself by being paid by temple worshipers for not making trouble for them."

"You know your gods very well, Padre," I commented.

"It is you who should know them," he replied. "Many of our Yoruba gods figure in the folk cults which still are practiced by descendants of the slaves in the Americas."

Practically all of the slaves brought to the Americas were purchased by ship captains from native African slave traders along the West African coast from Senegal to Angola. The tribes along this coast were not savage in the popular meaning of this word. They belonged to large and settled political entities, the Fula and Mandingo empires in what is now French West Africa, the Hausa kingdom in Northern Nigeria, the strong kingdoms of the Fanti and Ashanti of the Gold Coast, the regimes of Dahomey, of Yoruba and Benin in Nigeria, the kingdoms of Kongo and Loanga.

Under these West African rulers many intelligent persons used their wits in politics, trade, war and religion. The West Africans were not taught slavery by the European ship captains; they already practiced it on a large scale. Every man who amounted to anything owned slaves. Furthermore, every man who amounted to anything had hanging over him the threat of being sold into slavery if fortune turned against him. Slavery was the lot not only of the uncouth peasant snatched by marauders; those high in African society could also be victims.

Even the priests of the local religions were sold into slavery. "It is a commonplace among those who have studied New World Negro life," says Herskovits, "that African religion has shown greater resistance to white influence than any other phase of African culture. And to explain this one must again turn to African tradition. . . . Tradition has it that the most intransigent of the conquered were the priests of the indigenous local cults, who, because of their activities, were punished with what native idiom terms 'banishment' (slavery). In the New World these intractable priests continued their rites for their fellow slaves and instructed the next generation so their knowledge would not be lost to the people."[4]

Thus the intricate religious practices of West Africa crossed the Atlantic. As soon as the new slaves arrived they were introduced to Christian teachings through interpreters. Spurred by Mrs. Lobo's remark about the slave baptisms at Our Lady of Carmel Church, I visited the historic baptismal font where great numbers of slaves are said to have received the sacrament. Royal edicts made baptism of the slaves compulsory and missionaries gave much attention to stirring in their new subjects a genuinely Christian faith.

Yet there were factors that kept alive the religion of Africa. There was the element of force behind this Christianizing of the slaves. There was the fact that religion for the African was not a thing remote from life but an intimate part of his existence. Finally, there was the fact that occasionally there were spirited pagan leaders among the slaves who advocated holding with the religion of Africa.

We can understand, therefore, why the writings of the early days record the discouragement of the missionaries at the lapses of the slaves. Runaway slaves set up camps in remote areas and cultivated assiduously their pagan practices. Slaves in areas where missionaries were lacking also maintained religious rites.

Despite all these influences, however, the work of the missionaries had its effect and the great mass of Negroes in the course of generations became genuinely attached to the Catholic religion. The history of the Negro in Latin America is one of true love for the teachings and practices of Christianity.

Nevertheless there is the further fact of the retainment of links with the pagan past, witnessed today in areas where thorough formation in Christian living does not prevail. Examples of these deviations are voodoo in Haiti and the *candomblé* in Bahia.

All important is the absence of any real dichotomy, any sense of inconsistency between Catholic teachings and their African beliefs, so far as the untutored adherents of these cults are concerned. The Church is hostile to these practices and the police cooperate in making their pursuit unpleasant and dangerous. But their adherents, while holding to things Catholic, pursue unperturbedly their *candomblé* saints.

"Some of the Padres scold right furiously," explained Sabina, one of the *candomblé* "mothers" whom we visited, "but they don't understand. Why are they so mean to the good folk who come to our seances? Why are they so mean?"

Sabina and her followers profess to accept the God of Christianity and all that the Church teaches. But in addition there are the deities from Africa (and sometimes from the American Indian tribes) and these are very useful. They are, indeed, Catholic saints. Why not get their help? Here is the syncretism of voodooism and the *candomblé.*

"It is important to observe," noted Antonio, "that *candomblé* does not represent merely the application of a few African twists to a veneration of Christian saints. Quite the contrary. It is the pursuit to this day of a form of authentic animistic worship that has been in practice for centuries in West Africa, long before slaves were brought to America. This form of worship is substantially the same in Bahia and in Brazil generally and in the Caribbean. In the course of centuries, the names of Catholic saints have been given to some of these gods but the pagan worship has not changed."

"What are the elements that make up this worship, Antonio?" I asked.

"I would say that they are reducible to four. First, there are the gods themselves. Secondly, there is the 'feeding' of the gods, which in effect is the act of sacrifice in the cult. Thirdly, there is the personnel connected with the cult. Fourthly, there is the ceremony of possession. A fifth consideration is the Christian features that have been introduced into the cult as well as certain features that come from spiritualism."

"The thing people talk most about," I remarked, "is the period during the *candomblé* dance when various participants become possessed by the gods they invoke."

"Yes," agreed Antonio. "That you must see. I suggest that we go first to a festal hall of the *candomblé* when nothing is going on and take a look around. Then we'll go some night to a *candomblé* in action and see the participants become possessed."

Thus we agreed on our program. Bahia's present vogue as a center for the *candomblé* cult is not very old as such things go in Brazil. The first *candomblé* house was opened in 1830 deep in the woods outside the city. This was called Engenho Velho (Old Plantation) and was conducted by three women who became celebrated. At the turn of the century there were a score of such houses and today the total is placed at a hundred, frequented by an estimated 30,000 devotees. They are all independent one from another, each headed by a "father" or "mother" who gives the special character to his or her establishment.

It was interesting that Antonio decided that we should try to see the festal hall of Sabina because Sabina is the "mother" of a caboclo *can-*

domblé, an unorthodox development of the *candomblé* which brings in certain American Indians as saints.

We drove to an undeveloped section on the outskirts of the city and stopped at a well constructed house, evidence of prosperity. We left Antonio's car and walked into the front yard, neatly ornamented with flowers.

"Sabina! Sabina!" Antonio called.

"Halloo!" came a return from the house and a lady in her sixties appeared at the door. "Oh, it's you, Antonio. Come in, please."

We sat for a moment in Sabina's well appointed front parlor. She was a folksy person, evidently intelligent and more of the career type than motherly in her ways.

"I have brought you my friend," Antonio explained after the preliminaries, "because I wanted him to see the best appointed *candomblé* in the city. Would you have a moment to show him around?"

"Oh, my, Antonio, I am honored! Let's begin immediately."

We left the residence section of Sabina's quarters and went first to the festal hall, the main entrance to which was off a back street. The hall was some thirty-five feet square, which Antonio pronounced as standard size. It was without adornment except for a large colored print of an American Indian such as at home we would find on a life insurance calendar. This print evidently aimed to give a caboclo intonation to the establishment.

Sabina now stepped into the backyard and opened the door of a wooden outhouse. Sabina pointed to a rock on the floor. "This is Eshu," she said. "Before we begin each seance we placate Eshu."

Eshu! I thought of my Irish missionary friend in Ibadan, Nigeria, and his remarks about Eshu, "the mischievous minx."

"He is not the devil," explained Antonio, "but he can make trouble aplenty if he is not given attention. In Haitian voodooism Eshu is called Legba."

Certainly, represented by a rock lying on the floor of Sabina's hut, Eshu was an unprepossessing creature, filthy with the libations of liquid food that had been poured on him. Poultry strolled about Sabina's yard, a tiny pig was roped to a pole and a small peacock was quite disgruntled until Sabina gave it attention. We went back into the building.

"Now you must see the costumes of the saints," suggested Sabina. The costume room was small but quite orderly. A shrine in a corner niche contained a crucifix. The costumes were folded in bundles under a line of prints of Christian saints which hung on the wall and identified the African gods with whom they are linked.

The first print was of Santa Barbara. "This is the Christian identification of Shango, the god of storms," explained Antonio. "Sometimes Shango is identified as St. Jerome, sometimes as St. Peter."

Shango! In Ibadan I had passed Shango's *orisha,* the native temple.

Next was a print of Saint Anthony. "St. Anthony is the Christian identification for Ogun," explained Antonio.

"I saw his temple also in Ibadan," I remarked to Antonio.

"Yes," noted Antonio. "The slaves in this area were predominantly from Nigeria and thus it is the Yoruba or Ewe gods of that part of Africa that figure in the Bahia *candomblés*. In Haiti, I am told, most of the gods are from Dahomey though they have a relationship to the Nigerian or Nago gods."

There they were before us, Catholic saints who played the strange role of identifying African gods. There was a print of the Christ of Bomfim that identified Oshala; there was St. George who identified Oshosse, god of the hunt; there was St. Lazarus who identified Omolu, god of troubles.

Finally there were several crude representations of Indian gods who had no counterparts in Christian saints, such as Tapuya and Tupinamba. During the centuries the spirit of syncretism prompted the Negro lords of the *candomblé* to welcome deities of their caboclo confreres into their pantheon.

"Enough about the gods," said Antonio as we drove away. "Now we must arrange to attend a *candomblé* seance."

For this, Antonio chose a famous house in a convenient suburb that occupied the fazenda of a Frenchman named Gantois. This *candomblé* was once headed by the great "mother" Pulcheria and now belonged to Menininha.

"It is one of the best conducted *candomblés* in Bahia," explained Antonio, "so much so that it is difficult for outsiders to get permission to attend."

We entered the backyard of a rather large house and found half a dozen Negro women. One kindly old lady knitted in a chair. A couple of other women were preparing the supper. One woman was doing some wash while a large-boned, sloe-eyed girl hung clothes on the line.

"Is Mother here?" Antonio asked the girl. She stopped hanging clothes, looked at us quite deliberately and without a word went into the house.

"They want to know what you want," she drawled when she returned.

Antonio began to explain but she stopped him. "Go around to the festal-hall door," she said and returned to her clothes.

As we walked around the house I observed a burly Negro in his undershirt look out the window at us. When we reached the door it was he who opened it a slit and stood looking intently at Antonio.

"You remember me, don't you?" said Antonio. "I've been here for some of the seances. When is the next one?"

"There's one tonight," answered the fellow, looking for all the world like a night club bouncer. He hesitated a moment and made his decision. "Come back tonight. We start at eight."

Thus we had been put under the gleam of the fish eye and voted safe enough not to make trouble. Antonio was delighted; his worries were over. It reminded me of stories of how men used to buy bootleg liquor.

Circumstances made us late and we did not return until nine o'clock. "The sacrifices will be over," remarked Antonio as we drove along. "To the devotees, remember, feeding the gods, as the sacrifice is called, is more important than dancing to them though to onlookers the dancing and the sight of the dancers becoming possessed is much more dramatic."

"Just how do they feed the gods, Antonio?"

"The *candomblé* feast begins with the *matança,* the killing of hens or pigeons or other small animals and the pouring of their blood before the feet of the gods. This ceremony is private as is also the placating of Eshu."[5]

As we crawled gingerly up the very bad road to the hilltop we heard the drums. A couple of other cars were already parked and a hundred or so Negroes milled about outside in an air of excitement. When we reached the door we found the ceremony in full career. The brightly lighted festal hall was packed with over two hundred onlookers and the circle of dancers moved counterclockwise in the hollow square in the center. The drums were lively but I was to find that they were not at all hot as yet.

A tall gentleman of the perfect butler type, neatly dressed in gray suit, came over and conducted us to the section on the wooden benches reserved for the special guests.

"This festal hall is one of the best in Bahia," explained Antonio. "It is a new building constructed for the purpose. Since it corresponds with the plan of Engenho Velho, the master *candomblé* plan in these parts, it's evidently correct. It's made of brick covered with plaster and has a solid tile roof."

The walls of the hall were painted but not otherwise ornamented except for three niches high above the crowd. Each of the niches was illumined with an arc of electric lights. The central one contained a large crucifix. The one to the right contained a statue of Our Lady with a couple of vases of flowers before it. I could not identify the statue in the third niche but it also had flowers before it.

On each side wall were three glassless windows through which the wind blows almost with violence so that the hall remained pleasantly cool all evening. On three sides the crowd filled every foot of space outside the hollow square and black faces peered in through every window. The men occupied one side, the women the other.

Most of the onlookers were neighborhood Negroes but there were special guests. In front of us sat a well dressed Negro with sharp, intelligent face accompanied by two policemen. "He's evidently a high ranking police official," whispered Antonio. There were four Brazilians of mixed blood and several whites. None gave signs of active participation but a number made large offerings at the end of the evening. Across the hall in the women's section were some well dressed Brazilians and several foreign women.

On the fourth side of the room between the entrances for the participants sat the major officers of the seance. Most important, of course, was "mother" Menininha, the spiritual head of the Gantois *candomblé*. Her Portuguese title is *mãe-de-santo,* "mother in sainthood" which indicates her role as the mother in leading her followers to sainthood. Menininha occupied a double-width chair because she is extremely broad and fleshy. I watched her during the evening. She displayed no air of haughtiness or imperiousness, no attempt at glitter, no smirking sophistication. She gave every bit the impression of being a kindly mother.

On Menininha's right stood the muscle man of the afternoon, now in a dark suit that made him quite proper. His trousers needed pressing, however, and he wore a generally tousled air. Despite his attempts at fervor and unction, I kept my conviction that his greatest opportunity came in the hour of trouble. Several men who sat on Menininha's left were *ogans* of the ceremony; they provided prestige and money.

An interesting man was the *iye tebexe,* who directed the dance. He called out the songs, initiated each fresh refrain and with his iron gong fixed the basic rhythm for the music.

Then there were the drums. They were the authentic hollow-log African type, the heads stretched with cow-hide. An official battery of drums is always three: large, medium and small. For me, the most fascinating person at the seance was the drummer boy of the big drum. He used a single heavy stick in his right hand and with his left struck the drumhead with his hand in a marvelous variety of ways. His performance was sheer wizardry. Physically he had the form for a lightweight boxer, lithe as a leopard, with thin hips and no stomach. As the evening wore on the drumming of the entire trio rose from enthusiasm to exultation and of course, as was intended, played a major role in making the seance a success.

And now for the "daughters-in-sainthood," as they are called. As I was taking in the details of the scene they were earnestly concentrating on their quest. Each was seeking to call down the special god, or "saint," to which she was devoted, get him to enter her head and take possession of her, thus riding her as a horse.

Circling before us to the rhythm of chanting and drums were twenty to twenty-five women. I recognized immediately the sloe-eyed girl who, when we came in the afternoon, was hanging out the clothes in the backyard. In the circle also was the white-haired grandma, whom I had seen knitting in the rocking chair. She was probably seventy, with handsome face and large, strong body. The others varied in age from a child of twelve, slight of build, to women in their twenties, thirties, forties, fifties, tall, short, thin, extremely fat.

All were modestly and charmingly dressed in old Empire style, though with no costume jewelry. None gave the least indication of exhibitionism, of melodramatics. One lone girl had modern dress, a loose sweater and a black, tight-fitting skirt. She could have been a university student. She was awkward in her movements, lacked the rhythm of the others, but was deeply absorbed and entirely without pretense.

"They'd make a nice group of ladies for a parish sodality," I remarked to Antonio.

"Most of them are plain women of the city with a religious bent," Antonio observed, "dressmakers, domestics, or sweets vendors. They have little money and yet pay their way in the *candomblés*. In their ignorance they are quite unaware that this is paganism almost as it came from Africa centuries ago."

"I suppose men have traced all these practices to their sources."

"Quite so," noted Antonio. "Half a dozen details have been pointed out to me as African. First, the circle of women rotating in a counterclockwise direction is precisely as it is still done in Africa. Secondly, the worship through specific dances for each specific deity is traditionally African. Thirdly, the method of sounding the basic rhythm with an iron gong is African. Fourthly, stirring the emotions with wild, intricate orgies of drumming is African. Fifthly, the calling of the gods with specific songs is African. Sixthly, the practice of becoming possessed as a means to establish contact with the gods is directly from West Africa's animistic worship."

The drums got hotter, the voices of the singers, which lacked good timbre, became more piercing, the dancing became more furious. Menininha sang a bit part every now and then and her voice was sweet and warm. Meanwhile she watched the revolving line and the evolvement of the emotions of the individuals. Some became quite violent and had to be protected by companions from falling or from snapping their heads too sharply.

Each new song was initiated in a clear fresh voice by the director and continued for fifteen or twenty minutes with alternating solo and chorus, again in traditional African style. As a woman showed signs that her god was taking possession of her the drums took up the specific rhythm of the god—Shango, Ogun, or other of the deities.

Finally Menininha had signaled to eight dancers in the circle who had shown signs of possession to retire to the dressing room. During their absence there was a period of surcease. Then, with a burst of climactic singing and drumming, the strange procession of possessed ones returned in their triumphal finery.

Two were made up as the Christ of Bomfim who identified the god Oshala, one represented St. George who identifies Oshosse, god of the hunt, two represented Santa Barbara, the identification for Shango. Three, then, came out with the ugly hooded costume of St. Lazarus who identifies Omolu. One of these three was the old lady of seventy. A second Lazarus was the child of twelve, and the third a stout woman whose violent energy likewise astounded me.

Each of these eight whom the gods had mounted and were now riding was accompanied by a woman caretaker, and quite wisely so since now came an apogee of violence. The eyes of the group were glassy, the minds evidently in a stupor, but the emotions were afire. As their specific drum rhythm was played, they shook and stamped and were taken by convulsions. One lady had to be held for a minute or so by four of the caretakers till she quieted and then continued in her dancing. The drums came alive with their astoundingly complex rhythms, the singers shouted and the onlookers joined in the surges of excitement.

"What such a night can mean to these people always puzzles me," Antonio commented on the way home, "but one has only to witness a *candomblé* to realize that every last one of the participants experiences a terrific emotional shake-up."

Just what is the explanation for the phenomenon called possession? Herskovits says, "Scientifically, the phenomenon of possession in Negro cultures, at least, is as yet unsatisfactorily explained, largely because of the almost complete absence of adequate reports on the background and incidence of specific cases."[6]

It was one o'clock when finally I reached my room in the beautifully peaceful residence high above Bahia. I looked out on the bay where a silent moon put a gleam of unearthly loveliness on the waters.

It was over four hundred years since the first men of color were brought into this harbor from Africa. Antonio the student dwelt on the emotional impact of the ceremony we had witnessed. The scientist puzzles over the causes of the phenomenon. What can a missionary take away from such a shattering experience, I asked myself, other than a profound realization that after four centuries the Negro in Brazil still represents for world Christianity as well as for the Brazilian Church a great unfinished task?

Chapter 5

World of the Cattle Range

CATTLE, CATTLE, mile after unending mile. Father Gardner and I sat by the side of Carlos Ferraz who guided the privately owned Cessna in which we were flying over that legendary cattle country, among the best in the world, known as the Southern Pantanal.

"Pantanal" is a Portuguese word for flood plain. If you look at the map of southwestern Brazil you'll find along the Paraguay border a long succession of lowland areas, each called a pantanal. All this is in Mato Grosso, the "Great Forest," a huge, pioneer state which, while it has immense woodlands, is characterized more by great plains of the savanna variety that provide fine pasture for millions of cattle.

Brazil currently possesses fifty million head of cattle with Minas Gerais State and Rio Grande do Sul the two major centers. Together they raise 40 per cent of the herds. Yet almost every sector of the country has cattle areas. The Amazon Valley, both along the Atlantic Coast and far inland possesses moderately important cattle ranges. Most picturesque is the cattle country of Mato Grosso.

"The cranes make me nervous," commented Carlos. "One of them could easily be sucked into my propeller if it came too close."

The bird life was tremendous. The cranes to which Carlos referred were single large white animals that floated quite high on the air waves. The majority of flying creatures, including great flocks of cranes and spoonbill herons, were much lower. On the banks of the Rio Negro another species of wild life was visible—scores of huge alligators that dozed lazily in the sun.

"They never bother the cattle," explained Father Gardner, an American Redemptorist who was at home here. Over the grazing areas as far as the eye could see the steers nibbled placidly. Most of them were widely scattered but occasionally there would be a small concentration. Once we saw two mounted cowboys but otherwise the scene was bereft of humans.

"Teams of fence builders work incessantly stretching wire," observed Father Gardner, "but this is something new. In days gone by men sometimes could not determine within miles the location of their borders and cattle roamed wild."

"The grazing lands look like immense stretches of damp green moss," I remarked.

"The fact is," replied Father Gardner, "they are damp most of the year. When the rains come the beasts are sometimes up to their necks in water; indeed, a number of animals drown each year in the process of moving to higher ground."

The first ranch center that came into view was that of Miranda Estância, originally an English foundation and an important one in the area. The great house with the intricate cluster of smaller structures about it made a pleasing pattern in its setting of rich green lawns. In the corral a small herd was being branded.

The city of Campo Grande is the trading center for this region. The entire Mato Grosso was hopelessly isolated until the Northwest Railroad was built to unite Rio and São Paulo with the vast southwestern hinterland and eventually to join Brazil to Bolivia. Brazil lacks fuel except for its forests and thus one of the sights of the interior is to see a wood-burning locomotive chug across the plain in the night shooting up a golden shower of sparks 30 feet into the air.

To the Mato Grosso in 1930 came the Redemptorists from Brooklyn and today they have five colossal parishes in the state. Two of these are in Campo Grande and its environs. One is at Aquidauana (Ah-kee-dow-ána) where Father Gardner is pastor, a parish as large as Long Island that counts a million head of cattle within its confines. The fourth is in Miranda, still further westward, while the fifth is on the Paraguayan border.

We now flew over the Rio Aquidauana and saw a second beautiful center, the Fazenda Rio Negro. Finally we sighted our destination below us, the charming property of Antonio da Costa Rondon whose guests we were to be at Fazenda Tupaceretan, an Indian name that means, "God passed this way."

"We have been in the air an hour," remarked Father Gardner. "It takes eight days by ox-cart to cover this same route from Aquidauana, and four days on horseback. You can well understand why each of these fazendas has become a world to itself."

It became clear to me as well why each of these great cattle ranches, as in our own American West, represented so genuinely the dreams, the energy, the very life blood of the personalities involved. I was not surprised when Carlos led us almost immediately to the attractive and rather costly chapel on the front lawn before the *casa grande* and showed us two well made bronze statues standing outside the chapel.

"These are Don Ciriaco and Dona Thomazia, the inspiration behind this enterprise," explained Carlos. The affectionate tribute on the plaque prepared by the son, Don Antonio, to his father explained that Don Ciriaco was the great pioneer of the Southern Pantanal. He lived but a short life of fifty-five years, from 1849 to 1904.

"Men said neither cattle nor anything else could be raised in the Pantanal," commented Carlos. "It was too wet. Don Ciriaco proved them wrong and made millionaires of all his children."

"Dona Thomazia was a wonderful woman," said Father Gardner. "She is a legendary figure on all the Da Costa Rondon fazendas because she devoted herself not only to her family but to all the workers. Tupaceretan has the reputation of giving the best treatment of the region to its peons in a region which, because it is one of the richest cattle areas in Brazil, has a high reputation for good treatment of the workers."

"And Don Antonio has in his wife Sofia," continued Carlos, "a perfect helpmate who likewise gives herself unsparingly to her household and to the workers."

"However," noted Father Gardner, "the era of endless years in the back country is past. Don Antonio, as you know from our visit, has a lovely home in Aquidauana and a de luxe apartment in São Paulo where Dona Sofia serves him well as a gracious complement in the social whirl. They have three delightful children who will not grow up to live here among the snakes and alligators."

Since husband and wife were in Aquidauana where we had already visited with them, we were welcomed at the fazenda by the *capitaz,* as the manager is called, and treated well by the handsome, motherly Indian lady who is the family cook. In the center of the great grassy plaza near the residence stands the corral with divisions like the slices of a pie. At its heart is the branding and castrating shed.

"In the shed is the famous vice-like contraption called the *brete,*" explained Carlos. "The animals pass rapidly from one of the sectors of the corral into the shed and are immediately gripped motionless by the *brete.* In a trice the job is done on them and they are projected into an opposite sector sound in life and limb but with their dignity and equanimity badly shaken. Finally, to their great relief they are passed back to the carefree life of the range."

Don Antonio has built up good quality stock, as have his neighbors, by crossing the local cattle with the Zebu from Vellore in South India. Low cattle prices made herding of inconsequential importance until World War I. Today cattle raising in Brazil represents big business in which great fortunes are made.

The *capitaz* has all the dealings with the peons. His office reveals the paternalism that governs life on the Brazilian range. He has one room with shelves loaded with medicine, for he is the pharmacist. Another intriguing room is heavily laden with leather goods for the cow herders —saddles, harness, whips and the like.

"Since the division of Don Ciriaco's lands among the children, Tupaceretan is not among the largest of the fazendas," this capable gentleman explained. "Yet we have four retiros, each one fenced separately and counting thousands of head. The staff totals fifty peons with their families, which gives us some two hundred people in the colony."

"Just what does a cattle peon receive in the way of treatment?" I asked Carlos. He summed up the living conditions as follows:

1. Salary. Each peon receives 1,800 cruzeiros monthly, which by current exchange was $35.

2. Dwelling. Each family has a home, on this fazenda a neat and commodious dwelling. There are special quarters for the single men.

"There are two colonies," explained Carlos, "the old and the new. The new houses, situated very pleasantly above the lake, are built of stuccoed brick and tiled roof, with four rooms per family, designed for light and air and supplied with electricity. The older houses are wooden with thatch roofs. All of these latter are being replaced."

3. Firewood. This is supplied gratis.

4. Milk. This comes gratis.

5. Meat. Animals are slaughtered three times a week and the peon can purchase it at one cruzeiro per kilo, that is, at one cent a pound.

6. Household supplies. Don Antonio buys supplies wholesale and sells at cost to the families. "It is genuinely at cost," explained Carlos, "Don Cipriano set the tradition of not making money on his men."

7. Cattle raising. Each peon can own a few head of cattle and raise them for his own profit, providing he does not let this interfere with his work for the *fazendeiro.*

8. Garden. Each peon and his family can maintain a small vegetable garden.

9. Schooling. We visited the neat schoolhouse for which the teacher is hired by Don Antonio. The teacher has a home next to the school.

10. Religion. There is Mass monthly by the circuit-riding Padre at the beautiful chapel. In good weather the altar is rolled out to the chapel porch and a nave is provided by the great outdoors. "Family and employees gather in the open," explained Father Gardner. "We work hard to get proper religious instruction for the youngsters on the fazendas."

"Are these cattle workers a religious people?" I asked Father Gardner.

"Let's visit some of them and you'll see," replied the priest. "Their way of life and long tradition is against any very well disciplined religious practice but we Redemptorists are constantly meeting evidences of their earnestness and their piety. The cattle world is a world apart. There are casual workers who enter it for a while and then leave it but they are recognized by all as not really belonging. The main body are in it for generations and will accept no other way of life."

In keeping with custom, we stood at the gate of the first house we approached and called to the family inside. A young wife appeared at the door and smiled happily as she saw us.

"Padre!" she cried to Father Gardner. "You are the priest who married us last May. Please come in."

The young girl ran to the mantel and took down a photograph that showed her in her wedding veil, her handsome cowboy by her side. "We were married in the church in Aquidauana and you performed the ceremony, Padre."

"This happens often," Father Gardner explained. "They journey days for a church marriage since we strongly urge that they make a great deal of the occasion. God bless you, my young lady. You have a beautiful little home here."

Indeed it was a neat establishment in one of the new houses. "Agostinho is out on the range," she explained. "He will be back in a few days."

In the next house the mother, with definitely Indian features, brought us to the family bedroom to see the shrine. "There is a shrine in every one of these homes," explained Father Gardner.

This house demonstrated the problem the *fazendeiro* faces in providing four rooms to people who for generations have been accustomed to only one. The front room, bedroom and kitchen were neat enough but the fourth room contained only a great pile of huge slabs of strange, contorted reddish black material scattered over the floor. It was a large store of Brazilian *charque,* sun-cooked beef which thus preserved is kept for months. "What wonderful *charque!*" Father Gardner exclaimed, to the satisfaction of the housewife. "Many a pound of that I've eaten," he added for my benefit, "while riding the *giro,* as we call the circuits."

At another spot along the lake stood the older wooden houses with their thatch roofs. A one-legged man with his wife and half dozen children received us with enthusiasm. Immediately he also brought us to see his bedroom shrine. When we had concluded our pleasant visit his eldest son, Isaiah, eleven years old, volunteered to lead us back to the *casa grande* by the path along the lake.

Isaiah was a child of the pantanal.

"You don't go swimming in the lake, do you, Isaiah?" Father asked him.

"Oh, yes—often."

"But aren't you afraid of the alligators?"

"Oh, none of the boys worry about them; we just keep away from them."

"Is there any fishing?"

"Wonderful fishing!"

A spanky, white headed, red and black bird perched in front of us.

"What is that bird, Isaiah?"

"That is the washerwoman."

Parakeets in profusion flew about us but a bird Father Gardner did not recognize passed near.

"What do you call him, Isaiah?"

"That's a water chicken."

"What are you going to be when you grow up, Isaiah?" we asked the boy as we were about to leave him.

"I'm going to be a range rider like daddy was before he lost his leg," the youngster replied immediately.

"God bless you, Isaiah."

"Thank you, Padre," replied the youngster as he bowed solemnly, and dashed away.

Don Antonio's family fishing camp occupied a very pretty spot along the Rio Negro.

"It seems uncomfortably close to the alligators," I commented.

"But the fish are fantastically plentiful," countered Carlos. "Don Antonio is a great fisherman. Besides, you are much too preoccupied with alligators; let me show you a much more formidable beast."

Not far from the stables Carlos brought me to a cage with heavy bars in which a hefty young jaguar, its massive mouth heavy with teeth, lithely shifted back and forth in unceasing movement.

"This is Dona Sofia's pet, Nero. It was picked up as a tiny cub and played about the house like a cat for a little while. Now it's a child no longer."

The jaguar or puma is called locally the *tigre* (teeg-ray). Sooner or later it figures in every conversation in the cattle country.

"One fazenda estimates that in years past it lost a thousand head of cattle a year to jaguars," explained Carlos. "The beast has been pretty well cleared out of the established grazing country."

"The famous Sacha Siemel, known as the Tiger Man, used to live in Miranda and was a warm friend of the Padres," remarked Father Gardner. "His wife is the daughter of a Philadelphia banker. When jaguars were more plentiful, Sacha carried on a thriving business in these parts conducting American tourists on hunting trips and guaranteeing them a bag."

In the afternoon we bade farewell to Fazenda Tupaceretan and after a forty-minute flight reached Fazenda Taboco, the ace ranch of the area.

"The story goes," said Father Gardner, "that once this property was as large as Portugal. Today it is composed of sixteen divisions and is said to possess three hundred miles of wire fences. The full complement of cattle is 40,000, tended by some one hundred fifty peons."

Doctor Renato Alvia Ribeiro, the proprietor, met us with his jeep and drove us to the *casa grande.* A company of peons were saddling their horses for the day's final operations. The animals were well built —no nags among them—and several were quite spirited. I watched one big-boned cowboy soothe his beast, mount him and then reach down and pull up a youngster wearing only cotton shorts. He dropped the boy in the saddle in front of him. Once he was sure the horse would be steady he gave the reins to the boy and they cantered off over the plain.

"This is a great country for small boys," laughed Doctor Ribeiro who was also watching.

These peons wore broad-brimmed, flat-top leather or felt hats, a bandana around their necks, and bloomer-like trousers, most of them of light color, pulled in at the ankles to fit into the beautifully tooled leather top boots that cost a pretty penny and custom-made by the town cobbler. They wore woolen shirts and most had wide belts with tooled leather sheaths for their knives. A couple carried guns. A number were equipped with cat-o-nine-tails to use as whips, a supply of which I had seen in the capitaz's store at Tupaceretan. Some had lassoes.

"What do they do of an evening with time on their hands?" we asked Doctor Ribeiro.

"They play a great deal of music. The mouth organ, the guitar and the accordion are their instruments."

"Dona Sofia is particularly popular with the cowboys because she plays the accordion so beautifully," commented Carlos.

"They love folk songs, mazurkas, polkas," said the Doctor. "They're good at fitting improvisations of words to the old tunes. Their music is very beautiful as they sit about the camps after sundown."

"Are they skillful riders?" I asked.

"They handle themselves splendidly during the cattle roundups," explained the Doctor, "but few have the dexterity of the rodeo performers of North America that I have seen in the movies. It is my dream to go to the United States some day and witness a great rodeo."

"You meet many of the cow men here, don't you, Doctor?" remarked Carlos.

"Yes, the great cattle corridor some 1,200 miles long that extends from Mato Grosso to the cattle markets of São Paulo passes through Taboco. From November to February two or three herds a week each with a thousand head or more put up for the night here. Only three or four cowboys accompany a herd and it is tremendously fatiguing. The journey takes forty days and more."

"Most of these cow men are loyal workers, aren't they, Doctor?" said Carlos.

"They have a passion for their calling, quite as does a sailor or a lumberjack. No offer, even when it means substantial betterment, will take them off their horse. With their horse they want a wife, a home, a family and thus most of them are very attached to their fazenda. In times of danger they stand by us as policemen and soldiers as well as cowboys. They love us and we love them," concluded the Doctor heartily.

Home again in Aquidauana, Father Gardner and I followed up on Doctor Ribeira's comments regarding the cowboy's love for his horse.

"In point of fact," said the American, "the jeep is penetrating into the cattle world though the cow hand doesn't like it. Among us Redemptorists there is less emotional attachment to the horse. Recently Father Sheridan and Father Finn made a *giro* of a couple of hundred miles in a jeep with one of our parishioners as driver. They covered more fazenda posts in ten days than I on horseback covered over the same route years ago in thirty days. The driver could deposit each priest in a different post an hour or so apart and thus the jeep in effect did double duty by serving two different missionaries at the same time. Wherever there are roads, the missionary horseback rider is on the way out."

"And what a pity!" exclaimed Father Ellinghaus almost bitterly. "The jeep is the tool of a new generation that is soft compared with the early men who made tremendous journeys by horseback and thought nothing of it."

So as everywhere else in the world, the old-timer speaks disdainfully of the younger bloods. There has been nothing soft about the work of the American Redemptorists in the hinterland of Brazil. In January of 1930 Fathers Francis Mohr and Alphonsus Hild reached Aquidauana by the sputtering, wood-burning railroad and soon with many companions were becoming closely acquainted with the tropic heat and red dust, the plains and jungles of the Mato Grosso. In 1935 a second Brazilian unit began work in beautiful, green Parana, the southern state with a milder climate but equally primitive ways of life.

"It is an interesting story," one of the older Padres reminisced. "A story of young city priests from Brooklyn, Boston and the Bronx, from Pittsburgh, Providence and Baltimore who didn't know what *mato grosso* meant until they found themselves riding through the deep forest. They had never seen fleas or ticks until they were bitten by them. They'd grown up to think that hammocks were for summer afternoons on the back porch and now found themselves lying in them in the darkness of the jungle where the strange night noises could mean a tiger or a cobra. They had never dreamed that a sun could be so hot, a saddle so hard, a jeep so ornery, or beans and rice so monotonously tasteless."

Today the American Redemptorists have a strong foreign missionary tradition because a heavy percentage of the priests—over one in four—has served overseas. Most of the outstanding leaders in the United States have worked in Brazil or other foreign fields. One afternoon Father Gardner brought me to see St. Joseph's Chapel in the Mato Grosso village of Morrinho, built by Father William Gaudreau, who is now the Superior General of the Congregation of the Most Holy Redeemer at its world headquarters in Rome.

Ninety per cent of all Brazilians live in the coastal areas and for them the interior is to this day a forbidding frontier world. I met two young ladies in Campo Grande who were from Recife on the Atlantic far to the east. "This is the wild west," they remarked quite disdainfully. "It will be pleasant to get back to civilization." So likewise commented a young housewife from São Paulo, in Campo Grande with her husband. "I am in exile here," she confided. "Everything is so crude and rough."

But despite this repugnance for the interior on the part of pampered city folk, Brazil is witnessing today a strong movement into its vast empty lands. Besides the Amazon Valley, of which we shall speak later, there is this region where we now find ourselves, referred to as the West and embracing the Mato Grosso and the neighboring state of Goias. Here, vigorously pushed forward by President Kubitschek, the new centrally located capital of Brazil is under construction. Posters on the walls of Rio read, "Go West!" The government, which sponsors the movement, calls it the *Marcha para o Oeste,* the March to the West.

I witnessed some of the more vivid aspects of this march while visiting the New York Franciscans in Goias, a long narrow state that would stretch from Florida to Ontario. The federal government has, among other things, opened a great farm colony there called Ceres and the enthusiasm of the settlers is enormous. "This colony came from God," a group told one of the Franciscans who works with them. "We had no hope. Then we came here and though it is hard, now life is completely changed. Now we have hope."

Some five thousand families, set up on seventy-acre allotments of land, are assisted by five thousand additional families that thus provide a total of 50,000 inhabitants in the colony. A second colony, Rubitavia, is operated by the state of Goias, and counts 25,000 inhabitants, and is another parish of the Franciscans.

"It is like a modern version of *Westward Ho!* to see truckloads of settlers enter Goias," explained Father Ronan Giehl of the Franciscans. "Sometimes the newcomers journey a thousand miles. Soon they are raising rice, beans, cotton, corn for hogs, in some cases coffee. The huge areas that are opening give us missionaries a tremendous job of circuit riding but everywhere we encounter the happy excitement of men reborn."

"Where will all this lead?" I asked Mr. Leonard Cross, a former American vice consul in Rio, now with a development company in Goias.

"Many of us feel," replied Mr. Cross, "that the eventual opening of the Amazon Valley will come about not by expeditions up the Amazon but by this progressive advance both westward and northward through the wilderness. Manáos, the city halfway up the Amazon, is 4,000 miles from Rio by boat but only 1,700 miles by air. The beeline overland penetration by the advancing frontier of settlers has already progressed almost a thousand miles. Thus the Amazon will be conquered by a flanking movement of truckloads of grimy homesteaders, the foot-soldiers of civilization, moving up through Goias and Mato Grosso."

The political center of Goias is Goyania, the pink-cheeked baby boy among the state capitals of Brazil. It has a spanking new capitol building, a beautiful cathedral, a few busy thoroughfares but most of all great areas of streets crisscrossed in neat squares and nothing but the jungle in the future city blocks.

Anapolis, with 50,000 inhabitants, is the largest commercial center in the state. Here the Franciscans have their center from which they care for many parishes in southern Goias. In Anapolis they have erected the very substantial St. Francis of Assisi Preparatory College and the thriving parish with the Portuguese name of Senhor Bom Gesus—the Good Lord Jesus.

The pioneer work in Anapolis goes on in a section of bad repute known as Korea, with Father Dominic Coscia of Brooklyn in charge. As we approached his chapel I noticed its side wall disfigured with large letters of black paint which read, "Hail to Stalin!" "Down with Yankee imperialism!"

"This is how the local Reds greeted me when I began work here in 1952," explained the Padre. "I've left it all as a challenge to the churchgoers who are still angry about it. The chapel is too small anyway and I need all my money to enlarge my school that is growing like a weed."

"Are the Reds strong here?" I asked.

"Quite strong. When I arrived, one out of every four inhabitants of the parish was hostile to the Church. The percentage is now less. There were Spiritualists, Masons, Protestants (principally Presbyterians and Adventists), Communists. That man in the front yard across the street from the church is a Red; let's meet him."

We sauntered over to the man at the fence.

"Good morning, Celso," greeted Father Coscia. "This is my friend from America. We're talking about the ugly slogans on the side of the church."

"I don't think they're ugly," replied Celso unsmilingly. "What annoys me is to see women kneeling all day long in front of that statue on your lawn."

"Well, patience, Celso," the Padre answered with a chuckle. "They're praying to Our Lady of Fatima for sinners like you."

"Are the Reds just cranks or are they dangerous?" I asked as we walked away.

"In some parts of Brazil, and this new country is to be included, they are dangerous. Communism is outlawed but party followers are said to total a million. In centers like São Paulo they have able leaders and hold important posts in the unions. Let me introduce you to John de Sá the barber. He is one of my first conquests. He was one of the angry ones and, since he was born with a bitter tongue, he was a formidable enemy. Thank God he's with us and not against us."

John was all smiles as we entered his shop. His eyes filled as he told me of the recent Family Communion Sunday when families totaling in all a thousand persons went to the altar. "In my family there were twenty of us, Padre, twenty!" he explained and his eyes glistened with emotion.

We went into a simple room behind John's barber shop and visited his dying mother, a wisp of a woman fading away.

"These people have great love of their parents," Father Coscia observed. "In confession they will accuse themselves of the mortal sin of disrespect toward their father or mother and will pass over other offenses as of light nature."

Next we went to Leander Rodrigues the shoemaker who, because in a horseback country, had as much business with saddles as with shoes. Leander brought us to his home behind his shop where he lives with his wife and four sons. He was a very alert and intelligent person, most gracious and benign. He enjoyed immensely Father Dominic's teasing.

"This is the laziest man in our Men's League," began the priest.

"But Father Dominic is such a driver," countered Leander.

"Not at all—I only want to see you and the rest of the men maintain your self-respect."

"That you do surely, Padre," replied Leander, and turning to me he continued. "The whole neighborhood has changed since Padre arrived. The Reds had us on the run; we had no one to make us keep our chins up. Now we defend the Church at work, on the street-corners and in the bars. A short while back the Communist newspaper attacked the priests as fleecers of the poor and a group of our men secured dynamite to blow up the Red plant. Padre caught them in time, told them he'd disband the League if there was any violence and sent the ringleaders home to bed."

"They are great chatterers, these fellows," said Father Dominic. "You should hear them at their Monday night meetings."

"What happens, Leander?" I asked.

"Our Monday night discussion meetings are the backbone of our movement. Of our 200 members at least eighty show up every Monday. Father Dominic is very clever in starting us off with the story of what some man has said or done and before we know it we are arguing madly. When President Vargas committed suicide, for instance, we discussed his act for hours."

"What did you decide on it?" I asked.

"That it was wrong, of course. But at first many of the men were for saying it was right."

Father Dominic was quite evidently pleased with Leander. "These men are wonderful," he remarked. "Spark them to the cause of the Lord and they will die for Him."

On our way home we dropped in to see Dona Euripides Siquiera and her sister Dona Abela. "Both are faithful servants of the poor," explained Padre before we entered. "They are of a good family from Bahia. They haven't a penny. Dona Euripides is a seamstress and Dona Abela a midwife and they give away everything beyond enough to keep themselves alive."

We drank the inevitable cafeçita in the frayed gentility of the front parlor. "Dona Euripides is head of our Legion of Mary," explained Father Dominic. "These women, eighteen in all, are taking the parish census and are uncovering plenty of work for me."

"People are very frank about their matrimonial irregularities," observed the mild old lady. "There is always a sense of regret but hardly ever any shame."

"Dona Abela has performed over a thousand deliveries in the parish," noted Father D. "She takes many a case without pay—indeed, she often ends up by spending more than she can afford on the mother and babe."

"The big fight is to stop abortion," volunteered the younger of the two sisters. "They think I am so fussy in refusing to have a part in it. With most of the women it is solely a question of the inconvenience of having a child. They are seldom worried about a birth out of wedlock. Here among the poor of this new country people are immune to moral indelicacies; they are influenced by few social sanctions in these matters."

To Father John Francis Granahan, the Franciscan Commissary in Goias, the principal foe of the Church in Brazil is spiritualism.

"Brazil is the number one spiritualist country in the world," Father John Francis stated. "The very sensitiveness of the Brazilian and his credulousness through lack of religious training makes him an easy victim. The estimate of a million spiritualists in Brazil does not seem too high. These people have a hunger for prayer and answer it by going to the spiritualists."

"But what about the Church, the classic home of prayer?" I asked.

"These particular people have never known the Church as the home of prayer. A man I met some years ago told me that he was lonely and empty and spiritualism answered his need. I was astounded when this man told me the story of the Good Samaritan as if I had never heard it before, unaware that it came from the Bible. 'A man fell among thieves,' he said, 'and a priest passed him by—that was the Church. Then the Samaritan came and bound up his wounds—that was spiritualism.' Every time I read that Gospel in the Mass I think of this man."

"What is the answer to this situation?" I asked.

"No other argument will be effective but devoted social action. Pope Pius XI used to cry out with the words of Christ—*Misereor super turbam.* 'My heart bleeds for the multitudes.' Brazil's multitudes have got to feel Christ's hand of sympathy on them through the Christian lives of their fellow men. They must come to know every church and chapel once again as the home of their Lord of love. That's not the situation at this moment, though it is steadily improving."

Chapter 6

Where Man Is the Rarest Animal

THE SUN'S RAYS had lengthened and their heat had lessened. The waves of the Tapajoz were smaller since the following wind, though still pushing our sturdy whaleboat powerfully toward its destination, had become milder. I leaned against my backrest, facing the stern where Brother Paul was operating the outboard motor and Enrique Oti assisted him. Thus I could view the grandeur of the river as it fell away behind us.

The scene at waning day was idyllic. The river's waters were a beautiful blue like the open ocean; the sky was flawless. Hugging the left bank, the right bank was all but invisible. The mottled green of the Amazon jungle shone placidly on the nearby shore, broken on rare occasions by some evidence of humanity. The thin line of the far shore was beyond identification. Several trim two-masted river boats were skillfully tacking their way down stream. Smaller vessels with rich orange sails reminded me of the breathtaking beauty of off-shore craft at Ancona on the Adriatic Sea.

"The Tapajoz is rated the most beautiful of the branches of the Amazon," remarked Brother Paul. "Ocean vessels on the Amazon turn into the Tapajoz to fill their tanks with its crystal-clear water."

Brother Paul, head of Dom Amando College at Santarem, was new enough in the Amazon country to be still under the glow of his discovery that many features of life in the neighborhood of Santarem belied the evil reputation of the Amazon Valley. The Brothers of Holy Cross, with headquarters near Notre Dame University in Indiana, a short while ago assumed responsibility for the only Catholic secondary school on the Amazon along the thousand-mile stretch between Manáos, in the heart of the Valley, and Belem, the thriving city at the river's mouth.

"Santarem needs to reorganize its Chamber of Commerce, Brother Paul," I observed. "The world has no idea of the attractions it has to offer."

"Certainly it is a pleasant place to live in," Brother replied. "There are no insect pests that are the dread of great areas of the Amazon. The climate is glorious; during six months of the year, from August to February, very little rain falls and the sky is azure for weeks on end. Fresh breezes from the Atlantic, 400 miles away, keep the atmosphere endurable. Though we are only a few degrees from the equator the highest temperature ever recorded is in the middle nineties. The lowest, which is freezing for the local gentry, is 65. Weather men tell us our yearly average is 78."

Brother Paul was bringing me from Santarem, on the Amazon, to Belterra on the Tapajoz, a four-hour ride upstream by small boat. Belterra is headquarters of the St. Louis Franciscans who are spiritual custodians of some 300 miles of the Tapajoz River, under the leadership of the Bishop of Santarem. Along with Fordlandia, Belterra is celebrated as site of the huge rubber-growing experiment of Henry Ford.

Looking north in Brazil from the brilliant cities of Rio and São Paulo, from the long established areas of the northeast and the far south, and even from the as yet pioneer areas of Mato Grosso and Goias, the Amazon Valley is regarded by most Brazilians as beyond the pale of habitable territory. The Great North, as the Amazon is called, evokes a sense of dread far deeper than that which the ordinary American citizen experiences when he thinks of Alaska or sub-arctic Canada. Going north for the Brazilian means moving into tropical heat and not into the cold. It is not merely a matter of rugged living but of a sinister struggle with deadly disease and terrifying dangers.

Thus the ordinary Brazilian eliminates from his thinking three quarters of the territory of his fatherland. For the watershed of the Amazon is 75 per cent of the area of Brazil. Politically, the North is smaller, but it embraces more than 40 per cent of the national territory.

The early Portuguese called the Amazon the Mar Dulce, the Freshwater Sea. Traveling the river in small boats, they experienced the sensation that was mine as I journeyed with Brother Paul on the Amazon and Tapajoz; the dimensions even from bank to bank were so great that they thought of the area as a sea. Yet it consists of a main stream 4,000 miles long and 1,100 tributaries. Ten of these are larger than the Rhine; seven are a thousand miles long. If the mouth were at New York, the Amazon in a straight line would have its beginning 1,200 miles out in the Pacific. Its arms would reach far into Canada and down into Mexico. The flow through its embayment of many mouths (technically there is no delta) equals that of twenty Mississippis, a volume of sixty billion gallons per hour.[1]

Popular concept paints the Amazon Valley as a huge swamp that in the rainy season goes under water. Such ideas come from the fact that even those who live in the Valley often know only some segment of one or other of its rivers. Six long months make up the rainy season and the rivers run hog-wild. "As the rainy season comes on," explains Willard Price, "the river grows in majesty and terror. It uproots great trees and sends them thrashing downstream, or riding concealed just below the surface, a dire peril to shipping. It forms great *igapos,* flooded forests, dismal wastes deserted by animals and birds. It spreads out to make swamps as big as Texas. It broadens to incredible proportions. At some places it becomes three hundred miles wide."[2]

Surely this all suggests swamp country. At Manáos high-water mark is sixty feet above low-water mark. But the fact is that all this inundation, totaling an estimated 23,000 square miles, is less than one per cent of the Amazon Valley. Ninety-nine per cent of Amazon country is terra firma. Indeed, two-thirds of all Brazil is highlands with an altitude from a thousand to five thousand feet. Much of the Amazon is open grass country larger in area than the celebrated pampas of Argentina.

But what of the famed rain forest of this part of the world? It is definitely the real thing. The three major rain forests of the world lie in West Africa, Indonesia and South America. The largest is the South American hylaea (from the Greek meaning "wood") which extends through more than a million square miles of the Amazon and Guiana river valleys from the Mato Grosso of Brazil north to the Caribbean coast.

It is during air flights over the Great North, particularly in regions of the main Amazon artery itself and its mighty tributary the Madeira, that I have had my best views of the renowned three-story jungles of this part of the world. Naturalists have divided the vast tangled mass, the greatest unexplored area of the globe except Antarctica, into various component parts unrecognized by the casual observer. There is the first "story," the struggling smaller trees up to sixty feet high in the perpetual gloom beneath the canopy. Then there's the second "story," sturdier trees from 60 to 120 feet high that interweave to form the canopy top. Finally there is the third "story"—the giants of 120 to 200 and more feet high whose crowns proudly burst through the canopy into the sunny upper air.

In every square mile of this profusion there are thousands of species of trees, myriad other plants including lianas 500 feet long and two feet thick, myriad insects, thousands of marvelous birds, thousands of larger animals that live their lives at given heights and never venture up or down to "storys" that belong to others. It is a strange, fascinating world of wonder and of terror for the poor human who certainly has no normal place there.

Man is the rarest animal in the Amazon country. There is one man for every two square miles. Why this scarcity? "Much too simple," says Preston James of Syracuse University, a great authority on Latin America, "is the answer commonly given to the problem of sparse population in the Amazon—that the climate is unsuited to settlement by Europeans. Contained in the thick forests of the area there is a wealth of resources, some already exploited, some awaiting use. . . . Here we find again and again illustrations of the disaster which follows the attempt to collect the fruit without planting the tree; here is a land abundantly endowed with resources only waiting to be collected. The planting of the tree, however, requires so much labor and so much capital that the establishment of the more permanent and intensive forms of land use seems to be impossible."[3]

Thus Professor James joins those who say that the Amazon Valley has not yet been conquered because man, or better, society, has not tried hard enough. Of the two factors, labor and capital, it would appear that labor is the more critical need. A demonstration of this point lay at hand for me. Brother Paul was easing our whaleboat up to the Belterra dock and within a few minutes I was enjoying the warm hospitality of the St. Louis Franciscans in this great center where Henry Ford tried and failed to grow rubber. He did not fail through want of money or scientific skill; he failed to solve his labor problem. In 1946, after seventeen years of effort, Ford sold his $15,000,000 investment to the Brazilian government for $250,000 and called his managers home.

In morning breezes that had the softness of Hawaii, Father Martin conducted me through the Belterra plantation. The Franciscans operate here a parish of 5,000 souls, for the most part composed of families of plantation workers. We drove through miles of mathematically laid out groves of rubber trees. There are two and a half million such trees in Belterra and Fordlandia. The two of us walked in the shady glades and saw the milk-like latex dripping tranquilly into the precisely placed cups on the white-barked trunks standing in the immaculately clean parks. Workers with almost mechanical precision collected the latex or performed the other established chores. No one was pressed, no one faced any of the fearsome dangers of the *seringueiros* of the wild rubber tree areas. When noon came the men lolled in groups in the shade and their children brought them hot lunch from their simple but attractive little homes nearby.

It all seemed a dramatic duplication of the rich rubber plantations that I had visited in Malaya and Indonesia.

"This looks like a triumphant success," I remarked to Father Martin. "Why did Ford pack up and go home?"

"Evidently he became convinced that it wasn't worth the bother," came the casual reply of my St. Louis companion.

In substance, this is the truth of the matter. In 1929 Ford, struck by Harvey Firestone's success in growing his own rubber in Liberia, acquired two huge tracts on the Tapajoz, Fordlandia and Belterra. They totaled three million acres, as much as all the land planted to rubber in Malaya.

Years were lost with false starts in getting the right techniques. But money, brains and patience solved all these problems. The first pound of rubber ever produced came from the Amazon back in the nineteenth century but no one before had ever sought to apply to the Amazon the scientific principles that had brought such huge success in Southeast Asia and that had ruined the rubber industry in the Amazon. Ford sent Doctor James R. Weir to Singapore to bring back two thousand seedling descendants of Amazon rubber trees grown from the seventy thousand seeds that Wickham, the British conspirator of Kew Gardens, had smuggled out of the Amazon. After new experiments to readapt these specimens to their land of origin, cultivated rubber plantations came into being here on the Tapajoz.

But this was only part of the problem. What of the labor? Ford really never solved that. His plan from the start was a labor victory on the Tapajoz like his victory in Detroit. He treated his men royally as to salaries, as to conditions of living. But he never learned to understand the Brazilian caboclo. Why work seven days a week, asked this shrewd Amazonian philosopher, if you earn a week's salary in one day? The caboclo is not immoderately lazy, but money has never in itself been his objective. Ford spoiled him, labor agitators embittered him. The laws of social change were not employed properly to turn the caboclo into a modern worker.

But most important of all, there were too few caboclos. No means could be found to induce new labor to come to the Amazon. Ford could produce only a tenth of the rubber he needed. He sold out and pulled out.

"And now what are the Brazilians doing?" I asked.

"They are handling the labor problem Brazilian style," was the answer. "Their plantation operation keeps to modest proportions and serves above all to train small operators in the Valley to use improved methods for rubber production. Each worker gets a home of mud and palm leaves which costs the government about twenty dollars to build and gets his needs except for food and clothing. Instead of the two to five dollars a day Ford offered, the caboclo gets 40 cruzeiros a day, or about 65 cents U.S. This means tight squeezing but it's what he is accustomed to in these parts."

"What happens to the rubber?"

"Brazil since the war has built up a great rubber-manufacturing industry that is second only to its production of food and textiles. The rubber from these plantations is superlative. Brazil's auto tires are now counted by the million and go all over the continent. Best of all, we are only at the beginning."

Brazilian leaders, let us note, possess the brain power to know what they need if they are properly to develop the Amazon. They have launched a sound plan that can succeed. The question is now principally a political one; can they so create through political action a climate of confidence and conviction that will lead the necessary elements in Brazilian and non-Brazilian society to cooperate in bringing the human resources and financial resources to the Amazon for a successful development enterprise?

One evening at Belterra, Doctor Armando Nadler sat down with us and made the plan for a greater Amazon come alive for us. Nadler is a highly trained agronomist, a quiet man of studious bearing who works with the Instituto Agronomico del Norte, popularly known as the IAN.

"When Mr. Ford relinquished his plantations to the Brazilian government," explained Dr. Nadler, "they were placed in charge of the IAN. This organization disposes of considerable funds. Best proof that Brazil is determined to develop the Amazon lies in the fact that three per cent of the revenue paid into the Rio treasury by every municipality in the nation is set aside each year for use in the Amazon Valley. At present this provides 700,000,000 cruzeiros annually."

"Dr. Nadler, what about the biggest question of all, the human equation? How does the IAN expect to get adequate population to settle in the Amazon?"

"Padre, we feel that in this as in all the problems of the Amazon the solution depends on the quality of our thinking and our planning.

"Today to the great masses of the Western world, not only in Brazil and the Americas but in all Europe, the Amazon is a hell hole, a last-ditch stop only for the desperate and the despairing. How can we alter this popular conception?

"First must come creativeness and research. In this period in which we now live, the Amazon is a place for a relatively few intelligent and resourceful men. It is a huge land area but with much poor land. It is an area of incalculable riches but riches withheld from us by great obstacles as yet unconquered. Intelligence is needed not merely to exploit the Amazon but to discover the secrets for exploiting it.

"Then will come the period of courageous pioneering. To a degree this period is already with us. The Japanese are promising people for this. That fine Japanese boy, Enrique Oti, who came up the river in the boat with you is, as perhaps you know, the son of Sakae Oti, the celebrated farmer-extraordinary of this region. Dr. Camargo and Oti working together have demonstrated that jute can be made to yield phenomenal crops worth hundreds of dollars an acre.

"Finally, when the various factors have been worked out, we are hoping that the good news will go abroad in all the world: 'Hear ye! Hear ye! The Amazon is no longer a hell hole; the Amazon is a happy place to live; the Amazon is a profitable place in which to work and own a home!' In that day and only then will the millions move into our Valley."

A wrinkled Madre, forty years in Brazil, showed me through the men's ward of the Salesian Sisters' hospital at Porto Velho, far up the Madeira River in the Amazon Valley. In the two lines of beds lay forlorn wrecks of humanity, each seemingly more broken than his neighbor.

"They are either rubber workers or river men," Madre explained. "They are brought in to us from the forests ninety per cent dead. They are tough and often pull through."

"What has happened to them?"

"Most suffer from wasting diseases—malaria, amoebic dysentery, malnutrition. This man here was bitten by a snake; it's a miracle that he is alive."

"What kind of a snake?" I asked in fascination.

"A *pucarara,* the deadliest in the Amazon. It belongs to the rattlesnake family but has no rattle. It is not long—hardly more than six or seven feet—but thick-bodied and strong. This seringero was out hunting. He saw the *pucarara* before him but at that moment heard a stir in the tree above and was afraid it was a tiger. He took a quick glance up and the snake hit him so hard he fell over. As the snake pulled back the man shot him. He dragged himself out to a path and happily two friends brought him into the village. There a missionary chanced to be handy and by clever work with hot packs the priest drew off enough of the poison to save him. Then we got him here in the hospital to finish the job of saving him."

"Do many die from snakes, Madre?"

"A number, though not all from poisoning. The greatest enemy of the people is the anaconda, a huge constrictor that can be from twenty to forty feet long. Actually it kills very few human beings in any region in a given year but it is such a terrifying monster that the very thought of it fills the local folk with dread."

"Is South America as fearful a place for snakes as some of us imagine?" I asked Madre.

"I wouldn't know," she replied, "but here's Dr. Macedo. What would you say, Doctor?"

"South America has some bad spots and the Amazon is one of them," said the young doctor, interning here in the back country for experience with tropical diseases. "Our continent ranks next to Asia as the worst in the world for snakes. Some thirty to forty thousand people a year are killed by snakes around the globe. Twenty-five to thirty-five thousand die in Asia. Three to four thousand lose their lives in South America. Africa doesn't compare with South America for deadly snakes—not more than five hundred to a thousand deaths a year occur there. North America reports three to five hundred a year and Europe about fifty."

Thus I left the Salesian hospital with a lecture on snakes. Death from deadly snakes does not result solely from presence of the snakes but, as well, from the failure of a population to protect itself. It is only of late years that public health workers in the Amazon have ushered in a new day, not only by provision against the relatively remote peril of deadly snakes but against far more dangerous deadly microbes, thanks to which disease runs rampant in the area.

In Manáos I visited Mercy Hospital, an establishment with 300 beds conducted by the Daughters of St. Ann, the first Sisters in the Amazon Valley.

"Our group came out from Italy in 1885," explained the Mother. "Then the hospital was only a military post with twenty-nine beds. Some of the older Sisters here remember the days when we could do little more than console the dying. Thank God we have passed beyond that stage."

Particularly since World War II Brazil has been working hard to clean up the Amazon and the United States Department of Health has cooperated in this effort. In 1942 the Serviço Especial de Saúde Pública (SESP) was established and physicians, engineers, nurses and others moved into the Amazon both from the United States and from South Brazil. At Belem the Evandro Chagas Laboratory was set up for research, a basic need to fight disease in an area of medical ignorance such as the Amazon.

In the broad sense of the term, Indians in Brazil run into millions if one embraces with the word everybody who goes by the term caboclo. By the stricter definition, Indians, that is, "wild" Indians following tribal life, run to not more than 150,000.

"Four centuries of exploitation of the Indians," explained one of the Salesians at Manáos, "accounts for much of the violence of these tribes that normally are not bloodthirsty. Anger and fear motivate them. A couple of our Salesians attempted some years back to go among the Chavantes of the border region of Goias and the Mato Grosso. Abused by the whites, these tribesmen in times gone by had crossed into the forests beyond the River of the Dead and swore eternal hatred toward all outsiders.

"The two missionaries, Padres Pedro Sacilotte of São Paulo and John Fuchs of Lake Lucerne, Switzerland, studied the Chavantes tongue for two years. They journeyed hundreds of miles by canoe, by horseback and afoot, familiarizing themselves with the region. Finally, on November 1, 1934, bearing gifts, they made a first contact with forty to fifty Chavantes on a riverbank. In less time than it takes to tell it, the ferocious nomads fell on them, killed them, and left their remains for their canoe men, who had stayed out in the river, to lay away in lonely graves."

Eighteen years later, on July 23, 1952, the Brazilian Chamber of Deputies formally honored as its guest Padre Colbacchini, another Salesian. The Salesians had not been discouraged by the murder of their confreres. Padre Colbacchini's title to fame was the winning of the Chavantes. After years of effort, he and Brother Fernandez had fraternized with the Chavantes on the River of the Dead. It was a visit similar to that of Padres Sacilotte and Fuchs. Instead of death, however, Padre Colbacchini found friendship. The dreaded Chavantes had put aside their hatred at last and made peace.

Despite instances of systematized Indian killing, Brazil's recent record is among the best of the continent for treatment of the aborigines. In 1910 by Presidential decree the Brazilian Service for the Protection of the Indian was established. Candido Mariano de Silva Redondo, remembered as General Rondon, was the distinguished director of the service. Unfortunately, the General, a modern positivist so far as his spiritual outlook was concerned, was hostile to the missionaries and stood for leaving the Indian in his pagan beliefs. Otherwise as a friend of the Indian, General Rondon was a giant. He was a soldier, a civil engineer, a geographer and an anthropologist. He knew the jungle and its dwellers thoroughly, had a rare gift for making friends with the Indian, and worked out an ambitious plan to aid him. Today, for economic reasons among others, the tendency of government in the Amazon is once again to encourage the missionary to guide the Indian.

The forest Indian and his brother the caboclo have been for generations the special object of solicitude of the missionary. Today some 1,300 priests, Brothers and Sisters labor in the Amazon. Of the 350 priests, the majority are necessarily in the larger centers but in almost miraculous fashion the missionary, scarce article though he is, is found in every remote sector and usually has an intimate knowledge of the Indian.

Take as an instance, Padre Protase, a German Franciscan whom I came to admire while in Santarem. He is probably the greatest living authority on the Indians in the sector between the Amazon and Brazil's northern border where it meets Dutch Guiana. He is particularly familiar with the border area known as Guianas Paraenses that counts 8,000 Indians divided among some eighty tribes. With the group of Divine Word scientists who publish *Anthropos* he has prepared a monograph on the Tiriyo tribe of this sector.

"Is there danger going among these people?" I asked.

"The first requisite is to win their confidence," Padre Protase replied. "The first hour has great importance in this respect. They must be convinced that the missionary has come for *their* sakes, not his own. I gather information systematically, according to the rules of the scientists, but this is all secondary to my work for the Indians themselves."

"Are there many missionaries like you who are studying the tribes?"

"Unfortunately no. Three groups contribute to knowledge of the Amazon Indian—government officials, professional scientists and missionaries. Of the three, the missionaries have the best opportunities because they know the Indians of the far interior most intimately. Missionaries as a class, however, overlook the task of systematically gathering data according to the rules of the scientists. Good work in recording information is being done by the Capuchins of the Upper Solimoes, which is the section of the Amazon River nearest Peru, and the Benedictines of the Rio Branco, one of the poorest and most isolated sections, near Venezuela and British Guiana. The Dominicans and the Precious Blood missionaries on the Rio Xingu have made important contributions.

"The study of the Amazon Indians has only just begun. The interior is still one of the great unknown areas of the globe."

Understandably, most missionaries are consumed with the imperious urgency of meeting the crying spiritual needs of the long-neglected people of the Amazon. Keen, imaginative leaders such as Archbishop Albert Ramos of Manáos and Bishop Florian Louvenau of Santarem are striving desperately to provide their flocks with the bare essentials.

"Our first aim," says the Bishop of Santarem, "must be to cover as much ground as possible. Many of our priests spend their lives in endless journeying along the rivers, riding their horses for days into the back country. The people of a given village see a priest at intervals of from once a month to once in six months. For the rest of their existence their worship of God and the conduct of their lives is left to themselves."

Because organized religious life for so many has been so poverty stricken for so long, a festive occasion on the Amazon becomes an extraordinary outburst of spiritual feeling. The visit of the pilgrim statue of Our Lady of Fatima to the Amazon in the course of its journey around the world was marked by explosive demonstrations of affection and devotion. Brother John Boyle of the American Holy Cross Brothers told me of the spectacle as he witnessed it in Santarem.

"It was perhaps the most thrilling experience of my life," explained Brother John. "I don't know how to begin to describe the utter jubilation of the occasion. The entire population of the surrounding country worked for days to prepare the city. The statue of Our Lady came by boat·downstream from Manáos. How do you think Our Lady traveled? Naturally in a *rede,* a hammock. She had made the overnight trip like a true Brazilian. From the shore we could see a woman standing guard, tenderly swinging her back and forth. What Brazilian would not have given his right arm to be in that woman's place!

"Our Lady was carried in procession through Santarem's densely

Forward March!—Joaquin Blanquero walks six miles along the railroad track every morning from his father's farm in the country and is never late for class at Santo Tomas Parochial School in Temuco, Central Chile.

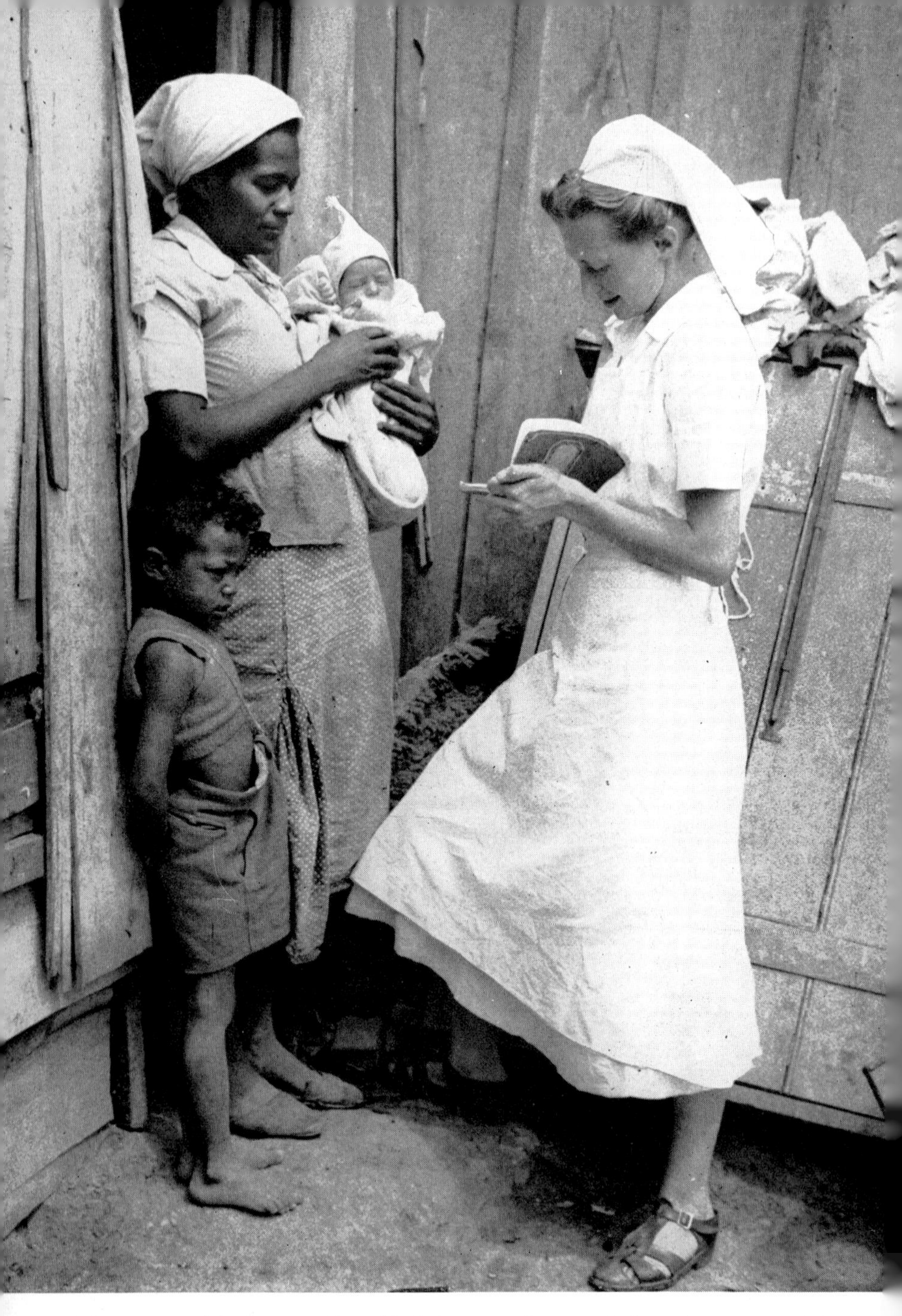

A better world—Among Brazil's laity are thousands keenly aware of their country's social problems. A Grail team nurse in Sao Paulo makes a house to house visitation aimed at serving the great city's needy families.

Blessed milk—Fathers Keenan and Callahan of the American Redemptorists in Paraguay bless UNICEF milk served to their 2,000 school children. Below, Chilean boys drink U.S. surplus milk from Catholic Relief Services.

Schools—San Marcos University, Lima, is the oldest in the hemisphere. These young men aim to be paleontologists. Below, Maryknoll Sisters teach at Lima's first parochial school, named after Lima's beloved St. Rose.

The Andean Corridor—This wild plateau country is beautiful in a harsh, desolate way. Hardy cattle, horses, donkeys and sheep are part of every landscape. The llama, alpaca and vicuna belong to the upper mountains.

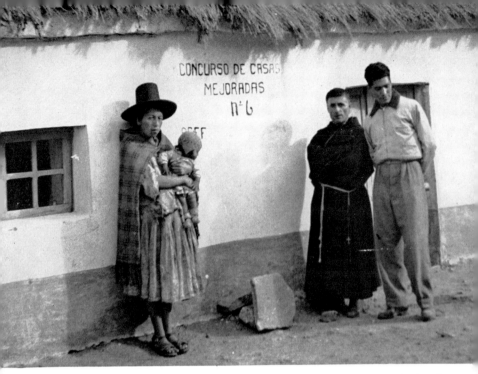

House with windows—The Christ Schools in Bolivia hold a better homes contest in Coipasi. Above, windows introduced into the adobe walls of an Indian home. Below, Indian housewives try out the modern flatiron.

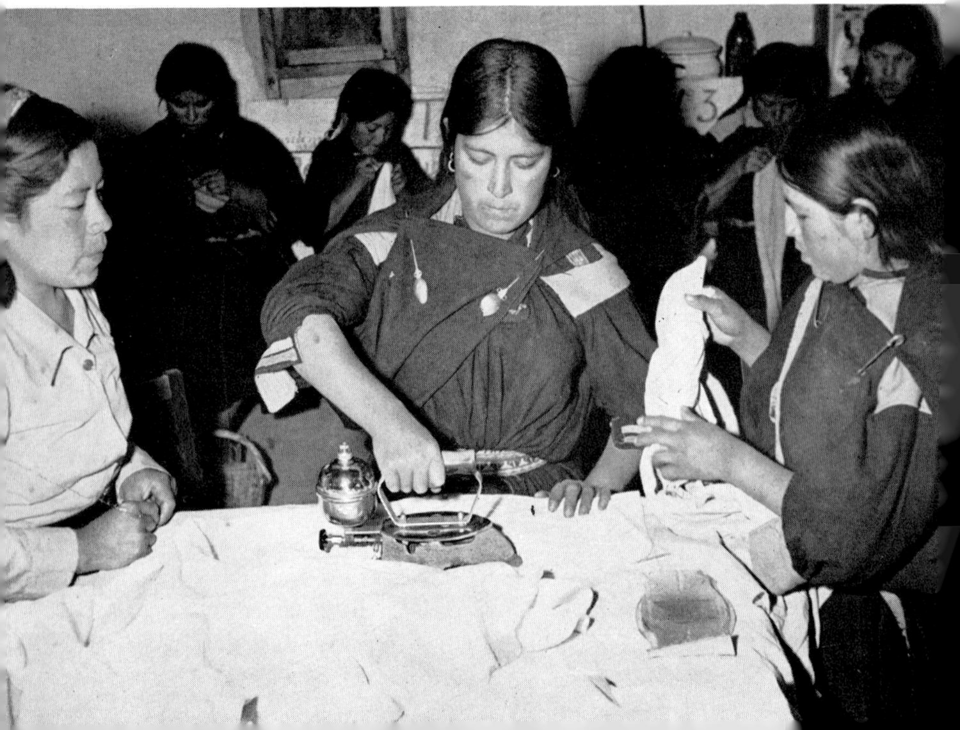

Wild rubber—Father Joseph Flynn of Cleveland examines a shipment of 300 pound balls of wild rubber, the latex gathered drop by drop from jungle trees, ready to journey from Bolivia down the Amazon to New York.

Holiday in the country—Fiesta time in Panama calls for happy excursions to rural villas where placid oxen substitute for the modern automobile. The women folk wear the beautiful Panamanian costume, the pollera, of white cambric richly ornamented with brightly embroidered flowers, birds and garlands.

Sick call—Bishop Charles Brown, a native New Yorker, journeying as a Maryknoll Missioner into the Bolivian mountains to a dying Indian.

Indian teachers—Expressionless but deeply earnest, these men train in Azangaro as religion teachers for the villages of Peru's altiplano.

Perfect poise—The Guatemalan market woman carries her basket on her head with the same aplomb that the American housewife carries her bag on her arm. Guatemalan dress is notable for its lovely color combinations.

Younger set—Natty looking Ecuadorian student nurses get a lesson in nutrition at their Quito training school. Below, a lively chat between the girls at Colegio Monte Maria of the Maryknoll Sisters in Guatemala.

Cardinal's theatre—The cultural theatre of Monsignor Salcedo's radio schools in Colombia is named after Cardinal Crisanto Luque of Bogota. Over 6500 radio schools bring learning and religion to the mountaineers.

Benignity—The Mayans dwell today in Yucatan (southern Mexico) and in Guatemala. Many a Mayan grandmother is the guide and mentor of a houseful of hacienda children who love her for her kindly warmth and devotion.

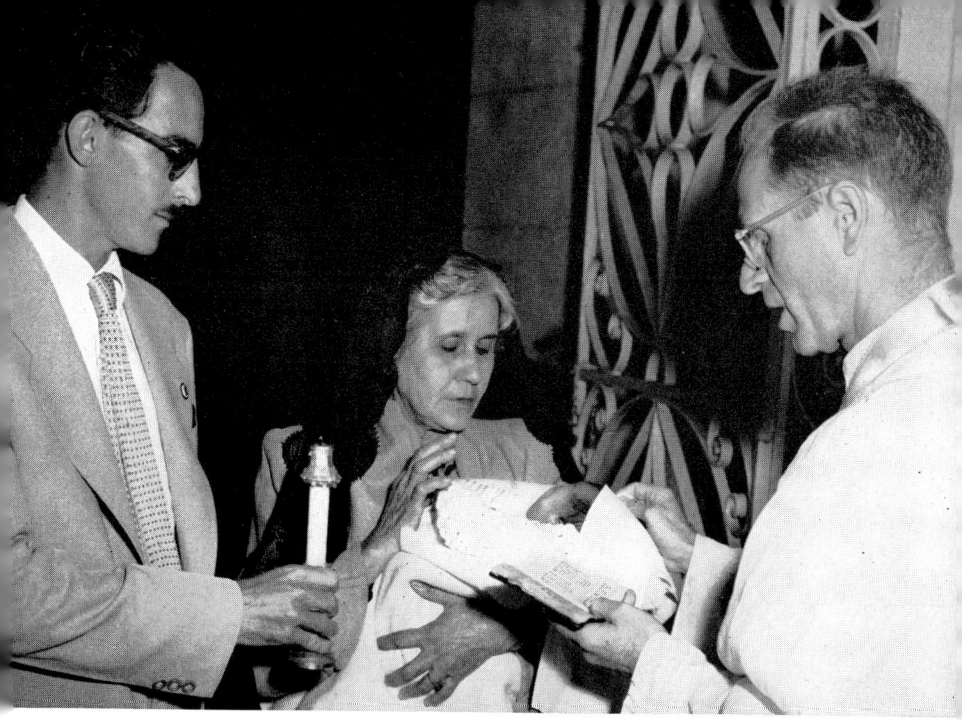

Young Christians—A Havana matron is sponsor for an infant receiving baptism from Father John McKniff of the Augustinians. Below, Father George Hogan of Maryknoll gives First Communion to a youngster in Peto, Yucatan.

Mary had a little lamb—as cute as it could be. She brought it to school with her one day. Tommy didn't approve. Thus boys in the Bolivian Pando have the same problems with girls as everywhere else in the world.

packed streets and the exultation was electric. All sang the hymn that told the story of Fatima. At every pause someone would cry out, "Vive Nossa Senhora!" and the crowd would burst forth, "Vive!" Someone would call out, "Let's all clap our hands for Nossa Senhora!" And all would clap. "Wave your banners!" would come the cry, and the forest of banners would wave madly.

"For hours this procession to the Cathedral went on and then came long ceremonies in the square. The grand procession was held at night from the Cathedral to the stadium. This was by candlelight, the candles set in decorated paper shades like little Japanese lanterns. In the stadium there was much singing and many inspiring addresses. When on Monday the statue left by plane to visit the Indians of the Xingu River, the mass sorrow at parting was poignant in the extreme. Tears poured unrestrainedly down thousands of cheeks as the plane disappeared over the horizon. Bishop Florian voiced their farewell. 'A fond good-bye to the Pilgrim Virgin,' he cried. 'But be consoled—Our Lady truly came to us with the statue here in Santarem, but now only the statue goes away. Our dear Lady stays with us!' "

Brother John caught the true import of the delirium of these people of the Amazon at the visit of the Pilgrim Virgin.

"Everyone among the Americans here experienced in extraordinary fashion a sensible awareness of the Blessed Mother's presence on this occasion," he observed. "I think this was because we were sharing so wholeheartedly in the very vital piety which seems natural to the Brazilian people. If we can manage to gain a little of their fervor and give them in return the intellectual convictions that in North America we have from careful instruction and well organized spiritual life, the work of our Holy Cross Brothers here in Brazil should prove a very wholesome experience both for us and for the people we hope to teach."

The most unique religious ceremony of this kind in which I participated took place far up the Amazon from Santarem in the mission of the Canadian Franciscans a few miles from Iquitos. Iquitos, 2,400 miles from the mouth of the mighty river, is the headwaters port for ocean-going vessels and lies within the confines of Peru. With Father Rodolphe Guibord of the Franciscans, I had journeyed by tiny river launch from Iquitos to Indiana, the Franciscan center for this pioneer region. On the fifteenth of August, the Feast of the Assumption of Our

Lady, the people of this area participated in a beautiful boat procession on the Amazon.

The largest launch, on which rode Bishop Laberg with a number of the Fathers including myself, carried the statue of Our Lady mounted on a throne atop the cabin roof. Behind us followed a fleet of some thirty large family canoes in double file, each crowded with occupants, all of the boats decorated with paper streamers, flowers and branches of green. At the Perez farm some miles down the river we tied up to the shore and the four bearers of Our Lady struggled up the 75 foot bank. The rest of us followed and, forming into a procession in the high field above, we walked through a herd of tranquilly munching cows to the palm leaf canopy built by the Amazon River caboclos of the neighborhood for the outdoor Mass of Assumption Day.

Toward its end a caboclo at the edge of the crowd took the cover off a stone crock he had thoughtfully brought up from the river and served water to many grateful worshippers about him. Then we sat in the tiny spots of shade under the small trees in the field and took lunch, the huge river before us, a thousand miles and more of tropic jungle in every direction about us.

Less than fifty of the priests of the region were born in the Amazon Valley. Candidates for the priesthood undoubtedly will be found in the Amazon some day but at present less than a hundred seminarians are under training. Local vocations to the Sisterhoods are more numerous but the Amazon is definitely a foreign mission field for communities of both men and women from Europe and North America.

I had my most exciting school experience in all Brazil in the parish of the American Redemptorists in Belem. Principal field of these Redemptorists from St. Louis is the city of Manáos and the two hundred and fifty miles of villages on the shores of the Amazon upstream from Manáos. Our Lady of Perpetual Help Parish in Belem counts 30,000 souls, most of them wretchedly poor.

Belem with its quarter of a million inhabitants, the great port at the mouth of the Amazon, is ninety miles from the open sea and only a few miles below the equator. It has large modern sections with fine squares, broad and shady boulevards, luxurious tropic vegetation and handsome buildings.

But my best memories of Belem turn about the less pretentious parts of the city, the sprawling slums of the poor. These people are city folk, at least by adoption, and hence do not class as caboclos. One of the points of distinction is their passion to give their children some schooling. The parochial school cares for 600 boys and girls and there are small government schools in the district. But the most extraordinary phenomenon is the presence of thirty small private schools within the parish confines, always crowded with youngsters whose parents gladly pay monthly fees to get their children educated.

"Some go without food to meet their school dues," explained Father Ronald Weninger. "On their part the kids put up with unbelievable conditions to get a little book learning."

Father Ronald and I made the rounds of these extraordinary institutions. There was Pedro's school. Pedro is a cripple with a bright, kindly face, warm penetrating eyes and a devotion to his youngsters that is legendary. He would well symbolize the master teacher of the ages who has always conveyed so much love as well as learning to his pupils.

The school? It is the front parlor of Pedro's little home, a room seven feet by seven, into which he squeezes two shifts daily. We saw the afternoon shift, which I counted as we stood near Pedro's desk and found to total twenty-four boys, squeezed in so tightly that they seemed to be sitting in one another's laps. There was a cordial, homey air in the sardine-box cubicle. Father Ronald quizzed two youngsters who bounced up smartly and answered alertly and exactly.

"They answer well, Pedro," remarked the Padre.

"Pedro teaches us well," volunteered one of the boys enthusiastically. Here was a schoolmaster who had captured the hearts of the boys who literally sat at his feet.

Another front-parlor school we visited likewise was conducted by a cripple, a lady who was a hunchback, neat and smart in her yellow dress, sharp and intense in her manner, quite evidently an earnest good person. At our next stop we found Maria das Dores out on the street talking to two girl friends while her thirty children sat idle in the room. The house was quite unkempt.

"Maria is not too bad a girl," ventured Father Ronald, "but she finds it a problem to do a hard day's work."

Best school of all was that conducted by three Negro women, the three Marias—Maria do Rosario, Maria de Lourdes and Maria da Asunção. They had 150 pupils and kept perfect order in the several rooms of their house where they held the classes. Maria de Lourdes was the spark, the genius of the enterprise. She is slight of build, quick moving, clever, decisive, able for many tasks in a small compass of time. All three sisters are daily communicants.

"The three Marias get the heaviest fees in the parish," explained Father Ronald. "Their rates are 20 to 80 cruzeiros per child per month, according to the grade. That would be 32¢ to $1.24 per child in U.S. money. The other schools charge 10 to 40 cruzeiros a month—16¢ to 64¢. For our families, these are heavy payments."

With Father Ronald I visited some of the families in the poorest sections of the parish, the Vila de Barca (Boat Village), and Val de Caes (Dog Valley)—wretched squatters' settlements among the most notorious in Latin America.

"I suppose most people in a neighborhood like this feel that life has cheated them," I remarked.

"Yes, but usually without bitterness. Take Vicente, the village cobbler. Let's go over to his house and you'll see."

Vicente, benignity in his smile and warmth in his voice, greeted us as as we entered. His motley cobbling bench was set up in the front room that should have been his parlor. We met his attractive wife and their four beautiful children.

"I'm a hard luck Joe, Padre," he remarked almost immediately in the local Portuguese equivalent. "That's why this wonderful family of mine is condemned to live over the stinking vapors of this unhealthy marsh."

"What are you going to be, son, when you grow up?" Father Ronald asked Franco, the eldest boy.

"I want to be a cornet player," he replied immediately.

"And you, Maria?"

Maria was shy and had to be coaxed. Finally she said, "I want to be a nurse and help Sister in the clinic."

"What about you, Luis?"

"I'm going to paint beautiful pictures," Luis replied in a way that suggested that he had it all figured out.

"And you, Miguel?—Perhaps you haven't made up your mind yet."

"Yes I have," answered Miguel, the youngest. "I'm going to be a doctor and cure people."

"But how would these children have such wonderful ideas?" I asked in surprise.

Vicente's eyes filled as he burst out fervently, "They get them from their mother. Everything lovely in this house comes from their mother."

"Best thing in the parish," said Father Ronald as we walked home, "is the enthusiasm of the men. Hardly one of them went to church when we Redemptorists arrived a few years ago. Yet in 1953 for the Eucharistic Congress of the Amazon here in Belem, two thousand of our men marched in a solid mass to the city stadium. The Archbishop was delivering a radio address on the platform as they entered and dropped his text to exclaim, 'My dear friends of the radio audience, we are witnessing a rare sight here at this moment. A body of two thousand fine men with their Padres from North America at their head are walking four abreast into our midst.' "

SECTION TWO

Lands of the South

• • ● • •

Chapter 1

New Day for the Argentines

ONE DAY IN 1954 while in Buenos Aires I stopped into a downtown restaurant for lunch. A gentleman sitting by the window kept glancing my way and toward the end of his meal came over to my table.

"Excuse me, Padre," he asked, "would you by chance be a North American?"

I replied in the affirmative and with quiet deliberation my interrogator undertook to relate his connections with Catholic parishes, colleges and dignitaries in the course of his years of schooling and entry into his career which was that of the law. As he was about to leave me he lowered his voice and leaned toward me.

"Padre, I have a law partner who for political reasons had to get out of Argentina and who is now teaching in New York. I cannot trust my correspondence to the mails. Would you consider carrying a letter to him for me?"

I gladly accepted the letter, which was delivered surreptitiously to my residence. I left Argentina and the Peron dictatorship and at the New York end established a pleasant acquaintance with this exile. A few months after the September revolution of 1955 I received in the mail one day a formidable document making me the beneficiary of an air travel life insurance policy for $12,500, taken out by this individual before his flight from Idlewild to Buenos Aires.

"Needless to say, I don't expect you to collect," explained a message. "I merely want you to know that I am returning to Argentina, once again a land of the free."

Argentina is overwhelmingly European. Of its 17,000,000 inhabitants, 90 per cent are from Europe, 8 per cent are of mixed blood and 2 per cent, a segment of some 300,000 souls, is Indian. But the predominance of Europeans is heightened by the distribution. The lovely provincial city of Córdoba, almost at the mathematical heart of the nation, is the dividing line between the modern European area and the older, thinly settled mountainous northwest and the Andean piedmont where there are districts running to 50 and 75 per cent mestizo.

One evening in the vivid mountain city of Salta a government official from Buenos Aires, a *Porteno* as such citizens of the capital are called, engaged me in conversation.

"It is like being in a foreign land here," he commented, "I am from a family that is Spanish on both sides; here in the mountains two out of every three men have Indian blood in them."

Most Argentines regard such comments as in poor taste but the fact remains that men are found in Argentina as elsewhere who take furtive glances at their fellows and assert their separation from them by blood.

Far to the north in Misiones Province the Divine Word Fathers do excellent work among tribal Indians. In Formosa and Chaco Provinces on the Bolivian border there are thirty to forty thousand Indians. In the Salta area Franciscans maintain Indian missions while Newquen Province in the foothills of the Andes counts splinter groups belonging to eleven different tribes.

Today there are but 3,000 Indians below the Rio Negro in southern Argentina. As late as the 1870s Indian raiders stole 40,000 head of cattle a year from the ranchers of the pampas. The government organized a campaign of annihilation in the years 1879-1883 and made great areas safe for settlement. It was one of those brutally effective operations reminiscent of our own Western plains repeated in a South American land destined to resemble us in many ways.

The hard core of old stock Argentines, as is the case with the old stock in the United States, represents but a minority today. The majority of the population has settled in the country within the past hundred years. The heaviest contingent has come from Spain. The Italians are next in number while French, Germans, Austrians, Russians, Irish, British and Swiss are likewise numerous.

Two-thirds of all the citizens of Argentina live today either in the capital or within the immediate hinterland of Buenos Aires, concentrated in the celebrated Humid Pampa, one of the richest crop and cattle areas in the world. In this small region are nearly 70 per cent of all Argentine railroads, 84 per cent of all the automobiles, 86 per cent of the acreage in money crops, 63 per cent of the vast herds of fine cattle, and 85 per cent of all the industrial production.

Buenos Aires, a handsome, modern metropolis of 4,000,000, is not only the largest city of Argentina and of Latin America, but the largest city of the Southern Hemisphere and second only to Paris among the Latin cities of the world. Certainly Buenos Aires is distinctly Latin; seldom does the atmosphere suggest a city in the United States. One handsome street or plaza reminds us of Paris, another conjures up memories of Rome or Milan, still others are definitely Spanish. Heart of the city is the marvelous Plaza de Mayo. The major artery is Avenida Rivadavia, named after a patriot leader of the early nineteenth century whose regime despite good intentions straightened the life of the Church. The great avenue runs for endless miles westward from its starting point by the harbor out through distant suburbs.

Buenos Aires harbor is one of the great ports of the world, with an average of 90 to 100 ships at moorage every day of the year. I remember it as the field of labor of Father John McFadden, a lovely old gentleman of the Columban Fathers who as chaplain of the Apostolate of the Sea is wonderfully well liked by the sailors. The tremendous docking facilities and formidable batteries of grain elevators create a dramatic sense of vastness.

Best thing in Buenos Aires is the people. In government circles the mood is formal. In the commercial core to the north of Avenida de Mayo there are business marts and tall office buildings where men hustle about after the manner to which we are accustomed in New York. Along the fine shopping streets the men and women are as smart and chic as the shops themselves.

In the homes of the families of wealth and culture, whether of old stock or of successful new arrivals, there is gracious living and a tradition for accent on character. Yet within the upper class today runs a current of subdued uneasiness, the recognition of a world that changes and challenges them. Typical was the comment of Señora Maria Gallegas at dinner in the Gallegas home. The family of eight had filed into the dining room at the customary hour of nine in the evening. The tempo among the young people was lively to the point of hilarity until someone mentioned trouble during the current strike at their uncle's plant. Immediately a hush passed over the table.

"It's all so sad," remarked Señora Maria, our hostess. "How wonderful it was when we were young. Mother brought us up to take it for granted that everybody we knew, rich or poor, was equal and we fraternized with the whole countryside. But now in recent years comes this unpleasant effort to make the lower classes feel hostile toward the upper."

Many of the Argentine upper class possess no great means. Yet many of the estates within fifty miles of Buenos Aires bespeak the enormous wealth that the meat-wheat-corn economy produces when conditions are normal. At least fifty families in Buenos Aires Province still have holdings of more than 75,000 acres. An Argentine multimillionaire will maintain not only a costly town house but a great country home set in a park with a swimming pool, polo field, and sometimes a golf course.

There are always the extensive stables. "We pamper our prize cattle like poodle dogs," explained Ricardo Miranda. "The placard over each cowstall carries a pedigree that reads like the ancestry of a titled family of Europe."

The more successful and the better educated in Argentina are not limited to those of Spanish stock. Many Italian, British and German names are prominent. There are 80,000 Irish in Buenos Aires who, while completely at home with the Spanish language and Argentine ways, have kept up their English to a remarkable degree.

One day in the Hotel Continental in Buenos Aires I was intrigued by the distinct Irish brogue in the hotel housekeeper's Spanish as she gave instructions to one of the staff.

"May I ask your name?" I ventured in English.

"Mary Delahanty," replied the woman. "How did you guess that I spoke English?"

"It wasn't difficult," I answered with a chuckle. "How long are you here?"

"My sister and I are in the hotel for twenty-four years. I am the night housekeeper and my sister is the housekeeper for the day staff."

"Do many of you of Irish blood keep up your English?" I asked.

"A great many. We have English-language newspapers and we have confessions in English at a number of the churches including La Merced a few blocks from this hotel."

A fuller appreciation of the immigrant population is obtained in the workers' sections of the city, the miles and miles of populous areas with their monotonously uniform houses.

"I love Buenos Aires," said Pietro Planamento of Naples in the course of a delightful chat one morning. "Whoever wants to work here in Argentina can do so. Everybody can have enough. There's no reason to be a Communist here. There's no reason anyway. The Communists want to destroy the family and put the state in its place."

"How much of a family have you, Pietro?" I asked.

"I have six fine children, the offspring of my wonderful little Argentine wife."

"Your wife, then was not born in Italy."

"No, Padre, Inez is of Spanish blood. It is always with deep emotion that I recall our humble beginnings. When we stroll along the street today, Padre, my friends say, 'Pietro, your wife dresses so well and walks like a queen. She must be from a fine family.' I laugh and say, 'Very fine indeed, amigo, she belongs to the nobility of the honest workers of the world.' "

"How did you meet her, Pietro?"

"I was dreadfully poor when I came from Italy, Padre, but I got a pushcart and became a peddler. I met Inez as I made my rounds. She was always sweet and smiling, beautiful as a lily. Soon I could rent a little store, I had a few pesos and I asked Inez to marry me. We ran the store together and we always had enough to send the children to school. Now Miguel, our oldest boy, is finishing college. This is the story of Argentina, Padre. All Italians here, even old Italians, feel young and strong. So likewise in New York, Padre, Italians can work hard and go to the top."

"What do you know about New York, Pietro?"

"I know that an Italian named LaGuardia was mayor of the city and another Italian named Impellitteri was also mayor. I know that at one time in the United States three great cities—New York, New Orleans and San Francisco—all had Italian mayors. I know that in the United States many Italians have made a great deal of money, own their own homes, and get elected to positions in the government."

Wonderful as Argentina is, the greatest tales of all that pass from mouth to mouth among the plain people are about our fabulous dreamland to the north.

Argentine history has its romantic turn. In the beginning the area was the ugly duckling of the South American continent because it had no gold or silver mines, nothing but pampas. The Spanish searchers for wealth passed it by. Those who approached South America by the east coast sailed unseeing past the pampas, seeking the Inca Empire. They mounted the Plate River and left their boats in Paraguay before making the agonizing journeys overland to Bolivia and Peru. Their successors soon found that it was far easier to use the west coast route.

Thus Paraguay, Uruguay and Argentina were long the neglected backyard of the Spanish realm in the Andes. Asunción, today the capital of Paraguay, was the primary settlement center of all this area but not very important. Such Argentine cities as Salta and Tucumán were founded from Lima, while Mendoza was founded from Chile. Buenos Aires was settled in 1580 but for two hundred years it counted for little in the South American world.

As we peer into this otherwise dull gray record of the Plate River past, two exhilarating events present their bright gleam of promise. The vessels of the ill-fated expedition of Pedro de Mendoza, aimed at founding Buenos Aires, touched the pampa shore in 1535. The expedition was a tragic failure but for one thing—seventy-two horses and mares, surviving the tortures of the ocean journey from Spain, abandoned ship to run wild on the vast empty plains. This was event number one. Seventeen years later, in 1552, occurred event number two. Out of another vessel from Spain came seven cows and a bull and they likewise took to the open grass country.

These horses and cattle made history. They multiplied in miraculous fashion. Soon vast herds of both in almost astronomical numbers were plunging and veering over the pampas on a continent that had never known a horse or a cow till the coming of the Spaniard. Scattered settlers built a trade in horse and cow hides, tallow, salted beef that continued for some three centuries.

Out of this business developed one of the most unique and colorful types in all Latin America, the *gaucho,* or South American cowboy. The term is distinctive of the Plate River country, though used in Uruguay and the southern provinces of Brazil. The gauchos were of Spanish or mestizo stock, long led a lonely and precarious existence in the world of the pampa, and developed a body of crafts and folkways that constituted a distinctive gaucho culture. The strongest motif in Argentine art, music, poetry and literature is this inimitable native son of the pampas, the gaucho. Today in actual life he has practically disappeared from the scene.

Argentina is celebrated today for its huge production of some of the tastiest beef in the world. Men forget that even in the recent past this beef was far from being high in quality. For centuries Argentine cattle consisted of scrub animals that ran at will on the vast, unfenced range, bred without care and principally for the hides.

In 1877, a momentous event took place. The first refrigerator ship left the Argentine with frozen meat for England. The meat was so poor that the importers couldn't get British buyers. The shock proved a blessing in disguise for the Argentine *estancieros* who resolved thereupon to remove the stain from the national escutcheon. They purchased herds of high-grade Herefords in England, carefully bred them in fenced-in pastures, made war against the cattle tick that gave fever to their herds and, finally, revolutionized the feeding by sowing a huge acreage of the Humid Pampa to alfalfa.

Alfalfa! Here is the stealthy invader into the pampa economy that brought the downfall of the herdsmen, always bitterly opposed to the entry of the agriculturalists. Alfalfa had to be planted on plowed land, then cut and delivered to the herders. Even for care of the cattle, many more hands were needed than during the days before modernization. Thus at last the *estancieros,* interested only in animals and in reserving the rich pampas solely to grazing; thus at last this ultra-conservative class wanted immigrants.

This was an epoch-making decision. As early as 1856 the first agricultural colony from Europe had been introduced into the Humid Pampa. In that year a group of 208 Swiss families was established at Esperanza, a long distance north of Buenos Aires because the area of choicest land was not avilable. The herding families disapproved and for twenty-five years blocked the wheat growers who felt it a sacrilege to employ exclusively for livestock raising the pampa's quarter-of-a-million square miles of deep, rich soil, one of the world's most fertile farming areas.

Now came a change; the herder needed the farmer. Both he and the gaucho scorned the actual work of farming, but the *estanciero* encouraged farming to implement the expansion and improvement of his grazing lands. The most effective way to prepare for the planting of alfalfa was to rent the land to tenants for four or five years as wheat acreage. The tenants were then required to turn over this land for a decade to alfalfa crops. Then once again the wheat grower came back with his family to his rude temporary shelter to plant his grain.

"But even today," explained Ricardo Miranda, an *estanciero* with a beautiful estate an hour's drive out of Buenos Aires, "cattle raising holds the primacy of prestige despite the increased importance of wheat and other cereals. Even in the districts of greatest wheat production, grazing land is never less than 40 per cent of the total area. Most of us have never become genuine farmers."

Some six million immigrants became citizens of Argentina before World War II. In the postwar world, which has been in great part a closed world to European emigrants, the United States has received the largest quota, a total of a million and a half. Canada and Australia have accepted substantial contingents of a little less than a million each, while Latin America has received 1,200,000. Of these, almost 600,000 have entered and remained in Argentina. Brazil has received 350,000, while Venezuela, the only other large client on the continent, reports a flow of 200,000.

One day in 1630 a caravan of ox-carts lumbered along the rough road out of Buenos Aires on its way over the pampa to Córdoba. Evening approached and the call came to set up camp. The journeyers had reached the little Lujan River, about fifty miles west of the city. The oxen were unharnessed and freed to graze in the open pasture of the treeless plain. The men huddled awhile about the fire of dried thistle branches and then went to sleep. It was just another night.

But next morning a strange thing happened. As the sun rose the men harnessed their oxen to their carts and broke camp. The animals lumbered slowly into action—all except one pair that refused to budge.

Shouting, cajoling, whipping were all to no avail. The headman ordered the *carreta,* or covered wagon, to which the animals were attached to be emptied and carefully reloaded, with due attention to the weight. But to no purpose. The oxen would not budge.

Finally it was noticed that the team would pull whenever one light box, that even the young Negro boy in the group could lift, was left off. The box was due for delivery to an *estanciero* along the route.

"Jose," called the headman to the boy, "take off that box and open it."

The rough teamsters gazed in wonder as the lid was removed. Within lay a small terra-cotta figure of Our Lady, garbed in a cope with a crown on her head, fashioned after the style of the artisans of Peru.

"Jose," said the headman, "Our Lady wants to stay here. You'll stay and take care of her till we arrange things."

And the story goes that Jose the Negro remained at Lujan as the life-long custodian of Our Lady. The rancher on whose land the incident occurred, Rosendo Oramas by name, welcomed the statue into his home and kept it for over forty years. Finally in 1671 the Bishop of Buenos Aires and the civil dignitaries assisted at its formal removal to a specially constructed shrine.

Already it was held in honor. Indians prayed before it and great favors were attributed to the intercession of the Mother of God as both redskins and colonials appealed to her here. Bartolomé Mitre, Argentine president whose mature wisdom assuaged the age-old bitterness between the peoples of the provinces and the capital, between gaucho and *Porteno,* prayed at Lujan. A large painting of Mitre kneeling before the statue of the Virgin hangs at the shrine. In 1887 Our Lady of Lujan was canonically declared the patron of the three republics of Uruguay, Paraguay and Argentina. Other great Argentine leaders—Belgrano, Pueyrredón, Martin Rodríguez, Viamonte—prayed for the nation here and in the hour of victory dedicated their swords here to the beloved Madonna.

In 1910 the tall spires of the present basilica rose 340 feet above the unbroken pampa and today buses by the score roll out from Buenos Aires carrying thousands of pilgrims for prayer. The entire town of Lujan is a gracious shrine to religion and fatherland with delightful colonial settings and museums that recall the past.

Lujan demonstrates how Christianity was built into the warp and woof of Latin America's republics. Nevertheless it was a restless, uneasy altar on which religion was enthroned in Spanish America. The cirumstances under which ecclesiastical administration in the New World was developed were most extraordinary. At the dawn of the nineteenth century, when the fight to dislodge Spain became a reality, the Catholic Church in Latin America had for some four hundred years been under the direction not of the Popes of Rome but of a sort of vice pope, the King of Spain, duly installed and empowered by the Vicar of Christ in an arrangement unique in all Catholic history.

"Remember," commented an Argentine priest to me in Buenos Aires, "for centuries not even a bottle of Mass wine could be delivered to the Church in Latin America without the permission of a Spanish officer."

Beginning with the second voyage of Columbus the flow of missionaries entered the New World. The Christianization of the Indians, pledged to the Holy See by the Spanish king, promised to entail a heavy outlay of money. The Pope recognized this and agreed in 1501 that all tithes collected for the Church in the colonies would go to the monarch. The really important concessions to the crown were made in 1508. In that year Pope Julius II accorded the following rights to Spain's rulers: (1) the right to select all the clergymen to occupy Church offices great or small in the New World, though reserving an approval of the choices to the Holy See; (2) the sole right to approve construction of churches and monasteries in the New World; (3) the right to decide the boundaries of all dioceses; (4) the right to sanction each new mission activity.

By way of usurpation, the Spanish king soon was exercising further rights: (1) the approval of all decrees made by clerical councils and synods in Spanish America; (2) approval of the publication in Latin America of all papal decrees, papal bulls, and permissions for ordination; (3) intervention by government officers in all affairs of the colonial Church other than matters of doctrine.

The Holy See's grants and concessions became known as the *Real Patronato.* No concessions in the records of Christendom compare with the *Real Patronato* in their all-embracingness. "Allowing so much control to the temporal power," explain Fathers Bannon and Dunne in their history of Latin America, "opened the way to a number of possible abuses. There were such in the Indies, but, by and large, it must be said to the credit of the Spanish kings that they used their privileges quite loyally."[1]

Some distinguished figures on the European scene took a more severe view than do our two American confreres of Spain's control of the Church in Latin America. Cardinal Giustiniani, the Papal Nunzio in Madrid, wrote as follows to Cardinal della Somaglia in Rome in 1826, "The restrictions which were imposed on the ecclesiastical authorities in [Spanish] America suffice to subvert all the principles of Canonical Jurisprudence, and create in Spain a species of Anglican Supremacy."[2]

In Argentina, as in the rest of Spanish America, the defeat of Spain and the refusal of Spain to recognize defeat, with Spain's consequent refusal to permit the Holy See to assume the direct leadership of things spiritual in Latin America, created an administrative vacuum. Thus it was quite natural that in the postcolonial period the new rulers would expect to continue the same theory of government in spiritual things as operated under the Spanish. To accept anything less would be, the new governments felt, a humbling admission that their position was inferior and second class as compared to that of old Spain.

Their clerical friends in the New World felt the same. In 1810 when the first governing junta took over Argentina, local churchmen advised the junta to assume the full prerogatives of the *patronato* as belonging to them as successors to Spain. Indeed, when Latin American governments showed themselves conciliatory, Rome in some measure accorded them these prerogatives. In 1874 Pius IX conceded to the president of Peru a temporary right of patronage "such as was enjoyed by the grace of the Apostolic See by the Catholic kings of Spain before Peru was separated from their authority."[3]

The early rulers of Argentina quickly undertook to legislate for the Church much as they did for the state. Manuel Rosas, the strong gaucho dictator who ruled from 1835 to 1852, was sympathetic to religion but gave orders to the priest quite as he did to the army officer. He specified the church services for every national holiday, for every military victory. He decreed against long sermons (not a bad move, surely) and told the preachers what they should preach. He ordered that his portrait be placed on church altars, be incensed during ceremonies and solemnly carried in processions.

One reason why for one hundred fifty years the government authorities, down to the latest outburst of Peron in 1954, have dealt so arbitrarily with religious matters is this heritage of muddled thinking from the past. Political leaders have blown hot and blown cold, some bestowing favors, some aiming to restrict or destroy, but great numbers have been misled regarding the basic principle, namely, the division of authority as regards the things of God and the things of Caesar.

"However clever Peron is in many ways," explained a dignitary in Buenos Aires in the prepersecution period, "he is an ignorant upstart as regards the role of religion in the life of a people. He throws an occasional bone of privilege to the Church or Churchmen but he shows no more regard for spiritual rights than for civil rights."

Thanks to the zeal of many fine Argentines, Catholic colleges and institutions of charity, particularly around the capital, became numerous and strong as the twentieth century advanced. The annual directory of Catholic organizations of social assistance for the city of Buenos Aires is a volume of over four hundred pages. As part of the plan to exalt the dictatorship, Peron undertook to gobble up large numbers of the Catholic institutions of charity. "Peron *cumple!*" read the great placards on many enterprises throughout the capital and the nation, "Peron achieves!" My first sight on arriving at the Buenos Aires airport was of two huge, handsome posters in the waiting room, one of Peron, the second of his wife Evita, with "Peron *cumple!*" emblazoned above them. My mind jumped back to the Rome of the then triumphant Mussolini of the early 1930s when everywhere the eye met similar posters of Italy's great-jawed dictator, always labeled with the words, "Viva il Duce!" In Buenos Aires a bitter social feud went on between Eva Peron and the women of the Argentine aristocracy. Whatever the merits of the contest, it gave further impetus to the Perons to take away their social enterprises from the Catholic women of the capital. All of these social activities were gathered into a huge quasi-governmental organization which became the special glory of Eva Peron who was sold to the populace as Argentina's angel of mercy.

Bishop Miguel de Andrea, Auxiliary of Buenos Aires, was one of the few who thwarted the plans of the Peronistas. His Excellency had built up one of the outstanding Catholic enterprises of its kind in the world in his Federation of Catholic Societies of Employed Women. It had an enrollment of 25,000 and possessed a large building as center, with residence quarters, cafeteria, recreation halls, sports fields, baths, medical services, library, vocational training courses, a beautiful chapel. When Peron undertook to take this over, by skillfully directing an appeal to the dictator through the mouths of thousands of working girls who asked to be let alone in their beloved center, the Federation headquarters was able to outlive the dictatorship in maintaining its original identification.

As the years passed, many Catholics came to be ashamed that the Church did not openly protest the abuses of the dictator. An Argentine priest visiting in Mexico remarked to a clerical confrere, "Here in Mexico you enjoy the blessed aftermath of a persecution; in Argentina we suffer the disgrace of peace."

But Peron saved Catholics from this embarrassment by attacking the Church, which he recognized as disgusted with his carryings-on. Shortly after this event an Argentine Catholic exclaimed to me, "Wonderful! Nothing else matters now so far as the Church in Argentina is concerned. What a stain it would have been on the pages of history if Peron had come and gone and the Church was recorded as having bowed to the blandishments of the dictator."

What did Peronism do to Argentina?

"Peron," noted an Argentine with whom I spoke recently in New York, "gave the laboring man in Argentina a sense of self-respect which he never before possessed. Never again will the shirtless ones be content to go back to pre-Peron levels. Peron deceived the men in his promises but he presented them with a new picture of what they have a right to possess. Those who follow Peron are forced to work hard for the laboring class or face their bitter hostility."

Here is one point of view. Others see untold harm in the class hostility Peron fomented. And there are still others.

"Peron," explained a young Buenos Aires doctor to me, "has awakened the Argentine layman to a keen appreciation of civil rights and religious rights such as he's never had before."

"But you've had dictators like Peron before," I countered.

"We've had dictators, it's true. But Peron has done two things to many of us. His attack on the Church after years of tramping on our civil liberties brought a mass reaction in Argentina which made it clear to most of us not only how highly we prized our rights but our religion."

"How many Argentines practice their religion?"

"While 93 per cent declare themselves Catholic, it is estimated that probably an eighth of the population goes to church every Sunday. Of these the heavy majority are women."

"How close a relation is there between religion and politics?"

"In Buenos Aires Province, which is the newer part of the country, I'd say 15 per cent of the population belong to the political right and are strongly conservative. Most of these are traditional Catholics, with the wives all practicing and a few of the men. Two thirds, some 65 per cent, represent moderate forms of conservatism and liberalism and thus constitute the political center. Most of these people would have no difficulty about declaring themselves Catholic, and a substantial minority practice their faith. Finally, 20 per cent are leftists of various shades to the extreme of communism. In this category we find a segment that is actively hostile to Christianity."

"What do you observe as the effect of Peron on these people?"

"Let's put it this way. Before Peron religion in Argentina was often characterized by pale, irresolute routines that got us nowhere. Since Peron the figure of the young layman proud of his Church and loyal to his faith is the order of the day."

This thought rang the bell with me because only the evening before, from Archbishop Mario Zanin, Papal Nunzio to Argentina, I had words that bore out the doctor's observation most forcefully.

"The choice seed in the Argentine Church is the modern young layman," declared His Excellency. "I attended a conference of Catholic doctors the other evening. The address delivered by one of the group had the force and depth worthy of a bishop and the discussion from the floor was most impressive. There are 7,000 Catholic doctors organized in Argentina. There is a conference of 34,000 Catholic teachers while there are similar groups from other walks of life. We can feel very proud of the vigor and the forthrightness of the new type of Argentine layman."

My finest recollections of Argentina are my contacts with this goodly company of dedicated laity. A portion of them were active long before the rise of Peron but the numbers today are far greater.

Among the veterans is Señorita Marta Zarroquin, still young and vigorous but with a career behind her of twenty-two years among folk whom we in the United States would call juvenile delinquents. Señorita Marta is one of nine children of a distinguished *Porteno* lawyer who saw to it that all his offspring imbibed deeply of the rich culture of Buenos Aires. Marta chose to devote a great part of her life to the delinquents.

"Just how is your work organized here in the capital, Señorita?" I asked.

"We are a body of seven teams of social workers bound together in a unit called the Protectorate of Minors. Our work deals in great part with the guidance of unmarried mothers and my particular team operates in the area served by the Rivadavia and Muñoz Hospitals."

"How do you make your contacts?"

"All young women in trouble who have no local family, that is, who are either from rural areas or from overseas, come to our attention. Our aim is to place them in work where they can support themselves and their offspring."

"I suppose they are hard to handle."

"No, for the most part they are well disposed youngsters but easygoing and ignorant, amoral rather than immoral, quite unconcerned about any public knowledge of their condition."

"What can you do about arranging marriages?"

"That is our great goal. Each of our seven teams is rated by its percentage of successes on this score and I am happy to say that ours is at the head of the list. The average of most of the teams is 50 per cent success in regularizing the marriages while our average has been 90 per cent. The chief work is with the young man and, usually, he is well disposed. 'Como non?'—'Why not?'—he'll say and we see to it that a Christian household is set up."

Though Señorita Marta did not say so, her unusual energy, I found, was the explanation for the high percentage of her team's performance.

Señorita Carmen Bellavista confirmed Señorita Marta's assertion that the amoral mentality rather than the immoral, the easygoing ignorance of the poor, accounted for a great deal of the ills in the slums of Argentina's cities. Señorita Carmen, slight of build, kindly and understanding, a tireless driver, is a lay missionary in charge of the Social

Work House of the Cardinal Ferrari Foundation, which possesses a sterling company of lay people making its impress on present-day Argentina.

"So many with spiritual problems are victims of economic problems, their own or those of people on whom they depend," explained Carmen. "I have just placed two children for a mother whose husband is in prison. She felt no shame about her husband's connection with prison; it was just a piece of bad luck that poor people have to face. She is from a world of low-wage earners here in the city who seldom see a priest, who have no chance for Christian instruction, who will never be reached unless we can create an army of lay apostles from among the more fortunate classes in Argentina."

To meet the needs, neither Señorita Marta nor Señorita Carmen nor any others dream of seeing in their time an adequate supply of priests or religious. For Argentina's 17,000,000 Catholics there are but 4,300 clergy of every category, one for every four thousand souls.

"First of all," Señorita Marta explained to me, "there is a basic shortage of clergy even if all were in contact with the people. Then there is the added handicap that great numbers of our priests are so involved in parochial and administrative routines that they spend much of their lives far from contact with the needy, particularly those who are not practicing their faith."

There are parishes in Buenos Aires and other cities that are as effective in meeting the needs of their people as are the finest parishes of Europe or North America. But they are the exception. The capital as a whole has an average of 27,000 Catholics per parish with seldom more than one or two assistants for each pastor. Vocations to the priesthood in Argentina are on the increase and the supply of clergy today is well ahead of what it was a generation ago but it is still lamentably defective.

"Ignorance through isolation from vigorous Christian living explains the growth of Spiritism and of Protestantism in Argentina," observed Dr. Angel Centeno, an alert young professional man who has won attention through his published articles on these two subjects.

"How seriously do Argentines take Spiritism?" I asked.

"Spiritism is probably making an even deeper impress on many lives than Protestantism. Spiritists frequently claim that they teach a philosophy, not a religion, and that Argentines may continue as Catholics and be Spiritists. In their meeting places they sometimes display the crucifix and prints of Our Lady. Only careful training can remove the idea here that Spiritism is harmless."

"Doesn't it take a certain amount of education to become a Spiritist?"

"It does and these people have it, even if they are ignorant of Christian teachings. Remember that 90 per cent of the Argentines are literate. Most Spiritists would rank as lower middle class but a goodly number come from higher levels of society. There are over 200 Spiritist centers in the country with three fourths of these in Buenos Aires. Their followers run to tens of thousands and represent for the most part people who are hungry for religious experience and who have been missing it from the Church."

Chapter 2

The Minority in Uruguay

IN 1516 Juan Dias de Soles, Chief Pilot of Spain, discovered the Mar Dolce, the great fresh-water sea that still forms ceaselessly at the mouth of the vast river system that enters the South Atlantic between what is now Uruguay and Argentina. Four years later, in 1520, Magellan discovered the river itself though it was Sebastian Cabot who, later still, gave the river its name—Rio de la Plata, the Silver River.

Juan Dias spotted a little off-shore island not far from the present site of Montevideo and decided to look around. He stepped on terra firma and almost immediately was devoured by the fierce Charrua Indians.

"That was the trouble with our Indians here in Uruguay," remarked a friend as we chatted one afternoon in Montevideo. "They were too fierce. They were among the bravest on the continent. We killed them all off—perhaps because they were brave enough in every encounter to fight to the last man."

Uruguay today has two and a half million citizens. It has enough mestizos, chiefly in its rural areas, to total 8 per cent of the population, while 2 per cent is Negro. The remaining 90 per cent, including practically all of the dwellers in Montevideo and its environs, are of unmixed European blood. The historical museum in Montevideo has its *Sala Indigena,* devoted to the primitive Indian, and Uruguay's great national poet, Zorilla de San Martin, has apotheosized the native in deathless verse. But the Indian is no more.

Uruguay has followed quite closely the development pattern of Argentina. For nearly two hundred years after the arrival of the Spaniards there were no fixed settlements within its borders. As a small country, (the size of North Dakota) it has always played the role of a buffer state between two antagonistic larger lands, Brazil and Argentina, much as Palestine was for centuries the buffer between Mesopotamia and Egypt.

The gaucho came first to Uruguay. As in pioneer Argentina, herds ran wild throughout a rich grazing area that until the early nineteenth century remained a public domain. The gaucho was interested only in hides and Uruguayan beef was without honor until the first two decades of the twentieth century when high-grade herds of Durhams and Herefords were developed.

Uruguay's grass was better than Argentina's and hence no alfalfa was needed. On the other hand, Uruguay's soil was poorer. Thus agriculture has never become important; no more than 6 per cent of its land is used for crop raising. Immigrants have settled here, but in small numbers. Uruguay's meat industry is second in importance only to Argentina's in all Latin America with Britain the major customer. Sheep are raised as well as cattle and wool looms large as an article of export.

"Of course we are proud of our meat," observed Heber Rico Monteverde during my first hour with him in Montevideo, "but it is the very wonderful way of life that our leaders have built for us here in Uruguay that in our estimation counts most. We think we have the best planned and best conducted state in the Latin American world."

Certainly to a North American Uruguay is a very appealing country. Heber and his very intelligent wife are two live-wire university students who have set up a happy home in Montevideo. When I was with them they already had a family of five children, including a babe of a few months who journeyed in the auto with us asleep in his cradle in the back seat.

"You can certainly be proud of Uruguay, Heber," I remarked to the man at the wheel. "Those who really know put it, of all the countries in Latin America, at the head of the parade in legislating and organizing a full-scale modern social welfare program."

"It's quite true," commented Heber. "It is regrettable that the great leader in all this, José Batlle (Bah-jay), was very unfriendly toward the Church. He introduced here the advanced ideas of French social welfare with its accent on secularization. Nevertheless, much as we regret the trend of his philosophy we recognize his great contribution toward making us a social minded nation."

"Uruguay has always been in the lead in taking care of the working people," I remarked.

"Right—before many other nations got to it we had the eight-hour day and a 44-hour week, we had unemployment compensation, a minimum wage law, prohibition against child labor, constitutional provision for labor unions and the right to strike. We had liability insurance, vacations with pay, retirement funds and old-age pensions. It all made an impressive line-up years ago when these ideas were new. And best of all, the laws did not merely remain on the books; they were put into successful operation."

"Don't forget what Uruguay has done for women," interjected Heber's wife, Señora Rico.

"Yes," said Heber, "Uruguay was the first South American country to give women the vote. We also have good working laws for women. Secularists would point to our early divorce law as well, though this is no advance since its principal effect is to destroy the family."

"I don't suppose you have many poor people," I ventured.

"Oh, yes, more than you might think. There are provisions for the sick and the needy, with excellent legislation on public health."

"This generally favorable atmosphere on things social helps the Catholic social program," remarked Señora Rico.

"Yes," nodded Heber, pursuing the point. "That is why we are so proud of UNCAS, the National Catholic Union for Social Action. This is one of the finest Catholic organizations for social action in Latin America. We also have among our practicing Catholics an unusually large number of men who are outstandingly public minded, many of them devoting their lives to social action. I am bringing you now to call on one of these gentlemen."

"What is his line?" I asked.

"For many years he has been a judge of the children's court of Montevideo. Recently he was appointed children's advocate by the Supreme Court of Uruguay. In short, he has passed his entire career aiding and defending children."

Thus began an acquaintance which I came to prize among all my Latin American connections. We stopped along one of the many quiet streets of Montevideo's better residential section, at the home of Judge Enrique Perez del Castillo, known to the people of Montevideo by the enviable title of the Children's Friend.

The very first encounter at the front door was a happy augury. A large, well-built woman with strong and kindly features answered our ring. Heber had telephoned ahead and hence my identity was already established. Yet I was not prepared for a greeting in English with a musical Irish brogue.

"Welcome, Father! I'm sure you've brought a blessing from North America for our home."

"And where, Señora Perez, did you come upon that Irish lilt in your voice?" I asked.

It was from Buenos Aires, as I might have guessed. She was the daughter of a businessman of Irish origin who had found success in the Argentine. The Judge as a young man had met her in Argentina's capital, recently graduated from the College of the Religious of the Sacred Heart. She returned to Montevideo with him and now I met the greater part of their brood of nine children, several of the younger girls the dearest little colleens ever, each with her mother's Irish eyes, deep as wells.

"You have a marvelous family, Señora," I exclaimed.

"We think so, of course," replied the wife. "But we don't only like our own children—we like all children. Shortly after Judge Perez and I were married the Judge was named to a post in the provinces. Before we were there very long the Judge had opened eight different cradle homes in the surrounding neighborhood."

Judge Perez sat in his chair, short and stocky of build, evidently a quiet and even a shy man.

"How did you develop this great interest in children, Judge Perez?" I asked.

His eyes lit and his lips curled into a beautiful smile.

"We worked in the country," he explained slowly. "It was a lovely place but there were no sports, no social activities to occupy us. It was easy, therefore, to take to helping children as a pastime, a hobby."

In recent years the Judge has concerned himself with the development throughout Uruguay of an organization called APAC—Association of Catholic Fathers and Children. It is a Latin American version of our Parent-Child Association and is active in many countries.

"He throws himself into it with enthusiasm," explained the Señora.

"Have you much of an organization?" I asked.

"There are 160 Catholic private schools in Uruguay," noted the Judge. "Of these, 117 have organized a branch of APAC. Montevideo counts 96 of the branches and we now have a circuit of monthly meetings in convenient colleges where the fathers gather to discuss the thousand and one problems that have to do with the bringing up of our young ones."

"Do you refer to individual difficulties parents have or to the more basic questions of the formation and education of children?"

"I refer quite definitely to the latter. I refer to the general current weakness among parents to leave to teachers and public servants and legislators the handling of their children. The father of the family has the basic right and obligation before the law to care for his children. Hence the parent should do the thinking and the studying and the discussing with other parents of what is best for the children and then he should do the fighting to see to it that these needs are provided. The teacher does not have these obligations; hence if something goes wrong it is the parents, not the teachers or the legislators, who have failed."

"You are championing, then, Judge Perez, the principle in Christian philosophy that recognizes the family as the basic unit of society."

"Precisely. I would like to promote a world movement for recognition in law of the family and not the individual as the basic unit of society. If the family is ignored, the individual stands alone and becomes the creature of the state."

Shortly after my visit to Uruguay, Judge Perez and the Señora visited the United States. The Judge, while in Washington, gave a conference under the auspices of the Organization of American States on his specialty, children's court practices in Latin America. The Judge, however, was primarily interested while here in visits to children's institutions. I went with him to the Good Shepherd Sisters in Peekskill who conduct for the State of New York a commitment home for delinquent girls, in which at the time there was a sizable group of Puerto Ricans. The Judge and his wife were with this latter group less than five minutes when he had the young women entertaining him vociferously with Puerto Rican folk songs and popular hymns.

"This has been my happiest experience in the United States," he remarked enthusiastically as we drove away.

The day after my visit to the Perez home I called on Mother Shaw and Mother McGloin at the College of the Sacred Heart. This school of the Religious of the Sacred Heart was opened only in 1947 on a property in the chic suburban town of Colasco. We drove to it along the Rambla Sur, the imposing ocean boulevard that links the line of superb beaches about Montevideo and makes the area one of the world's great summer resorts. "God gave Buenos Aires only mud for a coastline," remarked an Argentine enviously, "but He gave Montevideo these miracles of sand."

Mother Shaw despite her English name is of an old Montevidean family; her father, Carlos Juan Shaw, is one of the capital's prominent construction magnates. Thus she was quite at home when I mentioned Judge Perez and the many other local citizens who were so active in social and religious projects.

"We have witnessed a tremendous change, Padre, since my girlhood. Men today have learned to kneel down in church and to participate in the Mass with the missal in their hands as an intelligent act of worship."

"How true that is," said one of the gentlemen with me. "When I was young the few of us who went to church at all stood in the back with our arms folded as a sort of dumb act of loyalty to God but nothing more."

"The number of men now at church is still not high," explained Mother Shaw, "I believe it runs to some fifteen per cent. But they go into the pews and worship earnestly."

"When I was young," continued the gentleman who had just spoken, "such stories made the rounds as that of the man in the provincial city of Rocha who was the one and only man in town who went to church on Sunday. He was dubbed 'el catolico'—'the Catholic.' He was made out to be something of a phenomenon."

"But did the rank and file who didn't practice regard themselves as Catholic?" I asked.

"In most cases, yes," explained Mother Shaw, "though Uruguay has a small minority that denies all ties with Christianity. We have the distinction of possessing one of the great atheistic newspapers of the world, *El Dia,* founded by José Batlle. *El Dia* has long made a practice of writing God with a small g and referring to Pope Pius XII as Señor Pacelli."

Later in conversation with a group of Uruguayan Catholic leaders,

Roman Lezama Munoz, a lawyer in the capital, reminisced on this eclipse of Catholicism in Uruguayan life.

"Uruguay, like the other South American republics, had its Catholic beginnings," explained Avocado Lezama. "In 1825 when the so-called Thirty-three Patriots undertook to win our freedom they landed at Florida seventy miles from Montevideo and began by praying at the shrine of the Madonna of Florida, which was a replica of the Madonna of Lujan. In 1829 the first constitution recognized the Catholic religion as the religion of Uruguay."

"You began, then, with union of Church and state," I remarked.

"Yes, but as the years passed a great political struggle developed that involved the Church. In the Uruguayan back country, the conservative landowners and their gaucho followers became the predominant element of one political party known as the Blancos, the Whites. This party leaned toward support of the Church. The city dwellers of Montevideo became the predominant element in another party known as the Colorados, the Reds. The Colorados, who included the urban lower middle class and the intellectuals, were liberal-radical and anticlerical."

"How do you explain that?"

"So far as the educated are concerned, it is traced to weak Christian life and to our ties to France. Like Argentina, we did business with England but our strongest cultural influence was France. Thus our cultural thought became strongly attached to French secularism which aimed to expurgate religion from all public affairs."

"Weren't the Blancos able to counteract any of this?"

"Only in part. The Colorados prevailed in the elections most of the time and their legislation tended toward secularization of the institutions long connected with the Church. In 1863 the cemeteries were removed from Church control. For ten years from 1872 to 1882 the secularist trend was intense under the dictator Massimo Santos. In 1897 pressure began again. From the early years of the twentieth century under José Batlle systematic secularization became the order of the day. The constitution of 1919 established separation of Church and state."

"How far-reaching has all this proven in its effects?" I asked.

"It has had some very good effects," explained Luis Garcia Pardo, an architect who heads the Catholic Action men in Montevideo. "It has resulted in a religious life among a minority in the country that in recent years has become a very creditable movement. However, in a hundred different ways it has dechristianized public life in Uruguay. Christmas is now officially called Family Day, Epiphany on January 6th is Children's Day, Holy Week is called Tourist Week and Gaucho Week, the feast of Our Lady on December 8th is Beach Day."

"When recently your North American song 'God Bless America' was introduced into our schools," Rico Heber added, "the name of the Deity was removed and the song in translation became 'Oh, Bless America'."

"Yet you all seem to give recognition to the great contribution that Batlle and his followers have made in building modern Uruguay," I commented.

"Quite decidedly so," replied Rico. "We are proud of Uruguay and while we regret that these men have been victimized by French secularism we are delighted with their contribution to our country."

Rico's comment, I find, gets the backing of thoughtful students. Fathers Bannon and Dunne say of Batlle, "It can be said that with his rise to authority a new era began in the history of Uruguay. . . . It was the spirit of Batlle which made Uruguay social-minded and gave her the impetus in legislating for social reform and progress, that made her in these matters the leading nation of the world during the early decades of the twentieth century."[1]

My stay in Uruguay corresponded with the national elections. An interesting feature of the political campaign in this snug little democracy is the employment by the parties in their advertising not of names but of numbers. Thus Montevideo's streets were choked with posters and banners which by law could contain no pleading or provocative text but only huge numbers. Claims and attacks were limited to word-of-mouth and newsprint. Thus the eye met the emblazoned 14 of the Colorados, the 15 of the Independent Reds, the 63 of the Communists, the 80 for an offshoot of the Blancos, the Union Civica, which is the declared Catholic party. Evidently the Catholic group was campaigning vigorously since 80 seemed to appear very frequently. I encountered a smart-looking propaganda truck playing canned music and labeled with the Communist 63. I listened to the speaker and learned the two Communist Party planks: first, abolish the military treaty with the United States; second, cut the cost of living by 30 per cent.

The outcome of the elections to the national congress turned out as follows in percentages of the vote:

Group	*Percentage*
Colorado:	
Colorados	38.0
Independent Colorados	14.6
Total for group	52.6
Blanco:	
Blancos (Nationalists)	30.7
Independent Blancos	7.55
Union Civica	4.37
Total for group	42.62
Leftist:	
Communists	2.29
Socialists (bitterly anti-Catholic)	2.10
Total leftists	4.39

Thus the historic supremacy of the Colorados continues. The Union Civica with less than five per cent of the total places the formal Catholic vote very low but this does not seem to dismay the party's adherents.

"A characteristic of the Union Civica," explained Dr. Lezama, "is the high repute of its representatives in congress. Dr. Dardo Regules, the party director, enjoys great prestige as an unusually upright public figure. The party does not make a play for the popular vote. It represents men who want to act on current issues on the basis of political and religious principles. Many fine Catholics prefer to vote as members of other parties."

Montevideo is known for its strong atheistic daily but it is notable as well for possessing one of the great Catholic dailies of Latin America. This is *El Bien Publico.* Archbishop Antonio Barbieri, who is a keen and earnest public leader, had just chosen an able young man, Cesar Luis Aguiar, as editor and I visited him in his home.

"To fight, a newspaper is necessary," commented Aguiar. "*El Bien Publico* already has won its spurs both as a champion of Christian philosophy in public life and as a serious journal with high literary standards. We have built up a special Friday supplement on Art, Literature and Cinema that is unique in Uruguay."

"What is the philosophy of the Uruguayan press?" I asked Aguiar.

"Montevideo has over three quarters of a million population and no other city in the nation reaches fifty thousand. Thus the capital's newspapers, like most of its other institutions, dominate the scene. I would divide our newspapers into four categories. First, there are those that are declaredly against religion. In Montevideo *El Dia* stands alone in this class. Secondly, there are those that are indifferent toward religion. All the evening papers here are in this class; they indulge the lighter side of life with occasional serious articles on subjects enjoying current vogue.

"Thirdly, there are the papers that are benevolent toward religion without being openly friendly. These are the morning papers, with *La Mañana* the most generous. Finally, there are the Catholic papers and *El Bien Publico* is alone in Montevideo with a daily circulation of 60,000. Two provincial papers, one in Trinidad and the other in San José, reflect the strong religious spirit of their communities and are openly Catholic in tone."

"Religion doesn't get much of a place in Uruguay's press," I concluded.

"No, Padre. Men who practice their faith in Uruguay are a minority. But they are a tough-fibered minority, Padre, well able to take care of themselves."

"Well said," commented Heber Rico, who had accompanied me, after we had bidden Aguiar good evening. "There is an alert militancy about practicing religion here that for a long time has been on the defensive but that today is definitely assuming the offensive."

Federico and Hortenzia Soneira bore out this idea. This remarkable pair are the promoters in Uruguay of the Catholic Family Movement initiated in both Argentina and Uruguay by an Argentine, Father Peter Richard of the Passionists.

"The men and women in this movement seem almost like runners on their marks, waiting for the signal to go," commented Federico. "We have only to mention the idea of finer family life and better neighborhoods and they take up the theme with enthusiasm. People who have never done anything for others find themselves knocking on the doors of their neighbors, making their acquaintance, proposing plans to organize groups to help each other live better lives."

"Do you feel that the Catholic Family Movement is the first effort of its sort to awaken this enthusiasm?" I asked.

"No, not at all," replied Señora Hortenzia. "There is much more solid work going on at the neighborhood level here than many people realize. True, we are cruelly short of clergy but a great number of our Montevideans get splendid leadership from their priests. In Immaculate Conception Parish, for instance, Monsignor Carlos Freire has built up a remarkable block organization. I know because I am one of the block missionaries. In his huge parish the Monsignor has organized 400 blocks, each block with two women missionaries."

"What do you do?"

"Well, take our campaign last spring for the observance of Easter. My companion and I gathered families in our block into various homes. I gave fourteen public addresses to these groups—each of fifty or sixty people—urging them to make their Easter duty, instructing them for participating in the festivities, suggesting means to make Easter a happy occasion for their families and the neighborhood.

"Then for Our Lady's feast on December eighth, our block work brought together some six thousand people for a great open-air Family Mass."

"Is this special to Monsignor Freire's parish?"

"Not at all. Block missionaries everywhere in the city account for beautiful neighborhood achievements in attending the sick, caring for the needy, conducting block prayer, organizing festivals, plays, neighborhood sports."

Dynamic people like Señora Hortenzia compensate in Uruguay for that scarce commodity, the parish priest. Many a mission in the back country is a priestless project, the work of lay folk or of missionary Sisters.

Señora Rico's mother after raising her family entered a Uruguayan religious community and became known to the world as Madre Pia. One Sunday morning with her and Sister Josella Hahn, an intelligent and zealous member of the community from the United States, I journeyed into the country outside Montevideo and saw the rude mission station these Sisters had established among the farmers of the neighborhood. An old red barn had become a wretchedly primitive but clean little chapel while, by dint of great effort, neat new classrooms had replaced the crude school building that long had served here. The playground was alive with youngsters.

"Wonderful!" I exclaimed.

"But we can so seldom get a priest for divine worship," moaned Sister Josella. "These people are orphans without spiritual fathers."

Chapter 3

Not Quite Paradise

MYRTLE THE TURTLE hobbled sedately out of the shrubbery and moved over the well-cropped grass of the Redemptorist patio. Her wrinkled head swung easily from left to right on her thin neck extended well out from under her canopied shell, which was fully eighteen inches from front to back. The sage old centenarian was quietly enjoying an afternoon walk. She bespoke the peace and calm of the deep cloisters of this parish house built for the tropics here in the heart of Asunción, the capital of Paraguay.

"Myrtle's quite completely domesticated," commented one of the American Redemptorists. "She's been with us almost since our arrival in 1944."

"She doesn't seem to be at all infected with North American hurry," I remarked.

"No. She's probably taught us a lesson or two on hitting an easy pace. She's our substitute for tranquillizing tablets."

But little besides Myrtle bespoke a slow pace in this newly created center of the Parish of Our Lady of Perpetual Help. Since the Redemptorists entered Asunción from Brazil a little over a decade ago this huge plant occupying an entire city block had come into being. The church was large and beautiful and near it stood a modern parochial school, the only one of its kind in Paraguay. When we entered the social center attached to the school, housewives from the parish were helping the Sisters in the preparation of large vats of milk, part of the UNICEF feeding program in Paraguay for which milk powder is supplied to the Padres by the Paraguayan representatives of this United Nations agency.

"UNICEF milk does good work for our children," one of the Padres remarked, "as does also U.S. surplus food supplied through the Catholic Relief Services of New York."

I witnessed the splendid accomplishments of both of these agencies throughout Latin America. Catholic Relief Services in the six months from October 1957 to March 1958 distributed 33,000 tons of food and clothing in thirteen countries of Latin America, the appraised value of which was over $7,000,000.

"How many children do you feed?" I asked.

"There'll be a cupful of milk for each of the 600 school children in the morning shift and the same for another 600 who attend the afternoon shift. Then we have an additional thousand children in the three out-schools on the borders of the parish."

"A total of 2,200 school children!" I exclaimed in admiration.

"Which is not such a large number when you recall that we have 25,000 people in the parish."

"Are they anxious to give their youngsters an education?" I asked.

"Decidedly so. Only poverty stands in the way. It's estimated that 43 per cent of the children of Paraguay enter the first grade but only 3 per cent finish the sixth grade. We do better than that here but this is the average for the nation. There's no lack of love for schooling but the people are convinced that they've got to have their children's help to earn a living."

Thus Paraguay, which is often called the most beautiful country in South America, is scarred by poverty. Its climate is mild, its rain though plentiful is never unpleasantly or damagingly excessive, and its rich soil is prepared to yield abundant subtropical harvests. But this is not enough.

"A dream climate and a rich soil are not enough in themselves to save people from want," explained one of the Padres. "The Guarani Indians, who make up the main body of Paraguayans, are a gentle and friendly people very different from many of the tribes about them. Their land possesses the physical requirements to make it a happy, carefree countryside free from need. Hence it is tragic that Paraguay has known so much strife and suffering."

Asunción is a thousand miles by river from the Atlantic Ocean. Paraguay and Bolivia are the two completely land-locked countries of

South America. Paraguay is approximately the size of California, well served by rivers but since it is only thinly populated by a million and a half inhabitants it has but few roads and only a few of these are more than bullock paths. Most of the population lives in the eastern third of its territory.

West of the Paraguay River lies the vast area known as the Gran Chaco, which geographers compare to the Ganges Valley in India, a huge plain with scrub forest and sprawling streams. The Ganges possesses a thousand farmers per square mile and counts roughly a hundred million inhabitants. The Chaco, instead, is one of the most thinly settled areas of Latin America, principally because of its forbidding inaccessibility. Argentina, Bolivia and Brazil hold portions of it as well as Paraguay. Bolivia and Paraguay, the two countries least able to open it up, are the principal proprietors. In the 1930s these two luckless lands fought a costly boundary war here.

Catholic missionaries serve the scattered Indians and settlers of the Paraguayan Chaco, who number 75,000. The Salesians and the Oblates of Mary Immaculate supply the hardy missionary forces.

Deep in the interior, 125 miles west of the Rio Paraguay, are some thirty-five villages of Mennonites from Canada. Their Canadian home became an unhappy place for them because they were threatened with the invasion of outsiders and with conscription into Canada's army. Between 1926 and 1931 they picked up their possessions and sailed to another continent. Thanks to their rare agricultural skill, they have built themselves a new home in the Chaco. Of prime importance is the demonstration they are giving that men can farm successfully in this hitherto neglected area.

The eastern third of Paraguay is a low plateau that represents an extension of a formation that includes the province of Rio Grande do Sul in Brazil. The Brazilian portion is the home of thrifty farmers, but those on the Paraguay side still await the guiding hand of competent leaders.

"While the Paraguayan people are burdened with poverty," states Preston James, "the Paraguayan land goes on offering bounteous crops and a rich store of forest products. If the funds spent on armaments could have been spent on more productive ends, real economic values might have been created which would have brought prosperity to Paraguay, even if this country never was able to sink one productive oil well. The Paraguayan landscape, with its rolling hills, its rich green pastures, its waving palms, is still a pleasant one; except for the ambitions of some of its rulers Paraguay could have been a paradise."[1]

Thus from the pen not of the fanciful poet but of the judicious social scientist we receive this laudatory appraisal of a land usually rated as the most backward in Latin America.

There is still time to make Paraguay a prosperous home for its Guarani inhabitants. The first attempt to achieve this was launched some 350 years ago and is recorded in history as one of the classic mission enterprises of all time, the Paraguay Reductions.

Spanish activities in America had been in full swing for a hundred years and the first disillusionments had been experienced regarding the manner of civilizing and Christianizing the Indians. The task, it was seen, was not as simple as it had at first appeared. Half-way measures on the continent had failed. Greater devotion to detail, far longer sustained effort, much more careful planning was needed. The Jesuits in southern South America held a conference at Salta in 1602 and one of its pregnant conclusions read, "The zeal of the apostle is, like the individual bravery of soldiers, to be subordinated to tactics."

The tactic determined upon was the establishment of reductions in the region of the Paraná River, today shared as territory by Paraguay and Argentina. At that time the area was not assigned to any mission group so the Spanish king committed it to the Jesuits. The Society was given authority to assemble and govern all the Indian Christians independently of all other authority, to engage in an organized long-term *conquista espiritual.*

The formation of this "Christian Republic" began in 1610 and at its peak in the second quarter of the 1700s possessed thirty highly organized settlements totaling 150,000 inhabitants. By the time of the suppression of the Society of Jesus by the King of Spain in 1767—157 years later—three-quarters of a million Indians had been under Jesuit care in this enterprise.

While the Paraguay Reductions are the most celebrated, the reduction technique was employed among other backward peoples of the mission world. Almost a score of such enterprises were operated in the Americas alone, some of them under label of doctrinas or aldeas. All followed much the same pattern. All were designed as an instrument of formation for the Indian during his transition period toward full-fledged citizenship. The organization of the Paraguay Reductions was most thoroughgoing and many scholars have hailed as superb the formation techniques employed by the Jesuits during this century and a half and more of operation.

But why, after 157 years of guidance under the Jesuits, did the Guarani colonies fall asunder when the Jesuits were suddenly torn away from their Indians by the Spanish king? Why after five generations of tutelage did these Indians lack the capacity to continue the operation as civil communities of at least a portion of the thirty reductions? Why is it that today there is nothing but ruins consumed by the tropical jungle where all these establishments stood so long?

"It is certainly unfortunate," explained a Paraguayan gentleman to whom I put these questions, "that, regardless of the explanation, there should not exist today in our contemporary society some identifiable portion of the population to which we might point as representing at least the partial fruit of the efforts of the Jesuits. It is an error, however, to assert that the Guarani of the reductions reverted to wild tribal life when the Jesuits were taken away and the few missionaries who were sent to replace them proved inadequate.

"The Guarani formed by the Jesuits do exist today in the populations of Paraguay and northern Argentina. What was lost when the Jesuits were removed was not the culture instilled in the individuals. What was lost was the organizational network that kept specific communities operating as entities, producing, trading, instilling into each community the will to exist. When this organizational network disappeared with the Jesuit leaders, a few individuals reverted to tribal life, but very few. The majority moved away because the now unguided reductions proved unpleasant places in which to live, unprofitable places for the needs of daily life, badly located places in view of the new trends of life in the region. Thus the reductions themselves became ghost towns but the dwellers from them became good elements in other communities.

"The Reductions were not a failure. The low level of political and social life in the whole Plate River region during the generations following the suppression of the Jesuits explains why we know so little today about what happened to the inhabitants of the Paraguay Reductions. The tragic events of nineteenth-century politics in Paraguay explain why our population as a whole is in such a parlous state despite the excellent start which the ancestors of many of our Guarani received under the Jesuits."

Today two out of every three Paraguayans, some 65 per cent, are Guarani Indians. Some 30 per cent more, a little less than half a million of the population, represent marriages between Indians and sixteenth-century Spanish colonists. The remaining five per cent, estimated to have no Indian strain, include a few families of European immigrants who have come to Paraguay since 1870. Thus Paraguay is predominantly a bilingual Indian nation with Guarani enjoying equal place with Spanish. The political, social and economic leadership has traditionally been in the hands of a small Creole aristocracy of station and culture. The dictators of the postcolonial period came from this small class but the Guarani, while meek and obedient, have never been mere dumb cattle driven by masters to fight for causes that meant nothing to them. The Guarani have a deep love for the nation of Paraguay. This explains how they could be stirred to fight so bravely for their country and to die to the last man and the last woman in the holocausts of bloodletting that some of their wars have involved.

"Three strong-minded dictators dominated our history during the nineteenth century," explained the excellent Paraguayan gentleman to whom I have already alluded. "All three had a lust for power, and at least the first and third were consumed with a fanatical thirst for personal glory. All three were autocratic toward the Church and assumed complete authority over religion according to the fashion that they conceived Spain as employing during colonial days."

Dictator Number One of these three was José Gaspar Francia who held power from 1814 to 1840. Dictator Number Two was Carlos Antonio López, from 1844 to 1862. Dictator Number Three was López's son, Francisco Solano López, from 1862 to 1870.

Francia, called *El Supremo,* was a pitiless tyrant who had no faith in democracy as a form of government for Paraguay. He kept handy a picture of Benjamin Franklin, calling him "the first democrat in the world and the model whom we must imitate." He would then explain to fellow South American leaders of neighboring states that "these countries," his own and those of his neighbors, were not ready for the liberty that Franklin represented. Despotically he held within Paraguay for nine years the French scientist Bonpland who in his desire to study Paraguay's flora dared set foot within the country. Similarly he detained for six years two Swiss scientists who wandered like unwary flies into the web of this vicious spider. His hand fell strongly on the Church. When he died the fearful and ignorant peons performed superstitious devotions at his tomb lest he return and punish them for not propitiating his violent spirit.[2]

Francia was succeeded by López the elder, a more benevolent despot than Francia. He opened the country to the outside world. Since he would brook no authority in the land beside his own, he subjected the Church to an iron control of classic regalism. He had his brother Basilio made Bishop of Asunción, chose every pastor in the land, decided in each instance whether he would accept or reject the decrees of Rome regarding Church administration.

Carlos López's son Francisco indulged in the excesses of Francia a hundred times compounded. Besides being unscrupulously willful he was insufferably proud and viciously cruel. He had spent time in Paris and came back to succeed his father with a vision of himself as the Napoleon of South America. He brought with him from Paris a red-headed Irish girl named Eliza Lynch. Eliza ranks high among the crop of lawlessly colorful women who figure in Latin American history. She rode recklessly by Francisco's side throughout his wild career and supervised his burial when at last he committed suicide on the battle-field after the carnage of Cerro Cora in 1870.

Francisco López armed his Guarani and then provoked a purposeless war against Brazil, Argentina and Uruguay. This, the War of the Triple Alliance, was probably the bloodiest ever fought in Latin America. The pathetic heroism of López's deluded Indian followers is the only note of nobility in this whole sad period in Paraguayan history.

"The Paraguayans fought to the last ditch; they never surrendered. In one battle alone they left 6,000 dead upon the field, while the allies took only 350 prisoners, all of whom were wounded. Thus they literally fought to the death. . . . Women, boys, and girls took the place of men who had fallen. Women used as beasts of burden were, when exhausted, flung upon the roadside to die. Whole regiments came to be formed of mere boys of from twelve to fifteen years."[3]

Paraguay counted a million inhabitants when Francisco López came to power and at the end only 220,000 remained alive. Almost 80 per cent of the nation was destroyed. Since only 28,000 men survived and 106,000 women, there were almost four women to every man. Children totaled 86,000.

It is understandable that this violent period in their history is vividly present to today's Paraguayans. This was brought home to me by Bishop Ramon Bogarin, then the Auxiliary of Asunción, assistant to Archbishop Hannibal Mena Porta.

"Paraguayans are keenly conscious today of the terrific handicap from which we still suffer through the destruction of our nation under Francisco Solano López," he commented. "Yet the fighting spirit of the Paraguayans under López is something of which the nation is very proud. Indeed, despite their many woes, the remnant of the nation that survived the War of the Triple Alliance experienced a sense of exultation and a conviction of victory; they had not surrendered, they explained, they were bludgeoned into submission.

"This same fighting spirit prevailed when in 1932 Bolivia disputed our border line in the Chaco. Some 35,000 deaths occurred in the Chaco War because the Paraguayans battled like demons. Our victory over Bolivia was due in part to the latter's handicap as dwellers in high mountains forced to fight in the lowlands. But it was principally the tremendous will to win that brought us through."

Bishop Bogarin is a handsome figure, a keen mind and a fascinating talker who proves tremendously popular with the country folk and with the educated as well. He is a nephew of Archbishop Bogarin who, as occupant of the See of Asunción, was the great figure in Paraguayan Church life during the first half of the twentieth century.

"What has happened to religion in Paraguay since the days of the nineteenth century dictators?" I asked him.

"The situation has certainly improved since the early days of my uncle's episcopacy," explained His Excellency. "He became Bishop of Asunción in 1897 when only five years ordained. He died in 1949 after a career of fifty-two years. The clergy had been destroyed under López as well as the other elements of the nation and thus though a generation had passed my uncle still had a very limited personnel with which to carry on.

"The liberals repeatedly made bitter onslaughts against the Church. Their hostility made it very difficult to improve Church life. I recall well the days in 1929 when as a college boy I sat with the proreligion forces in the galleries of congress and joined in the demonstrations to get the government to permit the Holy See to increase the number of dioceses in Paraguay from one to three. It took days of wrangling to get the bill approved. With political opposition as it existed in Paraguay the union of Church and state proved a tragedy; the enemies of religion used government interference to block everything that might strengthen Christian life."

"When did you notice a definite change for the better?"

"At the time of the Chaco War. Despite the anticlerical climate there was a great deal of religion at the front. The priest chaplains in the army worked closely with the troops and out of the suffering the men of Paraguay experienced a return to the faith."

"Everybody speaks of the good work you've done to organize Catholic Action here in Asunción," I observed.

"In 1939 Catholic Action became a popular movement among the better elements. In 1949, 13,000 men of the capital made their Easter duty and some 25,000 women. Each year sees an improvement in this figure. One of our great gains has been the arrival of the American Redemptorists. They give us a splendid demonstration of the ordered and zealous parish life that can be created among our people through the vigorous leadership so frequently found in North American Church life."

"How rapidly are your clergy and Sisterhoods increasing?"

"Not rapidly as yet, but they are growing. The Church in Paraguay has the services of 270 priests today and some 320 Sisters. We have some sixty Paraguayan young men in training for the priesthood. In eastern Paraguay in 1949 we had 73 parishes that had no priests out of a total of 154; that is, we had vacancies in 47 per cent, practically one half. Five years later, in 1954, the vacant parishes were reduced to 60, which is 39 per cent, or two out of every five. The good trend continues."

"Where do your best hopes lie for future gains?"

"In the young men, Padre. We have some wonderful new leaders here in Paraguay. I'd like to show you their headquarters and have you meet some of them."

The Catholic youth headquarters are in downtown Asunción. An unusual concentration of men of fine quality in this center is due, I found, to this young bishop who himself is the embodiment of all that the new day calls for to build a vital Church.

The Bishop and I arrived at the headquarters early on a Friday morning and found the building already alive with a large number of young men.

"These boys are leaders in the Young Catholic Workers of Paraguay," explained His Excellency. "They have come here for a week-end retreat. They put up with pioneer conditions to do so, sleeping on the floor and taking pot luck for food during their stay here."

"Is the Y.C.W. strong here?" I asked.

"Quite strong and steadily growing as in other countries of Latin America. They now have twenty-eight sections in Paraguay. Meet some of these lads and ask them what they are doing. Alonzo, Miguel, Mario—this is a Padre from North America."

"Do you really do a job for the workers of Paraguay?" I asked.

"Decidedly!" replied Alonzo. "Our movement has produced some valuable leaders. Of the 280 delegates to the congress of the Confederation of the Workers of Paraguay not so long ago, thirty-two were Y.C.W. members. They were only a small minority, but they were largely responsible for keeping the Confederation from affiliating with the famous Peronist Central Trade Union called ATLAS."

"Our magazine *Juventud Obrera* (Working Youth) does fine work," explained Miguel. "Several times it's been honored with police raids for having defended the workers too well."

"We have a regular program," volunteered Mario. "It demands better housing for the workers, salaries adequate for the cost of living, freedom for trade unions, better conditions for young girls in domestic service, and so forth."

"They're grand boys," commented His Excellency as we left them. "Our student movement, Pax Romana, is also quite vital. Pax Romana is currently among the strongest university movements in South America. Among the 3,000 students at the University of Paraguay there is a strong unit of 200 Pax Romana members. Let's go to the office and meet Enrique Ibarra who has traveled considerably in South America for Pax Romana."

"How are our friends, the New Yorkers?" Enrique immediately asked with a smile.

"Fine, thank you, Enrique. Have you connections in New York?"

"Pax Romana certainly has. Mr. John Simon of the Foundation for Youth and Student Affairs on West 48th Street recently supplied a subsidy that permitted our international headquarters in Switzerland to give a group of Latin American leaders a three-month study journey to the university centers of Europe. It meant a great deal for the student movement in Latin America."

"How strong are the students in Paraguay?"

"In university life in Latin America today the Catholic group and the Communist group both have programs with definite goals. The Catholics are on the increase, the Communists on the wane. We feel at present that we belong to the winning team, the group with the biggest future."

"And to this university movement and to other international Catholic movements here in Latin America," interposed Bishop Bogarin, "little Paraguay has contributed an exceptionally large number of leaders. We have at least ten Paraguayans who currently occupy rather important international offices in social movements with headquarters in Europe."

"Perhaps it is because we are from a small nation that is bilingual," noted Enrique, "that we find ourselves so adaptable to participation in international movements. Then, I think the vigor of our Catholic activities here in Paraguay helps. Those of us who have journeyed through South America feel that Paraguay's Catholic movement, small though it be, holds first place on the continent for quality. We would rate Chile's second and Peru's third."

A source of inspiration for the new fighting Church of Paraguay is Roque Gonzalez de Santa Cruz, a native son of Asunción beatified by Pius XI in 1934. He was born in the capital in 1576 and as a Jesuit missionary preached to the infidels among his own people. One day as he spoke, hostile Indians attacked him and killed him instantly with a stone hammer. His body lies in Buenos Aires but he is especially honored at the Church of San Roque in Asunción. The young pastor of San Roque, Padre Juan Escalante, has some of the zeal of Paraguay's national saint. He studied social welfare in the United States and has developed well the social institutions for the needy under his direction.

"Illiteracy is rated at 75 per cent in Paraguay," explained the Padre, "and apathy tends to make the fight against want among the lower class an extra difficult struggle. I'd like you to see some of our poor. They're wonderfully good people but much too reconciled to their poverty for their own good."

"I suppose they include the housewives I saw scrubbing clothes on the river bank when I arrived."

"Yes, they and many others. When we talk of the poor in Paraguay we talk of the majority. We have splendid buildings like that of the Bank of Paraguay. But in terms of people, more important is the steady stream of barefoot folk who walk past its doors. We point with pride to the beautiful modern highway from Asunción to Villa Rica, constructed in great part with millions from the United States. But much more typical of our country are the dirt trails along which plod our rank and file in most parts of Paraguay."

We drove through the lush green lawns of the Parque Caballero in Asunción's upper city to a vantage point where we had a bird's-eye view of the famous Chacarita area, the slums of the capital. Then we descended the steep road and soon were at Padre Escalante's mother and child clinic. There we saw them, the faceless ones who live in the Chacaritas of every continent, off the main road of history, the meek and the accepting.

"Buenas tardes, Padre," called a high-pitched, feeble voice from across the narrow street.

"Buenas tardes, Doña Sabina," called back the Padre. "This is one of our octogenarians," he explained to me. "Let's pay her a moment's call."

Doña Sabina's house was a wattle and daub affair of two rooms, simple but very clean and tidy.

"Show the Father your shrine, Doña," Padre Juan suggested. It was a neat little niche in her bedroom with a statuette of Our Lady of Miracles.

"Every home in Paraguay has its shrine," Padre explained. "Sometimes it's to Our Lady of Fatima, sometimes to Blessed Martin de Porres, sometimes to Blessed Roque Gonzales."

"Everything is bare and meager," I noted, "but there's no evidence of stark misery."

"Correct," answered Padre Escalante. "We have some cases of genuine suffering among city people but in the nation as a whole there is little destitution. The climate is beautiful, the means to grow food are plentiful—less than one per cent of our crop lands are at present under planting. Yet we cannot be satisfied to leave the mass of the nation living at such a low level. Enterprises are needed to provide an economic base on which we can form our people to a fuller life."

Everyone interested in a better tomorrow for Paraguay expresses these same sentiments. I made a brief stay with the group of American Redemptorists who operate a mission station far from the capital along two hundred miles of the border between Paraguay and Brazil. Father Fitzpatrick of the town of Pedro Juan Caballero described the efforts he was making to encourage projects such as the Compania Americana de Fomento Economico, called CAFE for short, which is opening up some 450,000 acres of coffee plantations in his neighborhood that will employ 1,400 men.

"Projects such as these," Father Fitzpatrick explained, "conducted in modern fashion that permits the workers to give their families a chance to live as they should, are the urgent need of present-day Paraguay."

If the alert elements among Paraguay's leaders are not prevented from making themselves felt in the nation we shall see important improvements in the next few years. Indeed, this will be the case in the entire Latin American world.

"In the next thirty years," shrewd little Enrique Ibarra commented in Asunción, "Latin America will assume a high place in the public affairs of the globe. Within the world of Christendom, Latin America is going to shift from being a deficit region, dependent on other Catholic peoples, to an area that will be not only self-maintaining but a major contributor to things spiritual in the universe. After all, we represent numerically a third of the world strength of the Catholic Church."

"Do you see this day coming, Your Excellency?" I asked Bishop Bogarin.

"I do indeed," he replied. "And these vigorous laymen will bring it about. The Church in Latin America is like a great plantation reduced to a shambles by storms. Everywhere there's the debris of broken and dried-up trees. New trees are needed and, happily, these new and enthusiastic leaders will do the planting."

Chapter 4

The Fight for the Chilean Worker

AN UNBELIEVABLY UNKEMPT WOMAN stood at the entrance to the one-room hut of mud and boughs, two equally dirty children crowding shyly at her knees. The man of the house brushed past them and, prompted by Emilio, showed Father Coleman and me the dingy, squalid interior. I almost stumbled over a basket on the floor filled with a bundle of rags, involved in which, I gasped to discover, was a tiny tot a few months old who stared up vacantly at us from its crude cradle.

"When it rains," explained Emilio, "this dirt floor becomes a pool of mud."

Emilio Lorenzini was the leader of the famous Molina strike of 1954, headed by a group of Catholics of the labor movement known as the ASICH who won from the Chilean conservatives the title of "black Communists." He was one of the four persons thrown into prison by the Chilean government at the behest of the hacienda owners. The group was freed when Bishop Larrain appealed to Cardinal Caro of Santiago who in turn appealed for justice to the President of Chile.

Emilio was showing us the living conditions of the *inquilinos* who work on the cattle-raising and wine-producing *fundos,* the local name for the plantations of the lovely vineyard country of central Chile. We were at the moment visiting some of the most poorly housed in the Talca area, situated on Hacienda La Perla outside Molina. At sight of Emilio, their labor chief, a group of men quickly gathered.

"This is the wretchedness we want to do away with," Emilio said to them in the fiery clipped patois of the neighborhood, "Don't forget the meeting of the ASICH next Saturday." It was clear that here in this sector of the Chilean wine country a continuing battle was in progress for better living conditions and this vital young man was one of its leaders.

We drove down the road about a mile to the Hacienda Buena Unión and found there more workers' houses. In a three-room shack lived a family with ten children. Three youngsters slept in one room, three more in a second, while the remaining four and the father and mother occupied a larger third room. On the open floor of this third room the harassed housewife, evidently not too intelligent a person, coughed and sputtered as she tried to build a big enough fire to cook with.

"Every fire I make chokes me," she remarked querulously.

"The wood's not dry enough," her husband complained. "The *patron* makes us take our wood from the vineyard but the branches aren't long enough cut to burn." His difficulty seemed to be the proper concern of himself, the homemaker, and not of the *patron*, but evidently it was in the air to blame the owner for every inconvenience.

Outside a nearby house, as we approached, a neatly dressed young woman stood very straight, her husband by her side.

"May we go in?" Emilio asked.

"Why?" the woman answered him unsmilingly, looking at him with intense eyes. "Why show the strange Padres that we have nothing?"

"No need, Emilio," Father Coleman called quickly. "No need to disturb these good people. God bless you both!" he said to the two and their faces relaxed gratefully.

"Young couples like this," Father Coleman remarked, "are sensitive to being scrutinized for their poverty."

Next we rode to the Hacienda San Miguel where we saw a *conventillo* for unmarried transient men laborers. Following the established pattern of the *conventillo*, the construction consisted of a three-sided building with all of the rooms opening on a court. In each of eight rooms four or five men lived, a total of thirty-five occupying the *conventillo*.

In some of the rooms there was no furniture at all except straw on the floor. The men slept in sleeping bags. In others there were some crude bedsteads with ugly ragged blankets. There was one small window to each room. Entering into the dimness in one instance, Father Coleman surprised a man squatting in the semidarkness.

"Are you sick?" Father asked.

"No, just sitting," the man replied tranquilly and continued to fill his pipe.

Part of the space on the open side of thc court was occupied by a wall-less shelter with a tin roof. Here were six rough cooking grills, several of which were tended by men preparing food. Half a dozen other men stood idly by since it was past the working hours.

"Where are the toilets?" I asked onc of the men.

"We use the canal," he replied laconically, pointing to the slowly flowing stream twenty yards away.

"How much would one of these men earn?" I asked Emilio.

A discussion followed. On the better *fundos* each worker family gets a dwelling house with a little land for a family garden and vegetables. The father gets a cash allotment per working day plus an allowance in food, firewood and other needs. Some provision is made for the schooling of the children. On each *fundo* is a family chapel which sometimes is a sightly structure worthy to be a village church. The *inquilinos* attend this chapel, usually occupying a section separate from the *patron's* family. The larger *fundos* will count some two hundred worker families.

In the case of these unmarried workers of Hacienda San Miguel, the payment covers the individual only, since no dependents figure in the bargaining. The salary is 80 pesos a day, plus 35 pesos in food, which at San Miguel was spelled out as two 250-gram loaves of bread a day, one liter of cooked beans, meat twice a week, a kilo of sugar every two weeks and a quarter of a pound of coffee. In U.S. money this salary and food allowance represents 50 cents a day.

"As with peasant farmers all over the world today," Emilio explained, "it is the complete dependency of every phase of their life upon the goodwill of the patron that now irritates them. Many of the owners are very kind and generous but this is no longer enough. These men have heard too much about having rights as free men; they don't want to be dependent any longer on another man's favor."

These words sum up in a nutshell the current struggle of the Chilean countryside. "Chile's fundamental difficulty is the hacienda," notes Preston James, "and the rigid class distinction between landowner and landless tenant which that word signifies."[1] The struggle intensifies among every class of workers of Chile, the *inquilino* of the land, the *roto* who labors in the city, the mine workers, and, on the other hand, the conservative landowners, the traditional rulers of Chile, who have been joined of late by manufacturers and industrialists. But the real

Chile is still agricultural; forty per cent of the six million Chileans derive their living directly from the land.

The Talca area, some eighty miles from Santiago, where Lorenzini and his men maintain their union, is the finest section of central Chile, a lovely region with the classical grace of the Mediterranean. Its rich vineyards produce wines that rival the products of southern France and Italy. Chile is a curious stringbean of a country, stretching 2,630 miles from top to bottom, greater than the distance from Hudson Bay to the Caribbean island of Jamaica. A narrow middle sector of this huge length constitutes Chile proper and in this quarter 95 per cent of the population dwells.

Northern Chile is among the driest places on earth; it counts one of the few weather stations on the globe that has never recorded the fall of a drop of rain. Within its harsh desert wastes are the forbidding nitrate fields of the Atacama. Southern Chile is one of the rainiest parts of South America, a world of storms that possesses in its northern limits much of the charm of the German forests and Scandinavia. But as it protrudes southward it gathers up the winds, the cold, the barrenness, the compounded dreads of Antarctica. Some of the world's most primitive tribes, tiny vestiges of cultures past and dead, dwell in isolated spots of Tierra del Fuego at the southernmost extreme.

Neither the north nor the south are the real Chile; the core of the land lies at the center. Despite its charms, however, central Chile has its problems, which are both social and economic and which in great part turn about the hacienda. Recent figures show that in the rural provinces of central Chile north of the Bio-Bio River there are 82,000 land holdings and 93 per cent of these, or 76,600 out of the 82,000, possess only 11 per cent of the land. The remaining 7 per cent of the properties, with less than 5,400 owners, contains 89 per cent of the land. These are the haciendas with more than 500 acres. There are 375 properties with more than 12,000 acres each; these 375 haciendas possess 52 per cent of the privately owned land in central Chile.

Driving through this enchanting countryside in the mellow warmth of late November, the Chilean spring, the mood is set by the lush greens of field and meadow and copse, and the profusion of flowers. Only one acre in every ten grows food; the great portion of the terrain serves to raise animals—good cattle and horses. The herds of beautiful horses fascinated me, with their wide assortments from heavy mares to tiny, spindle-legged colts.

Seldom from the road do we spy a manor house. Often high, well-built walls line the properties for miles. Only by turning in through a great gate and following under a long canopy of trees do we come eventually to the great rambling country residence. Here dwells the *patron*.

Many of these properties in central Chile have been held by the same families for centuries and a strong tradition has kept the *patrons* close to the land. They enjoy life with the horse-riding gentry of their set, but, as well, the *patron* plays his role as an earnest, practical farm owner, joining with the *inquilinos* in the work of the property, the care of the vineyards and herds. It is this closeness to the soil that for long maintained the strong bond between *patron* and worker in Chile and kept absentee ownership at a minimum.

Today, however, this absenteeism is rapidly increasing. One cause is the investment by many *patrons* of a part of their wealth in industry and manufacturing. Another is the lure of town house life in Santiago. Today the gap widens between the *patron* and his *inquilinos* though the ties are still strong.

"Can the *inquilino* take his family and leave the hacienda any time he is not satisfied?" I asked Emilio as we drove away from the San Miguel Hacienda.

"Yes, he can legally," replied Emilio. "By Chilean law he cannot be bound to his master in any form of bondage. Yet there are few places in all Latin America where the tenant worker feels more closely tied to his hacienda than here in central Chile."

"How do you explain that?"

"Because almost every *inquilino* has great affection for his hacienda. He often works on land which his ancestors have worked for generations. From earliest boyhood he has been attached to all the family of his *patron*. He regards the estate owner as his protector. Even when he quarrels with the *patron* it is almost like a fight between blood relatives."

"Do you think the *patron* feels affection for the *inquilinos?*"

"Oh, yes! The *patron's* world is a larger world than that of the *inquilino* and hence he gives less love to his workers than he receives from them. Yet he takes pride in being regarded as their father. He would be ashamed to hear anyone say that he allowed his *inquilinos* to go hungry."

"Why, then, shouldn't it be easy to persuade the *patron* to provide a much better way of living to his workers?"

"That is quite a different thing. The *inquilino's* present miserable standard of living is, the *patron* will tell you, the age-old tradition. Change this way of living, educate the children, give them everything that people in towns have and you destroy the hacienda. For the *patron* it is a struggle between life and death."

"The *patrons* must react very strongly, therefore, against your efforts to form unions. Have you made much headway?"

"Most *patrons* are violently opposed to me," Emilio answered quite simply. "Today our union, the Federacion Sindical Cristiana de la Tierra, has half a dozen centers. The workers of some one hundred *fundos* are enlisted, seventy of which are in the neighborhood of Molina. Taking Chile as a whole we are not very important."

"What do you feel that your 1954 strike accomplished?"

"It was a small strike but it obtained big results. First, it made the workers confident that the Church was their friend because in our darkest hour Catholic leaders declared that our cause was just. Secondly, it increased the daily salary from 45 pesos to 90. Thirdly, the principle was recognized that *inquilinos* should get better housing."

Bishop Manuel Larrain of Talca, in whose diocese the strike took place, corroborates Lorenzini's opinion.

"The Molina strike was a small one," His Excellency explained to me, "but it accomplished the great purpose of establishing that the Church in Chile has a voice for the poor and stands with the workers. The Chilean *patron* is a good man but often lacks vision. He fails to see that, as Lenin himself declared, the ultra-conservative landowner is the best agent the Communists could have. By Christian teaching we hold for the rights of both the landowners and the workers. The mentality in Chile has too long been feudal and too often the priest seemed to belong to the castle alone and not to both the aristocrat and the commoner."

Panquehue, north of Santiago, is called the richest valley in Chile. Some twenty wealthy *fundos* represent the principal properties and by unstinting attention to both the *patrons* and to the *inquilinos* who constitute the majority of the 4,500 inhabitants in their parish, two young Maryknoll priests, Fathers Stephen Foody of New York and Bernard O'Brien of Chicago, won the goodwill of all. "Our Padres have worked miracles in winning esteem for the Church in the valley," declared Carlos Errazurriz, one of the *patrons.*

Heightened interest in the *inquilinos* became noticeable in the valley. A colony of attractive new six-room homes burgeoned forth on one of the *fundos,* each painted in deep red and gray and adorned with a grass lawn and flower beds. Half a dozen other *fundos* built new homes. A full-time social service worker was engaged for the *inquilino* families. The valley now has seven grade schools, five governmental and two private, including the parish school conducted by Chilean Sisters and caring for 240 children.

Raul Tagle operates a model *fundo* in Panquehue that specializes in fruit. I contemplated with admiration the precise patterns his ploughmen had made in executing the most modern designs in contour farming.

"It is definitely to my interest," Raul explained, "to improve the *inquilino's* lot. For instance, good clothes are psychologically very important and shoes are the countryman's symbol par excellence of progress. I want my men to have both.

"There is the question of a bed. There are two categories of people in the world—those who sleep in bed and those who don't. I want my men to belong to the first category.

"Then, a nicely furnished home makes for stability; a man is slow to pull up stakes when he has a home to which he is attached and which his wife and children also love."

"Men like Tagle," explained a university professor to me in Santiago, "represent the backbone of progress among the *fundo* owners. However, even they fall short in their thinking since they would base the solution of the problem not on the inherent rights of the workers but on the duty of the *patrons* as gentlemen to practice a benign and generous paternalism. 'I am a father to these people,' they say, 'I must treat them as beloved sons.' They by-pass any basic right these men may possess to be independent citizens."

A few of the more courageous among the *fundo* owners have gone this full distance. Near the city of Chillán, many miles south of Talca, a Maryknoll confrere, Father Cowan, brought me to the *fundo* of a young man of this advanced thinking. He occupied a property of 2,500 acres called Cuchu-Cuchu, held for some 200 years by his family of English descent and always worked personally from generation to generation by the head of the family. Tomás Cox, the present operator, learned his social theory at the Catholic University of Santiago, where he followed a graduate course in agronomy.

Young though he is, Tom Cox works quietly through magazine articles and discussion groups to enunciate the rights of the *inquilino* to a proper dwelling house, a proper minimum salary and a family allowance. He believes, too, that *inquilinos* should be free to better themselves by forming unions.

"Certainly here at Cuchu-Cuchu we live in happiness and understanding with our *inquilinos,*" explained Victoria, Tom's handsome blond wife who is a graduate of the Immaculate Heart Sisters of Villa Maria, Santiago. "We have thirty-five *inquilino* families, while eighty workers join us temporarily at vintage time. Let me show you how they live."

Father Cowan and I drove with Victoria along the *fundo* road to a section of *inquilino* homes. Flowering vines graced the walls and white quince blossoms bloomed at the gate as we turned in.

"The Acosta family lives here," explained Victoria. "The house is of stone and counts four rooms. Rosa! Rosa, are you home?" Victoria called. "We'd like to come in a moment."

"Wait till I tidy things, Señora Victoria," Rosa called back and we stood a moment on the porch, beautifully vine-clad and giving a view of several small fields, in one of which wheat was growing.

"Each family has ten acres of land for its use," Victoria noted. "Each is allowed to raise four large animals—two oxen, a horse and a cow. Besides, two pigs may be raised and as much poultry as desired. Tom must supply a food allowance for the whole family and the necessary firewood. There's a *fundo* store where the families may buy additional supplies and we keep the prices low. Each family man at present gets 85 pesos per working day which means 250 days a year. By the present poor exchange this is less than $100 U.S. a year, little enough it is true."

"Welcome, everybody," called Rosa, the lady of the house, "please come in. I'm sorry that my husband Carlos is not home."

Rosa showed us her parlor, dining room, kitchen and bedroom, four attractive, airy rooms, well equipped with simple furniture. In her bedroom she pointed to her neat little shrine to Our Lady.

"Rosa builds very beautiful altars," Victoria observed. "Every year for the Corpus Christi procession one of the three altars along the route stands in Rosa's front yard."

"Where do your children go to school, Rosa?" Father Cowan asked.

"We have a government school on the property," Rosa replied.

"It is so poor, however," explained Victoria, "that Tom plans to make it a private school so he can improve it."

"Tom has his heart set on being generous with his workers," remarked Father Cowan.

"He figures it as the sound way to keep pace with the changing times," replied Victoria. "Large numbers of men, he says, are not going to continue much longer to live in dependence the way *inquilinos* now live. He feels that it is only their lack of courage that keeps them from throwing off the outworn living conditions of the Chilean farm worker."

Some thousands of hacienda workers deserted their *fundos* in years gone by for pioneer sections of Chile, such as the Temuco region, where twenty per cent of the freehold farms are owned by former *inquilinos.* Thousands more went to the city where as urban workers, dubbed *rotos* in Chile, they are no better off than rural workers. Where, however, they have been able to join unions as factory or mine workers there are evidences that they have made certain gains. Unfortunately, most unions in Chile, as in Latin America generally, are strongly leftist.

The Communists of Chile since the 1920s have been an important element in the country's labor movement. For thirty years or more they have been the principal political force among the workers as a whole. The Reds have fought in every Latin American country for political influence; in some countries they have failed. Chile is one country in which they have very consistently succeeded.

"The history of the Chilean Communist Party, particularly since 1939," records Robert Alexander in *Communism in Latin America* "presents the best example in Latin America of how a Communist Party, with a relatively small membership and only limited popular following, is able to wield wide influence for a long period of time. Its importance has been due largely to the Communists' rigid discipline, their ability to play upon popular prejudices and issues, and their versatility in creating and exploiting the inferiority complex from which their rivals in the Chilean Left have suffered. . . . The only real answer to the Communists in Chile remained a social reform program which, beginning with an agrarian reform, would establish a firm economic basis for political and social democracy in the shoestring republic."[2]

Chile ranks first among all Latin American countries in per capita use of machine energy. Much of this energy is hydroelectric power from its mountains, but coal figures prominently as well. For metals, there are three major copper camps, all operated by North American capital. El Teniente, southeast of Santiago, is the best known of these, with two others in northern Chile, at Potrerillos and Chuquicamata.

Notable also is its steel production, which frees the country from importing any of this metal for its manufactures. The great steel center at Huachipato, a suburb of Concepción, is the number one industrial center of the nation. Here a quarter of a million tons of steel are turned out annually, about half the capacity of Brazil's celebrated Volta Redonda center, likewise developed with North American capital.

A dynamic Maryknoller from California, Father Mel Cowan, was chaplain at Huachipato when I looked in on this great enterprise.

"Huachipato is Indian for 'The Duck Trap'," Father explained. "There's no duck hunting here any more. The company holds 4,000 acres and its mills work twenty-four hours a day. The iron comes by sea from Cruz Grande, 500 miles to the north, the coal from the Lebu Peninsula, the limestone for the steel is brought in also by sea from 900 miles to the south. To keep this huge operation rolling, over 20,000 souls live here, including of course the families of many of the 5,000 or so workers."

"But all don't live in this little settlement," I remarked as we approached a heavy concentration of small, motley houses.

"No," answered Father Mel, "this is the old original section, called Huachipato Camp. The main residence section is in an attractive area called 'Las Higueras' which means The Fig Trees. It is beyond the hill, and thus protected from the strong odors of the steel processing. We'll see it later. Here in the Camp live poorer families who pay a rent the equivalent of 60 cents a month in U.S. money. An infant is dying in one of these houses and I'm due to baptize it. I suggest that you come along."

Father Mel knocked on the door of the Inostrozza family and we entered their two-room lodging, occupied by a mother and her two sons, both of whom were married and had their wives with them. The front room, about six feet by ten feet in size, served as sitting room, dining room and kitchen while the second, crowded with its double-decker beds, was for sleeping. The family had covered the board walls of the front room with wrapping paper on which they had pasted magazine illustrations.

"How is the baby, Señora?" Father Cowan asked.

"Poorly," replied the mother of the young men and evidently the head of the house. "We are desperate because it is Juan's first child."

Juan Inostrozza stood beside me, silent but alarmed. His young wife came forward, staring with frightened eye at the mite in her arms. A young man and woman, sponsors for the baptism, were likewise on hand and thus the room was well crowded.

"What does the doctor say?" inquired Father Cowan.

"He says it has pneumonia and he's given it penicillin, but he offers us little hope."

The tiny mite's face was blue and contorted. The sponsors knew their parts well and Father Mel proceeded with expedition.

"Elizabeth, I baptize thee. . . ."

The child coughed in anguish and a tear fell from the young mother's eyes. I was relieved when the little thing was returned to its crib in the double-decker bedroom.

"Courage! Trust in God's goodness!" Father Mel passed about the circle and his gruff heartiness gave new spirit to the anguished family. Here was the appeal to Christian courage, I thought to myself, that the Communists disdainfully label as the opium of the people. But all they can substitute for it is anger and bitterness.

"I must run," said Juan, "I'm due for my shift at the mill." A new peace on his face, he dashed out the door.

"Life is drab for these people," remarked Father Mel as we walked away. "But let me show you my happy shoemaker."

The old man, who lived a few doors away, greeted the young priest with a roar of delight and chattered endlessly. "I'm fit as a fiddle," he kept repeating. "I'll die if they don't let me go back to work. I've been happy all my life when I've been able to work."

"A few weeks ago he was at death's door," explained Father Cowan. "As I gave him the Last Rites I persuaded him to have a Church marriage to the common law wife with whom he is living and now both are happy."

The lady sat nearby rocking contentedly. The two lived with the shoemaker's son, a steel worker, and the son's wife. Their two-room shack was gayer in its trappings because someone had the secret of effectively using a little bright paint and some simple hangings.

"The steel company pays good salaries and thus draws folk from all over Chile," Father Cowan noted as we walked away. "I must bring you to some of the better-off people over in Las Higueras. This new residence section consists of five villages each built for 1,200 families, each village to possess a separate church. Unfortunately, the architect plans to accept the present poor condition of religion in this neighborhood as his measure for the future and insists that the churches should seat only 200 worshipers each. I am arguing with him presently for something larger."

It was immediately evident that Las Higueras represents the right side of the tracks here at Huachipato. The small apartment buildings stand on sightly new streets, along which even the comportment of the people differed from the seemingly shiftless milling of the populace in the less organized original settlement.

"Las Higueras counts 10 per cent *empleados,* or employees, and 90 per cent *obreros,* or workers," Father Cowan explained. "The distinction reduces itself to a matter of a little more education, a little more ambition and natural good judgment that aids certain of these men to move up the ladder of success."

"That reminds me of the immigrants who built our own United States," I remarked.

"Right. I'll bring you to the home of Ricardo Gonzalez, a typical example. Ricardo is earnest and thoughtful, a good-living man who, however, for years was not a church-goer because of a quarrel he had with his parish priest."

It was the end of the day and we found most of the family at home in their small but attractive apartment, with windows which looked out on green grass.

"Welcome, Padre," was my greeting from Ricardo, a heavy-built man in his early fifties. "We like to meet Padre Cowan's friends."

Ricardo's señora came in from the kitchen for a moment to shake hands and then served us tiny glasses of golden liqueur. Maria, a married woman with a bright little babe in her arms, joined our circle in the sitting room.

"You have a very pleasant home here, Ricardo," I commented.

"We like it very much," Ricardo replied. "I have fifteen years in which to pay for it but as a matter of fact I hope to complete the payments in six."

"You do not rent it, then," I noted.

"Most of these families don't rent; they are buying their homes on installment," broke in Father Cowan. "Las Higueras is not to be a company town, though its construction is financed by the company. These families aim to be independent owners of their own homes. Ricardo's, one of the better ones, will cost him the equivalent of $3,000 in U.S. money."

"Where are you from, Ricardo?"

"I drove a meat truck in Valparaiso, Padre," Ricardo replied. "I heard of the good salaries paid here at Huachipato, rated as the best in Chile, so I got a job with the company as a chauffeur. Now I've worked up to the post of weigher; I weigh the hot molten metal as the ingredients of the steel are prepared. It is quite a responsible job." A quiet gleam of pride shone in the good man's eye.

"Splendid," I commented, and asked, "How do the men like the company?"

"We don't feel particularly close to the company," Ricardo replied, "but we like the pay and the living conditions."

"I hear there's Communism at Huachipato."

"Yes, there is. Most men don't want it, are afraid of it, but a small number belong to the party and are well organized. The Red center is in Concepción nearby."

"How large a city is Concepción?" I asked.

"I think it's about a hundred thousand."

"We can find it in your atlas, Daddy," suggested Maria.

The group of us walked to the little hallway where, neatly aligned on shelves, were over a hundred books.

"Daddy does a great deal of reading," volunteered Maria, "and I've also read many of his books. I like the North American writers best."

My interest in my host mounted as I thumbed through his titles. A few were from Spain, some were English authors, but most were best sellers from the United States translated in Latin America. I noted Pearl Buck's trilogy on China, something by Priestley, several mystery stories by Mary Roberts Rinehart.

That evening in Concepción we returned to Ricardo's comment on the Reds with William Verbakel, a young Belgian now earning his living in Chile. From 1948 to 1952 he was national president of the Catholic Youth Organization in Belgium and continues here in Chile to be a student of Catholic social action.

"Some sixty militant Communists with admirable discipline are holding sway at present in the unions of the Concepción area," Verbakel explained. "There is as yet very little Christian social organization to oppose them . . ."

"Do you believe that this is true of Chile in general?"

"It's the general opinion," answered William. "The future of industrial labor will be determined in Santiago, Concepción, and Iquique, this last the center of northern Chile for the copper and chemical fields. Labor has a greater voice in Concepción and Iquique than in Santiago but in all three areas the Reds are predominant."

"What gains has the Catholic social movement made among industrial labor?"

"It has made a very good start but of course at the present moment it cannot dream of securing a balance of influence. There are plenty of Catholics among Chilean workers but few with any practical convictions on the social question."

"What do people like yourself feel should be done, William?"

This innocent little question led to hours of discussion. At the end this young veteran from the fighting lists of Belgium had formulated half a dozen conclusions. They went as follows:

1. *Education.* A substantial number of rank-and-file Catholics among Chilean workers need the formation of Catholic schools for the full appreciation of things Catholic needed for a national social action movement.

2. *A vital worker movement.* A popular movement at the worker level, free of all politics, is needed. Catholic leaders offer a plan of social and economic study and guidance. Now they must build cells of strength among the workers themselves.

3. *Social education of the clergy.* Without it there can be little intelligent encouragement of the workers.

4. *Socio-economic objectives.* All workers should be offered a set of Catholic socio-economic goals worth fighting for and must be trained in methods that Christians can use to obtain these goals. "An elite of young Chilean workers should be sent to Belgium for formation," proposed Verbakel.

5. *Family movement.* The Christian family movement is essential for this program.

6. *Trained foreign missionaries.* The precise social needs of Latin America should be made known to all foreign missionaries coming to the continent. "I know some Belgian priests here," explained Verbakel. "They know the Boerenbond of Flanders, our rural Christian social movement in Belgium, but they do not know that Chile has quite a different society from the small farmers of our Boerenbond."

Certainly it is in the air among Chilean workers today to better themselves by organizing.

"We have only to mention a plan for self-improvement and our workers jump at it," explained Father Cowan. "My cooperative is an example. I proposed a simple plan to buy meat. The first hundred members pledged 780,000 pesos in cooperative shares. The final subscription reached 1,800,000 pesos, at the time $6,000 in U.S. money. Today we have a full-time operator, Andrade Fuentes, and we hope to enlarge the venture to include a cooperative bookshop, a grocery store and a clothing store."

Thanks to Father Cowan's energy, Huachipato offered me a sense of hope and promise as regards the renewal of Christian living among the working men. Other witnesses, however, reminded me of the sober fact that many of Chile's workers, particularly in the urban areas, are far from possessing any great Christian impulse in their lives. One of central Chile's zealous bishops related to me some of the findings gathered in his diocese in the summer of 1957 by a team of fourteen university students from Santiago under the direction of two social-minded priests.

The inquiry carried on by these painstaking investigators turned about the nature of family life, religious practices and attitude toward the Church on the part of urban workers in three towns of central Chile.

According to the first conclusion reached, family life among these workers is at a pathetically low level. Of 56 marriages studied, in only two cases could it be established that the unions came about through elevated Christian motives. In thirty-four cases, which would be 60 per cent of the total, they represented for the worker a combination of sex motives and a general friendly inclination toward the woman. In twenty cases, according to the worker's explantion, the union was entered into solely for physical sex reasons with no love element evident.

The dominant concept established by the workers queried showed the wife to be a servant, to be ordered about at will, beaten as required and employed to satisfy physical desires. The worker's household rather than being conceived as a home in the Christian sense was regarded more as a place of habitation where he ate, slept, maintained a servant and companion. The wife seldom ate with the husband and seldom went out with him.

In a sampling of 500 families, 450 had children, 118 families had five or more children, 332 less than five. Abortion was well known and favored by 60 per cent of the men queried, though objected to by the remaining 40 per cent. A local bookshop in one town had considerable literature on the subject. There were very few unmarried mothers because the opinion was current in the area that no soul was present until four months after conception and thus no great moral harm was involved in early abortion.

The children were cared for exclusively by the mother. The boys became independent at fifteen years of age, the girls were more or less subject until marriage. As a rule the father exercised no formative influence in the home and the mother to a great degree was negative in her influence. An absence of delicacy on sex matters in the home was found to be prevalent. In matters of religion, a few instances of guidance were noted, such as the teaching of prayers and the sending of children to religion class but the great majority reported indifference on the subject. On the other hand, relatively few instances were reported of open hostility to religion.

What was found to be the situation as regards religious beliefs and practices? The following data summarize the findings of the team as the position taken by the workers. It might well be that the workers' wives would have reported otherwise.

Attitude toward religious observance: indifference regarding religion, 17 per cent; Protestants–nominal or practicing, 10 per cent; nominal Catholics, 68 per cent; practicing Catholics, 5 per cent.

Religious training: none, 31 per cent; Protestant training, 17 per cent; elementary training for First Communion, 47 per cent; good training, 5 per cent.

Existence of God: atheists, 1 per cent; indifferentists, 7 per cent; general belief in God, 75 per cent; formed belief in God the Father, 17 per cent. The workers when questioned on the divinity of Christ declared themselves 74 per cent as recognizing Our Lord as True God and True Man.

The Blessed Virgin: disbelief in, or doubts about Our Lady's power of intercession, 27 per cent; confused notions, 23 per cent; Our Lady Virgin and Mother of God, 50 per cent.

The Catholic Church: only a physical edifice, 25 per cent; general belief in the Christian churches, 21 per cent; the Catholic Church the true church, 47 per cent.

Catholic priesthood: in one or other way opposed to priests and the priesthood, 77 per cent; favorably inclined toward and understanding the priesthood, 23 per cent.

Baptism: baptized, 94 per cent; their children baptized, 85 per cent.

Prayer: never pray, 25 per cent; not since childhood, 23 per cent; sometimes, 32 per cent; pray daily, 20 per cent.

Attendance at Mass: never, 49 per cent; only funerals, 15 per cent; certain feasts, 30 per cent; weekly, 6 per cent.

Other Catholic practices: none, 49 per cent; processions, 40 per cent; Protestant services, 5 per cent; general Catholic practices, 6 per cent.

The university students who conducted the inquiry were from the higher social ranks and active in Catholic affairs. It is clear from their reports on the attitude toward the Church of the workers in the three towns visited that their contact with this little known element in Chilean society proved a soul-searching experience.

"It is completely clear and evident," wrote one of these young men, "that the Church does not reach the worker. . . . The priest, far from being respected and recognized as an instrument of God, is eyed with suspicion, as an outsider. Under these circumstances all that he stands for is regarded as false and given no consideration. Even when the worker has a thought of God, the Church as such is not understood, its doctrine bears no weight, and I feel sure never influences the worker. Thus the Church is attacked with ease and defended with difficulty."

"For the present-day worker," reports another of the team, "the Church is its priests. The worker has no inclination to participate in this organization that he regards as being managed completely by people alien to his milieu, managed by the rich."

"The Church and those who represent it," reads another report, "the hierarchy and the priests, are completely absent from working circles. For the workers the Church is something totally extraneous. They assume no position of open hostility but, far more serious, rather one of omitting it completely from any practical consideration. Workers of religious inclination experience great anxiety because they feel themselves abandoned by the Church. In labor problems it does not occur to any of them that the Church has anything to say; rather the idea prevails that it occupies itself only with devotion. They experience no guidance from the Church. The ceremonies, rites, organization, language and mentality of men of the Church are something incomprehensible to them."

In Santiago, Chile's handsome modern capital, the vital force of one of the best Catholic Action organizations in South America has its center. Its plan is based to a great degree on that of the Catholic Action movement of the Province of Quebec which is regarded as one of the best in the world. At the rectory of St. Augustine's Church in the heart of Santiago, eight priests, all under forty, have their residence and give full time to the Chilean movement. Three of the eight priests are attached to the General Sector; one priest, Father Rafael Larrain, is as yet alone in operating the Rural Life Sector; and four of the eight priests are attached to the Socio-Economic Sector which concerns itself with the working man. Linked to this third sector, though administratively distinct from it, is ASICH, a labor bureau that seeks to prepare Chilean Christian leaders.

A phase of the effort to help the working man is the cooperative movement. With Father Dick Smith, a Maryknoller from Buffalo, I called on Padre Maroto, director of the Catholic Cooperative movement in Chile.

"Our department began work in 1948," he explained, "and five years later had eighty savings cooperatives at different stages of development. We insist on both religious and political neutrality in this activity which must be administered in careful business-like fashion. Yet of course the whole enterprise is apostolic; it has already lifted hundreds of families out of animal squalor."

So far as organized effort is concerned, Catholic social action in Chile is only now making itself felt in the life of the nation. There were good men who forty years ago dreamed that they were to witness in their day a vigorous Catholic social movement that would have made Chile a continental leader in this field. They were deceived.

"Chile," said a daily paper in Valparaiso, *La Unión,* in 1911, "will be the American Belgium, which will offer to the world the beautiful example of social renovation through Christianity. To this end are pointed all our Catholic institutions of today: the university, the Christian social center, the library, the bookshops, all our circles and associations of religious, economic, social and political character."

In 1911 the working man in Chile was still in great part inarticulate but he did not blame religion for his wrongs. He still represented a factor securely woven into the country's fabric of Catholic life. The previous year, in 1910, at the First Catholic Social Congress, Archbishop Gonzalez Eyzaguirre founded the National Federation of Catholic Social Works and one of its branches was St. Joseph's Society of Workers, directed by Don Miguel Leon Prado. In this Society were fourteen sections in Santiago with a membership of 20,000 workers, and sixty-four centers outside the city enlisting another 15,000 workers.

Had the Chilean Church possessed a strong social program that spelled justice for the working man, it could certainly have proven itself the Belgium of Latin America. But Chilean Catholic leaders were found wanting.

"This [social] movement," writes Alejandro Magnet, "had in its favor the circumstance—which only later when it went wrong could be appreciated in all its force—that the laboring masses were attached to no other faith than the Catholic, and that the people, who still had acquired no consciousness of their power, or their rights, were a species of virgin soil, in which a good seed opportunely sown would have rendered a hundredfold harvest. The truth is that the good seed was not sown and soon the forces that were incubating beneath the false peace of that day destroyed those favorable circumstances which perhaps will never present themselves again."[3]

Why was the good seed not sown? Why were the Chilean people, virgin soil for the social idea, not impregnated with the doctrine forty years ago that would have led them as a people to great social achievement?

I asked these questions of a Chilean friend.

"The good seed of Christian social doctrine was not sown," he replied, "because the Papal teachings of our Christian social doctrine were not accepted by the leaders of that day, either here in Chile or in other countries of Latin America. Magnet repeats the story often told that during a social revolution in one Latin American country the revolutionaries raided a bishop's house and uncovered a large quantity of copies of Pope Leo XIII's *Rerum Novarum* hidden away in a storeroom. Maybe the poor bishop was an ardent advocate of Leo's encyclical but the story makes good telling by those who wish to imply that if the Pope's words had been preached from the housetops instead of hidden in the storeroom the Church would have been recognized as the workingman's friend and would not have been labeled as the workingman's enemy."

"What happened to Leo XIII's encyclical here in Chile?" I asked.

"It was accepted by a few, ignored by most, deliberately suppressed by another few who calculatingly recognized it as requiring substantial changes in Chile's treatment of the working man."

"The whole social question was ignored, then–is that so?"

"No, that is not true. Many good men talked of social betterment but forgot that remedies, not alone fine words, were needed. At the First Social Week of Agriculture held at the Catholic University in Santiago early in the twentieth century, it is symptomatic that not a mention was made of Leo XIII's *Rerum Novarum,* rated by so many as too severe an indictment of the hacienda owners."

"As a result, then," I commented, "the anti-Christian program beat out the Christian program in the race for the common people of Chile."

"Exactly. The situation called first of all for better food, clothing and living conditions and secondly for better education and culture for the working man. Those who called for a slow evolution toward respectability for the working man before he was to be given his rights lost out. The world social revolution that we've witnessed has settled that."

"What happened when Pius XI followed up on Leo XIII with *Quadragesimo Anno* in 1931?"

"For two weeks a group representing the Archbishop fought to have the new encyclical published in *El Diario Ilustrado,* principal daily of the Conservative Party and popularly regarded as the leading organ for things Catholic. They did not succeed. One of the editors said it 'was necessary to protect the Catholics from the imprudences of the Pope.' The Jesuits were criticized by the Conservatives because two of their members read excerpts from the encyclical on a ten-minute radio program. Thus, you see, Pius XI got the same treatment from the Catholic Rightists in the Conservative Party as did Leo XIII."

"And the conviction continued to grow in the working man that the Catholic Church belonged to the owners."

"In substance that was it. In 1911 a respected university professor, Juan Enrique Concha, said of the workers, 'The people are profoundly embittered, irritable, suspicious, distrustful.' In 1941 Padre Alberto Hurtado called attention to Concha's words. 'In thirty years,' he wrote, 'nothing has changed. Is it to go on forever that the people are to be "embittered, irritable, suspicious, distrustful"?' "

"Padre Hurtado, then, did something to remedy the situation."

"He most certainly did. At the time that he made the comment I've just quoted he added, 'Marxism has penetrated the people who legitimately desire better conditions. But where are the Catholic unions? Where the Catholic cooperatives? Where the associations for a just defense of the workers' interests? Marxism provides them. Catholics, no. Why? Not because the Roman Pontiffs have not spoken. Not because our bishops haven't repeated the teachings. The teachings have encountered no echo among the people for want of priests to consecrate themselves to this task.'

"Hurtado made a call in two directions, first for more clergy to meet the appalling shortage in Church leadership; secondly, for an organization to attack frontally the problem of the working man. This second effort brought about the establishment of ASICH by Hurtado's Jesuit confreres. It was the biggest achievement of Hurtado's very active career."

Few though they are, the clergy of Chile have responded very well to the call during recent years for "social awakening" and their labors for the worker are outstanding.

One September afternoon I went with Padre Piñero to Avenida Tocornal in the heart of Santiago. Padre Piñero is one of the team of eight priests at the national center of Catholic Action. Among his duties is the organization of the domestic servants, of whom there are 40,000 in Santiago and 100,000 in the remainder of Chile.

"Here we are, Padre," he said to me after we had walked a while. "Here is our Hogar de la Empleada, our Working Girls' Home which is the national center for the domestic servants of Chile. It is in its early stages of development."

Thus as with all others whom I encountered, there was the comment on the *newness* of his enterprise, the *note of apology* that the development was in its early stages. Padre had nothing to apologize for; the building was old but possessed an air of dignity and beauty and evidently the administration was well organized.

"I want you to meet Lina, who is the directress," Padre said as we approached the woman at the desk. "She is one of a staff of seven who conduct the organization. In order not to lose the spirit of their profession all seven are required to continue as part time domestics."

"How is the center supported?" I inquired.

"There are at present some 2,000 active members who pay dues of 20 pesos a month. In addition, the women pay small fees for services. Domestics are a relatively well paid class since in addition to their salary of 2,000 pesos a month, room and board goes with their job."

"Your principal concern, then, is to help them in their lives."

"Yes. We have a corps of thirty-four visitors who move systematically among the domestics of Santiago to be helpful to them. We encourage domestics to frequent the center. Every Sunday from three till nine there is dancing in the patio to which the girls may bring their boy friends. There are picnics to the country in which at times 500 girls participate."

Most celebrated of the institutions for the worker and his class in Santiago and all Chile is a foundation of Padre Hurtado's, the Hogar de Cristo. A rainy evening in October 1944, an old man in tattered shirt, his teeth chattering from a heavy fever, approached the Padre and asked him for the price of a room in a shelter. Padre Hurtado questioned him and, struck by his lot, spent a sleepless night thinking of him. The next afternoon in the course of giving a conference to a group of society women he told of his experience.

"Each of these men is Christ," he commented in his customary direct fashion. "What have we done for them? What has the Church in Chile done for its sons who walk the streets in the rain and sleep winter nights on doorsteps at risk of being frozen? These things happen in a Christian country. Tonight one of these men could die on your doorstep.

"The Protestants, instead, are the only ones in Chile who occupy themselves with this problem. The Salvation Army has hospices for these men and only a few days ago took up a collection to help them. How shameful for the rest of us!"

The effect was electric. After the conference, women gave him their jewels, one woman offered him a piece of land for a hospice, still another came that evening with a check for 200,000 pesos. Padre Hurtado found himself within a few days the unwilling director of the Hogar de Cristo which still continues in admirable manner its large-scale operations.

Father Dick Smith and I one morning passed through the generous confines of the celebrated establishment.

"When Padre Hurtado was alive," Sister Loretto, one of the original band in charge, explained, "he used to ride the streets at night looking for homeless men who didn't know what to do for a lodging and offer them a place here. We have 200 beds for them and they can stay up to eight nights until they've gotten a job and a room. We have a hundred beds for women, who can stay here up to five nights."

"You take in youngsters also, don't you, Sister?" asked Father Dick.

"Yes. Youngsters come to Santiago from all over Chile. We receive thirty to forty a day, many brought in by the police. Many of them are vagrants who act like tough little ne'er-do-wells. But Padre Hurtado was friend to them all.

"Indeed he was a friend to everyone, old or young. He formed an organization of 'graduates' and always wanted to see them when they returned. Some were successes, some failures, but they all loved Padre Hurtado. When he died one came in with a poem he had written to express his affection."

Bishop Manuel Larrain of Talca was a boyhood friend of Alberto Hurtado. The two possessed much the same spirit and have been known (and misunderstood) for the same devotion to Chile's working man.

"We are witnessing a new day in Chile," the Bishop explained one evening in Talca. "At Padre Hurtado's funeral, men of every political color in the Chamber of Deputies honored him for his devotion to the Chilean working man and to Chile's poor. Men still fight against granting rights to the *inquilinos* and the *rotos* but no one any longer doubts where the Church stands on the subject.

"And the Church as a consequence is free and vigorous in spirit with a growing number of wonderful young clergy who identify themselves with all that serves the good of their people."

One of my Maryknoll companions in Chile, Father James Sheridan, had much the same to say about Chile's clergy.

"These Chilean priests are interested not only in getting answers from their people to such questions as 'Who made the world?' They ask as well 'Has Señora Juarez's baby got milk?' and 'Is Juan Diego in prison for a just reason?' That's why they are beginning to win the devotion of the working man here in Chile."

SECTION THREE

World of the Andes

• • ● • •

Chapter 1

Soul and Body in Bolivia

IN THE BASQUE COUNTRY of northern Spain on the occasion of the fourth centenary of the death of Saint Ignatius Loyola, his Jesuit sons at a congress discussed among other things the spiritual needs of Latin America.

"I propose," said Padre Henry M. Huelin of the Society of Jesus, "that we undertake to organize a great national religious mission for the revival of the faith in one of the most needy lands of Latin America, the country of Bolivia."

Proposals like this have been presented before with little result. In this case there were factors that made a difference. First, Padre Huelin was himself an excellent organizer. Secondly, his first contact was with a human dynamo who was vitally interested in just such a project, the Papal Nuncio to Bolivia, Archbishop Ugo Mozzoni. His Excellency leaped at the idea and so stirred the Church authorities in Rome that they supplied the funds to transport a large team of preachers from Spain to Bolivia to participate in the enterprise.

Twenty-two missionaries made up this Spanish team, which included Dominicans, Redemptorists, Franciscans, Capuchins, Vincentians and Jesuits. In addition, eight Latin American countries sent contingents that brought the total to 148 preachers—98 in the mission band centered in La Paz and 50 in the Cochabamba mission band. Native-born priests who spoke the two great Indian languages, Quechua and Aymara, were added to these bands for the areas where they were needed.

Bolivia, it is well to recall, is the "poor little rich girl" of Latin America. Three fourths of her population of 4,000,000 lives in her mountain area which represents one third of her territory. Bolivia is immensely wealthy in large deposits of almost every known mineral, with tin leading the list and silver, gold, bismuth, tungsten, and copper following in the litany of her treasures in the earth.

But Bolivia to date has not been able to weld together a political society that can give it a government. "For four centuries now," a Bolivian remarked wryly to me, "Bolivia has been a land of the future." Some 55 per cent of the population is pure-blooded Indian, 31 per cent is mestizo and 14 per cent claims European blood. The Church's great weakness is its paucity of spiritual leaders, which come to less than 400 priests and some 450 religious Brothers and Sisters.

The Bolivian Hierarchy named Padre Huelin as General Director of the National Mission and Padre Edward Arcuso, S.J., resident in Bolivia, as Subdirector. In each of the eight dioceses and six mission territories a local organization was planned and for months before the period of the mission Padre Arcuso toured the nation ascertaining that every detail was properly organized. Three preparatory committees did advance work. These were the Publicity Committee, the Arrangements Committee and the Religious Census Committee. All Bolivia was divided into a huge checker board with the 200 parishes the basic units and the country's 750 churches the working centers for the preaching of the message of spiritual renewal.

The communities of Sisters in the nation took the census. In city, village and countryside they carried on their visitation day by day to house after house, family after family over a period of months. When eventually the preacher assigned to the given parish or community arrived he found an ordered body of data on the local spiritual situation as regards Baptism, Mass attendance, Easter Communion, marriages in or outside the Church, the level of local Christian family living.

Promotion of the National Mission began in January 1957 with an appeal for prayer and sacrifice that God would bless the effort. Hundreds of letters were sent to houses of contemplation throughout the world asking their intercession. Newspapers and magazines began to carry the word, radio stations took up the call and then in each locality posters appeared and neighborhood loudspeakers were installed.

Most important was the excellent word of mouth effort at the grass-roots level. The women and children were quick to respond. Then came the mounting indications that the idea was getting through to the men.

"What about this National Mission?" a worker would ask a companion.

"What about it?" the other would counter guardedly.

"Looks pretty good," the first would say.

"Yeh. Perhaps we ought to think about it."

The thoroughness of the Arrangements Committee played a part in making participation painless for the timid. In cities and larger towns improvised centers were designated for every neighborhood such as halls, warehouses, railway stations, markets and outdoor places of assembly such as plazas and even street corners. A network of loud-speakers was set up to carry the preacher's voice to every part of the community.

Six different types of mission were planned in all, to be employed according to the nature of the locality. First, a children's mission for youngsters eight to twelve years of age was to take place a week before the General Mission. The youngsters were to prove great propagandists among the older folks at home. Then there were the General Mission, the College Students' Mission, the Workers' Mission, the Employers' Mission, the Soldiers' Mission. These divisions revealed a practical understanding of Bolivian society.

Numerous though they were, the mission preachers could tackle only a given area at a time and months were required for the entire program. The General Mission in each given area lasted exactly fifteen days. The solemn entry of the missionaries in procession, singing the Litany of the Saints, took place on the eve of the first day. At the end of the procession the Bishop of the diocese publicly conferred on the preachers their missionary crosses with an exhortation to perform their labors zealously in God's name. In some of the cities, such as Oruro, the great mining center in the *altiplano,* the mayor of the city and other authorities participated and publicly conferred the title of Illustrious Guest on each of the preachers.

Each day of the fifteen, then, began with morning service which consisted of a dawn procession during which the prayers of the Rosary were sung through the streets. The populace found this a thrilling experience. Mass followed during which the missionary preached an instruction and a *fervorino*. The rank and file then went to work and in the evening gathered for the second service of the day marked with an instruction on the Commandments by one missionary and a sermon on the eternal truths by the other member of the parish team. Special conferences were scheduled for some evenings directed to the married men, the married women, the single men and the single women.

All this built up toward the grand climax of the second Sunday of the mission, the day for the great public worship. As many as possible were persuaded to go to confession, to rectify any irregularities in their lives, to reconcile themselves with God and to go to Holy Communion. The community cemetery was usually the scene for the final ceremony on Sunday afternoon. Afternoon Mass was celebrated for the souls of all the departed of the city and a powerful sermon on death in the presence of death stirred large numbers to the depths.

"Here was the great moment of the mission," one of the Maryknollers explained to me. "Many of the conversions of life were due to this function in the cemetery."

But still another function remained, that of wishing Godspeed to the departing missionaries leaving for their next station. A measure of the success of these two weeks of prayer and exhortation was the delirious enthusiasm that characterized so many of these departures.

The Papal Nuncio, Archbishop Mozzoni, seemed particularly impressed by the spirit of these leave-takings. "Some of them were extraordinary," he explained. "In the city of Potosí, where we thought the hostility of the leftists might injure the spirit of the mission but where instead the community fervor rose rapidly and to great heights, on the last day many of the men insisted on lifting the missionaries on to their shoulders and carrying them in triumph to the train amid the shouts of thousands. The priests were forced toward the end to lock themselves in their train compartments since excited groups threatened to carry them out anew for adulation. In Oruro thousands gathered in the streets for the departure and accompanied the preachers beyond the limits of the city."

"Were you yourself present personally at any of these gatherings, Your Excellency?" we asked.

"I partook in the greatest ceremony of all," his Excellency replied. "This was the closing day in La Paz on September 29, 1957. More than a hundred thousand persons gathered in the great Plaza of the Obelisk on Sunday afternoon. I celebrated the Mass and exactly at seven o'clock Pope Pius XII from Rome delivered his radio message to the Bolivian nation. The effect on the gathered crowd was stupendous. The joy and gratitude expressed at the end toward the preachers was unbelievable."

The special missions likewise achieved notable successes. The college students presented a problem since in many of the government institutions the directors and professors are Marxists and expressed no sympathy toward a reversion to religion. Yet the Mission succeeded in penetrating all these centers of study with admirable results. Some of the preachers were particularly brilliant and carried their audiences by storm. In Cochabamba 5,200 college students of both sexes attended and in La Paz the number reached 15,000. "I have a new respect for this Church of ours which we've been kicking around," remarked a university lad in the capital.

The Soldiers' Mission likewise did its special task well. In Cochabamba, which is a regional post of the Army, the mission was preached in the Senior War College and the Senior Arms College as well as in every barracks. In La Paz it was preached in twenty military centers including the Military College. The unforgettable event was the conclave in the La Paz Stadium, a soldier-worker gathering. The Army formed on the field and the workers filled the grandstands. The Papal Nuncio celebrated the Mass at which some hundreds of soldiers and workers received Communion. Hernan Siles Zuazo, President of the Republic, assisted at the function.

Soon the visiting preachers had gone back to their homelands and the handful of local clergy found themselves alone once again with their task.

"Do the after effects promise to be good?" I asked one of our Maryknollers.

"Quite decidedly," he replied. "Making due allowance for the short-term nature of much of the enthusiasm which accompanies such concentrated efforts, a great deal of enduring value remains. One figure alone is indicative, namely, the total of over 5,000 bad marriages that were rectified during the mission. Experience teaches us that many years from now Bolivians will refer to one or other of their confreres and say, 'He is a good-living man; ever since the National Mission of 1957 he has always been faithful to his religious duties.' "

What we may term an extra dividend from the National Mission was the special impulse given to Catholic Social Action among Bolivian workers. Special Workers' Missions were given in some twenty factories of La Paz, at some of which as many as 2,500 men assisted. But apart from these was the program organized around Padre Martin Brugarola of the Social Service Bureau of Madrid.

Padre Brugarola's schedule was so arranged that in no place did his visit coincide with the mission. As a socio-economic specialist he spoke to employers, intellectuals, priests and students in university circles and among business, industrial and agricultural leaders. He went likewise to the workers in factories, mines and farming centers. The aim of the hierarchy in capitalizing on Padre Brugarola's presence was to continue to bring home strongly to Bolivians the Church's interest in the social question. Important work was already in progress along this line under the Canadian Oblates, particularly among the miners.

Almost a hundred thousand men work in the bowels of Bolivia's harsh, mastodonic ranges and of these some 50,000 are Indians, prized for their capacity to work hard at high altitudes. The tin lodes in Bolivia are found at 11,000 to 16,000 feet up. In this thin air and bitter cold the Indian is at home and since prehistoric times he has taken metal out of the earth here.

At the turn of the century a Bolivian half Indian got possession of an abandoned tin mine. He worked it so successfully and manipulated his earnings so cleverly that when he died in 1947 he had a fortune worth a billion American dollars. His annual income for years surpassed the Bolivian government's. This was the fantastic tin baron, Simón Patiño. He with Maurice Hochschild and Carlos Aramayo constituted Bolivia's tin triumvirate who were hit so hard when the Bolivian government in 1952 nationalized their tin mines and established the government-run Bolivian Mining Corporation.

Financially the move was of doubtful wisdom. In 1957 a firm of New York consulting engineers working for the Bolivian government announced that by mismanagement the mines were on the brink of ruin. "Although the Corporation achieved an apparent book profit in 1955," says the report, "the government took 63 per cent of it, leaving insufficient funds for sound operation." Every business man will recognize here the tell-tale evidence of irresponsibility—acceding to the temptation to milk off the profits and thus destroy the working capital.

But politically, sociologically, ethically the nationalization was of tremendous importance for Bolivia. The Archbishop of La Paz praised the government on the step, calling it "an achievement of great statesmanship."

"The fruit of the labor of Bolivian miners was taken abroad without a just or humane compensation," the Archbishop noted. "We never have accepted, nor could we accept the fact that our own miners should be more profitable to other countries than our own." His Excellency expressed the hope—in vain, it would appear—that a "just, new and honorable management" would be instituted.

At this time the Bolivian Church through the initiative of the Papal Nuncio of that day, Archbishop Pignedoli, invited an able team of Canadian missionaries well trained in social action to take up work among the Bolivian miners. These Padres, Oblates of Mary Immaculate, established themselves in the area of the largest tin mines of Bolivia with center at Catavi not far from Oruro. The mines of Llallagua, one of the Oblate stations, produce 43 per cent of Bolivia's tin.

"How were you treated?" I asked Father Alexander Gaze, head of the band and today accepted as one of Bolivia's most capable social leaders.

"The men received us most cordially," he explained. "Fortunately we were at home with tough workers living a hard life under tough conditions and did not expect them to be either saints or courtly gentlemen."

"What happened?"

"We proceeded to live among them, to demonstrate that we belonged to them, that we lived in their world as a part of their world and not as interlopers who shared none of their problems and belonged outside."

To understand the meaning of these words one would have to see these mining towns and watch them operate.

"We don't get up with the singing of the birds," explained Pere Lefebvre of Llallagua. "It's the screech of the mine siren that throws everybody out of bed every morning, that gets these fellows to the pit head at six o'clock."

Some 6,700 men work in the great Llallagua mine. Crude trains bring the crews more than a mile into its depths, over 2,500 feet down. Within the labyrinth of its galleries the miners disperse like phantoms into the darkness. Throughout the day, then, the work is not merely brutal, with the roar of drills, the handling of huge chunks of ore, the tremendous heat, the suffocating odors. More, it is definitely dangerous.

"Those *llameadores,* the men who put the match to the explosion powder," commented Padre Pablo, "work with their lives suspended on a thread. A momentary distraction, a false calculation and, pouf!—they're just a piece of mangled flesh. We see the poor devils in the hospital when they're lucky enough to be still alive after an accident, their arms torn, their faces disfigured."

Then there is the silicosis, the deadly lung trouble that slowly builds up from the ore dust and destroys men's power to breathe, leaves them helpless in their huts to die.

"Why be surprised," asked Padre Pablo, "if in every mine fear has its expression not only in religion but in crude superstition? In a niche in a gallery we find a chapel to the Immaculata, Our Lady at work with the men in their subterranean world. But nearby also is Uncle Devil in his niche, a grinning creature of clay before which these same devotees of the Blessed Mother place peace offerings of coca, alcohol and tobacco to keep the evil ore from blowing them to bits."

Against this background of hard living it is not difficult to understand how easy it is for leaders to stir these men to violence. Juan Lechin, the leftist Minister of Mines, an ex-soccer star who holds the popular imagination in Bolivia, counts the miners as his political preserve. While personally refraining from attacking the Padres his Marxist movement undoubtedly was jealous of the growing prestige of the Oblates in Catavi.

"In September and October of 1953," explained Father Alexander, "the radicals decided that we were an unfavorable element and began attacking us. Our houses were searched twice by commando elements of Reds, we were publicly branded as gringo spies and were condemned at labor meetings.

"But we had no difficulty in our fight for fair play for the file so long as we showed no fear and answered the leftists when they attacked. One night at Llallagua Father Lefeb spirited in his statements that he enraged his opponents and they threatened to kill him. He signaled for the floor: 'I ask only five minutes, Mr. Chairman,' he said, 'to prepare myself to meet my God.' The hall-full of Indians cheered loudly and the incident was closed."

"Are the miners real leftists?" I asked.

"The miners are simple men who unknowingly follow the agitators like sheep. Hence four or five such agitators scattered through the hall can run the meeting, leading in the applause or in prompting howls of indignation as required. But the Padres get their turn by being courageous. At heart the men are sympathetic toward the Padre."

"Are you making headway in building religious practices into the men's lives?"

"We feel that we are. We understand very well that it will be a long, slow process. Low-level family life, coarse drinking bouts at religious festivals and other such traditions call for something more effective than mere admonitions. It is rather a question of carefully altering the point of view of the young, of giving the better elements in the mining towns some solid reasons for wanting to see things change. We need time as well as prayerful planning, clear vision and strong resolution."

The full tragedy of the weakness of the Church in Bolivia through the fewness of its clergy and the consequent lack of religious leadership for the latently strong and zealous lay forces which the Church possesses becomes evident when we consider this problem of the emancipation of the Bolivian Indian. Time and again Church leaders have outlined a program for aiding the Indian only to have the proposals come to nought through the greater strength of political, economic or spiritual opponents.

In the city of Cochabamba, pearl of the lovely Cochabamba Valley in the intermediate zone between the altiplano and the plains, lives Raimundo Gregoriu, an able and thoughtful Catholic lay leader who lives a couple of blocks from the Maryknoll Missionaries of Santa Ana Parish. Raimundo was born in Switzerland of a Rumanian father and a Bolivian mother of a wealthy family. He was brought up in Bolivia and from the beginning proved a brilliant student. At seventeen he wrote an article calling for army reform and was exiled to the Brazilian border. He returned to Cochabamba to a successful career as a lawyer and professor at the University of Cochabamba. He showed early interest in the role of the Church in Bolivia and through his political connections played a role in the writing of the Agrarian Reform bill of 1952-1953 which contained much that offered justice to the Indian but which was immediately misapplied by the leftist radicals to work injustice against the landowners.

At the Indian Congress at La Paz in 1953 Gregoriu did an outstanding job in demonstrating the Church's long history of concern for the Indian. He reminded his auditors that as early as 1883 Church authorities drew up a program of aid that would insure justice and advancement for the Indian. The politics of the times prevented any wide application of it. Pope Pius XI on the occasion of the centenary in 1925 of the birth of the Bolivian republic summoned the Bishops to try again to improve the spiritual and material life of the Indian.

"Not only is he abandoned," wrote His Holiness, "but he leads almost a life of servitude, subject to the deceits and vexations of every class."

The Primate of Bolivia, the Archbishop of Sucre, wrote a strong plea to the Bolivian people to consider the state of the Indian. In this document he refers to a memorial presented to him by a group of Indian leaders who asked the help of the Church in operating schools which the Indians planned building with funds they had collected. In this memorial appeared a plea which His Excellency said he quoted verbatim as an argument against those who denied that the Indian had interest in anything that had to do with progress.

"As the pastor of the parish is the soul of all his flock," wrote the Indians, "we see in him the true representative of God. For this very reason he holds all the authority necessary to labor for the good of our race, which possesses no other goal than to perfect itself in the service of God and of our fellow men. To this end our Reverend Pastors must aid us and lift us out of the stupid prostration in which in our present circumstances we find ourselves."

The plea did not go unanswered. In 1926 Archbishop Seiffert of La Paz launched a National Crusade for the Indian which called all Catholics to provide for the Indian masses strong centers of basic education through which new conquests could be realized in the economic, social and cultural fields.

Though President Siles and other distinguished Bolivians s
the Archbishop's plea, it was quickly bombarded by powerfu
tion from the *latifundistas,* the great land owners, by the an.....
and, strangely enough, by the national student federation under the leadership of Carlos Tovar, Minister of Public Works. Why this astonishing hostility to betterment of the Indian? "These men united," explained Gregoriu, "to support the thesis that the civilizing of the Indian constituted a social peril." Those two demographic statistics, the 86 per cent of Indian-mestizo population in Bolivia and the tiny 14 per cent of white population, proved a powerful argument for keeping the Indian from becoming a force in the country.

Archbishop Seiffert continued his fight for the Indians undismayed but his enemies were too bold and too strong. They finally forced him to resign as head of the see of La Paz.

A pastoral letter of the Bolivian bishops issued March 2, 1958, bears testimony to the sad fact that injustice and ineptitude still stalk the Indian peasant. Under the Agrarian Reform Law of August 2, 1953, many large estates were to be split up among the Indians who worked them, with just compensation to the landowners. Three things have gone wrong with this worthy plan and the Bishops call attention to them.

In the first place the landowners have not been compensated and have no immediate hope of compensation. By the middle of 1957, 14,000 landless Indians had received grants of land but thus far by high-handedly taking the land away from the legal title holders.

Secondly, the laws of social change have been so egregiously ignored that the Indians, suddenly thrown on their own with no knowledge of agriculture but simple sustenance farming which means raising only enough food to care for themselves, have brought about disastrous agricultural retrogression in the areas of the divided estates. A dairy farm near Cochabamba that used to yield 125,000 quarts of milk yearly now produces only 26,000 quarts because the Indians are not trained to produce an excess for sale. Another farm that employed 400 *campesinos* possessed 840 head of cattle, 600 hogs and 16,000 sheep, today counts only 25 cows, 20 hogs and 1,000 sheep for the same area. Perhaps the Indian families are far happier despite this heavy decrease but certainly there is strong evidence that they are drifting toward economic distress.

The third failure is by far the gravest. The Bishops report that application of the reform of 1953 "though acceptable in its guiding principles, degenerated in practice into an agrarian revolution of the Communist type." As a result, bureaucrats and grafters today have their hands on the throats of the new owners by involving the simple folk in unscrupulous deals. "From this agrarian revolution," the pastoral letter explains, "new landlords have arisen, harsher and more grasping than many of the former ones. They impose on the *campesinos* a yoke heavier than that of old."

Very wisely this document of 1958 takes into account past criticism leveled at ecclesiastics who have been accused of condemning the efforts of reformers and who insist on following themselves a do-nothing policy. "Let us save Bolivia, setting aside merely negative, destructive criticism," declare the Bishops. "Let us set an example of discipline, hard work and honor."

As examples of Catholic efforts to aid Bolivia's little man the Bishops cite the work of a Bolivian priest, Padre Julio Dumiri of Potosí who with confreres has worked hard to develop the cooperative movement for the *campesino.* In a land where voluntary agencies are frowned on as dangerous rivals of government bureaus, Padre Dumiri has met with government opposition, as have other organizers of Catholic labor unions and rural betterment programs. The Bishops bewail this opposition.

One well established Catholic movement has fared better. These are the Christ Schools of Potosí. The Bishops rejoiced at the glorious golden jubilee observances that were celebrated in Potosí in September of 1957. This admirable institution came into being in 1907, the creation of Padre Zampa of the Franciscans, as Catholic rural schools to serve the Indian. By 1932 they numbered more than 80 throughout the altiplano but the disastrous Chaco War in which Bolivia was defeated by Paraguay brought their ruin. Father Zampa went to his grave under the belief that his grand idea had been destroyed.

However, the Franciscans resuscitated the Christ Schools in the 1930s. In 1936 the Minister of National Education and the Prefecture and Municipality of Potosí came to their aid by setting apart the income from certain mining and farming projects for their support. In 1945 when a monument to Padre Zampa was unveiled in Potosí, 2,200 student delegates from sixty-five Christ Schools marched in the procession. Today there are over one hundred such schools with Sisters and zealous Catholic lay teachers.

A few Catholic parochial schools such as we know in the United States now exist in Bolivia. The first was constructed by a Maryknoll Missioner, Father John Lawler of New Bedford, Massachusetts, now a pastor in Lima, Peru, who led his parishioners of Santa Ana in Cochabamba to its achievement. The Christian Brothers of Mayorazgo near Cochabamba have a similar school as have the parishes of San Lazaro and Villa Vaca Guzman in Sucre.

Indicative of the modern enterprise of the Christ School directors is the interesting Coipasi Project for Fundamental Education inaugurated on May 9, 1953. Dr. Victor Montoya Medinocely, the technical director of the Christ Schools, underwent special training in Mexico and on his return to Bolivia obtained the enthusiastic assistance of SCIDE, the cooperative Bolivian-American educational service, for a fundamental education project in the Christ School village of Coipasi.

Coipasi is a community of 1,296 inhabitants some forty miles from Potosí. For a decade of years it had the distinction of having as the one and only teacher in its one and only school an excellent gentleman, Don Francisco Andrade. It was Don Francisco who proved the open sesame for the penetration of this traditionally unchanging Quechua world by the forces of change. "They want to help you," he explained to the village folk regarding the team of specialists from outside. "They want to make Coipasi a nicer place to live in."

The program directed by Dr. Montoya was five-pronged, as taught him in Mexico by CREFAL (the Regional Fundamental Education Center for Latin America): (1) health; (2) economics; (3) home; (4) leisure program; and (5) improvement in basic knowledge. Except for the guidance of the specialists, all of the program was to be carried out by the villagers themselves.

A sanitation office was set up and a plan for better drinking water was studied. On May 27, 1953, which was Bolivian Mother's Day, the program of education for the Indian women began, a literacy course for adult women who had never been to school. The class counted forty-nine the first day and six months later, on November 19, there were still forty-two when the examinations were given. The simple country women had made a beginning that was satisfactory beyond all expectations.

A start was also made at the Spanish language. None of the women and very few of the men in this Quechua-speaking community knew any Spanish. Groups were formed to acquire a little of this bridge language that would lead to a knowledge of the great world outside. Characteristically, the leaders began by organizing group singing of Spanish songs.

The majority of these farmer folk, both men and women, never read a book or newspaper of any kind. How could reading habits be formed? A modest little communal library was organized. On the tables a few periodicals, newspapers and pamphlets were placed, including picture magazines for these who could not yet read. Thus the cultural and social life of Bolivia began to penetrate Coipasi. The library was at the new social center and here of an early evening public readers without great fanfare would read aloud to groups who gathered. Thus curiosity was awakened for the contents of these previously unthought-of links with other people's ideas.

Cinema shows were first arranged in the village chapel. "We should have a more seemly place," suggested some. Soon the people were raising funds through the cinema shows to buy a piece of land for the social center and its construction became a village project.

Most popular of all were the village leisure activities. Volleyball, up to then unknown, came to town and caught the enthusiasm of men and women as well as the youngsters. Phonograph records were used for concerts of national music. Songfests became more and more frequent and soon the community had a greatly increased repertory. On August 6 of that memorable first year a selected company of villagers went to Betanzos, the provincial capital, and delighted everybody with a choral concert in two parts.

One day in November of 1953 Dr. Montoya proposed a small consumers' cooperative. He suggested four objectives: (1) to buy rice, sugar and other less used commodities; (2) to gain experience in ways of buying and selling that would secure better prices; (3) to provide an easy way to introduce new items into the village that were good for health and for the improvement of the home; (4) to strengthen the Coipasi communal cooperative bank. The Christ School directors loaned a small sum to purchase the first articles—rice, sugar, kerosene, matches, grease and the like.

But Dr. Montoya's finest dream was yet to be realized. He talked it over with Don Francisco. "We must find a means to make these people realize how wretched and ugly and dirty their houses are," he said. The team of specialists and Don Francisco decided to make a start. Three young families were approached and volunteered to improve their homes by talking over ideas with the team.

"See, Joaquin," began Dr. Montoya, "you are a tall man. The door of your house is so low and narrow that only by bending and turning can you let yourself through. People who build houses in other places make the door large enough that a man need not lose his dignity every time he goes into his home."

The young husband and the Doctor entered the house.

"See," said the Doctor, rubbing his hand on the wall and then walking to the door, "See how black with soot my hand is. The room where you live and where your wife cooks is so small and so confined that the house cannot help but be constantly filled with smoke. It is so dark that the soot accumulates unnoticed and nobody can even see the amount of dirt that hangs about you. If we were to cut into the adobe walls and put in a few small windows everybody would be delighted with the difference it would make inside."

So the process began, always with care not to suggest too much at a time lest even the more courageous Indians might rebel against the changes proposed. Finally, into the homes of the three families larger rooms and higher ceilings were introduced. At the Christ School carpentry center several windows with four panes of glass were made and brought to Coipasi, to be paid for on easy terms. They were introduced into the hitherto unbroken adobe walls.

The neighbors watched all this, some with uneasy foreboding, some with laughter and ridicule, but many with a stirring of curiosity and at least a silent recognition that there was merit in these new ideas. By skillfully avoiding any conflict with those whose minds remained closed and by leaving the discussions to the villagers themselves a successful beginning was made in home improvement.

The day of triumph for the home improvement program came in 1956. After a period of cautious experimenting Dr. Montoya got the happy idea to launch a home improvement contest in Coipasi and to announce that a committee of high government dignitaries from La Paz would serve as judges and award the prizes to the winning families. This news created a genuine stir. Now the villagers almost in unanimity took hold of the idea and for months applied themselves to the problem of making their homes measure up to what the judges would be looking for when they came.

The festive day dawned bright and clear. Coipasi made a pretty sight under the deep blue sky, tall eucalyptus and green willow trees waving amid the neat homes on their small cultivated plots. People wore their Sunday best—hooped petticoats, ponchos and shawls—and the local band played folk music on reed flutes. There was a great hubbub as a station wagon sped into the village with the judges, educational and Indian-affairs authorities from the capital. A procession led by the school children preceded the inspection and then the "commission" moved from door to door through the village.

Two outstanding features caught the eye of the judges, one outside the houses, one inside. Over thirty of the houses displayed immaculate white walls, some with new neatly laid thatch roofs, some with tile. Most had newly constructed latrines behind the dwelling. But the main attraction, indeed the contest's most widely praised feature, were the new windows. "How did you persuade them to introduce windows?" asked one of the experts who knew the problems of the Indian country. "They persuaded themselves," replied Dr. Montoya, in the most orthodox modern social welfare manner.

"My wife likes the windows best of all the changes," replied one Indian when asked, "because she can look at herself in them as in a mirror."

"If I didn't install the windows," said Don Lorenzo, a 35-year-old farmer, "people would criticize me for not caring to give my children a good home."

The second outstanding attraction for the judges was the raised stove in place of the traditional cooking fire on the floor. Almost all the households participating in the contest built new hygienic kitchens separate from their dining rooms, with the raised clay stove and chimney, and shelves for cooking utensils.

"We must confess," explained Dr. Montoya, "that as in the case of the windows, it is the motive of imitation rather than a sense of need or conviction that built many of these kitchens. There has been a direct relation between the householders' ages and outside social contacts and their use of these new kitchens. Young married couples with two or three small children employ the new kitchen for everyday cooking. The older women tend to keep their new stoves to look at and continue to cook on the floor."

For Dr. Montoya the day proved a happy culmination of years of anxious striving. "Most of the dwellings were below standard," he observed. "In fact, some families were living in almost subhuman conditions, not so much because of their extreme poverty as because of the complete lack of encouragement to lead a better life. Long-rooted habits made people indifferent to change, resigned to living in the unhygienic promiscuity of their mud huts. Whatever slight influence the local school had on the children was of very little if any value, since at home the influence of parents and elders was stronger."

After the tour the officials gathered in the center of the villages and awarded the prizes. One contestant received a washstand set (basin and bucket), others went away happily with new wheelbarrows or plows. Each received a diploma signed by the authorities, attesting to his progressive spirit and his love for Coipasi and Bolivia.

The joint efforts of SCIDE and the Christ Schools in this fundamental education project of Coipasi extended well beyond this little village. It is estimated that thanks to this program 85 per cent of the rural dwellings in the Potosí area have been improved. Coipasi's new streets, embellished central plaza, rebuilt church, its social center and sports fields have been models for the surrounding countryside. Indeed, they serve as basis for a similar program among the Aymara of Warisota, an initiative of the staff of Warisota Rural Normal School, situated on the immense plateau between La Paz and the Peruvian border, on which 350,000 pastoral Indians, all of Aymara stock, are scattered.

The principal effort to provide for the spiritual care of these Aymara has its center in the village of Las Peñas, forty miles from La Paz. One beautiful afternoon I drove to Las Peñas and watched a golden sun execute its wizardry on the line of mighty snow-covered mountains off to our right. Half a dozen of the peaks are over 20,000 feet high, and mightiest is Illimani, among the tallest of the giants in the mountain spine of the Americas that extends from Alaska to the Straits of Magellan.

As we arrived at Las Peñas a soft sunset glow gave a gentle beauty to the crude homes set among the trees. The parish is comprised of twenty-one communities. A first group of these is organized under modern Bolivian law, a second group is comprised of free communities under Aymara communal law, while the third group represents worker settlements on haciendas whose owner-patrons govern them under traditional hacienda law. At the time of my visit, the haciendas were in a bad way; only two of the twelve in the parish were in operation due to the leftist agitation against the rightist owners.

Father Bernard Ryan, the Maryknoll pastor, has enthusiastically joined the other enterprisers of the altiplano who are seeking to help the Aymara. With encouragement from the government he has installed a small model of the immensely successful radio broadcasting schools at Sutatenza in the mountains of Colombia which we shall visit later.

But good news comes from the city as well as from the country. La Paz, Bolivia's national capital, key to its mountain world, has the most curious of locations. It is a vast crater 1,400 feet deep that is a monster washout created by a slowly eroding river that through millenniums has cut into the surrounding plateau 12,000 feet above the sea. In this city, higher than Lhasa, the capital of Tibet, 350,000 people live. Archbishop Antezana has a score of parishes to serve these people—some of the parishes with more than 40,000 souls. Less than a hundred priests undertake the impossible task of serving the people in these parishes. It is not surprising that a bare five per cent of the city's population goes to Easter Communion.

Archbishop Ritter of St. Louis visited La Paz a few years ago and was appalled at its spiritual poverty.

"You can help us," the Papal Nuncio, Archbishop Mozzoni, said to him. "Send us some of your St. Louis priests."

Archbishop Ritter did just that. When he got home he wrote to sixty-two of his younger clergy ordained from five to ten years and asked if they would volunteer to go to Bolivia. Within a week forty of the sixty-two declared their readiness. In May 1956 the first group of three came to Bolivia, studied Spanish at the Maryknoll language school in Cochabamba and then took charge of a slice of the Maryknoll parish in the capital.

The parish of San Pedro counted almost 60,000 souls. The St. Louis sector with 12,000 people is called Christ the King Parish. It started with an open shed with galvanized roof as its only church. Mass is also offered out in the open air about a half mile up the hill in a slum area dominated by the Protestant Church of the Nazarenes. Father Joseph Gremillion of Louisiana in a recent visit had the moving experience of serving as pastor one Sunday in this pioneer neighborhood.

"I offered Mass for 250 persons, half adults, half children," he recalls. "They knelt and sat on the bare ground. It's uncanny how the Faith has stuck with these people. 'We are Catholic, our nation is Catholic,' they will tell you. 'We have it from the milk of our mothers,' they say. More North American dioceses should offer their priests to Latin America."

Chapter 2

The Voyage of El Hermanito

I AWOKE SHORTLY AFTER daybreak and from my cot on the deck I could see the jungle green of both banks of the river. I went up forward to our boat's snubby prow to watch the cool sun of the early morning touch the placid waters. Almost immediately an eighteen-inch fish, a silvery dorado, leaped from the depths a few yards in front of us and dropped back with a smack that in the silence sounded like the report of a cap pistol. It was our morning greeting from the Rio Madre de Dios.

I had left Bolivia's mighty mountains and now, though thousands of miles from the Atlantic, was only 500 feet above sea level. Over 70 per cent of Bolivia is lowland, an area of 300,000 square miles that begins at the Argentine border and reaches north well into the Amazon Valley where Bolivia meets Brazil. We were riding very close to Bolivia's northern line, in an area which Medaro Chavez, one of its biographers, calls the Bolivian Eldorado, the true heart of the South American continent. Again he describes it as the Mesopotamia of Bolivia because within its water-logged compass there is a tangle of thirty-two winding, twisting rivers, all of them in great part navigable and all of them garnished with an infinity of dark-watered arroyos, short feeder streams that make ideal private moorings for the river people.

The plague of the area is the thirteen great cataracts that effectively isolate the region from the Amazon Valley. Most imposing and beautiful is Cachuela Esperanza. Bolivia's military men look benignly on these blockades of rock and raging water; for them they are frontier fortresses that have kept the invader from grabbing Bolivia's territory. For the little folk of the area, however, the rubber extractors and the brazil-nut pickers, they are a Chinese wall that condemns the region to be a quiet backwater of the earth, a barrier against progress and the fraternity of peoples. Huge distances and mighty problems of livelihood have kept the world of the Amazon from flourishing. Bolivia's Pando Department and the Province of Vaca Diez would be at best the end of the line whether approached from Brazil to the north or from upland Bolivia to the southwest. The cataracts inexorably seal their fate.

But now the airplane brings new promise. It was by plane that I entered Riberalta, the quaint town with grass streets perched on a little bluff a hundred feet above the Beni River, harboring 8,000 people and serving as the center of the Pando. Here Bishop Thomas Danehy maintains headquarters for the Maryknoll Missioners who labor in the region. The Maryknoll Sisters operate a hospital here and carry on pioneer work on the rivers as collaborators with the Fathers.

Bishop Danehy proposed that I join two of the priests who were making the journey to Conquista, the largest rubber barraca, or plantation center, in the region. "The trip by boat will take as long as the rail ride from New York to St. Paul," noted one of the Padres. Thus on the previous day we had boarded the El Hermanito, the 40-foot shallow-draft Maryknoll river boat. It is named "The Little Brother" after Brother Gonzaga who was killed while captaining the boat when a huge tree fell on the vessel as it hugged the shore in following the meandering channel.

We were a happy party of seven aboard. The priests were two old friends of mine, Father Bob Fransen of Glendive, Montana, and Father Dick McMonigle of St. Paul, Minnesota. (Father Dick has since died a victim of cancer.) I made the third.

The crew numbered four and constituted a team of top efficiency. The commander was Pablo Villamor, a pleasant, good-looking young fellow who took the night shift and slept between decks in a hole that must have been stiflingly hot when the sun beat down. Pablo Jimenez was the co-pilot, a sturdy old Cavinas Indian who at work slouched around in blue denim overalls but who sported a pair of two-toned brown shoes for dress-up. The engineer was Napoleon (Napo) Barca, a reliable fellow who watches his motors carefully. He has a good-humored, puckish squint and an aptitude for clowning. He is the butt of Commander Pablo's jokes. Pablo calls him a bandit, steals his cigarettes, and plays innumerable tricks on him. Finally there was Olga Suarez, the cook, a likable person from Santa Cruz who when on shore works in one of the mission kitchens.

When we left Riberalta we had a little company of lepers aboard that we brought upstream to Aqua Dolce. Among them were two young men who were brothers and their mother, all victims. The father years ago had committed suicide when he found his family thus afflicted. A number of the other adults were married and had children, but all of the children were free of the disease. For this they could thank Carlos Ribeira, the practical nurse of the colony who was their devoted counselor and servant. He had just paddled the company downstream in a large canoe carved from a tree trunk and was now accompanying them back. As soon as we left Riberalta the fresh river breeze swept the sultriness out of the air and the day became enjoyable.

The river was low but Commander Pablo piloted skillfully, read the water's surface to avoid the shallows, and co-pilot Pablo sounded with a pole. Sometimes we swung from shore to shore quite wildly, following the erratic channel.

We stopped at Valparaiso with a sack of grain, waved to the folk at San Jose, bought watermelons and lemons at another village and finally said goodbye to our lepers whom we landed at Aqua Dolce. Night fell and we sat far forward on the deck in the tropic full moon. "The moon here in the Pando" remarked Father Dick somewhat poetically, "is the one thing that never disappoints us." It was a night for poetry. The air was soft and tender. One bank of the river was always in deep shadow, the other brilliant with light and according to the channel we glided from one to the other. Finally we set up our cots on the deck and I found myself surprisingly comfortable under a heavy blanket.

Now it was the morning of the second day. We said our Masses as we moved at an altar set on the deck and were prepared for a pleasant morning when suddenly the boat stopped. "I must clean the points of my motors," explained Napo. Immediately great swarms of the tiny but savage mariwi fly descended on us and we were soon badly bitten. It gave us a thrill to hear the engines turn over at last. Almost immediately the insect pests were gone and we were enjoying the delightful breeze. "This helps you to understand," Father Bob remarked, "what a purgatory it is to paddle at slow pace here in the still air."

The Maryknollers in the Pando are divided in their duties into town missioners, barraca missioners and river missioners. The squad assigned to the river work would seem to have the most rugged routines. There are four priests currently in this group. Father Ambrose Graham of New York City is the dean of the river men. In his early days he worked for seven and eight months on the upper Orton without coming out but is now forbidden to do this. His present assignment is the lower Beni not too far from headquarters. Father Sam Valladon of Oakland, California, covers several hundred miles on the Madre de Dios. Father John Flinn of Cleveland takes care of the upper Beni above San Pedro, while Father Jim Dyer of Ossining, New York, has charge of the Orton and Tahuamanu Rivers.

Each of these men has a boat and it is an interesting study in individualities to see with what a different eye each regards his boat. Father John Flinn, for instance, is a careful planner and a stickler for detail, with a strong mechanical turn. He has given his boat a name, the Santa Ana, and he has fitted it so that he can sleep aboard it, cook his meals regularly, and meet every emergency with his neatly assembled gadgets. His confreres admire him for being thoroughly prepared and well organized for his career.

Father Ambie Graham's boat in his days on the Orton had no name. It was a small twenty-five footer with minimum equipment and he slept ashore every night.

"Why did you use such a small boat?" I asked him as we chatted in Riberalta before my departure for Conquista.

"First of all," he explained, "a small boat was better on the Orton where there were so many shallows. Then, people were so hospitable. When I pulled up of an evening they always invited me to throw my bedding on their floor and sleep for the night with them. The old lady would brush away the dirt, taking care to get rid of the hog and chicken dung. They were careless with their housekeeping but the homes were never really dirty."

"What about food?" I asked.

"I always carried food. I had dried milk and cocoamalt which I could mix with water from the river. I had juices and spreads in cans. But so often people would kill a chicken for me and usually their meal was good. The women did my laundry for me and mended my clothes."

"Could you work with the people at night?"

"I had great success with movies which I showed with a small kerosene machine. No barraca boss however cool he was toward me dared interfere when I broadcast a call for a movie or slide film show; people came through the jungle for miles, sometimes by hundreds. I had a film on Our Lady of Guadalupe but the best was an old film on St. Francis of Assisi. Ugolino was the villain in the St. Francis picture; the example of the sinner was always Ugolino. Soon the bad deeds of Ugolino became famous up and down the river. Men would hunt me up and tell me with great excitement the lessons they had learned from Ugolino and how they now kept straight because of his misdeeds, 'And you didn't say a word to me, Padre,' they'd cry. 'It was the voice in the box!' "

"I suppose they'd rather have it out of the box," I remarked.

"Oh yes. They're tired of having the priest correct them. I noticed that if instead of conducting a religion class I'd hold a question hour of an evening the real hard customers in the settlement would attend in order to argue with me. They love to argue out here along these rivers."

I decided that they need more Father Ambie Grahams in this South American back country. What a thrill a good argument with a good-humored priest must be for these people. Life is definitely on the empty side out on the rivers. At the first sound of our motor as we broke the stillness, all stopped whatever they were doing. Whether an isolated hut or a river hamlet, young and old lined up in sight of the stream and gazed at us and our boat, continuing to gaze until we passed beyond their view. They were the watchers. The young returned our salute with vigor, the older ones displayed less enthusiasm. But only the barking dogs showed real joy.

"There is a note of disconsolateness in the patient but vacant stare of these people," I remarked to Father Dick McMonigle. "There is something melancholy in their uneven struggle with the jungle wilderness."

"True, and it is the unequalness of the struggle rather than any basic impossibility of succeeding that makes us who work with them feel sad," answered Father Dick. "There is a way to succeed in this jungle, a way to make life happy for parents and the kids, but these people don't have it."

"A way to succeed—that's interesting," I observed. "Most people say it's quite hopeless here."

"Don't misunderstand me," replied Father Dick. "I don't mean that it would be easy to succeed. Bolivia is a poor country, definitely unable today to provide a decent life for all its people. The aid it gets from the United States and the United Nations doesn't reach these northern tropical plains—we are definitely at the end of the line. But men who know say that the same crops could be grown here that are grown in Central America. At present 30 per cent of Bolivia's foreign expenditures every year are for food that could be grown within the country. This region could raise all of Bolivia's needs in coffee, pepper, chocolate, things now bought abroad. People could make a tidy living growing money crops on family farms."

"Are there any plans for this?"

"Very vague ones. The principal reason is illustrated by that little scene right in front of us."

The little scene to which Father Dick referred was a crew of mechanics working on a good-sized river boat pulled out of the water onto a playa of sand. Several of its metal plates below the water level were badly bent and the mechanics were taking them off to repair them.

"That's the Orton, which struck a huge log a few days ago and sunk. It's a worn out old boat, more than forty years in service here; if conditions were anywhere near normal it would be sold for junk. One of the best indications of the general decline of this area is the sad condition of the public launches that serve the rivers. Most of them date from the rubber boom of over forty years ago. Our oldest launch, the Tahuamanu, was built in 1896. Once there were forty to fifty launches in the neighborhood; now there are but a dozen."

Father Dick's remarks reminded me of some of the things Dr. Vaca Diez told me in Riberalta. Dr. Osvaldo Vaca Diez is the son of one of the pioneer builders of the Pando. He studied medicine in Paris and now has a daughter at college in the United States. He is respected as one of the upright leaders in the Bolivian North, a good man interested in the building of Christian family society in the region. I mentioned him to Father Dick.

"Yes, Dr. Vaca Diez knows the story very well," he agreed. "The Doctor's father has been called the Cecil Rhodes of the Bolivian North but his dreams have not as yet come true. Before 1890 old Antonio Vaca Diez presented to the Bolivian legislature a plan to introduce roads and steam navigation that would supply the need of communications that was keeping the area from developing. The need has not yet been filled. In Antonio's day there was the bright prospect of rubber riches but then the rubber bubble burst. Men here have never gotten over their disappointment sufficiently to make any new strong resolves for the area's prosperity."

We passed another beautiful moonlit evening on deck and moved along eventlessly until shortly after ten, when we docked at the port for Conquista. Carefully hung mosquito nets insured us a restful sleep and the next morning after early Masses we made the hour's journey afoot to the rather exposed plateau that provides a natural base for this number one rubber-extraction center in the Pando. Years ago it was the site of an Indian village where members of both the Araona and the Cavinas tribes lived. The Indians here were exterminated by a plague of dysentery.

Rubber operations are carried on currently in the Pando by several companies—Suarez, Soenenschein, Seiler—each of which operates its own properties and exercises a certain control over individual extractors which insures them a supply of rubber. Conquista is the property of Seiler, a Swiss firm. Over a thousand persons live within its domain of several hundred thousand acres either at the headquarters barraca, or in one or other of the eight field centers, the most distant of which is eight hours' journey by truck. The headquarters barraca is a busy village in itself, where seventy-two families live and all business operations are concentrated. A Maryknoll missioner is based here. He has a chapel seating 150 and an unpretentious residence, both buildings provided by the company. Father McMonigle had just been appointed here, thus becoming one of the barraca priests, the second of the three categories of Maryknollers in the Pando. This group lives with and follows the extraction workers.

We quickly sought out Mito Chavez, the local manager for the Seiler

Company. His Christian name is William and his nickname Mito would thus be the equivalent of our Bill. He was quiet and unpretentious in manner and impressed us by the clarity and good sense of what he said.

"You'll find nothing here comparable to the Ford plantation in Brazil or to the marvelous parks of cultivated rubber trees in Southeast Asia," he began. "We are breaking with tradition as you will see but up to now we've dealt only in wild rubber from the jungle. A single seringhero works three estradas at a time, visiting each twice a week. An estrada, or rubber-tree route for a normal day's work, counts about 150 trees scattered thinly through 75 to 100 hectares. Thus for each worker we need 250 to 300 hectares of wild-rubber-tree jungle, or 500 to 600 acres. It is clear that our business can operate only where there are vast stretches of jungle and our crews must be scattered through this jungle or they'd never get on the job each morning at daybreak. This explains our set-up with eight field centers all of them at considerable distances from headquarters."

"Mito," I interjected, "how about drawing us a map of the whole enterprise?"

"With pleasure," Mito patiently replied. He took a sheet of paper from his desk and with pencil and ruler prepared the map which is reproduced on the following page.

"The estradas," he continued, "are actively worked for fifteen years and then must be allowed to rest for eight years or the trees will be injured. Thus it happens that of our eight centers, four are resting this year and only four are active. Those resting are Batraja, Mate, San Miguel and Bella Vista. The active centers are Urubamba, with thirty-two families, Florida with twenty-seven families, San Felipo with twenty-two families and Junin with thirty families. Thus we have about 120 families at the field centers."

"You must have a big problem of supply," I remarked.

"Yes—each little community lives its life apart and gets only what we bring it. There is a fairly good road with seven bridges along the main axis from Conquista to San Miguel, 32 kilometers long. Mule paths link up the four centers off this main road. Junin represents a new axis 20 kilometers long. A mule path covers the 52 kilometers to Puerto Rico on the Orton River at the far opposite extreme of our

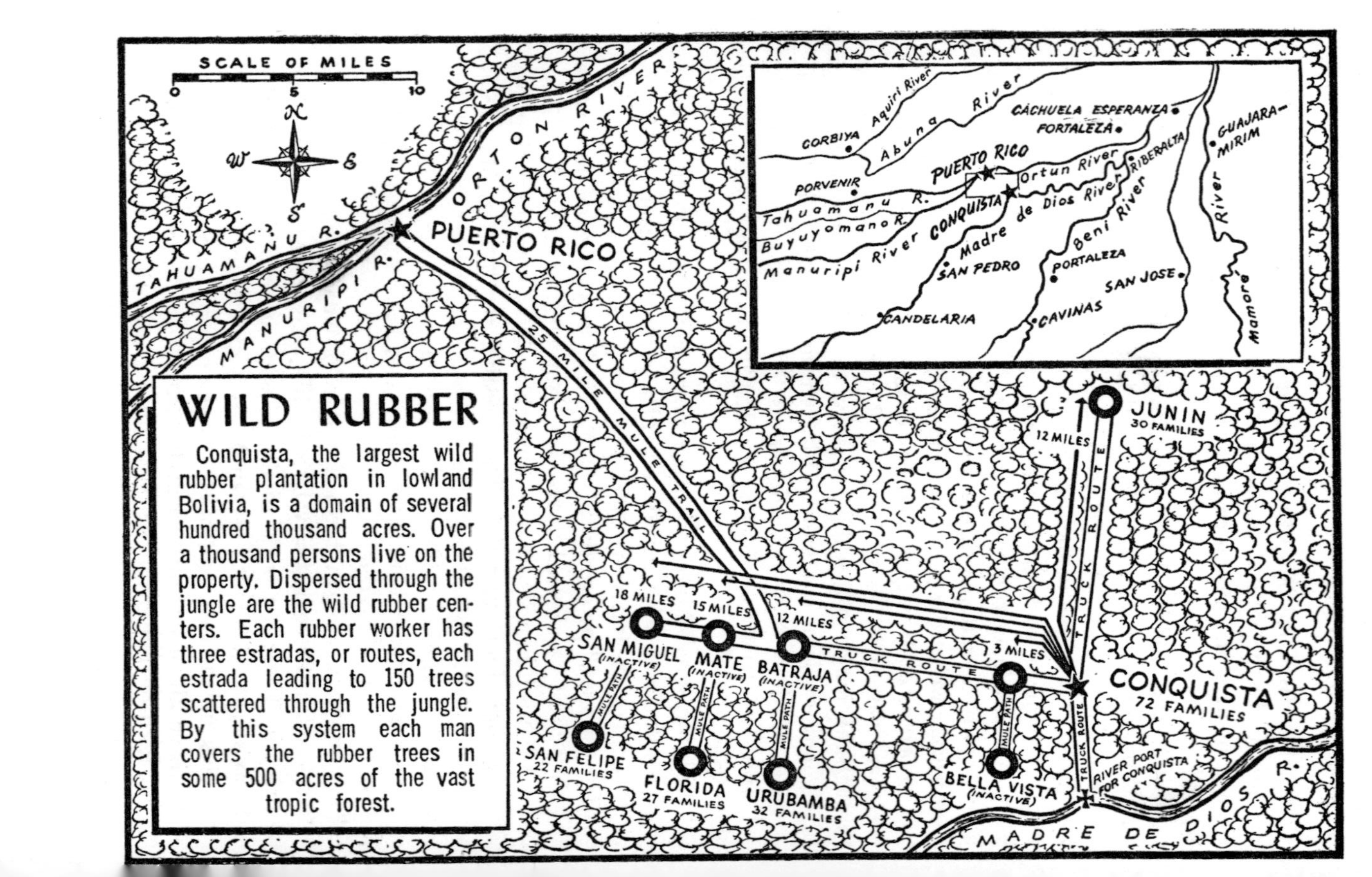

WILD RUBBER

Conquista, the largest wild rubber plantation in lowland Bolivia, is a domain of several hundred thousand acres. Over a thousand persons live on the property. Dispersed through the jungle are the wild rubber centers. Each rubber worker has three estradas, or routes, each estrada leading to 150 trees scattered through the jungle. By this system each man covers the rubber trees in some 500 acres of the vast tropic forest.

property. Every two weeks a truck brings supplies that are delivered to the company store in each community. This store is the only source for purchasing the family needs. The men buy on credit and they can get deeply into debt if they are not careful; most of them are not."

Here Mito was making indirect reference to notorious conditions which develop in the lives of many seringheros, namely, their heavy indebtedness to the company store that results in their practical enslavement to their proprietors. Even in this day and year, many proprietors in poorly policed backward areas send armed posses after seringheros in debt to them if they attempt to shift to other companies.

"Who directs these field centers?" I asked.

"Each is headed by a capataz appointed by the company. Health conditions are watched by a male nurse hired by the company who covers all the centers. Just now we have an excellent man named William Schmidt who is very devoted to the workers and their families."

"Are there teachers for the children?"

"The children come to the company school here at headquarters. This is directed now by Carmen Rosa, a very good woman from the Maryknoll parish in Riberalta. She has an assistant who is paid by the government."

"What is the work year in the field centers?"

"The principal rubber season is April to July, the time of hardest labor. During August and September the men grow food for themselves on the small farms allowed them by the company. October and November represent the second and shorter rubber season. December to February is the season for collecting brazil nuts. Everywhere where rubber trees grow there are also brazil-nut trees. The roasting center is here at headquarters."

"It is not an easy life is it, Mito?"

"No, it is an isolated and difficult life that we think is on the way out," he replied. "These company communities will then either be abandoned or become civil communities with a new economy. Let's visit the Seiler company's attempt to write a new chapter in Pando agriculture," proposed Mito with a smile.

We drove out in a truck to the fields in which the Seiler Company has 80,000 sapling rubber trees growing in plantation style. As we found while discussing rubber production in Brazil, an infinitude of painstaking research has gone into this development of South America's new plantation rubber trees to substitute for nature's own in the jungle. Between the rows were young coffee trees and cacao trees for the local production of the chocolate bean. Here at Conquista also were fields of rice as part of the Seiler program for diversified agriculture.

On the new plantation we met Branca Peris, a Catholic Czech who is the agricultural technician directing this program. "We are also taming the wild brazil-nut tree," he explained pridefully. "To reach maturity the brazil-nut tree requires 140 years of natural growth. By grafting slips from the wild trees onto other roots we can produce yielding brazil-nut plantations in fourteen years. Then the ugly labor of following the estradas to the wild trees will be gone, men can produce more, live a more normal life, and should be paid more. Thus science will open the way peacefully to better living conditions for the little man in the Pando."

Mito brought us to his neatly furnished home and now became the family man. We met Señora Chavez who was a member of the Children of Mary in Riberalta parish, and the very attractive Chavez youngsters. We took dinner in his separate eating pavilion that kept heat and odors out of his home.

"We are happy to have the Maryknoll Fathers with us," began Señora. "We have the Maryknoll Sisters in our neighborhood just now. We respect the Fathers very deeply for their devotion," she added with a smile, "but it is the Sisters who completely capture our love and admiration."

Two of the Maryknoll Sisters, Sisters Vivian and Maura Kieran, were actually on the Conquista property during our visit but had gone by horse to Florida at the far extreme of the property to visit the sick.

"On the rivers the people go crazy with joy at the approach of the Sisters," continued Señora Chavez. "It is the beautiful things that they do for the needy in the hidden corners of the back country that win the loudest praise in the Pando."

Sister Rose Mercedes and Sister Marquette had made the first journey to Conquista some years previously.

Sister Marquette explained to me that on this trip she and Sister Rose Mercedes made a ten-hour ride to San Felipo on horseback, with a pack mule carrying their hammocks and medicine. The capataz could find privacy for them only by letting them use the company store as sleeping quarters. "There'll be rats here," remarked Sister Marquette immediately, "I see soap and flour."

They hung their hammocks and sure enough, as soon as the light was out the rats came along the hammock ropes. But happily the mosquito netting was sufficient to form a barrier.

Father Tom Collins of San Francisco told me of a horseback journey he made with two of the Sisters to Lago San José. There they heard of a sick man in a bad way two hours further on. They continued on and found him in great pain from gall bladder trouble, arranged to have him brought to the Riberalta hospital for an operation. He still talks of their long ride to take care of him.

Great chattering squadrons of green parrots greeted us as our vessel left its Conquista mooring in the lovely afternoon and started downstream. The Pando rates as a land of the green parrot. Certainly if noise is any proof, friend parrot feels very much at home here. There were also beautiful flocks of white, black and white, and gray cranes that as evening fell went through their exquisitely graceful routines.

Next morning we found that since our passage upstream a small settlement of Chama Indians had moved onto a large playa in the river. They had come for turtles and turtle eggs buried in the sand. The Chama is a river tribe in the area. The Cavinas Indians are the most numerous Pando tribe—well built, robust, copper colored people who are arrogant, frank, affable, with expressive faces. They are intelligent and the missionaries have awakened some ambition in them.

There are some fifteen tribes in the Bolivian lowlands and only the Sirioni, who are very few, are savage and dangerous. While a man like our co-pilot, Pablo Jimenez, counts himself one hundred per cent Indian blood and practically everybody in the area has a strain of the Indian in him, all speak of the tribal Indians in quite detached fashion, peddling vague hearsay information regarding them much as men among us speak of gypsies.

For the last dinner on our speeding vessel Olga prepared a delicious serving of locro, which is a dish of chicken and rice enriched with eggs, tomatoes and potatoes. Father Sam Valladon, on the upper porch of the Maryknoll center house in Riberalta high above the confluence of the Beni and the Madre, chanced to see our boat as we forged down the home stretch and thus Brother Owen was at the port with the jeep for us.

"It feels like coming home," I remarked as we entered the house.

"We all find it the same," Father Valladon replied. "The whole town has warmed up wonderfully toward us since our first arrival a few years back. Today 30 per cent of the people of Riberalta attend Mass on Sunday and there is a generally keener religious life in town."

"How does this show itself?" I asked.

"Well, for one thing Church marriages have greatly increased. Ten years ago there was no great sense of impropriety about a common law marriage. Now both men and girls are ashamed of free unions. The young women are no longer contented with a mere civil marriage. Nothing short of a religious marriage satisfies them. Double households still can be found among those with money but the tendency now is to keep it quiet; the women involved are no longer proud of their role."

"We have some outstandingly fine families today," noted Father Tom Collins. "There are men like Ricardo Suarez of the rubber dynasty who was educated in England and came back an excellent Catholic. He and his wife and five children are almost daily communicants. Ricardo is a leader among the men and strong in St. Vincent de Paul work among the poor."

The new 1957 concordat between Bolivia and the Holy See promises to be very helpful in the six mission territories of the Bolivian lowlands that it seeks to develop. The missionary traveling through the back country can now perform marriages without formidable obstacles in the way of civil regulations. The schools are also greatly aided.

"Our people have a fighting interest in their schools," explained Father Collins. "When a rumor circulates that the government plans cutting back in any way on schools, particularly the parish schools which the people support in part by voluntary offerings, men and women gather immediately in fear and anger to draw up a petition."

"Even the plantation laborer is changing on this question of education," commented Father Tom Higgins who, with Father Steve Maskell, conducts the Carmen Commercial Institute in Riberalta. "Once a man would let his kid go to school until one fine day he would look at the youngster lying abed, realize how big he was and call to him, 'Get out and bring in the rubber—no more school for you.' But today the father is all too aware through sad experience of the need of book learning; he wants his boy to get an education."

One morning I went to Carmen Institute with Father Higgins. "Let's ask some of these boys what they have in mind for the future," I proposed.

The first young man we talked to was Francisco Tudela, a quiet solid student from Cavinas, the Indian reservation 600 miles up the Beni from Riberalta. He was seventeen years old.

"Did you study hard at Cavinas, Francisco?"

"Not particularly; the school wasn't much good."

"Why did you come here to Carmen?"

"Because I think I can be a good mechanic."

"Would you like to own your own business?"

"I never thought of such a thing. Nobody on the reservation owns a business, just a farm."

"Would you like to own a farm?"

"A small farm for food for my family, yes, but not if I had to hire other people. I'd just like to be a good mechanic."

"What do other boys like you at Cavinas think about the future?"

"I don't know. I never heard anybody talk about the future."

Father Higgins looked at me and smiled. "Francisco," he said, "reflects the spirit of the Indians and their reservation at Cavinas. Not much vision there."

Next boy was Alfredo Machu, child of a Japanese father and Bolivian mother. He was a leader in the school and a good athlete.

"What are you looking for in life, Alfredo?"

"I want more tranquility, better living."

"Do you want to work for others or for yourself?"

"I want to work for myself; I want to *own* something."

"What, for instance?"

"A truck garden that will produce vegetables to sell here in Riberalta."

"Will you work alone?"

"No, I want to employ others. But they'll have to work with hand tools; machines are too costly."

The third boy was Antonio Araos, whose father is a retired lawyer and his mother a music teacher in the government school. He is big boned and wears a confident smile. He entered with the sure-footedness of a boy encouraged by successful parents.

"Where do you live, Antonio?"

"My father has his cattle ranch at Santa Ana but a sales station here and it is here we are living now."

"What are you going to do?"

"I aim to own a cattle ranch in the neighborhood of Trinidad where cattle raising is profitable."

"What will you do with the cattle?"

"I'll bring a few overland to Riberalta with cowboys but I'd prefer to sell most of my meat directly to the airlines packing company for La Paz."

The fourth boy was Renato Jimenez, small of stature and only fifteen years old. His grandfather is a well-known lawyer in Riberalta.

"What do you think we should do about the future, Renato?"

"I think we must build up our school because we want to make the Pando Department and our nation great."

"How precisely would you help the nation?"

"I'd grow more food. We need much more food to save Bolivia from importing from abroad."

"What will you do about it?"

"I'm going to own a trading company to send foodstuffs from the Pando to the altiplano."

"What are you studying now, Renato?"

"I'm studying bookkeeping to keep the accounts of my business."

"Food is the thing, eh?"

"Food—but more than food, we need culture in the Pando—libraries with good books, schools on the rivers, better homes for better living, an electric light plant, water, sewage."

"You've put many good ideas in those boys' heads, Father Tom," I remarked as we left Carmen.

Bishop Danehy's dream for the Pando has been a socio-economic program to help develop a society of independent farmers. Toward this end he secured a land concession on the Beni for the Blanca Flor Project. This eventually is to be an agricultural colony where men will be guided in techniques and cooperation for a combination of sustenance farming and the marginal production of money crops. Father Jim Logue of New York City has a similar goal for younger men at San Rafael Training Farm. Time is needed for the fruition of these plans.

"Lack of faith in the Pando and lack of faith in themselves is perhaps the greatest enemy our people have," one of the missionaries remarked in summary. "The day that we can convince the young people here to stay and build a better Pando rather than run away, on that day the tide of apathy will turn. To hasten this day help from La Paz is needed, international help is needed. But all important, we must build up in these people the will to help themselves."

Santa Cruz is the traditional gateway to the Bolivian lowland, a city of 30,000. A company of Andalusians came here with their wives long ago and the Cruzenian, as the local inhabitant is called, is distinctive in all Bolivia, with his kinsmen scattered in the lowlands as far as the Pando. He is demonstrative, open, warm, gay.

Once the Cruzenian was isolated from the mainline Bolivians. He was called the camba or country hick. But now a highway 310 miles long climbs into the mountains from Santa Cruz to Cochabamba. It can mean such changes in the Bolivian Oriente that men say it may prove the most important road ever built in South America. In the opposite direction a railroad moves eastward to the Brazilian border and now both freight and passengers may journey all the way from Santa Cruz to fabulous São Paulo. Thus the Santa Cruz area, which has promising possibilities in agriculture, seems destined to be one of the most prosperous corners in Bolivia.

Santa Cruz held special interest for me because, quite as in the Pando, here a contingent of Maryknoll Missioners is growing up with the new day and entering enthusiastically into the problems of the people.

With Father Tom Foley of Belmont, Massachusetts, I listened to a small, shy man from Hungary, Señor Greku of the Bolivian Ministry of Development, explain why we should keep our eye on Santa Cruz.

"Santa Cruz has prospects of being one of the main centers of the South American continent. It is a natural focal point for international air communications, north-south, east-west. Locally there are huge riches. There are already 160,000 people in the area and in a decade or two there can be 500,000 gainfully at work here. I have found the best kaolin in the hills that I have seen anywhere outside Bavaria, of a quality that will make the finest porcelain. There is iron, gold, mica in the vicinity. There are great deposits of graphite."

"What are you doing here in Montero?" I asked.

"We have just completed a sugar mill that can refine the cane of 12,000 acres yearly. The mill can handle 250 four-ton truckloads of cane a day."

"Are you going to get that much very soon?"

"That depends on two things—the roads and the atmosphere of confidence and security that the government must create among the farmers here."

I saw the farm-machine pool established at Montero out of which machines may be borrowed by the small farmer. Time will decide how he makes out. Interesting experiments are in progress to bring 5,000 farm families down from Bolivia's altiplanto to work here in Santa Cruz. The Bolivian army has brought down a first contingent of Aymara Indians and a UNESCO team transported a body of Quechua Indians from near Oruro. Both experiments seem to be working well. Groups of Japanese and Italian immigrants likewise have tracts in early stages of development.

"But along with the new there is still the old," explains Father Joe Gribbs of Detroit who works in the large town of Warnes. Over a meal of wild pigeon shot by his houseboy he painted a picture of family living in this old area with its stirrings of new life. "The biggest things in most home circles in this neighborhood are not the latest seed discoveries or the chance to get a day's use of a tractor. It's two very old problems, alcohol and concubinage.

"We have two large sugar mills in the parish, which at first glance look like fine institutions. But the fact is, they turn out to be feeders for seven alcohol factories. Bolivia is still importing sugar for sweetening our coffee. Its own sugar in great part goes for making the much more profitable beverage alcohol which the locals buy pure and take fifty-fifty with water, a mighty powerful concoction. The chief curse of the neighborhood is drinking."

Father Gribbs is in good company in this attack on alcohol. In their 1958 pastoral the Bishops of Bolivia likewise have hard words for drink. They urge the clergy to guide well the campesino in his home life and his work, insist that he send his children to school, inculcate in him a sense of thrift and teach him healthy habits as regards his house, his food and his clothing.

"Above all," say the Bishops, "declare war without quarter against drunkenness, source of so much misery for our native people. Avoid by every means possible that our religious feasts degenerate into pagan, worldly orgies through alcoholic liquor."

I urged Father Gribbs to continue. "And evidently your next biggest problem is concubinage."

"Right. Too often the woman is unable to hold her man. To fight concubinage, we've decided that as a preliminary, wives should be taught to keep themselves more attractive to their husbands. So many use rouge and high heels only until they land a man, then abandon all notion of keeping smart.

"But for us the key remedy lies in maintaining the respect of the man for his own family. Father O'Brien and I set out to prove that it is possible to accomplish the impossible, to get the man to become a decent, church-going family partner. We decided to conduct a mission for the men. Everybody laughed at the idea. But the two of us took to our horses and made a house-to-house visitation throughout the countryside. We announced an unheard-of thing, church services for a week to which women were absolutely forbidden to come; they were to be strictly for men only.

"The idea worked. Every night for seven nights some 400 men rode into town, filled all the yards near the church with tethered horses and reported faithfully for the sermons and public prayer for men. At the men-only Mass on Sunday morning over a hundred men went to Communion."

"What were the after-effects?"

"Definitely encouraging. Only yesterday a local mechanic stopped in and said, 'Padre, tomorrow is my wife's birthday. I figure a way to make her happy is to go to confession and communion.' He was at the altar rail this morning with his wife. This is exceptional but everywhere in the parish it has become quite the fashion for the men to take new interest and new pride in maintaining a happy family life."

Devotion to Our Lady in Bolivia is a hidden wellspring of strength for managing the unmanageable man. The Santa Cruz area is fortunate in having at Cotoca one of Bolivia's best-loved shrines to Our Lady. Among other things Our Lady of Cotoca is patroness of the Bolivian Air Force. During one of my visits to Santa Cruz, a specially chosen air crew flew over Cotoca and dropped bouquets of flowers in homage to Our Lady. The next day Father Gus Kircher and I encountered one of the top officers of the base in Santa Cruz and Father Kircher congratulated him on the beautiful gesture.

"Padre," he replied, "every man in the service envied that crew for its privilege. Many of us may not be very faithful to our religious duties but every one of us has a deep love for Our Lady of Cotoca."

Chapter 3

The Indian Corridor of the High Andes

One of the unusual geographical phenomena of the globe is the two-thousand mile corridor in the high Andes that runs southward from the border of Colombia the length of Ecuador, Peru and Bolivia to the northern border of Argentina. The floor of this corridor is 8,000 feet above sea level in northern Ecuador but by the time it reaches Peru and Bolivia it is two and a half miles up, 13,000 feet, vying in height with the Tibetan plateau. In this corridor some ten million people live, of whom over six and a half million are Indians.

One of the most extraordinary ethnical phenomena of the world is these Indians. Men have despised them as dumb cattle, as hopelessly unresponsive, as useless in these smart modern times in which we live. Yet a thoughtful observer like Arnold Toynbee passed their way in 1956 and listed them among the earth's choice peoples as hardy pioneers.

"The Indians' home-grown civilization, arduous though it be, is admirable in its self-sufficiency," he writes. "Catching glimpses of the Indian at home," he continues whimsically, "I had the same impression that I once had when I drove out into the countryside from Quebec. If the modern civilized world should ever manage to wipe itself out by a perverse combination of technology, folly and sin, these earth-bound peasants would still be there to multiply and replenish the earth when the flood of poison-radiation had subsided.

"It would take perhaps barely a thousand years for the southernmost French Canadian peasant pioneers to run into the northernmost Quechua Indian peasant pioneers among the ruins of Miami, Florida, or Houston, Texas, and on that day the New World at any rate, would have been repopulated."[1]

The element in the Andes that prejudices so many against the Indian is dirt. "Ugly old mud-holes, aren't they?" a missionary remarked to me as we visited a village near Puno, Peru, where the mud and straw houses are windowless and lightless, smoke-filled and odor-filled, the nests of men with unwashed bodies and badly washed clothes. "But don't be deceived by this situation which in great part is due to the rugged climate, the stark poverty and the crudely harsh living facilities here in the mountains," he went on. "These people have some fine qualities. If we can help them solve some of their problems we'll find out how superficial this bad habit of uncleanliness is."

Victor von Hagen is devastating in his disgust at these houses. "Within, each house was as snugly warm as an oven and as filthy as an abattoir. Untanned cowhides stretched out on the hard baked-mud floor were the beds, the piles of blankets upon them emitting an overpowering stench. In one corner the untended fire consumed cow dung; on the blackened walls hung bright woolen festive clothes, with next to them the carcasses of flayed sheep. On the one hand we had the beauty of the land; on the other, the filth of these human habitations."[2]

To understand these people we should recall briefly their background. When the train crosses the altiplano from La Paz to the Peruvian border it stops near Lake Titicaca at a place of ruins called Tiahuanaco. A step from the station we find the vestiges of the city state of this name which is regarded as the cradle of the civilization of the Incas. Huge stone monoliths with intricate carvings stand on the plateau and look out on the gaunt waste. Most notable monument is the Gateway of the Sun. As I watched, an Indian drove his herd of llama under its mighty arch and seemed dwarfed to midget size. Already here in the cradle city a thousand years ago there was cultural greatness. From this neighborhood the forces moved northward that founded the imperial city of Cuzco, now in upland Peru. When the Spaniards arrived in 1531 the Incan Empire, called Tahuantinsuyo ("Four Parts of the Earth"), extended north to Quito, Ecuador, and south to Chile and Argentina. It probably counted 15,000,000 inhabitants.

The Incas ruled as despots and as descendants of the sun god. Cuzco had palaces and temples that rivaled ancient Egypt and a network of roads to the four corners of the realm that matched those of old Rome. Present-day remnants of them remind us of the Appian Way and the Via Salaria. Rome boasted a highway from the Scottish border to Jerusalem, a distance of 3,000 miles. The Incas matched this with an Andean road from Quito, Ecuador, to Talca, Chile, that was 3,250 miles long.

Incan society included nobles, priests and common people. Communists like to say that the Incan form of government resembled the soviets of the USSR, an exaggeration, but it was categorically collectivist. Incan society was evidently well and benignly organized under resourceful and vigorous governors. Every family had its house, its field, its flock. A sufficiency of everything was the rule with enormous irrigation systems, agricultural terraces on the mountainsides which even today strike us as stupendous. Regular taxes paid in manual labor provided smooth, efficient functioning of the state seemingly without abusive burdens. There was art and beauty to a remarkable degree but, curiously, no written records and evidently very little systematic training of the mind in the way of formal schools. The Incan culture never approached the greatness of that of Greece and Rome.

The Spanish impact on the Incan armies was probably like that of an atomic-equipped regiment hitting a fighting unit with outmoded World War II equipment. At Cajamarca, a spot in present-day Peru, the confident Inca Atahualpa with Ruminagui his commander secretly threw 5,000 troops around Francisco Pizarro's tiny Spanish company of 200 soldiers. But then the Inca made the mistake of accepting Pizarro's invitation to dinner. He came with a retinue of hundreds on his palanquin of gold ornamented with parrot feathers. Not the Spanish commander but a Spanish priest met him, Padre Vicente de Valverde. The Padre gave the Inca a brief lesson in religion, then explained that Pizarro represented the great king of Spain who in turn was rightfully authorized by the Pope to take possession of the Incan Empire.

How did the Padre get this knowledge, the Inca asked. "From this book!" replied the priest and handed the Inca a Bible. The Inca turned it over and over in his hands, then threw it to the ground.

This was enough. Padre Valverde retired with his Bible, Pizarro waved a white scarf, the hidden Spaniards leaped from their hiding places with infantry, cannon and cavalry and the carnage began. Pizarro personally saved the Inca from death. "He seized the Inca's long hair in his bloody hand, dragging him along like a bull on a rope." He then negotiated with the nobles for a roomful of gold as ransom for the Inca, got his gold and with dastardly ruthlessness put the Inca to death. By wit, by boldness and by weapons of another world Atahualpa was captured. In a matter of a few hours, or of a few days at most, the fighting spirit of the Incan Empire was broken.

That spirit has never to any important degree been revived, though there has been a series of bloody revolts, and there seems no desire among the Indians today to seek its revival. But it is probably this lack of spirit among the Indians that accounts more than anything else for the filthy huts, the faceless communities, the uninspired Indian society that inhabits the Andean corridor.

From the day of their defeat by the Spanish the Andean populations began to suffer for want of the very services which had been so well ordered in Incan times. The roads, irrigation systems and agricultural terraces which had always been maintained fell into disrepair. With deteriorated communications, food production fell off. Most important, leadership was lost.

It is incorrect to say, however, that the descendants of the Inca completely forgot the past. When the Great Liberator, Simón Bolivar, was en route to Bolivia, he stopped in the Peruvian mountains and a local Indian leader, José Domingo Choquehuanca, thundered across the plateau with a delegation of hundreds of horsemen to greet him. Choquehuanca's short speech in Quechua amazed Bolívar and today has its place in Peru as a literary masterpiece, a revealing evidence of Indian thinking.

"It was God's desire," this Indian declaimed before Bolívar, "to form from savages a great empire. He created Manco Capac. His descendants sinned and God sent Pizarro. After three centuries of penance God had mercy on America and created you. You are the man sent by Divine Providence. Nothing in the past can compare with what you have done. In order to have somebody imitate you, it would be necessary to provide them with a world to conquer. You founded five republics, which in the great advancement to which they are called, will elevate the esteem of your name to heights never yet attained by man. May your glory increase with the years as the shadows increase with the setting of the sun."

After 400 years, most of these six and a half million Indians still know little or no Spanish. From the Colombian border to southern Peru they speak Quechua. Below a line which runs through Puno on Lake Titicaca they are predominantly of Aymara stock and language, though Bolivia counts a considerable Quechua-speaking element as well.

Today the Andean Indian divides into four main groups: (1) the hacienda peon; (2) the free Indian; (3) the industrial worker in the mine or mill; (4) the evolved Indian who, while educated and in business or the professions, desires still to be considered a member of his people.

The hacienda peon follows a life similar to that of the workers on the fazendas of Brazil, the estancias of the Argentine or the fundos of Chile. It is estimated that almost 40 per cent of the highland Indians of Ecuador are hacienda peons, that rather more than 40 per cent in Peru are thus established, while in Bolivia the number runs to 25 per cent.

Some of the best types in the Andean corridor are free Indians. They include tribes or segments of tribes that have never been enslaved. To enjoy this privilege, many in generations past paid dearly for liberty by escaping to remote and difficult areas where life was very near to insupportable.

There are two classes of free Indian, the individual landowner and the communal farmers who hold lands and manage their affairs collectively. Celebrated among the individual landowners are the Otavalo Indians, a people numbering about 100,000 found in northern Ecuador near the Colombian border. It is not uncommon to find an Otavalo farmer who works 100 acres though some hold parcels of as little as two and a half acres. Nevertheless as a group they represent the best performance in the entire two thousand mile corridor.

The Otavalo contribution to Ecuador's economy is relatively unimportant. Most land in Ecuador belongs to the old hacienda system and produces so little food that, as in Bolivia, foodstuffs are a major import of the country. All the privately owned land is held by 3.5 per cent of the population.

Quite notable in the case of the Otavalo Indian is his spontaneous occupation with cottage industries so dear to the heart of the social economist. A generation ago he imported straw palm from the coast several hundred miles away and made the excellent straw hat bought by so many workers on the Panama Canal that it became known in the United States as the Panama hat. By 1952, however, this industry had fallen to 3.3 per cent of its former gross, a catastrophic loss for the Indians.

But Otavalono handicrafts are still very much in being. Every home has a loom. The Indians show rare skill in wool spinning, dyeing, weaving, embroidery and pottery, employing precolonial designs admired for their beauty in the markets of the world. Both the Andean Indian Program of the UN and the United States International Cooperation Administration (ICA) have sought to encourage these handicrafts by improving the techniques of the Indian mastercraftsmen and teaching them modern marketing methods.

The communal farmers in the Andes are a hangover from Incan days. Now a white governor is always in charge at the district level. Each of the communes is under an Indian alcalde and his Indian assistant is appointed by the governor. The communes are divided into *ayllus* or villages and thus the average Indian deals only with Indian officials. The isolation of many of these Indians is amazing and their general suspicion and fear of the outsider, including the modernized mestizo who may live quite near them, is very strong.

The land held by independent Indian owners and by the communes is usually the poorer and more isolated segments left over after the creation of the haciendas generations ago. Most Indians have tiny woebegone farms on steep slopes or on bleak arid punas in the upper reaches of the mountains. Enlightened self interest and a heightened sensitiveness to the lot of their less fortunate fellow citizens have prompted the governments of Peru and Ecuador as well as Bolivia to give attention to improving their lot.

"The Indian farmer is our greatest undeveloped asset," explained a very dedicated official in the government development bureau in Puno. "He makes up more than half of our population, yet he often follows his own laws and ways of conduct much as his forebears have done since the days of the Incas. He seldom pays taxes and takes no part in the life of Peru. He grows hardly enough to meet his own needs and sells only enough to buy a few odds and ends for the wretched way of life he follows. Men like myself would dearly love to help him. The course we should follow seems to be quite clear. But he himself is often the biggest obstacle to our repairing the damage of the past."

There is nothing surprising about the tendency of the Indian to rebuff his would-be benefactors; centuries have taught him to beware the Greeks bearing gifts. A most interesting example among many such efforts, this one with a happy outcome, is the so-called Cornell-Peru Project.[3]

Not so long ago I journeyed by a Peruvian plane above the breathtaking grandeur of the triple line of ranges that cross Peru: first, the Cordillera Negra, which is bleak rock; then the Cordillera Blanca with its snowy peaks; and lastly over the Cordillera Azul with its green vegetation and its cast of mystic blue haze. Almost four million Quechua Indians live in these ranges. I could discern far below the occasional green valleys flanking a stream, the crude pueblos, the mountain fields at weird angles, the threaded roads on the huge mountainsides like pieces of string pressing into a package.

In a narrow valley of the Cordillera Blanca is the Hacienda Vicos. In the early 1950s Professor Allan R. Holmberg, an anthropologist of Cornell University, combined with Peruvian scholars and officials to try to do something for the more than 2,000 Indians living in hunger and disease on this neglected hacienda. Holmberg and his group determined to avoid disrupting the community or creating confusion and anxiety. They found at Vicos an epitome of the Indian problem. The Indians were almost completely illiterate with only two per cent able to read or write and very few able to speak other than Quechua. Hunger was chronic, drink their only recreation. An epidemic meant death in almost every home. They were little better than slaves, despised by their neighbors, often commandeered by the authorities and carried away in trucks to do odd jobs when mere brute strength was needed. There was strong hostility among the hacienda Indians against the nearby mestizos.

Holmberg set as his first task to increase the food crop. So great was the need that the Vicosinos were eating their seed potatoes and stealing as much as they could from the hacienda. The Project proposed a credit plan by which it would advance the seed, fertilizer and insecticide on a fifty-fifty crop-sharing basis. The plan was first presented to the Indian leaders. Immediately the outsiders sensed hostility; the leaders evidently felt that any new plan would undermine their own favored position and turned it down.

Undiscouraged, the Project presented the plan directly to the peons at the traditional weekly meeting for assignment of work, the *mando*. The rank and file showed interest until one of the leaders condemned the proposal. Out of 125 present, nine signed immediately for the plan and thirty-one later. But then a campaign of rumors started, evidently encouraged in part by landowners and mestizos in the neighborhood who opposed any new ideas. Why had these gringos come to the valley? What strange reasons had they for offering help? Surely there was some scheme to cheat and exploit the peons. The Peruvian personnel in the Project fought valiantly to counteract all this but in the end only seventeen peons, the poorest of the poor, fighting opposition even within their own families, finally took the seed.

These seventeen had to follow instructions to the letter on every tiny detail. They had to disinfect the seed potatoes and the land, plant the seed at 18-inch intervals in rows three feet apart, apply guano as fertilizer, spray insecticides at set times, remove blossoms from the plants, cultivate, irrigate as instructed.

But their day of triumph was great. At harvest each of the seventeen had double the crop of his neighbors, huge healthy potatoes such as never were grown in the neighborhood. The next year 87 Indians took the seed, the third year 135 Indians. The Project had won the day and on the confidence it gained it has made Vicos into a model community with the best in schooling and health facilities.

"Foremost among all the purposes for the Project," explains the Project reporters, "has been the calculated endeavor to develop the Indians' self-reliance and change their own image of themselves—an image of serfs destined to poverty and endless unrewarding work."

The role of the priest in winning the confidence of the Indian to these betterment plans can prove vital. I drove out from Cuzco one day through beautiful mountain country to the ancient Incan village of Chinchero, 11,800 feet above sea level. Some 10,000 Indians live in the town and go out each morning to work the fields that fill the majestic valleys. The Peruvian government and the American government's ICA (originally Point Four) have developed here a village improvement plan and we met Señor Fernandez, the director, and Alicia Tamayo, the directress. Señorita Alicia, a large-built enthusiastic mountain woman with a broad-rimmed sun-bonnet hat and gingham dress, greeted us warmly.

"I spent ten months studying for my work with your Department of Agriculture in Washington and each time I think of it it is like reliving a dream. It was wonderful! And here we have been so successful. But you know we must give all the thanks to Archbishop Hermosa of Cuzco. We came here and began our project but nobody was interested. All said they would have nothing to do with it. 'This is terrible!' we declared. 'But I know what we should do,' I said, 'we should bring the Archbishop of Cuzco out here. He should speak for us to these people.'

"The Archbishop came out. You know he is an Indian like ourselves and we all love him. His address worked like magic. He talked for over an hour and he kept saying over and over, 'You must believe in these people, you must trust them. They are good people. Your Archbishop knows what they are trying to do and he knows they want to help you. They are good people; trust them.' When he finished everybody cheered him and we had won the day."

Señorita Alicia had paid a finer compliment to the Archbishop than even she appreciated. She had credited him with playing one of his finest possible roles in his relations with his people, the bringing to them of confidence and understanding. The priest, the missionary in particular, holds an enviable position among the mountain Indians. Almost everywhere they respect and trust him because through the bitter centuries they have had many evidences that he labors for them.

A Peruvian missionary expresses his sentiments thus: "Who would be a missionary if he did not have the hope that through his efforts the Indian would enjoy in some way the same opportunities and the same rights as other men?

"There is a grave at my door. It is of a Spanish missionary dead two centuries ago. Franciscans and Jesuits have long sought to aid these people. Time and trials have driven them out. We start again. I say Mass at dawn and work each day on the inconsequential things about me. How little my role seems, yet how great. There must be a man who loves the Indian not as a servant but as a brother. There must be many such men."

Today missionaries from Europe and North America work in the

Indian corridor. The Maryknoll Missioners, who have their headquarters for the southern mountain area in Puno, maintain parishes in such towns as Ayaviri and Azangaro among the Quechua and in Ilave and Juli among the Aymara. All of these communities count a heavy Indian population.

"We think highly of our Indian both as a man and as a Christian," commented Father Jack Byrne of Dunmore, Pennsylvania, who knows well the people of Ayaviri. "He is hard-working and pious, gentle and unspoiled."

I was deeply impressed by their unstudied devotion at morning Mass in Ayaviri's huge old Spanish church. Most are illiterate but more and more are learning to read. We find not a few engrossed in their prayer book as they kneel at Mass in the dim quiet of the early day.

At Azangaro Father Charles Murray of New Bedford, Massachusetts, is credited by his confreres with uncovering a number of priestly vocations among the Indian boys. "It is our young Peruvian companion, Padre Hernan Llerena, who has done most of the work," explained Father Murray. "For years he devoted every spare moment to the young fellows, strengthening their confidence, building their ideals."

Tradition has been against encouraging Indian vocations in this region of Peru but today in the minor seminary in Puno the Maryknoll Fathers count more than twenty Indian candidates in a total of thirty seminarians. "They are making a great mistake," remarked a Peruvian pastor in Arequipa in reference to this training school. "The Indian will never make a priest." Thus the incubus of the past works against all attempts at change. The Maryknollers already have two Indian priests prepared under their care, Padre Jose Vitulas whose father and mother are full-blooded Aymara, and Padre Claudio Colquehuanca whose parents are of Quechua stock.

The notoriously shy reserve of the Indian inhabitants of the village of Ichu, a few miles outside Puno, was broken down a few years ago by Father Dan McLellan of Denver, Colorado. His experience serves as a striking instance of the confidence that the Indian will place in his spiritual father.

Father McLellan went each Sunday to the humble chapel of this community of 5,000 and softened up the cold and distant stares among the elders by playing with the children and winning their adoring affection.

"Everybody in Puno says you are very unfriendly," Father Dan remarked to some of the men one day. "Why don't you be a little warmer with people? They wish you well. But does any outsider ever visit you here?"

"No one," one of the men replied.

"Why don't you have a road to the highway?" he asked.

"How would we build it?" someone asked by way of answer.

This was the beginning. It was true that the village, though near Puno, was completely isolated. After several meetings with the alcalde of one of the two *ayllus* and a number of other leading men Father McLellan persuaded them that they themselves could build a two-mile road to the highway if they made up their minds to it.

Father McLellan went to the Provincial Minister of Highways and secured the services of an engineer to lay out the road. The alcalde then put the traditional machinery to work within the *ayllu,* each man accepting responsibility for a given number of days' work on the construction or guaranteeing to hire a substitute in the event that he could not do the work himself. The government supplied tools and dynamite. Local pride was stirred and with surprising zeal the road was completed within a year.

Father Dan drove me along Lake Titicaca where fisher folk labored on the shore with their celebrated balsas, the reed boats special to these waters, the largest mountain lake in the world. The balsa is seaworthy for only a few months but a new one is easily made from dried fronds of the bright green reed which we saw men and women cutting at the lake edge as we passed.

Suddenly we turned off the main highway onto a narrow but new-looking road that led into the hills.

"This is the masterpiece of the men of Ichu," explained Father Dan enthusiastically. "The road was officially opened in July 1954 in the presence of the Prefect of the Province of Puno, the Mayor of the city of Puno and of Bishop Dettman. The notables of Puno who were present were greatly impressed to see the townsfolk of this notoriously backward community appear neatly dressed and sober. The fact is, two of the men showed up intoxicated and we locked them in a room until the ceremony was over. The building of the road gave these people a wonderful psychological lift and now they are talking of other improvements."

Father McLellan is the pastor of the principal parish in Puno and with several Maryknollers as helpers he has rejuvenated the spiritual life in this mountain city. "When the Maryknollers first came here there was one lone woman who came regularly to Mass. The Padres dubbed her Cathedral Kate. Today there are 3,000 on Sunday, or ten per cent of the gross population. Religion is taught by the Padres now in every classroom in town as Peruvian law allows. Communions of devotion have grown to more than 2,000 a month. We are making a systematic house to house visitation and despite rebuffs from many who have grown cold on religion through neglect the response is phenomenal."

Father Dan's great achievement in Puno is the organizing of the first signally successful credit union in Peru. "We began in 1955," he explains, "and in 1957 we recorded 3,000,000 soles in deposits, the equivalent of $150,000 in U.S. money. The astounding fact is that sixty to seventy per cent of the members are Indians. We thought it was to be for our parishioners but one day shortly after we started an Indian woman from a distant spot in the mountains, poor, ugly, plain as salt, came in with 3,000 soles hidden in her petticoats. She put the money on the table and said she wanted to be a member. Others have followed her."

"How do you explain it?" I asked.

"It's obvious," Father Dan replied. "The Indian is hungry for a way of living which he can put his faith in. He wants someone to trust and, frightening though it is for the responsibility it places on us, he is ready to trust us."

"Do they borrow as well as deposit?"

"Oh, yes. The average Indian loan runs from 1,000 to 3,000 soles for seed grain, for a bull, or for other farm needs. The Indians understand how loans work and are careful about keeping their commitments. No Indian—in fact practically no member of any group—has as yet defaulted on a loan."

"What did the Indians do before you opened the credit union?"

"To borrow they had to go to private persons who, because the risk here in the mountains is regarded as great, charge high rates. As to investing their savings, there is no established practice. Putting money in the bank is unknown. That's why the government looks upon our project as tremendously important."

"Where does the Indian keep any money he may save?"

"Here's one example: A young Indian from an *ayllu* beyond Ichu came to me recently and said, 'Padre, has my father been in to see you yet? I've been arguing with him for weeks. He has a big box of money hidden in our house and I'm scared sick. Some day someone will find out about it and steal the box or kill him for it. For weeks I've been trying to persuade him to bring it to you.' After a few more weeks the old fellow finally showed up with his money. To answer your question, most Indians put their savings in the Andean equivalent for our North American family sock, which most frequently is the multilayered mattress of animal skins on which they sleep."

Father Dan and his Maryknoll confreres are fully aware of their grave responsibility to insure the sound operation of their credit union. They have allied it with CUNA (Credit Unions of North America) of Madison, Wisconsin, and insist that everybody keep all the rules.

What happens when an Indian emancipates himself from the old ways and enters modern life? One August afternoon I made the acquaintance of Pedro Tupiño at our Maryknoll House in Lima and it proved an exhilarating experience. A great many Indians leave the rural altiplano and take up work in the cities of Ecuador, Peru and Bolivia. An average of 60,000 a year are said to settle in the neighborhood of Lima and a steadily growing segment of Arequipa is composed of newly arrived Indians. Most of these people take up lowly tasks and enter but slowly into twentieth century ways. But not so Pedro.

Pedro Tupiño is from a sector of the Canate Valley in southern Peru that was never conquered even by the Incas. His people spoke Kanki. Tupe was the only town in the area and from this town Pedro received his family name.

Pedro is small and lithe of build, Indian in features but with a face that, rather than deadpan, is highly expressive, marked by smiling, sparkling eyes.

"May I ask, Pedro," I began, "if you are an Indian?"

"Yes, Padre, I am an Indian. Frankly, Padre, many of my race when they come to the city are not proud of being Indian. They usually say they are mestizo. It took me a long time to bring myself to say without apology, 'I am an Indian.' Now I have conquered myself on this point and being an Indian is the guiding aim of my life."

"You seem to be a successful Indian, Pedro. You have a fine education and you operate a very profitable business."

"God has been very kind to me, Padre. I could very well have been today a peon in the mountains, barefoot, wrapped in a poncho, ignorant, illiterate, hungry and cold. Why have I received so much?"

"Just *why* did you receive so much?"

Pedro laughed. "I owe it most of all to my father. He was a simple peon but in everything that meant providing for his family he was wonderful. He was greatly respected by the townsfolk of Yanyos, where we lived. They would say of him, 'Tupiño is the only man born in Yanyos in a hundred years and there'll never be another like him!"

"What of your mother?"

"My mother, then, was a marvelous woman. She had very little education but she possessed the science of love and life. She must have had a thousand homely sayings that I can recite in great part and they became the philosophy of my life. She loved me dearly and for long she would not part with me to let me go to school."

"Did this set you back in getting started?"

"As it turned out, it did not. My oldest brother agreed with my mother. He was to our family in the things of the spirit what my father was in material things. He used to say, 'Men are like horses; you must not break a colt too young.' Thus I got no formal schooling until I was eight. Then I came to Lima to the American Methodist School where I studied in English. I was older than the boys in my class but each year I did two years in one. Then I went to the Peruvian School of Engineering and secured my degree by the time I was twenty."

"Did you get a job immediately as an engineer?"

"No, instead I got my first bitter disappointment. I felt that I knew my civil engineering so well that I set out with high hopes. I went immediately to the government service bureau and asked for a position. I sat in the outer office every day for weeks until finally I gave up in despair. They were not prejudiced against me because I was an Indian; there are Indians in government service. It was because I had no friends. You cannot have a government job without friends."

"What did you do?"

"I resolved that I would succeed in a way in which I would not need friends, that I would work for myself. Everything happened right for me. I went into the merchandising business and I made a great deal of money."

"And now you are a man of leisure."

"In a certain sense, yes. But I am not finished living. I wish to help my people. I keep saying to myself, 'I am in debt to other men.' I received a great deal from other men. I want my fellow Indians to receive the same."

"You believe in your fellow Indians, don't you?"

"Decidedly. I am sure that we Indians are as capable as other men. Take any ten thousand Indian boys and you will find that their minds are basically as intelligent as other men's, their wills are congenitally as strong as other men's though not disciplined by clear and formulated objectives such as cultivated people possess. Their emotions are stirred by different influences than other men's but, again, they are basically the same. I tell my fellow Indians that they must not be ashamed to be Indians. I would like to reach many of my own people, to give them assurance, to stir in them desires for betterment, to help them to take their rightful place in our great nation of Peru."

"Does the educated and successful Indian keep to his religion, Pedro?"

"He does, according to the degree that he keeps true to himself. Most Indians hold to their religion. Most keep away from the erratic ways of men without religion. We could not pray to the Blessed Mother if she were garbed in the modern dress of the worldly. So men will have no respect for us if we assume the ways of the worldly."

Chapter 4

Lima and the Catholic Continent

TROPICAL PALMS ornament the attractive patio of San Marcos University, one of Peru's proudest heritages. It was founded in 1551 and thus is the oldest university in the Western Hemisphere.

"San Marcos is regarded as liberal in spirit and some of its professors are leftish," remarked Padre Simone, my Italian guide, "but it is a commentary on the general state of religion among Peru's better classes that thirty per cent of the students here joined the men at the Catholic University of Lima in a public Communion service last Easter. Peru to many of us rates as the most Catholic country in Latin America."

San Marcos' reputation as "liberal and leftish" was well demonstrated in the attacks by a sector of its students on Vice-President Nixon during his visit of 1958. Back in the 1920s it grew out of such enterprises as the "popular university," when students of the university organized to give classes in various subjects to members of Peru's newly launched trade union movement. A number of student leaders supported the workers' campaign for an eight-hour day and the unionizing of labor. Outstanding among these leaders was Victor Paul Haya de la Torre. In 1923 the Peruvian President decided that the student-worker movement was a menace to the country and deported Haya de la Torre. In Mexico in 1924 Haya founded the Alianza Popular Revolucionaria Americana (APRA).

The Apristas, with Haya at their head, have proven an interesting phenomenon in Peru, where today they are the largest political group. They are hated by the Communists and until lately have been bitterly opposed by both moderate and extreme conservatives. They urge land reform, advanced labor legislation, industrialization, the incorporation of the Indian masses into the civic life of the nation. They are a classic example of how an aggressive social movement with radical tendencies can steal the thunder from the Communists and call down mountains of wrath from the world organizers of Moscow who know that they succeed best when they can pose as the lonely pleaders of justice for the downtrodden.

Father Weber of Germany, pastor of San Felipe, the flourishing parish of the Missionaries of the Sacred Heart in Lima, confirms the statement of Padre Simone regarding the relatively high level of religion in Peru.

"The educated Peruvian has a deeper Catholic culture than the North American or the German," he explained to me. "One never has to *prove* the faith here. Unlike the hostile elements in postwar Germany, there are no enemies here of the Person of Christ. There are anticlericals but seldom any anti-Christians. As to moral infractions, all are children of the *good* God and conveniently overlook the Deity as the *just* God. The dogma of punishment for sin is often quite completely ignored."

The basis for improvement on this latter score, the schoolmen seem to agree, is disciplined religious education. Father Morris of the Marianists of Dayton, Ohio, insists that the school's the thing for the molding of Peruvian society. The Marianists for almost a generation have conducted in Lima one of the best educational institutions in Latin America. Sancta Maria College has trained some of the outstanding leaders in modern Peru.

Another excellent school in Lima is Villa Maria, the top-flight young women's college and academy conducted by the Immaculate Heart Sisters of Philadelphia. It required a long day for my visit to these Sisters because in addition to their huge Lima plant with its enrollment of 1,200 young ladies of Peruvian upper-class society, the Immaculate Heart Sisters also conduct St. Anthony's School in Callao, the port of Lima on the coast, in which 900 children of families of modest means are educated free.

At Villa Maria Sister Gregoria chatted thoughtfully with me toward the end of the day. "These are the mothers of the next generation," she said, "in many of the households that will give leadership to this outstanding South American nation."

"What ideas do these young ladies have, Sister," I asked, "as to what makes an ideal Catholic family?"

My question intrigued her. "Let's ask them and find out, Father," she replied enthusiastically.

Sister decided on a sampling of some forty young women in the college department. The inquiry proved impressively successful. These young ladies sat down at their desks one morning and, each independently of the other, revealed remarkable consistency in sound instincts as they picked their examples of fine Catholic living.

Each young lady named a family, described it briefly and then proceeded to answer the question, "My reasons for considering this family outstanding." It was this item that proved so enlightening. Four characteristics were constantly referred to under this heading: (1) the mutual love and affection between husband and wife; (2) the household spirit of warmth and joy among parents and children and the strong family unity; (3) the active spiritual life within the family as a whole; (4) the dedication to service of their neighbor on the part of parents and children.

Parents everywhere can learn a lesson from the keen observation of these young ladies on the first of these characteristics, the mutual love and affection between husband and wife.

"To me," one young lady wrote of the family she chose, "the most important thing is the love that the father and mother show to each other. Although they are married for more than fifteen years, they act as though they were just married in the way they treat and care for each other, giving a living example of what married life should be."

"You can easily see," writes another young lady, "that the wife is very much in love with her husband; she is willing to do anything to please him. He in turn appreciates this and is very sweet with her."

"Mr. and Mrs. E. are a young couple with outstanding Catholic spirit," reads another report. "They are a wonderful example of perfect mutual understanding. I like the great love that husband and wife have for each other as well as for their children, four boys and a girl."

On the second characteristic, a household spirit of warmth and joy with strong family unity, several interesting examples were cited.

"This family is a little community with the motto one for all and all for one," explained the writer. "Love and affection among the children reign at every moment. One of the boys was very fond of riding and wanted a horse but his parents said it was too expensive a gift to give one child alone. When his brothers and sisters heard this they immediately offered all their savings to buy the horse. When the parents saw this act of generosity they gladly bought the boy his horse."

"The eleven children in this family," writes another, "show great unity and deep love for each other and for our Creator. From the eldest to the smallest they show great love for their parents. The mother in particular displays such happy good humor that you immediately feel at home in this large family."

"I like the way the children share responsibilities among themselves," says still another. "They understand the great need for mutual help which exists in the world today."

All the families cited are notable for the third characteristic, a family life of prayer.

"Catholic in all ways," reads a typical report, "rosary every night with all the family, prayers before and after meals, Mass every Sunday and Communion for all every first Friday. I like the family especially because the girls, instead of going out too frequently with friends, stay by the side of their mother who is sick with an incurable disease."

"The family has great devotion to the Virgin of Fatima," another comment reads, "and all go to Communion every Saturday and Sunday. One of the small sons, a two-year-old baby, was kidnaped and held in ransom. We can imagine the suffering this family endured. Yet the mother showed her truly Christian spirit by publicly forgiving the kidnaper."

It is notable that every family chosen is cited for the fourth characteristic, love of neighbor through works of charity.

"All the family partakes in wonderful Catholic Action work," says a report. "The mother among other things does a beautiful job among the old people of San Vicente. The two girls are catechists in the same parish. The father and boys are admired for the fine example they give everywhere. They make the poor people feel that they are not receiving charity but sharing in what the family has."

"Doctor B. has founded a leper hospital and supports it with his own money. He cures the poor free."

"The family I chose has eight children, four boys and four girls.

Parents and children give themselves generously. The eldest daughter has become a Visitation Sister. One of the boys takes an active part in a club to spread the Faith among the uneducated Indians of Peru."

One family was mentioned by the young ladies not once but four or five times and I decided to make its acquaintance. I found it consisted of Dr. Enrique Cipriani and Mrs. Isabel Throne de Cipriani with their nine children. They live in an attractive home across the street from the Immaculate Heart School and are a handsome couple, he sharp and intelligent, she svelte, smart, as animated as quicksilver.

"We are quite embarrassed to get such notoriety from the Villa Maria girls," remarked the Doctor with a laugh. "It's probably our daughters' classmates trying to be loyal."

"But as I hear it, Doctor," I replied, "the record is there; you can't deny it. What's the secret of it all?"

"We give much of the credit, Father, for whatever special enthusiasm for religion we have to the good Catholics of Long Island."

"Of Long Island?"

"Yes. Shortly after I got my degree as an eye doctor and Mrs. Cipriani and I were married, we went to New York for a year so that I could specialize. We rented a home in Long Island and were profoundly impressed by the wonderful Catholic life of the fine people whom we came to know in the parish in which we lived. We soon found ourselves having a delightful time at evening parties and socials.

"But what was more, we discovered that a number of the finest young couples with whom we mixed never failed, regardless of what the event of the night before might be, to appear in church next morning for Mass and Holy Communion.

"We took up the practice and when we returned here we continued it. It was somewhat unusual here. At cocktail parties people would ask how we could come to such affairs and go to Communion next morning. We merely laughed off the remarks and suggested that they try it themselves, that there was nothing contradictory about enjoying oneself and going to the sacraments."

"Did your militant Catholicism cause you embarrassment in your social set?" I asked.

"Quite the contrary," replied Señora Cipriani. "As the children grew up we found the neighbors very happy to let their youngsters keep company with ours. The young folks themselves seemed to pass the word that with the Ciprianis they were sure both to have a good time and to do the right thing."

This is quite what the Villa Maria young ladies implied on their questionnaires. Cecilia Gutierez, one of those who chose the Cipriani family as her ideal, wrote, "The Ciprianis are a model of a modern Christian family. In the atmosphere of their home it is natural in my opinion that the children will be true Christians guided by such wonderful parents. It would be splendid to find many families like this one who give their children such a perfect education to be devout and happy and united and to be good citizens of Peru."

Dr. Cipriani was a Founding Member and first President of the men's branch of Catholic Action in Peru. He does a great deal of free practice at the Children's Hospital of Lima. He is a member and leader in the Serra Club of Peru which aims, as in the United States, to encourage vocations to the priesthood.

Within his profession the Doctor is President of the Consortium of Catholic Doctors in Peru and the founder of the free clinic of Saint Camillus. He is likewise a delegate of the Association of Fathers of Families of the Catholic Colleges of Peru.

Mrs. Cipriani besides carefully raising her family has a similar chain of charitable connections. She is President of the Society of St. Camillus which aims to care for the needy in the Barrio of Buena Muerte. She engages regularly in house to house visitation for social work, helping families with matrimonial problems, in the education of their children and in organizing Christian family life.

The Opus Dei has recently been organized in Peru and both the Doctor and his wife are active in this almost exclusively lay movement to build a high level of spiritual and cultural excellence into the personal lives of lay leaders of the nation.

From Isabel, the eldest daughter, I secured through Sister Gregoria a paragraph on the spiritual life of the Cipriani family. "Papa and mama go to daily Mass and Communion. Every Sunday all of the nine children old enough to be able to go attend the 8:30 Mass at Santa Maria Church and go to Communion together. We recite the rosary together every evening. We practice the Nine First Fridays and the Five First Saturdays. We children have charities that we take care of. We are very much united and earnestly pray for God's blessing on our family, above all through the good example of our parents."

Many young ladies of Villa Maria and other colleges that train the upper class find their way into active charity about Lima. In years gone by practically none took up nursing since, as in other Latin American countries, it is only recently that this service career has assumed a standing to attract upper-class young women. This prejudice against nursing is now disappearing. Many take the six-week course in practical nursing offered by the Red Cross and become Gray Ladies in the hospitals.

Some of the young college women undertake service activities. I discovered that Laura Galligo-Lecca and Carmen Barua had established a clinic in a poor section and I sought them out.

"How did this come about?" I asked them.

"The credit goes to the Villa Maria Sisters," Laura explained. "They changed our whole outlook on religion. When Carmen and I graduated we determined to make use of our lives for the poor. We talked over our ideas with Marcela Gonzales, a cousin of Carmen's and also a Villa Maria girl, who is a social service worker and operates a family relations bureau. 'You'll succeed,' said Marcela, 'if you know how to keep your feet on the ground and be practical.' "

"We tried to be practical. We went to the officers of the Banco de Credito and secured from them rent free a small store that could serve as quarters for the clinic. We got a commitment from a young medico whom we know, Dr. Jorge Vega-Cristi, to let us send him from the clinic for free treatment ten medical cases three days a week that needed professional care. Other young ladies joined us and the Consultorio San Pedro went into business."

"How long are you open each week?"

"From three to five each Monday, Wednesday and Friday but the clinic is only our base of operations. The real work is done visiting families in this really miserable slum area."

"What kind of problems do you strike, Laura?"

"Our biggest problem is broken homes," replied Laura with the enthusiasm of a true devotee. "Marcela Gonzales guides us carefully in everything we do. In 85 per cent of the cases it is the fault of the man. Drink does not figure too often; it is lack of attachment to his home and his family that prompts the man to be unfaithful. We must try to do more than merely visit these families. They need better houses, better food, better pay, better life. We'd like to talk to the Archbishop. We now know our little neighborhood very well; we know everybody who lives in it. Now someone bigger and stronger than we must help in solving our neighborhood problems."

Small enterprises like Laura's and Carmen's are not unusual in Peru but it goes without saying that the organized governmental effort which this modern state is undertaking represents the major contribution in social improvement. Increasingly important, however, is the role that the Church in Peru is playing in the larger centers.

The city of Lima has sixty-seven churches, some of which are among the finest structures in the New World. There are marvelous exteriors and interiors that represent the work not only of architectural and artistic greats from Spain but the achievements as well of native skill. The enormous two-towered cathedral is particularly imposing. Nevertheless modern Lima is short of parishes through the shortage of clergy and short of church edifices because of the huge expansion of the city. The beautiful new quarters of the National Seminary of San Toribio, the oldest seminary in the Western Hemisphere, now has some 300 candidates but the outflow of priests is still meager. Most of the clergy is foreign and the largest unit among the clergy from overseas is Spanish. Nevertheless some of the outstanding new churches are the work of non-Spaniards. The Missionaries of the Sacred Heart who are Germans have erected San Felicé Church, a distinguished achievement. The Marianists, the Carmelites, the Maryknollers represent North American contributions. But the unfilled voids are still great.

In view of these handicaps it is a pleasure to find that the Christian life in a number of Lima's parishes is vibrant and forward looking with a definite consciousness of their social mission. One such is the Parish of San José conducted by the Spanish Carmelites. Over a side entrance near the church is a sign which reads "Social Service Center." One morning with my fellow Maryknoller, Father John Lawler, and Señorita Maria Rosario Araoz I passed through this entrance to a memorable experience. In a sense we were viewing the handiwork of Señorita Rosario since it is due to this remarkable citizen of Lima that both Church and state in Peru are social minded in such definitely Christian fashion.

"Thanks to Señorita Rosario," explained Father Lawler, "a number of the better organized parishes of Lima are establishing social service centers to help build up better living conditions for the poor. The Carmelite Fathers here at San José have one of the best parish centers in the city."

We came upon an inner court. All the rooms abutting on the court were devoted to the social center. Evidently the lively bustle of a typical morning's activities was in progress. Women, many of them with children, moved in and out of doors, waited in the patio or were attended by the staff in the various offices.

"Señorita Rosario!" cried a woman's voice. "What a happy surprise!"

"Señora Isabel!" called the Señorita, and the two women embraced affectionately.

"Father, this is the director, Señora Isabel Gonzales," said the Señorita as she introduced the gracious, smiling lady who approached us. "We are all proud of the work she is doing."

"We have only to follow Señorita's wonderful leadership," replied Señora Isabel.

"This is point number one in the success of a social center," Father Lawler remarked to me in a low voice, "—a capable director." I found that the Carmelites were certainly fortunate in Señora Isabel. She is a widow with sufficient means to give all her time to social work. At the time of our visit she was President of the Women's Branch of Catholic Action in Lima, a natural leader with quiet self-possession, cultured, devoted, unassuming. The San José Social Center is her special task.

"There are two divisions in our work here," the Señora explained. "They are medical care and domestic science. The latter is an outgrowth of the former. Men, women and children who need aid, particularly medical attention, are often found by our social assistants living under wretched conditions. So often mothers know nothing about conducting good homes. In our simple little domestic science department here we have a model kitchen and other means for teaching. Out of this direct aid comes the opportunity to form good Catholic family life."

"You have social assistants, then?"

"Yes, we have two full-time workers who receive the standard salary. They are the only paid members of our staff. One of them is here this morning; you must meet her. This pair of zealous young women, trained under Señorita Rosario at the Social Service School, provide our main contact with the families of the parish. They keep careful records here at the center and do a thoroughly professional job."

"How do you provide the medical aid?"

"A group of doctors in the parish gives us each a small portion of his time. Dr. José Pinelo, a pediatrician, is here this morning. Come, let us meet him. He spends two hours each week with us."

Dr. Pinelo, a hearty, robust figure, shrugged off my word of commendation for his generous assistance. "This idea of a social service center puts a very fine touch on parish life," he remarked. "Now that we see it in operation, it seems most natural to make medicine work for the Gospel. I get a great deal of pleasure from my weekly visit here."

"Who takes care of the domestic science division?" I asked the Señora.

"A group of women with the necessary skills handles the classes in homemaking," she replied. "Some are from outside the parish. It is very encouraging to notice the large amount of discussion around the parish that these classes have created."

"There are no priests in evidence," I remarked. "Do they have a role?"

"Quite decidedly," replied the Señora. "Every two weeks the two social assistants and I meet with the pastor and review the program and problems of the center. The clergy of the parish are available at all times for the spiritual problems that arise; they conduct classes in religious training and visit the homes of families with troubles that can best be faced by the man of God."

A moment later when we had bidden goodbye, I could not help stopping for an instant on the sidewalk and looking up once again at that sign over the gateway—"Social Service Center, Parish of San José." What a mountain of accomplishment will be achieved, I decided, when ten thousand such parish centers are set up in the lands of Latin America.

"Señorita Rosario," I asked, "how do you explain the development of this unusual idea in Lima?"

"All doors are open to Señorita Rosario," volunteered Father Lawler with a smile. "From the Cardinal of Lima down, she has been able to make clear what tremendous things can be done for religion through social service at the parish level."

During the next few days I found out much about Peru's social program, one of the best on the continent. However, it was Señorita Rosario's clear-minded conciseness that summed up neatly the country's principal tasks.

"Peru's social problems," she explained, "may be reduced to five. They are, first, illiteracy; secondly, there is the general low level of cultural life, social life and physical health; thirdly, there is the instability of the family, particularly in the direction of illegitimacy; fourthly, there is a series of special urban problems, chief of which is housing, a field that Marina knows so well; fifthly, there are the special rural problems, all of them heightened by the dispersion of our rural people over such a wide and inaccessible mountain terrain."

At every step the National Social Service School came into the conversation and I was happy to be able to visit it. The establishment occupies a property that was once the residence of a wealthy family. We met members of the staff and a number of the students. The atmosphere is informal and friendly but at the same time there is strict discipline with careful attention to the modern professional techniques. It rates as one of the best schools of social service in Latin America.

"The school from its beginnings has made no secret of the fact that spiritual principles should play a part in the life of the social assistant," explained Señorita Rosario. "Its founder, President Benevides, was a man of strong Catholic instincts and so arranged things that the three directors to date, of whom I am the third, were encouraged to maintain a distinctly Catholic atmosphere. Thus it is unique in all Latin America; it is one hundred per cent governmental and one hundred per cent Catholic. When I took my post I received the assurance that I would be free to give our students a strong religious motivation in their work."

"To what degree do the young women who leave here carry this motivation into their careers?" I asked.

"I would say," replied Señorita Rosario, "that seventy-five per cent of our graduates live actively Christian lives."

On the large administration desk in Señorita's office where we sat I noted a small plaque bearing a neatly inscribed text in Spanish: "The Son of Man is come not to be ministered unto but to minister. Math. 20:28."

"That's a very apt ideal for a social worker," I remarked.

Señorita Rosario smiled. "I give one of these plaques to each of our students when she finishes her course."

There is a private and personal matter in Señorita Rosario's life which I must mention as evidence of the deeply practical character of her dedication. Señorita is of a good family though without any abundance of this world's possessions. She lived with her two sisters in the family residence in a section of Lima that had come to be inhabited by large numbers of people of the lower middle class and a great number of the very poor. The section was without a nearby parish church. Señorita Rosario decided to remove this deficiency. She went to Cardinal Guevara and proposed to him that he establish a new parish in her neighborhood. "My sisters and I have decided," she explained, "that if Your Eminence can secure a group of missionaries who will serve our part of Lima, we shall turn over our residence to them as their temporary rectory until they eventually may build a home for themselves."

And this came to pass. His Eminence secured the services of Maryknoll for this pioneer task and Father John Lawler was sent to be the first pastor. Señorita Rosario met him at the airport on his arrival, gave him the keys to her house and a considerable sum of money which she had collected to start the new parish.

"But where will you and your sisters live in the meantime?" he asked.

"We are nicely provided for," replied Señorita Rosario. "My sisters have taken a small apartment and I have set up a bed in my office at the Social Service School."

Happily, Father Lawler proved a very capable organizer. In almost miraculous fashion under his guidance the parochial plant of St. Rose of Lima came into being. Thus the Rosario sisters were able to return to their family home. In this woman Peru and the whole Catholic world possesses an outstanding example of a thoroughly able and finely inspired social worker.

"Señorita Rosario," I observed one day, "I am struck by the Catholic atmosphere in much of the activity for the public good here in Lima and in other centers of Peru. In your opinion, how characteristic is this of the continent as a whole? Do you feel that Latin America may rightly be called a Catholic continent?"

The Señorita smiled. "The doctors differ on this question," she replied. "I belong to a minority that contends that the continent can no longer be rightly termed Catholic, though the vast majority of the population is nominally Catholic. We discussed this matter at the International Catholic Action Seminar at Chimbote."

Chimbote is a port in Northern Peru that smells strongly of fish, a down-to-earth corner of the Latin American world where in 1953 some 300 delegates representing vigorous lay leaders prepared a thoughtful self-evaluation of the Church's strength in Latin America. Señorita Rosario was among the participants.

"The majority at Chimbote," explained the Señorita, "declared that Latin America should be called a Catholic continent. This Catholicism is, they noted, more the survival of a Catholic tradition than the product of a currently active Catholic life within the population mass of the continent.

"I stood rather with the minority that did not necessarily reject the more preponderant view. Rather we felt that Catholics were making a mistake in labeling as Catholic the present way of living in Latin America. The current condition of things is the fruit of nominal Catholicism. It represents not so much the absence of Catholicism as its unfelt presence. Even where Catholics frequent church and the sacraments they often fail to live by Christian principles in their conduct of public affairs. Thus the world in looking at us gets a false and inadequate impression of Catholicism. Our average Catholic behaves in his surroundings much as does many a Protestant, a Liberal, or any other person with only a partial appreciation of the full richness of the Christian heritage."

In various parts of Latin America I met other delegates to Chimbote. All were impressed by the frank, even devastating, analysis of the present weaknesses of the Church and the realistic goals that the delegates set for themselves.

"I think the major contributor at Chimbote," said Señorita Rosario, "was Dr. Horacio Terra, the architect from Montevideo, one of the leaders in the Church in Uruguay. Dr. Terra used the surgeon's knife on the sick Church in Latin America and, just as ably, expertly prescribed the cure. In the end it was all very heartening since it made clear that, badly off as we are, the more alert elements in the Latin American Church have for a generation now been building back strength into the weakened structure.

"Every religio-social project of Latin American Catholics like these social welfare centers and other promising undertakings we see here in Lima, are a step in the right direction. We decided at Chimbote that our greatest single peril in Latin America lies in the possibility that the millions of plain folk who are now in rebellion against their hard lot will decide before we have a chance to prove the contrary that Christ's Church has no interest in a just way of life for them."

Dr. Terra and his confreres at Chimbote enumerated seven causes for the present unsatisfactory condition of the Church in Latin America. They all make sense. They sum up as follows:

1. *Geographic causes.* Bad geography scatters the population of Latin America—180,000,000 today but still thinly distributed—over a vast area made difficult by mountains and by rivers that too often run dry or flow in the wrong direction. Thus the Church, as well as the state, in great areas suffers from the bad distribution of the inhabitants which calls for huge dioceses, sprawling parishes and consequently accentuated individualism and isolation.

2. *Racial and ethnic causes.* Latin America is no homogeneous whole. It is best conceived as twenty republics as different from each other as twenty European nations, with ethnic groups even more diverse than are the Negro and the white in the United States. Peru is an example with its small sector of European stock, its world of the mountain Indian and its substantial mestizo element.

3. *Social causes.* Weakness comes from poor family life, from illegitimacy that sometimes reaches to fifty and eighty per cent, caused by widespread irregular or nonexistent marriage ties. Over half the population rates economically between moderate poverty and desperate indigence. Nominal Catholics of wealth create social problems by widespread refusal to accept the papal teachings on land tenure and the rights of the laboring man.

4. *Political causes.* There is union of Church and state in Argentina, Bolivia, Colombia, Peru and Venezuela and varying degrees of separation in the other nations. But whether there is union or separation the Church almost everywhere is subjected to limiting legislation in the Spanish and Portuguese tradition of suffocating the ecclesiastical control.

Rarely do Catholic clergy and Catholic people experience the freedom to initiate a spiritual, educational, or religio-social program for action without subjection to substantial interference from political authority.

5. *Psychological causes.* Latin American society, the Chimbote delegates noted, is younger and more immature than many men think. It has as yet failed to digest properly the social requisites of democracy. Strong individualism in civil affairs results in an overindividualistic Catholicism as well. A truer concept of the Christian apostolate is needed for better Christian life.

6. *Pastoral causes.* The paucity and poverty of formation in the clergy has worked harm. Too often in the past the priest permitted himself to act as a mere functionary, a "sacramentarian" performing spiritual acts for fees. Too often today the people as a consequence so regard the priest.

Frequently the economic condition of the clergy is parlous. The Church no longer is adequately state-supported anywhere but yet the tradition among rank and file Christians persists that the faithful have no role in Church support. Support of charitable enterprises is too often an exclusive privilege of the wealthy and is not a living practice of the rank and file.

7. *Communications causes.* The absence of adequately organized means for mass delivery of the Good News to the people, the delegates explained, was a major factor in ignorance and misunderstanding regarding the Church in Latin America. Sadly inadequate use is made of the radio, cinema, television, newspapers, magazines, books and modern propaganda in general. Financing represents only a part of the problem; much more important is the absence of a widespread conviction of the value of these instruments for the successful heralding of the Christian message.

"What did you decide to do at Chimbote after you toted up all these causes of weakness?" I asked Señorita Rosario.

"We decided to continue to do what we have been doing now for years," answered the Señorita. "We determined to continue the fight to overcome the weaknesses. Remember, Padre, the Church in Latin America is no longer losing ground; it is winning back lost ground. Heaven knows there is a lot yet to be won but despite all the prophets of doom we are winning it."

This is the word that one picks up from people like Señorita Rosario everywhere in Latin America. Dr. Cipriani during my visit with him had the same to say.

"The new era of religious life in Peru dates from the Eucharistic Congress of 1935," explained the Doctor. "It is not sound to speak of 400 years of Christianity in America as if it represented four centuries of steady growth with our present condition the net total of this steady growth. The faith in Peru was strong in colonial days, was sadly weakened by events of the revolution and languished through the nineteenth and the first third of the twentieth centuries. Peru's faith of this generation is new and still growing."

The delegates at Chimbote fixed seven basic objectives for Catholic Action that have been renewed at other assemblies large and small. They are as follows:

1. Build a stronger Christian family
2. Awaken Catholic initiative to modernize higher education
3. Improve popular education at the community level by:
   a. Stronger religious education
   b. Grade school education for all the poor
   c. Schooling for the Indian
   d. Greater enlistment of the rank and file in social organizations
   e. Higher standards of living for the Indian
4. Strengthen the economic life of Latin America according to Christian principles
5. Bring men together more in Christian brotherhood
6. Promote Christian social principles in political life
7. Promote Christian principles in world affairs

Dr. Horacio Terra recommended five common-sense ways to work for Latin America:

1. Work for all men; stop dividing men into saints and reprobates and working only for the saints. This will only save the saved.
2. Work for the family but put the family to work for good outside the family circle.
3. In today's complex society, practice Christian tolerance toward every man's creed.

4. Work with others shoulder to shoulder, brother to brother; fraternalism breeds love, paternalism exasperates.
5. Limit your work to no single nation, race, society; give it the all-embracing beauty of Christ and His Gospel.

Bishop Larrain of Chile was at Chimbote. He sent the delegates home with words from Cardinal Newman's "Second Spring" ringing in their ears: "The world grows old, but the Church is ever young."

"When your confreres ask you what you saw at Chimbote," Bishop Larrain concluded, "tell them you saw the vision of the new day that is dawning."

Chapter 5

Colombia's Voice of Freedom

THE GONG rang through the corridors of the Tunja seminary. "Class dismissed," said Padre Alfonso Navia and his students filed out. One slight-built young man stopped at the professor's desk.

"Padre," he remarked quietly, "this is all very interesting, these principles of radio transmission. I'd like to come to your room this evening and get clear on some points."

"Good, José, come by all means."

That evening and on other occasions during his years of training, José Joaquin Salcedo consulted with Padre Navia, his physics professor, and by the time he was ordained to the priesthood in 1947 he had acquired a strong taste for radio mechanics. Bishop Luque of Tunja assigned the promising young man to cut his clerical teeth in a difficult post among the mountaineers so prevalent in his diocese at a village called Sutatenza.

Sutatenza, in Colombia's mountain province of Boyaca, was a pueblo with hardly more than forty inhabitants, though the parish for which it served as center counted more than 8,000 souls. That was the way in the mountains. There were a few small villages of forty to a hundred members, many hamlets of three to ten families, hundreds of scattered homes in the labyrinthine heights in which usually a dozen or so human beings dwelt, isolated from their fellows. It was a typical sampling of life in the Cordillera Central, highest range in Colombia, a massive wall some 500 miles long, much of it 10,000 feet high with peaks at 18,000 feet and topped with perpetual snow.

Such folk had the good qualities of plain, rough people the world over. They were basically honest, loyal, religious. They suffered then, from the handicaps of people deprived of training and of any hope or incentive for bettering their lot. Sutatenza in particular was notoriously backward through drink, its men given to violence.

Padre Salcedo resolved to make himself helpful. He mingled among the *campesinos* and proved himself apt in winning their trust. He soon held their allegiance. He proposed that the parish build a social hall. On the given day, fathers and sons in great numbers appeared to do the building, carts dragged in the lumber and supplies, mothers and daughters prepared the meals.

The hall was a success. On Sundays in particular people gathered from near and far and came to know each other better. But Padre Salcedo, his eye on the ensemble of 8,000 persons within the parish confines, realized he was reaching but a small portion of the whole. He was wont to look out among the mighty peaks and across the deep, broad valleys dotted with innumerable peasant huts, marked at frequent intervals with small clusters of dwellings and here and there by larger conglomerations of houses that under the sparkling sun shone like distant fairy villages. A tracery of roads led up from each valley bottom, skirting giddy precipices as they neared the top. Below his home the road cut through the breathtaking grandeur past a shrine called Purgatory Chapel and came at last to Sutatenza, dramatically perched on the finest site of all.

"It is very beautiful, certainly," he would conclude, "but this maze of mountains serves as prison walls to cage in men's minds and hearts from growth and better living. If we could only reach these people and teach them."

Both government and Church had long felt thwarted on this very score of their teaching mission. Schools there were but few could attend them due to the impossible terrain. Illiteracy was in places eighty per cent and worse. The consequent handicaps were enormous.

Then more and more strongly came the conviction to Padre Salcedo that the lessons he had learned from Padre Navia for the diffusion of the voice by radio could be adapted to solving the enigma of mountain ignorance.

In 1948 he passed the word among his people that he had a plan to set up at Sutatenza a little broadcasting station and to provide at many spots in the mountains small centers equipped with receiving sets where he could speak to them and teach them.

Happily, the people believed in him. He was but a boyish priest only twenty-seven years of age at the time but they responded enthusiastically to his call. He asked each family on a given Sunday morning to bring to church with them a lamb, a hen, or even a few fresh eggs. Both he and the people were astounded when, on the day selected, they found gathered at the church a goodly flock of lambs, some 800 hens and mountainous piles of eggs. All this foodstuff was loaded next morning on borrowed trucks and conveyances of every sort and carefully transported to Colombia's capital city, Bogotá, eighty-five miles away, to be sold. With the proceeds were purchased the first small radio transmitter (today a museum piece at Sutatenza) and the first batch of receiving sets for the mountain centers.

Thus was born an idea that has developed into one of the most unique educational institutions in modern times. The Radio Schools of Sutatenza have become, not only in South America but throughout backward areas in many parts of the world, a pattern for revolutionizing the lives of scattered peoples.

When recently I undertook to appraise this unusual phenomenon my task began not out in the mountain country but in a tall building in the heart of the alert, modern city of Bogotá. The eighth and ninth floors of the Colombian Savings Bank Building in Bogotá are the organizational headquarters of Monsignor Salcedo's project, now called the Acción Cultural Popular—the Popular Education Movement. Luis Bernal Escobar, a most personable gentleman, is the Secretary General and conducts an operation that possesses the smartness and the crisp efficiency of a modern business enterprise and yet the warmth and humanness of a neighborhood social circle.

"Today the Accion Cultural Popular," explained Señor Bernal, "represents perhaps more than a million dollars worth of equipment and property devoted to the operation of over 6,500 radio schools located principally in mountain areas but found in every part of Colombia and maintains auxiliary programs for the *campesino*. When the new radio station at Sutatenza was constructed it was the third strongest in South America."

"Does Monsignor Salcedo still play an active role in the project?"

"Very much so. With the growth of the movement he has shown his ability to grow with it. Though still a young man he reveals a remarkable capacity for sound and imaginative administrative thinking."

"What part do the ecclesiastical authorities play?"

"The president of the ACP is still the Bishop of Tunja but since the occupant of the see of Tunja when Monsignor Salcedo began his work is now the Archbishop of Bogotá, Cardinal Crisanto Luque, His Eminence as well as the fifty and more bishops of Colombia have adopted this project as their own."

"I understand that the government has a stake in the operation."

"Our movement is completely independent of government control," replied Bernal, "but the authorities from the beginning have recognized its enormous value for the nation and have cooperated in substantial fashion."

Besides the general administration, other phases of the operation are handled in the Bogotá headquarters. Bernal showed us the radio theater where professional talent found in the city can be enlisted for entertainment and other programs. There is a large correspondence department where 1,500 letters of inquiry from country people are handled daily.

Without further ado I drove away from urban Bogotá out across the rich green savanna country of the valley about the capital. After sixty miles of level road we began to ascend into the highlands and were soon in the world of Monsignor Salcedo. I wafted a prayer to the Madonna as we drove past Purgatory Chapel amid some of the grandest mountain scenery in the world. "Welcome to Sutatenza!" boomed a smiling, rich-voiced, heavy-set gentleman who came toward us as we alighted in the little piazza of the storied village. It was Professor Ismael Loperat, Director of Radio Pedagogy, whose cordial hospitality reflected the gracious warmth that characterizes this extraordinary Colombian enterprise.

"I want to see the *campesinos* learning their lessons," I said immediately to the Professor.

"Right!" cried Loperat enthusiastically. "It is the really worthwhile thing we have to show you."

We left Sutatenza in a road-worn car and made our way into a little valley. We stopped at a break in the vegetation and took a path that led away from the highway.

"The key to everything we do at Sutatenza," explained Loperat as we walked, "is the local leader—the *auxiliar inmediato.* This person may be a young man, an older man, a young woman, an elderly one, but all the great machinery of organization that we have built up has been in vain if the local leader has not the warmth, the patience, the discipline, the generosity to help his group of *campesinos* to learn each day's lesson as it comes over the air."

"How is the leader at this school?" I asked.

"She is very good—Rosa Gomez, a young girl of the neighborhood about twenty years old who works in earnest."

We came to a clearing on which stood a one-room hut. Class was in progress, a group of nine boys and girls and three housewives gathered about a table. Rosa stood at the little blackboard. An instruction in writing was coming over the air—clear, precise, in quiet modulated voice. Rosa crayoned the words on the board as the voice directed. At a break in the radio voice, it was Rosa's turn to repeat what had been said and then she hurriedly glanced at the papers before her pupils to see how successfully they were following the instructions.

I was particularly struck by a woman of fifty years who was painstakingly writing her day's words in a large, childish but firm hand. Her face was weather-worn but possessed a bright contented look and there was excitement in her eyes.

"What is your name, Señora?" I asked.

"Señora Transito Barto, Padre."

"How long are you here in school?"

"Ten weeks, Padre. I do very poorly."

"No, she doesn't," corrected Rosa in a soft voice, "She is the best in the class."

Both the children and the housewives took our intrusion with unfaltering calm and continued to work unconcernedly. I remarked this to Loperat.

"This is typical of these mountain people," he replied. "They have no pretentions to great accomplishment but on the other hand they possess a spirit that is completely unbowed. Whether young or old, they are never simpering or uncertain. They are deeply grateful for kindness but bitterly resent the tiniest evidence of patronizingness or disdain."

"Is this the usual size of a radio school?"

"Yes. The ideal for a local leader is ten to twenty persons. Some run to as many as forty but this is an unwise number for good results."

"Is this the typical set-up of a school?"

"Quite. The quarters are a little better than usual since often we merely use the front porch of a mountain home. There are ten standard items for every one of our radio schools. First, there is the crucifix. Secondly, there is a print of the Blessed Virgin, Seat of Wisdom. Third, there's the radio receiving set with its antenna."

"Who supplies the radio?" I interjected.

"Each group of families must buy their own. Naturally they are inexpensive in type. Monsignor Salcedo negotiated the purchase of the early equipment in New York City but European firms now do the manufacturing. The receiving set costs about $14.00."

"Please go on with your enumeration."

"The fourth basic item is the gong, the famous piece of iron rail hanging in the open which when struck with a hammer resounds so clearly throughout the neighborhood. Fifth is the clock, since the correct time is important for contact with the Sutatenza broadcasts. Sixth is the blackboard. The table and benches, seventh. Eighth is the study equipment—copy books, pencils, maps, other teaching needs which each local leader must request with careful precision each month when he or she sends in the report. Ninth is the school register which, simple though it is, is given emphasis to underline the importance of enrollment and attendance."

"May I interrupt again, please?" I put in. "Is attendance at these radio schools merely a matter of casual goodwill or is there an attempt at systematic training with examinations and some form of recognition for good performance?"

"There are two categories of schools," replied Professor Loperat. "Of the 6,500 schools some 2,500 are controlled schools in which the organization is sufficiently disciplined that monthly reports authenticated by the parish priest and supervised examinations allow for true judgment on achievement. An office at Sutatenza carefully keeps Kardex records of each such school and certificates of achievement are sent to the *campesinos* who make good. Naturally they are very proud of these certificates."

"What is the tenth item of standard equipment, Professor?"

"The tenth item is a sports field. Often this can be only a corner of a farmer's yard but if, as at this school, we can find room for a basketball court we are very happy. We conceive every radio school as a sort of neighborhood social center with leisure programs aimed particularly at Sunday, and serving the whole neighborhood as well as those enrolled in the school courses."

In the course of my stay at Sutatenza, the radio school that attracted me most was that conducted by Señorita Concita Sastake. Señorita Concita was 78 years old. She was a retired government school teacher who, the Professor explained, enthusiastically volunteered to open a radio school in the living room of her home.

Loperat and I left our car by the road and walked to Señorita Concita's place along an arbored pathway that brought us finally to her pretty cottage. We approached unnoticed and found the Señorita bent over a young mother whose infant was plumped on the bench beside her, the old lady guiding slowly the hand of the younger woman as she made her first letters on a sheet of paper. Señorita Concita exclaimed with pleasure when she discovered us. "Welcome!" she cried. "And pardon me for not seeing you. This is always a thrilling experience teaching a grown person to write her first words. The first time they can inscribe some such expression as 'Mama Mia' on paper and then read it back, tears of joy often roll down their cheeks."

"Señorita Concita has started a second career as a local leader for our radio schools," observed the Professor.

"All my life I've loved to teach," explained Concita, "and this idea of gathering people about the radio is heaven-sent."

Naturally the little class at the Señorita's was specially privileged in having one so skilled to guide them. We noticed the advanced stage of the youngsters under her direction. One eight-year old read prose and poetry to us with ease and feeling.

"Don't these agile minds make older people like you envious?" I asked the housewife.

"No," she replied. "Instead it makes us very happy. We realize that now our children are not going to grow up in ignorance as we did."

"I note that there are only women and children at these classes," I remarked to Loperat as we walked away.

"Yes, during the day the men must work. There are four hours a day of radio class work. From six to seven each morning is the class for men. From three to four in the afternoon is the class for women and for children who cannot attend school. From four to five in the afternoon, then, is a special service for the armed forces. There are forty-seven military barracks in Colombia, each with from 200 to 500 enlisted men, 63 per cent of whom are rated as illiterate. By government arrangement these men may follow the radio class. Finally, from five to six each evening is a repeat class for men."

"How much training can you give the local leaders?" I asked Loperat.

"Naturally they are seldom like Concita who, aged though she is, is a finished teacher and in the comfort of her home can do practically a professional job. Since we need thousands of such local leaders we choose steady types whose chief qualities are their earnestness and readiness to learn the simple techniques of a radio class monitor. The training of many has to be done at the parish level. But for the Parish Aids, who are the top sergeants for pastors to guide the local leaders in each parish, we conduct two courses a year of four months each in the Campesino Institute at Sutatenza."

"How many radio schools would be found within a given parish?"

"There are as many as 150 to 200 in some parishes."

"How wide a gamut does the ACP educational program run?"

"Principal objective during this first decade is the fight against illiteracy. Religious instruction has a major place. But perhaps you'll be surprised to learn how ambitious we are. At headquarters in Bogotá we have half a dozen special educational secretariats and important programs have been organized in agriculture, health, domestic economy and sports. The ACP has a score of agricultural experts on its staff."

Behind the air programs and complementary to them lies another huge field that is receiving the cooperation of UNESCO. This United Nations organization has supplied four educational experts for the preparation of text books and literature that are essential if the hunger for reading and study awakened by the literacy campaign is to be satiated. These four experts, at Monsignor Salcedo's insistence, are Christian Brothers, headed by Brother Fulgentius of Mexico.

On April 11, 1953, Pope Pius XII thrilled every citizen of Colombia by speaking from Rome on the occasion of the inauguration of the new Sutatenza station. "The radio," declared His Holiness, "is a precious gift of the Lord . . . Colombia, Catholic Colombia, the nation of the Sacred Heart of Jesus and of the Virgin of Carmen, has seen clearly its problem. Dispersed throughout your immense and rugged territory—where even today communication is not easy—thousands and thousands of our strong-hearted sons, sound and generous like the soil which they daily fructify with the sweat of their brow, could not in normal fashion be served by the beneficent presence of the minister of the Lord or of the educator of their intelligence.

"A priestly mind and heart provided the solution. . . . Today we behold these most modern and potent installations that make possible a full-scale radio movement and insure the efficacy of your teaching labors.

"Our blessing on all the friends, sympathizers, benefactors of Radio Sutatenza, our blessing on all the good Colombian people, and, finally, on the new installations . . ."

While world leaders from the Pope down hail the achievements of the Accion Cultural Popular, a plaque near the great Sutatenza antenna reveals that Monsignor Salcedo in his hour of uncommon triumph has been mindful of the source from which he drew his inspiration. He pays a tribute of gratitude to Padre Alfonso M. Navia, C.M., Professor of Physics and Chemistry who opened the Monsignor's eyes to the possibilities of radio. "It is the rare physics professor who is thus honored by his pupil," commented Loperat.

Mario the chauffeur drove me down the mountain road to Chocontá to catch my bus to Bogotá. His eyes shone with joy as I told him how much I thought of his beloved Sutatenza. His last words to me bespoke the solicitude of the *campesino* for every wayfarer who must turn his back on the mountain world and enter the city. "When you get to Bogotá, Padre," he said solemnly as he pressed my hand, "watch out for the thieves; they are very dangerous in Bogotá, Padre."

Bogotá possesses a majestic setting, spread out on a broad green valley partially encircled by Andean ranges. It is only four degrees from the equator but because it is almost 9,000 feet high it enjoys a cool invigorating climate the year round. It is a happy combination of rich colonial monuments, including sixty churches, and tall modern buildings on broad new thoroughfares.

In the Latin world Bogotá is called the Athens of America and deserves the title since for generations it has been a home for exquisite

Spanish literature, writing and speech noted for classic purity. When the revolt against Spain came to Bogotá it got its spark not among the downtrodden but in the literary circles where the call for freedom rose in finely cadenced phrases. Many brilliant journalists have written in Bogotá newspapers and have helped to create the local tradition of columns of electric writing with each day's breakfast coffee.

In view of such tastes it is not surprising to hear that five of Colombia's fifteen universities are in Bogotá with the National University occupying a University City of fifty acres. Oldest of these and highly influential is the Javeriana, founded by the Jesuits in 1622. Its solid vitality is representative of the strength of the Church in Colombia as a whole.

Quite as Colombia as a nation ranks among the topmost of the Latin American world, so likewise does the Colombian Church. Currently it possesses a hierarchy of fifty-one members headed by the outstanding Cardinal Luque; and counts a body of 3,500 priests and 11,000 Sisters. Its Catholic educational system is the largest in Latin America and operates 3,000 schools with 275,000 students. It possesses particular strength at the secondary level. Of the approximately 600 secondary schools in Colombia, some 400 are private Catholic institutions. In recent years the Church has made great strides in the social field, notably in its service of the laboring man.

Colombia's population is distributed within its confines in most unique fashion and this uniqueness affects the organization of the Church. Some 91 per cent of the country's inhabitants, that is, almost twelve of its thirteen millions, live in 30 per cent of its territory and this 91 per cent is organized as the established Church in Colombia. The remaining 9 per cent of the population lives in 70 per cent of the area, in many places with a density of less than one person per square mile and (in the "backyard" of Colombia's territory, the vast plains country and jungles that constitute segments of the Orinoco Valley and of the rim of the Amazon Valley) a cultural level that rates in some spots among the lowest on the globe. Wisely enough, the Church regards this 9 per cent of the population as mission territory and has organized it in Apostolic Vicariates and Prefectures. Some 250 missionary priests and 650 missionary Sisters labor in this mission territory.

The 91 per cent of Colombia's population in the area of the established Church possesses a personnel that, while not sufficient for its needs, is for the most part well above the general average for Latin America. This developed area, which is 130,000 square miles in extent, is twice the size of New England. In South America as a whole there is an average of approximately 4,600 Catholics per priest while in Middle America as a whole the average is 5,000 per priest. In the Archdiocese of Bogotá there is a priest for every 2,119 Catholics; in the Archdiocese of Medellin 2,591 Catholics per priest; in the Archdiocese of Manizales 2,728 per priest. Best record is that of the Diocese of Santa Rosa in Antioquia with a priest for every 1,876 Catholics.

However, dioceses along the Caribbean shore are not so fortunate. The Archdiocese of Cartagena has but one priest for every 6,023 Catholics and the Diocese of Barranquilla one for every 5,676 Catholics. This sector of Colombia is Caribbean in influence, was in colonial days an active African slave area and has given only limited attention as yet to improving the Negro elements in the population.

Of all the regions of Colombia, the Department of Antioquia is the most interesting. I boarded a plane at Bogotá and in an hour had been hurtled over the saw-tooth ranges, over the Magdalena Valley and had landed in Antioquia. To me, Antioquia's people represent one of the rare phenomena not only of Colombia but of all Latin America.

"Antioquia," commented Padre Felix Restrepo, rector of the Universidad Javereana, when we spoke about this area, "is often called the Ireland of Latin America." I think it might also be called a mountain edition of Canada's Province of Quebec. It contains an admirable people who throughout their history have striven as consistently for freedom as the Irish or the folk of Quebec, a people who possess a naturally high morality and a passionate love for the ideal Catholic home, who have families of sixteen, eighteen, even twenty children, who put their Catholic faith before everything else in the world and practice it with fidelity. The area counts an abundance of rugged priests and saintly Sisters who labor not only in Antioquia but throughout Colombia. "Antioquia," explained one of its priests in its capital city of Medellin, "furnishes almost two-thirds of all the religious personnel of Colombia."

Coffee is the cornerstone of Colombia's economy and the growing of fine Medellin coffee is the specialty of the Antioquenian farmers. They are thrifty resident owners who love their superb countryside and the hypnotic fascination of its eternal spring. The cottages are as sharp and neat as Swiss chalets, garnished with their hedges and blossoms and flowering bushes. Many homes have wide verandas fringed with yellow creepers, green lawns, a majolica fountain in the garden, a nook of precious orchids.

My objective in the Antioquenian country was to visit Bishop Builes of Santa Rosa and the foreign mission seminary which he founded. Like all Antioquenios the Bishop was proud of his homeland. "The religious life of Antioquia," he explained, "is built about the Blessed Sacrament and devotion to the Sacred Heart. Great crowds fill the altar rails on First Fridays but in some towns the practice of daily Communion is extraordinary. The shrine town of Marinella, for example, which has a population of 8,000, has 2,000 at Communion every morning. In Yarumel, which is a city of 20,000, there are a thousand communicants daily."

The Yarumel Foreign Mission Seminary, high in Antioquia's mountains, is the only institution of its kind in South America. "It didn't seem right," Bishop Builes explained, "to have so much faith in Antioquia and to have no foreign mission seminary. In 1927, on the Feast of Saints Peter and Paul, the same feast," and he gave me a smile, "so dear to Maryknollers, the decree of foundation was signed in Rome. So, since Maryknoll was born in 1911, we are sixteen years its junior."

Today the Yarumel society counts over a hundred priest members, 35 missionary Brothers and over 400 candidates. The Holy See has assigned the society's missionaries to care for four mission territories within Colombia.

Antioquia possesses another notable institution in the Bolivarian Catholic University of Medellin. This great educational center possesses some of the finest science laboratories in South America but it is in quite a different field that we record its importance. This is in its development of Workers Evening Schools and in its provision in a number of ways for the educational advance of men of humble origin. Much of this effort both in Medellin and throughout the nation has been done through an organization called Catholic Social Action, the present national director of which is Padre Vincent Andrade, S.J.

Padre Andrade has made an important contribution toward a Christian orientation of the Latin American labor movement. In 1946 Padre Andrade with the encouragement of the Bishops of Colombia guided Catholic laboring men of the nation to organize the Colombian Workers' Union, the UTC, which played a useful role in breaking the back of the once-powerful Communist controlled international CTAL, the Confederation of Latin American Workers.

Vicente Lombardo Toledano of Mexico is credited with making this organization Communist-dominated from 1940 on. As spokesman for the CTAL, Lombardo, though always an "independent Marxist" was throughout World War II the most powerful Communist trade union leader in the Western Hemisphere. The Latin American Communists reached the zenith of their power in 1945 and 1946. Their political parties had influence in almost every country. They had members of Congress in six countries of South America (Argentina, Chile, Uruguay, Peru, Venezuela and Colombia) and in three countries of Middle America (Mexico, Costa Rica, Cuba). But from then on their star waned. In recent years they have suffered severe defeats in many countries. By 1954 they no longer represented an immediate peril in any country though this is not to say that the Communist apparatus, that has a long history of effort in every Latin American country, will not again become menacing.

Colombia as an industrial nation has witnessed social injustices among its workers and many of these workers, Catholic though they were, joined the leftist ranks of protest. The CTAL Congress in Cali, Colombia, in 1944 was Communist-dominated. Padre Andrade attended the Congress as representative of Catholic workers of Bogotá but when he demanded the floor to argue with some of the delegates he was refused permission to speak. Leftist leaders did not hesitate to attack him in the press.

But Padre Andrade was due to have his day. He and many Christian elements in Colombia persuaded the workers to see that their true interests were not going to be served by the Rebs, that they should protect their birthright by possessing their own union. In 1946 this came into being as the Union de Trabajadores de Colombia, the UTC. Colombia's hierarchy continues to be strongly social-conscious. In the spring of 1958 Cardinal Luque of Bogota and the fifty-one Bishops of Colombia issued a new pastoral letter setting forth the needs for reform in property ownership, workers' wages, labor-management relations and housing. The pastoral urged the Colombian government to expropriate the land from large properties for less fortunate citizens. It reminded workers of their obligations as well as their rights but enjoined employers "not to treat workers as slaves." "The first obligation of management," said the Bishops, "is to provide a just salary to workers." The current average per capita income in Colombian cities is $4.40 a week while in rural areas the actual money return apart from the supplied food and lodging is 60¢ to $2.00 a week. Most important, the Bishops praised the trade union as such, "without which individual workers would be powerless in upholding their just claims on management."

Several Catholic efforts have been made in other Latin American countries to urge the workers to take steps to remain free from Communist and radical entanglements. Such is the ASICH movement in Chile of which we have spoken and the Rerum Novarum movement in Costa Rica. It is good to note that efforts have been made by the AFL-CIO to encourage non-Communist unions in Latin America. In 1946 Serafino Romualdi was appointed to represent United States labor in Latin America. Through his efforts the Inter-American Regional Organization of Workers (ORIT) has united non-Communist and nondictator unions as the American affiliate of the International Federation of Free Trade Unions. This is the world trade union force that opposes the Communist-dominated WFTU—the World Federation of Trade Unions.

It is heartening to witness the consistent interest of Catholic hierarchies throughout Latin America in trade unionism. Robert J. Alexander in his analysis of Red activities in Latin America sums up well the reasoning behind this concern of all moderate elements in Latin America. "Although there is a tendency abroad," he says, "to deprecate the Latin American trade unions, the fact is that they remain the most powerful mass organizations in Latin America today. They are a vital part of the Latin American social revolution and are perhaps the only institution in the region which can challenge the role of the military as the principal determinant of public policy and government. The Communists do not underrate their importance."[1]

My friend Padre Juan Alvarez Mejia of the Colombian Jesuits dwelt upon this basic question of Latin America's social problem in Bogotá one evening. "The only way to make sure," he commented, "that the Communists do not trick the workers, peasants and intellectuals of Latin America into giving the Reds the absolute power they seek for their Communist revolution is for the Christians to lead the revolution themselves. We must call for the reforms and fulfill the dreams of world social justice that our Latin American brothers who are in want are so rightly seeking."

Many persons in high places as well as low are thinking such thoughts today in Latin America. The New York *Times* in an editorial early in 1958 noted the fact that in the course of four different movements to overthrow dictatorial governments—in Argentina, Colombia, Venezuela and Cuba—the Catholic hierarchies in these four countries forthrightly made statements on the rights of the people to struggle for justice and freedom.

After the World Eucharistic Congress in Rio de Janeiro in 1955 the Bishops of Latin America organized what today is called CELAM, a word formed from the title in Spanish which we translate as Latin American Bishops' Conference. Continental headquarters are in Bogotá and already an imaginative program of continental activity has been launched. The second vice-president of the Council, Bishop Manuel Larrain of Talca of Chile, with characteristic aptness interprets the meaning of the move.

"The era of Robinson Crusoe is over," he says, "Catholic Action in Latin America and the work it inspires—press, TV, movies, radio, education, and so forth—must be organized on a supranational plane. We must pass . . . from a phase of national isolation to one of inter-American cooperation."

As to the goals, His Excellency sums them up in terms of human need. "Latin America is on the threshold of imminent and radical reforms," he explains. "Shocking social inequality, the existence of immense proletarian and subproletarian masses living in inhuman conditions, the monopoly of land-ownership . . . and the general lack of social awareness on the part of well-to-do Catholics—all show how urgent it is to take a definite stand in this regard. With us or without us, social reform is going to take place; in the latter event, it will take place against us."

SECTION FOUR

The Rise of Protestantism

• • ● • •

Chapter 1

The Rise of Protestantism in Latin America

LETICIA VAN HISSENHOVEN and seven other young ladies make up one of the distinguished Legion of Mary teams that carry on house to house visiting in the poorer sections of Bogotá.

"What kind of people do you meet?" I asked Leticia.

"The most interesting person I've encountered thus far is a shoemaker who is a Protestant," she replied. "He is a very religious man. He can recite the Protestant version of the Bible by the page, he comments on it in a way that shows that he has absorbed the passages in great detail and evidently he finds great spiritual satisfaction in their beauty."

"Is he a born Protestant?"

"No, he was brought up a Catholic here in Bogotá and studied the catechism a little when he was a boy, but explains that he had forgotten the lessons. He came across a piece of Protestant literature and found the minister very anxious to help him when he approached him. Apparently he was hungry for religion, had drifted from his own and the Protestants seemed to fill the void for him."

"How has he received you?"

"He talks very earnestly with me and seems surprised to hear things about the Church that are new to him. He shows no desire to come back but we are hoping he will attend our day of spiritual retreat this spring."

From the Rio Grande to the Straits of Magellan a topic of conversation in many circles these days is the rise of Protestantism in Latin America. It was a pioneer idea in 1910. Today it is represented by a contingent of some six million followers in the total population of one hundred eighty millions.

"Latin American Protestantism," writes one of its leaders, Alberto Rembao, "represents the most fertile portion of the mission world cultivated by the Protestant mother churches of Europe and America. The proportional growth of our world missions during the period 1900-1950 has been one to six—that is, for every convert at the beginning of the century we now have six. The relative increase in Latin America is one to ten and the proportion is rising.

"Latin American Protestantism is no longer an imported product. It possesses a national community in each country, directed principally by South Americans. In other words it is a spiritual reality that has taken flesh in South America."

The Protestant advance in Latin America may be divided into four stages:

First stage: From the period of Latin American independence to the Mexican Reforma (1860)

There was no flow of Protestants to Latin America during the three centuries of Spanish colonialism. "In those brave days," a Spanish friend explained to me, "to get aboard a ship for America a man had to prove that no member of his family had been condemned by the Inquisition for two generations." In Protestant nations, the feeling against the Catholics was quite as hostile. When the Dutch got control of the seas of Asia they destroyed the Catholic missions in Ceylon and the Celebes and elsewhere along their routes. It was Pilot Adams, an Englishman on a vessel caught within their waters by the Japanese, who sowed suspicion against the Spanish missionaries in Japan. In

1570 the Huguenot pirate Jean Sore captured a Portuguese vessel carrying forty Jesuit missionaries bound for Brazil and threw all forty into the sea.

At the time when the Latin American countries were gaining their freedom Protestants were engrossed in their first missionary triumphs in the Far East in the persons of men like Robert Morris. But a vanguard reached Latin America. Rivadavia, the Argentine leader, welcomed Anglican immigrants and employed two Protestant missionaries, James Thomson and William Morris, for his educational reform. O'Higgins, the great Chilean general, called Thomson to Chile and rewarded his labors with his country's highest decoration. Sarmiento, then frankly anticlerical, encouraged Rev. Mr. Goodfellow in his missionary efforts and promoted the erection of Protestant churches in order that they might be, he said, "a lesson sculptured in stone to the effect that our country will never turn itself into a Catholic cloister."

A factor overlooked by so many who study the Latin American scene is the role that Latin American Liberals like Sarmiento, rebellious against the Church, have played for over a century in opening the way for representatives of Protestantism. Often Protestants were warmly welcomed by men who were nominal Catholics and did not intend to renounce their Catholicism but who took the view that this was a way to carry on their fight with the Church in public life.

"It is a historical fact of Hispanic America of the nineteenth century," a South American Protestant explains, "that when Protestant missionaries from Anglo-Saxon America arrived in the twenty republics of the glorious Iberian branch they found hundreds and thousands of persons who, while not baptized as Protestants felt proud to call themselves Protestants in spirit. They were the Liberals who received the Yankees with open arms."

The uninitiated outsider needs to know that the political party terms of Conservative and Liberal carry far more significance in Latin America than Republican and Democrat do in the United States. There is a philosophy behind Latin American politics that in most countries involves the Church. The Conservative or rightist along with many other characteristics touching his politics usually has defended the Church and the Liberal or leftist has opposed it. With the passing of time many men desired to be neither rightist nor leftist but preferred a moderate center. North American politics are better expressed in Latin America by these moderates of the center than by the Liberal or Conservative parties.

Second stage: 1860 to 1914. Entrance and official establishment of the Protestant churches

During this long half century the various churches sought legal recognition. They established themselves in the capitals and in certain larger cities, with lesser development in the back country.

The legal position of religion in Latin American countries involved two general considerations, namely, the legal position of the Catholic Church as the official religion of the new republics and the legal position of the Protestant churches. A great deal happened during this half century in many countries to secure sufficient recognition for the Protestant churches that they might freely function and carry out publicly their evangelism.

Much more important, however, a great deal happened during this half century and during the remaining decades until today to alter the official position of the Catholic Church. Protestantism was seldom involved directly in this struggle but has gained decidedly from it.

The constitutions of the new republics after independence all considered the Catholic Church the national religion with exclusion of all opposing creeds. That of Chile (1818) declared the inviolability of the Catholic Church "without permitting any other cult contrary to the religion of Jesus Christ." The Provisional Statute of San Martin proclaimed in Peru (1821) explicitly guaranteed the supremacy of Catholicism. Mexico's Congress of Chipalcingo (1813) committed the country "to maintain concordats with the Holy See in order never to admit into the country any religion distinct from the Catholic." Guatemala's document was most explicit: "The Catholic religion which we have inherited from centuries ago and which we have professed in the intervening centuries must be conserved pure and inviolable, keeping alive the religious spirit that has always distinguished our country, protecting its ecclesiastical ministers, their persons and their property."

The change from this position began with the Mexican constitution of 1857. Various changes in other countries followed. In 1925 Chile by amicable negotiations relinquished its concordat with the Holy See and declared separation of Church and state. To jump ahead to the present day in order to conclude consideration of this point, we may note that currently nine of the twenty republics have established the principle of separation between the spiritual and temporal powers. Three are in South America—Chile, Uruguay and Brazil. The remaining six are in Middle America—Mexico, Nicaragua, Honduras, Panama, Puerto Rico and Cuba. In the remaining countries a major or minor degree of superiority of position is granted to the Catholic Church but freedom of worship is accorded to Protestantism.

Certain of the countries have sought at times to limit the freedom of Protestantism. These were Ecuador, Peru and Paraguay while Peron at certain periods had restrictions against Protestants as well as Catholics. Colombia since 1945 has forbidden Protestant action in its mission areas and has restricted activities outside Protestant places of worship. When Dr. Searle Bates wrote his analysis of the situation in 1945 he could say that in South America "the field is completely open to the action of the churches."[1]

It is important to explain that this change came about in most countries of Latin America through the movement for the complete laicization of civil society.

"About the middle of the nineteenth century," explained a professor at the Catholic University of Lima as we reviewed this question one day, "relatively small groups throughout the continent undertook what at that time seemed the titanic task, impossible of realization, of gaining control of the key posts in public education, in domestic affairs and in the army itself in order to rid them of all forms of influence by men with spiritual approach to the things of life. Most of the citizenry, including many of the clergy, saw clearly enough what was up but pooh-poohed the entire affair. 'In countries so solidly Catholic such as ours,' they said, 'such efforts are condemned to failure before they start.' But these elements succeeded. Now we are the witnesses and the victims of these cohorts of laicism. Thanks in great part to our easy-going forebears, in large sectors of Latin American life today, religious indifferentism rules the roost."

Up to the beginning of World War I, Protestant gains from this state of affairs were quite modest. "In 1914," states Dr. Latourette, the historian of Protestant missions, "the results obtained by the Protestants in Latin America were not impressive. . . . Their total followers in the republics barely reached a hundred thousand, a figure much inferior to the returns of missionaries among the Negroes in the British West Indies and the Guianas."

Third stage: 1916-1938. Unification of forces, preparation of programs, fixing of objectives

Latin America was rejected as a mission field at the great Protestant mission congress of Edinburgh in 1910. A group of Americans, however, met at Cincinnati in 1914 and decided to go it alone. Thus the Conference of Panama in 1916 came into being. Here took place the first continental planning that henceforth was to mark the common efforts of most of the organizations, today numbering nearly a hundred, that work in Latin America. At Panama the appellation Evangelical was determined upon as possessing a more positive connotation for Latin America than Protestant. Surveys were made and fields were searched out that could be described as most abandoned by the Catholics. Work among the Indians was determined upon as a specialization. A systematic development of well placed secondary schools was proposed. Medical work was discussed as well as plans for Biblical institutes and theological seminaries.

Conferences similar to Panama were held at Montevideo in 1925 and at Havana in 1929. The Committee on Cooperation in Latin America, now so expertly set up in its Fifth Avenue offices in New York, came into being during these years.

Substantial though not phenomenal gains were made during this period. The missionary body increased to some 3,000 with over 10,000 Latin American collaborators while the Protestant body in Latin America was now estimated at 1,600,000. Non-Catholic writers opposed to the Latin American venture and some Catholic journalists were wont to ridicule the small results obtained. But these were decades of quiet preparation that were to pay large dividends, some of which are still being collected.

Fourth stage: 1938 to present. Period of massive, systematic effort

In October 1938 the Protestant world mission congress was held in Madras, India. Already at this early date difficulties for mission work on the world's major continent, Asia, were being experienced from two forces, exacerbated nationalism and Communism. The situation prompted Doctor John Mackay, then President of the International

Missionary Council and today still the articulate head of Princeton Theological Seminary, to make a strong plea to the congress that Latin America be recognized as a major mission field.

The plea was almost prophetic in its implications. The years that followed witnessed catastrophic setbacks throughout Asia and thousands of missionaries have been turned toward Latin America. Millions of dollars are now working in Latin America that probably would have gone to China or India if these fields still held the promise of twenty-five years ago.

During 1939 to 1941 a number of distinguished North American leaders including John R. Mott visited Latin America, discussed problems with local directors of various societies and with Latin American Protestants. In the United States and Canada a stepped-up propaganda campaign made all familiar with the new stature acquired by the program to reach the peoples to the south. "It was rather exciting," commented a South American Protestant in retrospect. "In launching a campaign North Americans are such masters; we watched the development of details in admiration."

With the coming of World War II the Good Neighbor Policy of President Roosevelt took on the urgency of a patriotic duty. U.S. government staffs in each republic mounted to many hundreds to meet the requisites of the war effort. U.S. spending in Latin America became prodigious and U.S. popularity reached an all-time high. At home it was easy enough to make American citizens Latin America-conscious.

Developments during the war and since followed established lines:

1. Latin American and North American Protestants were prepared for key posts.

2. Technically correct mass communications media for best effectiveness were worked out, including the modern instruments such as radio which win friends in Latin America by their very modernness as well as by their message.

3. An avalanche of written propaganda was produced. Brazil, for instance, became the country of heaviest Bible distribution in the mission world. The literature at first was not always well prepared but was warm and human, inviting the common man "to step across the street" and take a taste of North American Christianity.

4. Oral preaching and lecturing was engaged in heavily, more out-

side than inside the churches in order to get to the crowd. Big-name preachers were widely advertised. House-to-house visitation was standard equipment.

5. Stress was laid on educational institutions. Today over 500 secondary schools are in operation, many aimed at the ambitious young without social background or financial means. Scholarships get them started and the more promising ones get their chance to continue to North American universities. Perhaps as few as five per cent become Protestants but all the others may to a degree be counted on as spiritual fellow-travelers.

6. Medical work, including many beautiful hospitals, have a place in the program as well as other institutions of mercy and service.

Recent surveys of the results of this intensified effort indicate that so far as the body of followers is concerned the countries of Latin America have doubled, tripled, and some even quadrupled their numbers in the last twenty years. The statistics employed in these pages are, unless otherwise noted, those compiled by Dr. Frank W. Price, Librarian of the Missionary Research Library in New York City.[2] In the following table, summarizing twentieth century growth, the entries are taken from other standard sources. While Dr. Price's are all-inclusive, this table excludes the British, French and Dutch colonies.

	1903	*1925*	*1938*	*1952*
Foreign missionaries	1,438	2,951	3,949	5,688
Nationals in ministry	6,000 (?)	6,094	10,132	7,800
Houses of worship	1,000	3,940	12,441	20,000
Members	100,000 (?)	500,000	1,300,000	2,700,000

The 1957 total, from figures in the 1958 edition of the *World Christian Handbook,* quoted by Dr. Price, is 6,131,500. This total includes the British, French and Netherlands colonial areas which count 329,500 Protestants. The ten countries of South America report 2,714,000 Protestants and the 12 self-governing political divisions of Middle America report 3,088,000.

Brazil possesses the largest Protestant community, with 1,776,000. The new West Indies Federation is next with 1,187,000. Four other nations report substantial figures: Mexico with 911,000; Chile with 370,000; Argentina with 364,000; and Haiti with 313,000. The sixteen remaining Latin American countries are credited with a total of 881,000 Protestants. The 6,131,500 Protestants in Latin America represent 3.4 per cent of the total population of 180,000,000.

"Protestantism experiences particular satisfaction in this accomplishment," a Spanish professor in one of our Catholic colleges remarked to me. "For centuries the Latin world has presented a solid phalanx against the Reformation. The theory has prevailed that there was some sort of functional incompatibility about the doctrines of Luther and Calvin as regards penetration of this sector of Christianity. Latin America seems to have disproven this contention."

There is a note of triumph in the Latin American Protestant over this development in his world. Rembao, whom we have already quoted, says, "Now Protestantism here is so active, so visible, so militant that the skeptic and the statistician has only to count its followers. . . . Protestant communities are entering their third generation and we no longer suffer from the stigma of being called renegades as was once the case."

As to missionary personnel, Dr. Pearce Beaver, formerly head of the Missionary Research Library of New York and now at the University of Chicago, finds the percentage distribution of the 15,000 United States and Canadian missionaries overseas as follows:

Region	*Percentage of Personnel*
Africa, south of the Sahara	25.2
Latin America	25.07
Eastern Asia	20.83
India, Pakistan, Ceylon	13.97
Near East, North Africa	4.97
Southeast Asia	7.12
Pacific islands	2.81

Thus according to the official lists one in four of all North American Protestant missionaries overseas is in Latin America. However, those close to the scene explain that this tells only a part of the story. Only a portion of the staffs are included in these figures. "Taking into account all of the imponderables," a specialist in the Protestant movement explains, "it is not far from the true picture to say that in 1957 there was a Protestant body of ten thousand foreign missionaries in Latin America."

The indigenization of the Protestant churches in Latin America is proceeding rapidly as a policy of prudence and practical operation. Hence the figure given above for native-born ministers is to be regarded as decidedly low.

The Protestant effort has represented a varying intensity and degree of success in the different Latin American countries. "I would say," my Spanish professor answers on this point, "that in eight countries there has been a noticeable amount of success. These eight are, in the order of the statistics, the following: Brazil, Mexico, Chile, Argentina, Haiti, Cuba, Puerto Rico and Guatemala. In another group of countries, the effort has been strong but the results not equally commensurate. These are Peru, Panama, Colombia, Nicaragua, Bolivia and Paraguay. Finally, in seven countries only superficial results have been obtained, namely, Uruguay, Ecuador, Venezuela, Costa Rica, Honduras, Salvador and the Dominican Republic."

A final characteristic to be noted in the current effort of Protestantism in Latin America is the frequent employment of extreme virulence in the attacks on Catholic Church teachings and practices. A private survey made for administrative purposes by persons with wide acquaintance with religious life in various parts of the world lays stress on this point.

"Neither in India, China nor Japan," the survey reads, "does Protestantism encourage its missionaries to attack Buddhism, Hinduism, Confucianism or Shintoism with the violent accusations that in Latin America it levels at the Church of Rome. One has only to visit its libraries and bookshops and examine its books, pamphlets and throwaways to note that so frequently primary attention goes not to the beauty of the Protestant way of life which Protestants purport to announce, but to rendering injury to beliefs and practices that the Catholic holds sacred. In open-air preaching and Sunday school teachings the habit of making Catholic ways the primary point of attack appears so consistently that one can only conclude that a calculated policy exists that has been established at central bases of tactics and strategy.

"Often it was explained to us by moderate Protestant leaders that such practices were engaged in only by more fanatical sects whose unworthy activities are disavowed by the major churches of Protestantism. This we found to be incorrect; a considerable number of missionaries representing sects which in other parts of the Western world hold the regard of knowledgeable Catholics and the general public seem, once they reach Latin America, to be bitten by a noxious bug that prompts them to peddle the hateful baggage of ugly calumny and twisted half-truth that they must know to be improper misrepresentation."

Personally in wide travels through Latin America I have encountered many Protestant missionaries. Those whom I like to remember are the individuals who (while following loyally their calling as representatives of a divided Christendom, the very contemplation of which is heartbreaking to those of us who yearn so deeply to see it one) sought to render warm respect to every Christian, be he priest or peasant and to Christian faith in Latin America wherever they found it. If such men see themselves impelled to tear down the walls of another man's belief I feel that they do it rather in sorrow than in anger or disdain. Certainly they do not resort to unworthy methods.

Chapter 2

South American Protestantism

THE TEN REPUBLICS of South America possess a Protestant population of 2,714,000. Brazil is the unchallenged leader with 1,776,000. Argentina and Chile have approximately the same Protestant membership, 364,000 and 370,000 respectively. The three smallest groups are found in Venezuela with 18,000, Uruguay with 10,000 and Ecuador with 5,000. The remaining four countries muster a total of 141,000.

Protestantism in Brazil. During my stay in Porto Velho, far up the Amazon Valley on the distant Madeira River, I was treated on several evenings during the week to strident singing in a house over the back fence. Here in this family residence on the edge of the jungle the small group of Baptists in town gathered for services and hymns. Protestants are everywhere in Brazil.

The first Protestants to enter Brazil were sent by John Calvin but most did not stay. One who did was Jacques de la Balleur, a theologian and eloquent preacher, a student versed in Spanish, Latin, Greek and Hebrew. He was hung as a heretic in Rio de Janeiro in 1567. Thus Europe's religious wars had their chapter in Brazil.

The Flemish controlled a portion of the coast from 1630 to 1654 and their Protestant missionaries worked effectively among the natives. "Many were the Indians," recorded Padre de Barros, the Jesuit, "who were as Calvinistic and Lutheran as if they had been born in England or Germany. They called the Church *moanga,* that is to say 'false' and the doctrines *morandubas ahares,* that is, 'lies of the Fathers.' "[1]

The first Protestants of the modern period came in the early nineteenth century. England made a treaty with Portugal in 1810 that provided chapels for its subjects and the arrangements served as well for

German immigrants to points in the south. Under Pedro II greater freedom was obtained and Kidder and Fletcher, missionaries from the United States, reported of Brazil, "There is no Catholic country on the globe that shows greater tolerance or greater sympathy to Protestants." Most of the larger churches established themselves during the second half of the nineteenth century and many Protestants played important roles in education and social welfare during the period of the Church's great struggles with the Liberals.

Bishop Agnello Rossi, a specialist on Protestantism in Brazil, explains that Protestant immigrants from 1820 to 1947 totaled only 3 per cent of the whole, which means that easily 95 per cent were Catholic. But while similar Catholic immigrant bodies that came to North America brought their priests with them and built a sturdy religious life for themselves, the Brazilian groups did badly on this score and thus the faith among them often languished.

Ardent proselytism brings Protestantism to possession of 3.5 per cent of the Brazilian people today with over a thousand foreign missionaries and 3,500 native-born ministers. Their theological students total over 1,500 in thirty houses of training. A Spanish seminary professor who visited some of these seminaries was impressed by the high order of their organization. "Their training course is planned to the last detail and is carried out with precision," he explained. "In many of the schools nothing seems lacking, neither good libraries, nor ample living quarters (including cottages for married candidates), nor residences for the professors (many of them graduates of foreign universities), nor sports facilities for both faculty and students. When one recalls that major seminarians for our diocesan clergy in Brazil total but 1,200 (though there are more such candidates for the religious orders), these 1,500 Protestant candidates give us reason for thought."

Top consideration among Brazilian Protestants goes to training. Emile Leonard calls the Sunday School "the great instrument of Brazilian evangelism." By recent report there are 8,065 Sunday Schools with 36,355 teachers of both sexes and 554,453 in attendance.

Some 20,000 Brazilian children attend Protestant grade schools but the special strength in education lies in 85 secondary schools with 36,000 students. The churches operate also five nurses' training schools, seven colleges and the only Protestant university in Latin America,

Mackenzie of São Paulo, with an enrollment of 7,000. Though the majority of the students in the higher schools are Catholic, a condition of acceptance is that they follow all courses in religious instruction. Mackenzie University counts 30 per cent of its faculty Catholic.

Of the 221 radio stations in Brazil, Protestant programs are scheduled on 100 that broadcast to 60 cities in 18 states. On a national television quiz show similar to our $64,000 Question, the first person to choose the Bible as her subject was a Baptist housewife from São Paulo State whose remarkable performance caught the attention of the nation.

Brazil as the largest distributor of Bibles among the mission countries of the world has in Rio its own Bible publishing house in a building as large as a football field. For the decade from 1942 to 1951 it reports the prodigious total of 11,221,898 Bibles and portions distributed. The figures have since gone higher. Literally tons of Protestant magazines are in circulation with a total of 191 titles.

As I moved about Brazil I found constant evidence of a consciousness of the Protestant effort. The very fact that many of the churches employ highly effective techniques in such intelligent fashion places in the hands of thoughtful Catholic leaders a powerful instrument to call the laity from easy indifference. Bishop Rossi as leader of the National Secretariat for Defense of the Faith has established local units everywhere which find it easy to challenge Catholic church-goers not to be outdone in zeal by their Protestant neighbors.

In Campo Grande in the Mato Grosso I said Mass at St. Anthony's Church. Father Corrigan, the Redemptorist pastor, had explained to the congregation the previous Sunday that Mormon missionaries were making house-to-house visits through the parish and that Catholics should give them proper evidence of their knowledge of their faith. After Mass a mother of a family came into the sacristy to explain to me at length and with evident satisfaction how well she had refuted the Mormons who had called.

In Anapolis in the Goias Father Dominic Coscia of the Franciscans spoke of the excellent Protestant hospital in the city. "When I first took up work in my parish," he explained to me, "I used to visit my sick parishioners when they went there. One day, however, Dr. Farnstone stopped me in the corridor and told me not to come any more. I explained that it helped the faith of my people to have their pastor call on them when they are ill. 'How can you use such an argument with me?' he answered. 'We are here to tear away (*arancar*) the Catholics from their religion.' "

In Pirenopolis, also in the Goias, an American Franciscan related to me an incident that was duplicated in other countries. On a feast day morning when the townsfolk were crowded into the square before the church ready for the procession, a Protestant with his truck equipped with a loudspeaker drove into the square and undertook to broadcast a condemnation of the ceremony and spoke deprecatingly of what he referred to as "worship of Mary." The priest went over to the truck and at first the missionary asserted that he would continue because it was a holy thing to break up such an improper gathering.

"If you were back home in Hartford, Connecticut," the priest replied, "you wouldn't stoop to such a crude procedure. Why do you do it here?" Evidently the thrust hit its mark because the young man drove off.

A pastor in a town in Colombia told me of missionaries who followed a procession in his parish with their truck and ridiculed the townsfolk through their loudspeaker. A third priest in Guatemala, one of my fellow Maryknollers, told me of a similar experience during Holy Week in the Cuchamatanes Mountains.

Protestantism in Uruguay. Protestant sources indicate that a total of 20,000 followers represents a generous estimate of membership in this country that is so advanced materially but in which such a large portion of the population has lost its religious sense through materialism.

Protestantism in Argentina. "The presence of Evangelical missionaries here," writes the Argentine Antonio Sagarna, "is not, cannot be an offense to the Argentine people who, thanks to the vision of eminent Catholics, have held liberty of conscience and of worship sacred in their history, their institutions and in the normal course of their lives."

Despite such statements, Protestants say that while they encounter "no crude fanaticism or brutal persecution" in Argentina, "the Catholic press and radio commentators carry on a continuing campaign of lies and calumnies against our activities."

Protestants in Argentina total 450,000 to 500,000 with a strong concentration in Buenos Aires. Some outstanding training institutions are found in the city, which is regarded not only as a national but as a continental base. The faculty of the Evangelical Theological Seminary on Calle de Camacua has been described, correctly or not, as the "ideological brain of South American Protestantism." The Baptist and Lutheran seminaries are likewise strong in well-trained faculties.

Since Buenos Aires, with Mexico City, is a major printing and publishing center for Spanish Latin America it is understandable that the Protestants should use it as a base for production of literature. The Editorial Sudamericana is technically one of the most modern printing establishments in the Western Hemisphere while the Baptist publishing house is the best this active sect operates south of the Rio Grande. There is a wealth of bookshops. "What an extraordinary sight greets one who looks into the windows of La Aurora Bookshop!" commented a visitor to Buenos Aires. "Side by side are books by Bishop Fulton Sheen and the Spanish mystics and Protestant literature from both North and South America." La Aurora is the Methodist book center.

Ward College, conducted by the Methodists, draws many Catholics. One of the outstanding Protestant service institutions in the country is the famous Boca Mission near the docks, founded by William Morris over a half century ago. Its free meals, dispensary, schools, playgrounds, open-air theatre have taken care of many newly arrived Spanish and Italian immigrants. There are classes in typewriting, arithmetic, English and other useful courses that help prepare some 1,500 young people to get jobs.

My young lawyer friend, Dr. Angel Centeno, by his down-to-earth analysis of the practical effects of Protestant efforts has helped stir many in Catholic circles out of their complacent disdain of Protestant efforts. He was among those who emphasized to me the great opportunity the Protestants possess through the relative paucity of Catholic contacts with great masses of the population.

"Would you say that hunger for religious experience has anything to do with Protestant successes?" I asked him.

"Frequently it has," he replied. "Recently we had here the Reverend Hicks, an American evangelist and faith curer who couldn't speak a word of Spanish, who did all his work through an interpreter. Despite this he had audiences of up to 50,000 people at the Buenos Aires Stadium several times a week for two months. I attended some of his sessions and visited him at his hotel in the course of preparing articles for the press. The huge crowd, the personal attraction of the speaker, the great numbers of the sick, some of whom were flown in by plane from as far away as Misiones Province, the spell of the mighty host of voices when all were invited to join in the congregational singing was deeply moving. For me, most important was the willingness of tens of thousands of nonchurch-goers to accept the speaker. Hicks told them to have faith in God and showed no hostility to the Catholic Church. Some clerics pooh-poohed the performance and disciplined Catholics said it left them cold. But they forgot that great numbers of nonchurch-goers who went through idle curiosity were hungry of spirit and encountered a stirring religious experience."

"Did Hicks help build up Protestant ranks here?"

"I suppose he did. But I would gather that much more enduring work is accomplished by the quiet house-to-house evangelism and by the service centers. Let me show you some of the neighborhood spots in the suburbs where Protestant groups do street preaching that seems to be effective."

The Doctor and I drove to populous lower middle class neighborhoods in the outskirts and he indicated corners at which on Sunday mornings the street preachers set up their pitch.

"They'll get sixty to seventy people at one of these pitches on a Sunday," he explained. "The sessions are usually quiet and gentlemanly. The effective work is done by indirection. A certain delicacy is employed in expressing disbelief in confession, in the intercession of the saints, in the wisdom of a celibate clergy. Protestants, the speaker will say, honor Mary as the mother of Christ the Great Teacher; by innuendo he makes it clear that he does not believe that Christ is the Son of God or that Our Lady has from God any special role of intercession."

This routine goes on not only in the cities but in the remote country areas. A priest in the mountains beyond Salta told me of Protestant headway on the Indian reservations.

"For want of clergy our Indians have long been cared for by superannuated priests who can just make it to the church on Sunday to say Mass for the faithful who come in from miles around. Recently one of our teachers found sizable groups of Indians at distant spots who had set up Protestant services. 'How did this happen?' the teacher asked in astonishment. 'We have come to see more clearly,' replied the simple people with enthusiasm. 'The minister visits us, our Sunday devotions are so beautiful. We pray, we sing, we like it.' Why can't Catholics who are so many do more for these people, even if we have no priests? We are an army without generals and generals without an army. Someone must do some reorganizing."

Padre Elizalde, a pastor of Ciudadela in the Diocese of La Plata, found an answer that is growing in popularity. He organized what he called the Diocesan Oblates to train young laymen and lay women who go in teams into the rural areas.

"We need the missionary spirit," commented Señora Maria Leon as this ever-recurring subject came up in a conversation at her home one afternoon. "We need many Catholics to do what my Protestant paperboy did the other morning. When he delivered *La Nacion* to my door I found that he had put inside it an advertising sheet from his neighborhood Protestant church. I felt impatient with him and sorry for him but I said to myself, 'We Catholics need his spirit; I would never have thought of promoting religion the way that boy did.' "

A parish priest outside the capital made an interesting comment. "People won to Protestantism speak of its attractiveness," he noted. "They talk about the concerts, the social gatherings, the happy contacts with Protestant leaders as if this never happens among Catholics. I wonder if possibly we don't make ourselves too dour and severe. I noticed the other day in the Buenos Aires cathedral the sign that hits your eye the minute you step inside: 'Women are forbidden to enter without veils.' Why not change this a bit? It might read, 'Welcome to the House of God; come properly veiled.' "

Oddly enough, this same thought had occurred to me as I saw the prohibition at the cathedral door. At the cathedral entrance in Rio de Janeiro the text of the sign comes nearer to the spirit proposed by my young Argentine friend. "If you love God," the Rio sign reads, "don't enter His house with sleeveless dress or in decolleté."

In either case the major task remains; namely, to get the unchurched millions, whether in silks or rags, to come seeking the Kindly Light through the church door.

Protestantism in Paraguay. Protestants in Paraguay are reported to total some 23,000.

Despite the low membership, Protestant institutions in Asuncion stand out prominently. I visited the beautiful buildings of the International College of the Church of Christ. The ensemble was breathtaking.

The Baptists pride themselves on having in Asuncion the most complete group of social works found in any of their Latin American missions—a hospital with 150 beds, clinic, primary schools, Biblical institute, school of practical agronomy, a strong program for family life and social life, large batteries of well presented promotional pamphlets and leaflets.

Protestantism in Chile. Padre Ignacio Vergara, S.J., who with Padre Humberto Munoz has made studies of Protestantism in Chile, arrived recently at a total of 681,000, "including the militants, candidates, sympathizers, and so forth." The official Protestant figure in the *World Christian Handbook* of 1958 is 370,000.

Protestants are quite satisfied with their gains in Chile. "It would be difficult," writes one, "to find a country where the moral power of Protestantism is so patently evident as among the Chilean Evangelicals."

German and English Protestants entered Chile in the late nineteenth century. The Germans established themselves on the southern fringe of Central Chile in cities such as Puerto Montt and Valdivia and have made a deep impression on the whole region. Many sought to protect their national character and their Lutheranism but today it would appear that not more than 25,000 maintain their original faith. The English have likewise entered in great proportion into Chilean life and few formally maintain themselves as Anglicans.

The major churches have made some gains and maintain well developed institutions. The Baptist College of Temuco has engaged in more than twenty-five years of intensive work and has built a following. El Vergel in Nueva Imperial is the crowning achievement of the Methodists in Chile, a vigorous, self-supporting center for agricultural training. The Adventists are very proud of Mariposas College of Chillan.

The real Protestant force in Chile, however, as in other Latin American countries is the Pentecostals. Chile has its own special development in this division of Protestantism, the *Canutos,* a sect found also in Brazil, Venezuela and in other Caribbean countries.

One of my Maryknoll confreres newly arrived in Chile describes taking up work in Gualleco—a long-abandoned parish in central Chile

—in the 1940s, and making his first tour by horseback among his scattered country folk. Along the way he invited everybody to Mass and each replied with a friendly smile and an agreeable *"Como no?"* ("Why not?") But at one point he called to a boy leading a team of oxen.

"How about coming to Mass tomorrow, son?" he asked.

The youngster hesitated a moment, looked from the priest to his beasts, and then said stoutly, "I never go to Mass."

"What's the matter, son?"

"I am a *Canuto,* I don't pray to statues."

This was his first contact with this unusual group that is quite strong in rural Chile. It is an autochthonous, economically independent, strongly proselytizing body, quite contagious in its influence on many simple folk. It had its start in Valparaiso in 1910 but gets its name from one of its famous early preachers, Canut de Bon.

Its religious meetings are classical examples of highly emotional gatherings at which the preacher with agitated shouts stirs his flock and the flock reacts with continual interruptions of "Alleluia! Amen! Praise be to God!" As the tempo mounts individuals feel inspired, fall to the floor in trances, are called on by the preacher to reveal to the brethren what they have received from the Spirit. If the preacher has done his work well, every member of the flock goes home thrilled by the wonderful experience.

The *Canutos* of Chile are reputed among their neighbors as exceptionally honest and law-abiding. They refrain from liquor and gambling. They support their church generously and never let their brother *Canuto* suffer want. "The best carpenters in Temuco," explains a Maryknoll missioner in that city, "are *Canutos.* They have worked hard to learn their trade, they give an honest day's labor, they are never off the job on account of drunkenness, because they do not drink."

Padre Vergara quite understandingly explains that such sects prove the existence of "immense spiritual riches in the people of Chile." The Chilean *roto,* like the pauperized masses in the England of John Wesley and like other bodies of the earth's disinherited, possess a great spiritual receptivity, a hunger for God. Unsatiated by thc traditional Church, that would feed them if it were vigorous and vital, they gladly accept a substitute religion.

Protestantism in Bolivia. Combined Protestant strength in Bolivia is estimated at 29,000. The statutes of the Christian Evangelical Church in Bolivia, which is a union of the various sects, were approved by the Bolivian government December 11, 1954, and thus Protestantism obtained recognition as a juridical personality.

Protestantism in Peru. Protestants number 73,000. In Lima, best known Protestant schools for the upper classes are Maria Alvarado College and San Andres College. The American College, though it began under Protestant auspices, is now independent.

The largest single unit of Protestants in Peru is far from the capital, high in the Andes on Lake Titicaca. Here the Adventists have some 25,000 well trained followers, principally Quechua Indians in the neighborhood of Juliaca. They operate a network of 150 elementary schools, two secondary schools, a small hospital of 30 beds that is favorably spoken of throughout the region, clinics, a training school for religion teachers. Their propaganda efforts seem very effective, with best results from the door-to-door visitation work of Indian missionaries.

The group is eclectic—a serious breach of its laws against drinking, gambling, blasphemy leads to dismissal. This same situation prevails in other parts of Peru. "The Protestants have a good reputation here in Cuzco," explained one of the teachers in the Christian Brothers College. "Their followers have the name of being very moral and of fighting alcoholism." Again in Ayaviri one of the Maryknollers remarked, "We have very few Protestants but they have a reputation for morals. Of course if a Protestant here commits a grave moral offense he by that very fact becomes immediately an ex-Protestant."

In January 1945 President Manuel Prado canceled all Protestant propaganda among the Indians in Peru and made the following statement: "The Constitution protects the Catholic religion. The nation spends large sums for the development of Catholic missions [among the Indians] and their activities should not be vitiated by diverse forms of religious propaganda."

This appears to be a quite categoric condemnation of Protestant activities. However, previous to January 1945 the President was already in consultation with North American Protestants regarding an enterprise which while highly commendable as a scientific project would, he knew, be open to criticism from Catholics as introducing Protestant missionaries into the Indian area.

The organization in question is the Summer Institute of Linguistics which has a connection with the University of Oklahoma. This enterprise got its start through the Rev. William Townsend who was invited by President Lazaro Cardenas of Mexico to provide language specialists for work in Lower California and in Yucatan. Even if the linguistic technicians exercised roles in Mexico as Protestant missionaries as well, this would have represented no problem for Cardenas who at that time was fighting the Catholic Church.

In 1945 the Linguistics Institute began work among the Peruvian Indians. By recent reports the personnel totals 136 North Americans who are "linguists, doctors, pilots and technicians" with a large staff of Peruvian helpers. The organization has made contact with 24 tribes and operates 32 bilingual schools. It possesses a vast radio network, five airplanes, and much modern scientific, sanitary and technical equipment. The principal training center for the tribal Indians is at Yarinacocha, near Pucallpa, a community on the banks of the Ucayali which is being developed as a key city in the Peruvian Amazon for the new overland route from Lima.

The Catholic missionary bishops of the region have written categoric condemnations of the project, principally on the score that the Yarinacocha training center serves for Protestant penetration. Padre José M. Cuesta, S.J., has prepared a survey which is more serene in tone than the episcopal statements and reaches three conclusions: (1) the Summer Institute of Linguistics is, in addition to being a scientific and linguistic organization, likewise a propaganda organ of evangelical Protestantism; (2) the training course at Yarinacocha for tribal natives while technically under the government is de facto operated by Protestants; (3) the government should consider the propriety of thus acting contrary to Peruvian tradition and the constitution.

Almost an allied question to that of the Linguistics Institute is the encouragement given by the Peruvian government to the Le Tourneau Caterpillar Tractor interests for a huge development work in the vicinity of Pucallpa. The objection of the local episcopacy arises from the fact that Le Tourneau is a zealous Protestant from the Mississippi Valley who is happy to aid the Protestant missionaries in the course of promoting his own interests.

Le Tourneau is the master of the "big wheel." He has received a concession of a million acres of jungle near Pucallpa on condition that he build roads. He has brought in his huge "big wheel" equipment that rapidly cuts roads through the forest. By his contract he promises to protect the faith and the practice of the faith of the people who will settle on the land he clears. With Catholic missionaries missing, however, and Protestant missionaries ready, the situation points toward gains for Protestantism. Certainly, the Peruvian government would find it hard to refuse the aid of men like Le Tourneau in this boom area of the Peruvian Amazon.

Protestantism in Ecuador. Protestants in Ecuador do not total more than 5,000. "Our work in Ecuador," one report reads, "is dishearteningly slow, more so than in any country along the Pacific Coast." Some progress has been made in Guayaquil, the port city, but Quito the capital has proven quite difficult.

Yet in Quito is located one of the outstandingly successful propaganda projects of the continent. This is Radio Station HCJB, "The Voice of the Andes." Forty mission societies cooperate in support of this powerful instrument, with a strength of 50,000 watts, that broadcasts 24 hours a day seven days a week in seven languages and boasts of over a thousand programs a month. Its program material is consistently high grade in the cultural, educational, political and entertainment fields.

President Galo Plaza granted the contract and provided land for the project. It serves as the official voice of the government, broadcasting sessions of congress, governmental information and special events such as the inauguration of the president. Yet this in no way hinders it from providing heavy religious programs including daily prayer, Bible lessons, meditations, hymns, Protestant church news. Speakers are free to present positivist or laicist views but nothing Catholic. The Church is not mentioned even in criticism on the Spanish or Portuguese language programs which are beamed to the entire continent but the policy is otherwise for the Quechua programs. The Panamerican Christian Network of which it is a part hooks up at times for global broadcasts.

Centers for Protestant Indian work in Ecuador are Ambato and Riobamba, gateways to the jungle. In Ecuador the great Andean wall drops away quickly with consequent difficulties for communication. Several Catholic societies work among the tribal Indians, most celebrated of whom are the Jivaros, fierce warriors renowned for bringing home the heads of their enemies, shrinking them, and collecting them as North American Indians collected scalps. Visiting at the center of the Missionaries of St. Joseph in Ambato I talked with Padre Ottarino, one of the veterans of the Rio Napo country.

"All but a thousand of our people are Indian," he explained, "and now almost all these Indians are Catholic. The exception is the small Auca tribe which refuses to receive the Fathers." I was to recall this conversation later when in January 1956 five young American Protestant missionaries were massacred by the Auca Indians. The tragedy drew wide attention. The wife of one of the young men wrote the story for North America and it proved a best-seller.[2]

Padre Pedro Suarez, S.J., was martyred by the Aucas in 1667. They have proven an object of fascination for many zealous men wont to contemplate the world's most difficult tasks, the Gospel's most insurmountable barriers. Similar tribes are found in other parts of the Amazon. We have already dwelt briefly on the death of the two Salesians, Padres Sacilotte and Fuchs, at the hands of the Chavantes in Brazil and the final triumph eighteen years later of another Salesian, Padre Colbacchini, among these same Chavantes.

What type of American boy volunteers for this unusual task as a Protestant missionary? Jim Elliott, one of the five killed by the Auca, came from a Scottish family with a home in the shadow of Mount Hood, Portland, Oregon. Each morning the father read the Bible to the children in the breakfast nook and bade them live by it. Jim determined to be a missionary and went to Wheaton College in the suburbs of Chicago to prepare. He took up wrestling to make himself physically strong. "I wrestle solely for the strength and coordination of muscle tone that the body receives while working out," he wrote rather solemnly to his mother, "with the ultimate end that of presenting a more useful body as a living sacrifice." He became the college wrestling champ. He studied Greek "preparatory to translating the Bible into some unwritten language." At college "the challenge of the dread Aucas" appealed to him and thus he moved toward Ecuador.

Pete Fleming, second of the five, born in Seattle, Washington, was a letter man in basketball and golf, possessed an unusual knowledge of the Bible, took his M.A. in literature and planned to be a professor until he decided on Ecuador.

Ed McCully, eldest son of a Milwaukee bakery executive, was a star in football and track at Wheaton, won the 1949 championship in the National Hearst Oratorical Contest, studied law for a while at Marquette University and then chose Ecuador.

Nate Saint, born in Philadelphia, had an older sister Rachel who read him missionary adventures when he was a boy and an older brother Sam who was an air pilot. Nate went to South America as pilot of the Missionary Aviation Fellowship and thus got his assignment as pilot for the Ecuador group.

Roger Youderian came from a ranch near Sumatra, Montana, studied to be a teacher in agriculture, and as a paratrooper made the Rhine jump and was in the Battle of the Bulge. He first thought of a missionary career while in the service and thus ended up in Ecuador.

All five of these men were married and when death came their young wives had a total of nine children. The approach to the Auca turned about the use of the airplane, called for months of reconnoitering and many attempts to make friends by dropping gifts from the air. A sand spit in the Curaray River became their landing strip, fifteen minutes' flight from their advance post of Arajuno. First step on landing was to build a nest-like hut 35 feet up in a tall tree but in a matter of days all five were massacred by the distrusting Auca.

Protestantism in Venezuela. Venezuela today has, according to Catholic estimates, 40,000 Protestants. "Though the major churches of Protestantism are not particularly strong here," reads a statement, "on the other hand, the restless and terribly contagious carryings-on of the Pentecostals, the Adventists and Jehovah's Witnesses can, in the long run, undermine all solid religion among the uneducated. The strength of the Pentecostals resembles that of Chile."

The dictator Guzman Blanco, who despoiled the churches, expelled the religious, secularized the cemeteries and introduced divorce, welcomed the Protestants. In his early years the succeeding dictator, Vicente Gomez, likewise granted full freedom, though with dictatorial caprice he withdrew it partly during his last years. Complete freedom of movement exists today.

Protestantism in Colombia. The Protestant body in Colombia is placed at 46,000. The open employment of the usual methods of proselytism that characterize the Protestant effort elsewhere on the continent has been suspended in Colombia.

General Mosquera is credited with the first "friendly overture" in 1861 that permitted the official entrance of Protestant churches into Colombia, though Protestant rights had been recognized since the 1820s. The Presbyterians founded the American College in Bogotá in 1877. Advance was slow and at the Congress of Panama in 1916 the Colombian delegates reported that the churches could only wait patiently for better days later on.

A change came in 1930 with the rise to power of the Liberal Olaya Herrera who had once been a Sunday School boy of one of the Protestant sects. Shortly after, one of the missionaries could report, "We enjoy complete religious liberty and the influence of the Evangelical churches is making itself felt." World War II brought still greater gains so that at its end a Protestant missionary could write as follows about the years 1935-1945:

"The last decade has registered a progress never before witnessed by the Evangelical churches of Colombia. There are now more houses of worship and better ones than our missionaries of twenty years ago would ever have dared expect."

But in 1946 the Liberals lost the election and the Conservatives required the Protestants to give up all the extralegal privileges they had enjoyed under the Liberals.

Why is there insistence on the strict letter of the law? A prominent professor and writer in Bogotá had a comment on this point. "Certainly a factor in the situation," he noted, "is the methods employed by some of the North Americans during the recent period of freedom. Protestants in the United States would be surprised to know how shrewd Colombians are in distinguishing between the various missionaries who come among us. The major sects are usually (though unfortunately not always) represented by individuals who consistently observe the proprieties. But many of the so-called fringe sects come with crude, ugly and distasteful tactics. One word sums up their attitude toward us. That word is disdain. These people awaken not only our anger but our contempt."

The constitution of 1886 provides for freedom of religion: "The state guarantees freedom of conscience. No one shall be molested on account of his religious opinions nor shall anyone be compelled to profess beliefs or to observe practices against his conscience. The freedom of all cults which are not contrary to Christian morals or to the law is guaranteed."

The Conservatives chose to forbid open propaganda in the streets and through the press, radio, television and public motion pictures. Protestant activities continued and hence by an instruction from the Ministry of Government on January 28, 1954, the restrictions were stated again: "Non-Catholic nationals or foreigners resident in Colombia, whether ministers, pastors or simple faithful, may not proselytize in public, nor use means of propaganda, outside the locale where the cult takes place."

Referring to activities among the quarter of a million Indians and other inhabitants of Colombia's mission territories, this same instruction was still more restrictive, stating that Protestant ministers were to "exercise no public missionary nor educational work, except for the children of non-Catholic foreigners."

Still another factor enters into this picture. This is the mortal contest between the Conservatives and the Liberals in Colombia that in times past has reached beyond the ballot box to sanguinary feuds throughout the countryside.

On April 9, 1948, a massive outbreak between Conservatives and Liberals occurred when a popular Liberal leader, Jorge Gaitan, was murdered in downtown Bogotá in the course of an insurrection. The Liberal masses of Bogotá, who idolized Gaitan, maddened by fury, descended on every building or individual associated with the Conservatives whom they blamed for Gaitan's death. Further, the destruction spread into the rural areas, immediately awakening reprisals by Conservatives and stirring up lawlessness among quite another group, the back country bandits.

The result has been a decade of sickening violence in Colombia. A letter to New York dated March 11, 1958, from a trustworthy source in Bogotá contains the following sentence, "The number of murders, either for political reasons or out of banditry is mounting steadily. The last report I heard was that 280,000 people have been killed in these 'skirmishes' in the past eight years."

A by-product of the Conservative-Liberal political war has been an exacerbation of the hostility between many strongly religious Catholics who are Conservatives and the Colombian Protestants who stake their future on open advocacy of the Liberal cause. Among the immense property damage involved since 1948 is included homes and houses of worship of Colombian Protestants. Among the tens of thousands of lives lost certainly Protestants are to be counted.

The organized protests of the Protestants against the treatment accorded them in Colombia have included a listing of Protestant "martyrs," persons, at this writing totaling eighty, who Protestants hold have been put to death for their religion. The eightieth death was reported late in 1957. Father Eugene K. Culhane, S.J., of *America* while in Bogotá in January 1958 investigated it and reported his findings.

"I checked the story," he writes, "of the eightieth and the latest martyr claimed by the CEDEC *Bulletin* of December 10. Juan Coy, a Protestant, 'a peaceful, law-abiding citizen, who had never been active in politics,' had been arrested 'for holding private worship for a small group of relatives and friends' in his home in Saboya. On October 29, the day after his release from prison, he was found dead from a rifle shot. There were no witnesses. Conclusion: 'With the death of Coy, the number of Protestant martyrs in Colombia reached eighty.'

"The truth of the matter is that Juan Coy's family, ardent Liberals—as are 99 per cent of Colombian Protestants—had been feuding with another gang in town, who were Conservatives. In the preceding three years, two of Juan's brothers had been killed, presumably by the other gang, each of them after heavy drinking. A week or two before Juan's death, a young man of the other faction had been mysteriously slain. Juan's mother, sister and remaining brother, when asked their opinion after his death, stated that in their firm belief he was killed, one—by the other group; two—for 'political' (i.e., feud?) reasons. This information was given by Dr. Enrique Sanchez Millair, of the Ministry of Justice."

No Colombian in his right mind seeks to justify this dastardly bloodletting. But certainly it seems a twisting of the truth to give the impression that these eighty Protestant victims have been felled in an otherwise peaceful countryside for the sole reason that they are Protestants.

Chapter 3

Middle American Protestantism

MIDDLE AMERICA embraces a dozen self-governing political divisions and a number of dependent territories under the British, French and Netherlands flags. For convenience and completeness we include here as well dependent areas not embraced by the term Middle America.

These dependent territories have the following Protestant membership: (1) the Guianas, French and Netherlands Antilles, 225,000; (2) Bahamas and Virgin Islands, 57,000; (3) Bermuda, 19,000; (4) British Honduras, 27,000; (5) Falklands, 1,500. Total Protestants listed here come to 329,500.

Among the remaining territories, the recently established West Indies Federation possesses 1,187,000 Protestants in a total population of 2,954,000. Thus the Federation's Protestants come to 40 per cent of the whole. Puerto Rico, while a part of the United States, is listed as a self-governing unit in Middle America.

Central America. One afternoon in San José, the capital of Costa Rica, I knelt near President Figueres as with ease and grace he read an act of consecration of the Costa Rican nation to the Sacred Heart of Jesus. A hundred thousand citizens knelt around him in the stadium at this closing event of the Second National Eucharist Congress.

Figueres is not a religious man and is married to a lady from the Hudson River Valley who is not a Catholic. Yet this public act of prayer by the head of the government is regarded as quite normal in this country where Catholicism is the state religion. Of the other Central American states, Panama by its Constitution of 1941 recognizes the Church and prescribes religious instruction in its schools as requested by the parents. Nicaragua exercises the right of patronage, which means that the President has a say in the nomination of Catholic bishops and the government pays a small salary to the clergy. El Salvador in its 1950 constitution recognizes the juridical personality of the Church but places limits on its freedom. Honduras has separation of Church and state but by no means ignores the Church; complex regulations govern its conduct. Guatemala, while friendly since the 1954 revolt against Communism, still has its hostile legislation on the books.

In Central America's six little countries with their total of 11,000,000 inhabitants, Protestantism possesses some 291,000 followers. Guatemala has the largest representation, with 143,000, while Costa Rica's 11,000 is the smallest.

One quiet Sunday in the city of David in the deep interior of northern Panama, I went about town with an American Vincentian missionary who knew the nooks and crannies and was impressed with the number of places of worship large and small which serve as centers for Protestant effort in this region. The priests who attend the San Blas Indians south of the Canal likewise encounter Protestant work among them. However, principal activities are centered in the population concentration about the Canal.

Costa Rica possesses only a small Protestant group. However, this little aristocrat among the Central American states holds the respect of Protestant leaders and some of the churches are making its capital their Caribbean base. The large Protestant radio station, "The Voice of the Caribbean," technically and financially very strong and operating after the pattern of "The Voice of the Andes," is located in San José. Here also is a large union publishing house, El Caribe, which serves a wide area. The publishing group called LELA (Literatura Evangelica Latino-America) likewise is based here.

In addition to these institutions aimed to serve the continental movement in general, efforts are made to reach the local people as well. As reaction, a small Catholic radio organization has come into being in San José and rank and file Catholic families have taken steps against door-to-door proselytism. Some thousands of cards are posted on homes which read: *"Esta familia es catolica: se suplica a los protestantes no la molesten."* ("This family is Catholic; Protestants are requested not to trouble it.") The American Conventuals are making an important contribution by building up their new school, the Colegio de San

Francisco, which offers Catholics a strong center for English language training, a desideratum that prompts many Latin American families to send their children to Protestant schools. "We treat the boys here in much the way that we are accustomed to do in the United States and the school spirit is marvelous," explained Father David, the rector. Some 40 per cent of the Franciscan Conventuals of the United States are in mission work.

Protestantism counts 38,000 followers in Nicaragua. The Baptist hospital in Managua enjoys a high reputation for its splendid staff and the Baptist college, in the capital, one of the Protestants explained to me, "competed for excellence with the Jesuit college in Granada."

The Baptists, however, possess only a minority in Nicaragua. The major unit in the Protestant family belongs to the Moravians out on the Meskito Coast who have worked here industriously for over a century, since 1849. (The Moravians, it is interesting to recall, were the first Protestant sect to preach the Gospel and had little company in this activity until the end of the eighteenth century.)

The Meskito Coast does not get its name, as one might suppose, from the notorious hard-biting insect. It comes, rather, from an Indian tribe that has long lived along this 350-mile eastern shoreline bathed by the waters of the Caribbean. It is a remote and meager region possessing a labyrinth of lagoons that in the lusty days gone by provided perfect hiding places for pirates.

When the first band of American Capuchins arrived in 1939 the Moravians were quite active and Catholic ministrations in the area had been poor for a period of many years. Bishop Niedhammer, the present Capuchin leader, came with this first group. A born missionary, he fell in love at first sight with both the long neglected people and the hurricane-ridden area and today Catholic life has been restored.

At Siuna the Maryknoll Sisters have the Capuchin idea to stir the people to do better for themselves and their families as they conduct a school that seeks to give these country folk a spark of initiative. Fathers Roderick Brennan and Norbert Elsman, with whom I stayed during my visit, operate the mission and have worked wonders persuading men to use plows, to practice foresight that will keep their families from starvation.

"What are your relations with the Moravians?" I asked Father Roderick.

"We can speak only well of them," he replied. "They have trained native workers and feel deeply for all these people. Some day, God willing, the things that keep them separate from us will pass away."

The government of Honduras gives chilly treatment to the Church in that it has disowned practically any connection with it. The constitution of 1936 guarantees free exercise of religion to all and Searle Bates in his study of religious freedom states that in Honduras Protestantism encounters less opposition than in other Latin American republics. Divorce is legalized and cemeteries are secularized. The Protestant population is reported as 22,000.

El Salvador, smallest of the Central American republics, possesses a modest Protestant movement, with a total of 29,000 followers. The Baptists represent the only major church with a vigorous program but the Pentecostals, notably the Assemblies of God, have recently attracted the greatest attention.

Guatemala presents quite a different picture as regards Protestant strength. Its total of followers reaches 143,000 in a population of 3,500,000, with concentrations in the larger centers.

"We recently made a survey of our cathedral parish," Bishop Gonzales of Quezaltenango, second largest city in Guatemala, explained to me. "We found that 13 per cent of its population has Protestant affiliations. Of the 20,000 couls, 2,700 were reported as interested in one or other Protestant sect."

With a national average of 4 per cent, the Bishop's example is exceptional. Nevertheless it dramatizes the growth of Protestantism in certain segments of the population.

Since the days of the dictator Rufino Barrios, beginning in 1871, the Church has faced strong Liberal opposition in Guatemala. In the late 1940s clever leftist leaders began to flirt quite boldly with Moscow. With the help of outsiders, including the United States, the leftists were overthrown and Castillo Armas came to power in 1954. Most of the old restrictive legislation against the Church remains on the books but a strong new feeling toward greater appreciation of spiritual values has awakened in the nation.

"Turning the country over to the Communists was going too far," explained Walter Widmer, a Guatemalan graduate of Santa Clara University in California. "Even the more extreme Liberals were not prepared to set up an anti-God regime. Their fight with the Church has been aimed not against principles of dogma or morality, but at the control of the politico-social institutions. In the old Spanish regime the Church controlled all of these institutions—education, hospitals, charitable organizations, the registration of births, marriages, deaths, the custody of our mortal remains in the cemetery after death. The new concept of the state that came with the French Revolution brought a struggle with the Church on this control. The Liberals see this control as the essence of the struggle and in the fight they of course invade areas unquestionably belonging to the Church. But while a few of them give lip service to atheism, these are very few indeed, so much so that when the Reds reared their heads here, the majority cried, 'Oh no, not this! We are against clerical pretensions but we are not against God.' The Reds created a swing back toward religion and toward the Church in Guatemala."

Some Guatemalan Liberals look with kindly eye on Protestantism as Christianity without the Church. "Guatemala is one of the widest open countries in Latin America," reads a Presbyterian statement of 1947. "Her Liberal governors do everything necessary to insure religious freedom both in theory and practice. The relations of the Presbyterian mission with the government have been marked by the warmest cordiality."

Some twenty-five different groups coordinated by a comity pact are at work in the country. A memorial presented by the Protestants to the government in July 1954 spoke of the "200 North Americans" in their personnel ranks but there were in addition over 300 Guatemalans among their missionaries, a total of more than 500. Thus Protestant forces heavily outnumbered the approximately 153 Catholic priests and the 178 religious at work in the country at that date.

The united hierarchy of the six Central American republics in their joint pastoral of May 27, 1956, allude to this question of personnel. "Our basic problem, which cannot be ignored," the bishops say, "is that of vocations and the formation of a sufficiency of good priests eminently apostolic in spirit. Not that we do not already possess many good priests; it is rather that the field of labor is so immense. To care for it we require an increase of at least one hundred per cent in selfless workers of the Gospel."

Protestantism in Mexico. The first morning of my initial visit to

Mexico City the driver of my taxi had his wife in the front seat with him and the pair of them related instances during the religious persecution of the 1930s when they helped hide priests and participated in other ways in the underground of that day. "Every family has its stories, Padre," the driver remarked. "Those who suffered are still heroes among us." A well-to-do family in a provincial town showed me the secret room in their extensive home. "This is still called the priest's room," the head of the house explained. "We had anxious days when we had a priest on the run hidden here." A bishop with whom I stayed was the prison cell companion of a priest who was shot at the time of Father Pro. "With a knife," His Excellency recalled, "he cut a calendar into the wall and canceled out each day on it until his last. He had marvelous courage."

Catholic Mexico still lives in the aftermath of these days of struggle. The religious garb is still forbidden. When in 1955 I visited Colegio Guadalupe, conducted by the Benedictine Sisters of Achison, Kansas, Mother Mildred, the very capable president of this school for 1,800 girls, wore lay dress. "It was heartbreaking for us to put aside the Benedictine garb," she explained. Happily, good friends among Mexico City's society matrons warned the Sisters against wearing dowdy, tasteless garb as a substitute. "It would only convey the impression," they explained, "that Sisters are people who don't know how to pick out proper clothes." Mother Mildred made a handsome figure with her well groomed gray hair, her black suit and her shirtwaist tastefully ornamented with a red and white flower design.

In no other Latin American country is there a history of such bitter strife between the state and the Church as in Mexico. Mexico is strongly Indian and during the colonial period the Church was the only protector of the Indian. The Mexican Indian has had an ardent love for his Catholic religion and a simple trust in the priest. In the Church-state struggles great numbers of Indians stood unquestioningly with the priest.

The major contest began with the coming to power of the Liberals in 1855 and more specifically with the constitution of 1857 and the consequent War of the Reform. The revolution of 1910 was a renewal of the contest but some of the bitterest battles occurred in the 1930s. Avila Camacho on coming to power in 1940 did much of the effective work to calm the storm. "In most extraordinary fashion," a Mexican gentleman explained to me, "the Church-state conflict melted away when Avila Camacho uttered three words, *'Yo soy creyente'* ('I am a believer'). His declaration that he was a Catholic worked magic in appeasing the anger and soothing the anxiety." The postwar period in Mexico has been marked by religious peace and by a remarkable resurgence of religious life.

Protestantism received encouragement from many of the Liberals. Benito Juarez, the "Father of the Reform" took the position that his fellow Indians should be "Protestantized." He charged Churchmen with failing to educate the Indian and said the Indian needed a religion that would "teach them to read and not to waste their earnings on lighting candles to the saints."

Other Liberal leaders, such as Lerdo de Tejada, Ocampo, Carranza, Madero and Calles were friendly defenders of the Protestants or their public promoters. Calles at one time took a position against them but not for a long period. Portes Gil and Lazaro Cardenas were friendly.

Avila Camacho in addition to declaring himself a believer made other declarations favorable to the Church but never for that reason unfavorable to Protestantism. "There is no religious problem in Mexico," he stated. "Our Constitution recognizes, among other liberties, the liberty of all religious believers and in our country the great majority of these belong to the Catholic Church." Miguel Aleman, Camacho's successor, was friendly to the Church and likewise a friend of Protestantism since his mother was a fervent Methodist and he himself had attended Protestant Sunday School.

The *Christian World Handbook* for 1958 reports the Protestant figure for Mexico as 911,000 in the current population of 30,000,000, or 3 per cent of the whole. Protestant activity in Mexico today is at an all-time high.

"The breakdown of our Protestant mission work in the Far East and the Pacific," wrote Baez Camargo in 1949, "has proven a genuine gain for Mexico. Already the number of missionaries and the economic resources have increased substantially in our direction. New societies have entered Mexico; young workers have come to reinforce the labors of the veterans, who work more and more with Mexican cooperators."

Greatest Protestant attention is given to the capital but at least half a dozen other sections of the country represent areas of major effort. The Presbyterians take first place in the size of their operation with establishments in twenty-two states organized into nine Presbyteries, the equivalent of Catholic dioceses. The Presbyterian Publishing House in Mexico City is a huge enterprise. The Presbyterian Church operates four secondary schools (in Mexico City, Veracruz, Merida and Campeche), eight Bible schools for training its ministers and a number of hospitals and other institutions.

Methodism is highly pleased with its Mexican development. "With the exception of Brazil," a recent statement reads, "the Methodist Church is making its most rapid and solid Latin American advances in Mexico."

The Baptist Church has had greater difficulty than other sects because its program of religious instruction in its schools runs counter to Mexican law. Adaptations have been made and the program has been changed to include other lines of effort. The Baptist Publishing House in El Paso, Texas, is one of the major Protestant establishments of its kind serving Latin America. Impressively substantial physical plants are a characteristic of the efforts of a large number of the more than thirty Protestant societies at work in Mexico.

Most ambitious of all the projects promoted by the Protestants in Mexico is the Federal District headquarters of the Summer School of Linguistics which has its link with the University of Oklahoma. As already explained, this organization had its origin through the initiative of the Rev. William Townsend and the sponsorship of President Lazaro Cardenas. Its quarters in Mexico City are in the Wycliff Bible Translators' Institute. Its staff of specialists totals 200 to 250, some with fixed residence in the capital while the others are scattered throughout fourteen Mexican states where vernacular language problems are prominent. The scientific achievements in the way of dictionaries, grammars, folklore studies, Bible translations are formidable. The Institute's 1955 catalog lists 362 titles, not all of these pertaining to Mexico but all bearing on pre-Columbian culture. Here is authentic science put to work by Protestant enterprise.

Protestantism in the Dominican Republic. Protestants entered this Caribbean land in 1889 but characterize it as "the neglected land" since even today their staff is small and their efforts quite restricted.

The total Protestant membership is listed as 23,000, in a population of 2,000,000.

An outstanding Protestant institution is the International Hospital of Trujillo which enjoys high prestige for its fine techniques. The nurses' training school connected with the hospital likewise is known for its high standards. "Our young ladies," explains a staff member, "work not only in the principal cities of the country with the Department of Health and on the sugar plantations but likewise are sought after in other Latin American lands and even in the United States."

The Protestant radio station HIN operates daily programs such as "The Voice of Prophecy" and "The Voice of the Gospel." The literature program follows established lines. A visiting Catholic describes his experience in a bookshop in Trujillo where the zealous Protestant clerk asked him if he was an "Evangelical" and then delivered a sermonette to him on reading the Bible and on "giving himself completely to the Lord."

Protestantism in Haiti. Haiti figures as a field of special Protestant success since within its population of 3,000,000, its total membership is calculated at 313,000 better than 10 per cent.

Little happened of note in Protestant annals until the U.S. Marines landed in 1915 for their stay of twenty years as policemen and bookkeepers for the disorganized regime. Latourette observes, "Protestant presence in Haiti cannot be called effective until that fact." Landsheer states, "Protestant influence in Haiti developed from the North American occupation of 1915."

"The occupation," writes a Protestant missionary, "constituted a source of benefits for Haiti. Its presence served to teach the people their first lessons in tolerance and good neighborliness. Our activities have developed since then at a rhythm which grows stronger each day. It has been—as in Cuba and the Philippines—one of the beneficial results of the presence here, even though only temporary, of the greatest Protestant power in the world."

Much more important for actual gains, however, would seem to be the stepped-up activities of Protestant groups during and since World War II, encouraged by elements in the Haitian government for the social and economic advantages that their poverty-stricken people might obtain. Dumarsaid Estime, as Haiti's Minister of Education, invited Frank Laubach, originally a missionary in the Philippines, to introduce into Haiti his celebrated system for conquering illiteracy. When he became President in 1946 Dumarsaid asked a Baptist missionary then heading the Haitian Independent Bible Society to push the development of education throughout the country. This gentleman was given the freedom to choose other Protestants as his assistants.

Protestantism in Cuba. Protestants in Cuba total some 200,000 or 4 per cent of the population of 5,000,000. The recent survey of a group of Cuban Catholic Actionists characterized the composition of the Protestant body as follows: (1) the majority are culturally of a lower level, belonging to rural areas and isolated barrios; (2) a minority, but by far the most important element, comes from the younger sectors of the population, of middle class stock, often well off financially, who today are not ashamed, as in times gone by, to belong to the Evangelical family. It is this second element that gives the cachet to Protestantism in Cuba.

Cuba and Puerto Rico were the only Spanish colonies in which, thanks to the petition of a colporteur of Bibles, Pedro Duarte, Protestants by royal cedula were permitted to establish themselves, although under severe restrictions. Little use was made of the permission except by a few Episcopalians.

The strong influx came after the American occupation in 1898. In addition to contingents of the various churches and the YMCA, large numbers of the 2,000 American teachers who entered the island were Protestant. Their supervisor was Mrs. Alice Gordon, a former missionary in South America. The country has been regarded as a key approach to the Latin American world. "We must consider Cuba," wrote Mr. Brooks, a Methodist missionary, some years ago, "as a gateway to the rest of South America . . . A well organized mission in this country would greatly strengthen the cause of Protestantism in all the other republics."

Today the total of Protestant missionaries, counting the churches which report and those which do not report, is estimated at 1,200. Particularly since World War II the Pentecostals have put considerable forces to work in the countryside. The major churches use few non-Cubans now in other than administrative posts.

The special strength of the Protestant effort is its great network of well organized colleges. In 1956 these totaled 98 with an enrollment of 14,000 students. Catholic colleges count an enrollment of 67,000 in 245 centers but the profound impact made on Cuban life by the Protestant educational system must be recognized.

"Today," runs a Catholic commentary, "Protestant colleges such as Candler, Buenavista, San Pablo of Camaguey, the International College and La Progresiva of Cardenas have acquired national rank and their alumni figure in the country's economy, in the magistracy and even in the Secretariat of Education. From the technical and pedagogical viewpoint some of these schools compare with the best among the Catholic institutions.

"Unquestionably, La Progresiva College represents the intellectual center of Cardenas. Its professorial body is eminently capable, counting brilliant and highly specialized staff members. Its zone of influence extends far beyond the city limits. Its alumni are found everywhere in the republic and its professors are called everywhere to give conferences. It is no exaggeration to call it the most important Protestant center in Cuba."

The same authority notes the following regarding these Protestant colleges: (1) the possession of a well prepared teaching personnel conscious of its duties; (2) the emphasis given to the English language (Catholic institutions such as the University of Villanova conducted by the American Augustinians in Havana are ably striving to meet this need); (3) the prominence given to sports; (4) the moral discipline which Protestant schools seek to maintain; (5) the financial generosity that insures good salaries to professors and numerous scholarships for students; (6) solicitude in placing their graduates, either in careers in the United States or in remunerative posts in the homeland.

A most interesting and almost wholly unexpected reaction from the growing recognition of the strength of Protestantism in Cuba is a movement of vigorous apostolic effort on the part of younger elements among Cuban Catholics.

"Cuban Catholicism today," states the recent Catholic Action survey, "finds itself in a better position and better prepared to defend the faith than ever before. A great forward step has been taken though much remains yet to be done. Catholic Action lately has given backbone to the Catholic lay apostolate and Catholics generally have at their disposal a better stock of religious information and better practical guidance. As a result, the Catholic position more frequently receives consideration and respect at the hands of public opinion."

Protestantism in Puerto Rico. The Protestant population of Puerto Rico percentage-wise is admittedly high. Over 6 per cent of the inhabitants, 147,000 in a total of 2,350,000, have enrolled in one or other of the sects.

"Protestantism," states a European Catholic student of the question, "has naturalized itself in Puerto Rico to a greater extent than in any other country of Latin America." In less than half a century the greater part of the Protestant pulpits in Puerto Rico have passed into the hands of Puerto Ricans. The Presbyterians, as an example, state that they no longer have any church on the island assigned to a North American minister. The record of the other churches runs high on native-born ministers. "Probably in no other area of the world," states a Protestant writer, "have we been witnesses to such an advance in such a short period of time."

Catholic clergy on the island total some 350 while the auxiliary religious, both Brothers and Sisters, who assist them bring the figure of those who seek to meet the spiritual needs of the Catholics to well over a thousand. Of these, some 600 are from the United States, the largest concentration of American Catholic personnel in any political division of the world outside the United States mainland. However, a great portion of this personnel has been in the island a relatively short time, a fact which leads the European Catholic authority already quoted to comment on the poor performance of the Church in the United States in meeting the Puerto Rican situation.

"Without caring to do injury to North American Catholics," he states, "whom I admire greatly after my happy sojourn among them, I regret to say that they are culpable in part for the state of affairs in Puerto Rico. During many years the number of priests sent from the United States (responsible for the spiritual care of its colony) was entirely insufficient.

"In the educational effort, things have gone better. Many parishes have an adjoining parochial school. Hundreds of Sisters from the United States occupy Puerto Rican classrooms. Catholics have opened colleges and the Catholic University in Ponce is now a glorious reality.

In this field the North Americans enjoy well merited prestige everywhere in the world."

American Catholic leaders in Puerto Rico place the blame on U.S. government policy for the spiritual turn of events. "Puerto Rico," writes Bishop McManus, the American Redemptorist who heads the Diocese of Ponce, "is a Catholic people that is the victim of a group of officials who, abusing their power and the public funds, have undertaken to destroy the beliefs of the inhabitants . . . United States policy has aimed from the beginning to destroy the philosophy and religious traditions of Puerto Rico. For this, it merits no other name than that of the spiritual killer of that nation."

Since 1899 Protestantism has been free to establish itself in Puerto Rico without restriction. This has led Millham to observe that the island provides a "living example" of what Protestantism can accomplish when it is able to operate "under equality of conditions with the Church of Rome."

The Protestant churches, contrary to the policy in Cuba, did not undertake to establish a network of private schools. Rather, they have operated well organized teacher training institutions that have supplied large numbers of the public school staffs throughout the island. The educational administrators from Washington have almost always been Protestant. "From the beginning," states José M. Lazaro of Puerto Rico, "the Protestants have been in possession of the key posts in education. Only once during fifty years was the educational commissioner other than a Protestant and some were former Protestant ministers."

Protestant effort in Puerto Rico has gone into hospitals, clinics and dispensaries. Outstanding institutions are Ryder Memorial Hospital of Humacao; St. Luke's of Ponce; the hospital of the Brethren in Lares; Saludy Vida of Mayaguez; the Presbyterian Hospital of San Juan.

An additional point of difference between Catholics and Protestants in Puerto Rico has been the collaboration which many of these Protestant hospitals have given to the program promoted by the government since 1937 for birth control and sterilization. The "Catholic conscience" has been regarded as the major obstacle to the program.

SECTION FIVE

Vignettes of Middle America

• • ● • •

Chapter 1

Knock on Any Door

WE DID NOT KNOCK because there was no door. The structure we entered in the heart of the slums of the city of Colon in Panama was a *barracone*. It consisted of a long, unlighted corridor of single-room apartments. Each room had a small window looking out on a dark alley. One toilet at the end of the corridor served the score or so of families. There was likewise a single water spigot to which the families came with containers to serve all their cooking and their washing needs.

Part way down the corridor, Father Lynch gently tapped on a door panel. There was no sound from within, no response to the knock. The priest tapped again. Still no evidence of life.

"It is Father, Miriam," Father Lynch called through the door, "I have a visitor to see Maria."

Now the key turned in the lock and an anxious Negro face peered out through a slit of the cautiously opened door.

"I'm so sorry, Father. You usually come in the morning. I thought it was someone tricking me."

"I'm the one to be sorry that I had to frighten you, Miriam. This is an American priest friend. I want him to give Maria his blessing."

"How kind you are, Father Lynch!"

A bed stood at right angles some three feet from the door. On a tipsy little table near its head stood a smudgy oil lamp, easy prey for the careless pass of a hand to upset it and start a flash fire. A few feet beyond hung a piece of sheeting which served as a curtain for a second bed. A tiny kerosene cookstove stood near the window. No ornament broke the unrelievedly bleak walls.

Lying in the first bed was a large-boned but emaciated Negro woman, her dull eyes half closed, who struggled for breath. She had a cancerous obstruction in her throat that was inviting death. Father Lynch had anointed her the previous day. This was Maria. Miriam, who now stood at the foot of the bed, was a somewhat younger woman but already in her sixties.

"We've been together so many years," Miriam murmured, "ever since the fire."

"She refers to one of Colon's great fires," Father Lynch explained, "that destroyed many tenements years ago."

Maria strove to describe her desperate state but the words would not come out. The priest quieted her, smiled at her reassuringly.

"Just remember your lovely prayer that you've repeated to me so often, Maria—'My heart beats with Christ's heart, with sweet Mother Mary's heart.' Live each moment to offer that heart beat, Maria. Soon God will press you to His Heart."

Miriam went to the head of the bed, stroked Maria's forehead tenderly. Each of us priests gave Maria a blessing.

"Good night, Maria. Good night, Miriam," whispered Father Lynch. "God love you."

A shoal of youngsters spun and shrieked in the street outside. We walked, each with his own thoughts, until a couple of blocks further on Father Lynch stopped at a sidewalk door that should have led into a shop but which instead opened into the one-room apartment of Margarita.

"Good evening! Good evening!" cried Father Lynch as he swung back the door and faced a little old lady in a big chair who evidently was practically blind but who immediately on hearing the voice cried out "Father Lynch!" and gave forth an avalanche of gay words and laughter that ended with, "There's only one Father Lynch in all the world."

"Ah, there's only one sly and foxy Margarita in all the world!" retorted Father Lynch.

A young lady who stood cooking at a kerosene stove that burned full blast joined in the laughter.

"Violet, how do you happen to be here?" Father asked.

"I come every day at this time and prepare Auntie a meal," the girl replied.

"How, conceivably, can you do all that you do?" remarked the priest in evident admiration. Violet, he explained later, was a "saint," a Legion of Mary girl who gave every spare moment outside working hours to the sick.

"How old are you, Margarita?" I asked the bright-eyed lady.

"Ninety-two, Father," she replied. "No longer able to dance the pollera but I find my way to St. Joseph's every morning."

"For more than sixty years," intervened Father Lynch, "Margarita has visited the sick in this neighborhood and she has made more people laugh than a circus clown. God be with you both. Good night!"

"You have all kinds in the parish," I commented to Father Lynch.

"Yes—all kinds of good people, Father, and most of them poor. St. Joseph's is the best parish in Panama for the religious life of its people; ninety per cent of the families have been married in the Church. We Vincentians are proud of it."

Before I knew it I was several flights up a giddy outside stairway of a multistoried building of cheap apartments. Finally we stepped onto a slanted porch so rickety that I wondered if it would hold. We turned a corner and were in the one-room apartment of an aged couple, Emilio of Martinique and Maria of Guadeloupe, both French speaking. Maria stood over a pot on the stove.

"What an honor!" cried Maria. "You must take some of my delicious soup."

"No. This American Father wants only the pleasure of meeting two wonderful people like you. They have raised eight fine children, Father, who now are scattered about Panama. They have never had much except their spirit of gaiety but as you can see, they have a simple but very gay little home here."

True enough. The room held considerable furniture but was particularly notable for its bright ornamentation.

"No one need feel sorry for that couple," remarked Father Lynch as we left. "They have the fine good humor of their race. There is a small colony of Guadeloupians here in Panama that operates a benefit society, principal task of which is to bury the dead. Like most of the world's little people, life for them adds up to a sprinkling of joy, much patience, a great deal of hard work, the thought of God and eternity, and then the grave."

I recalled often this evening with Father Lynch as I journeyed through Middle America. This complex area of mainland and islands between the northern and southern continents counts over fifty million inhabitants. Immensely wealthy families are among them, learned people, men of great talents. But for me the fondest memories turn about the millions who rank as the shirtless ones, the plain folk of city and country, who have little and expect little but who deserve the main attention of us who appreciate the things of the spirit. We can count them still on our side but they can easily be captured by the angry radicals of evil intent unless we insist on making their lives more meaningful.

A parish that reminded me of St. Joseph's in Colon was El Cristo of Havana. El Cristo is in the heart of the Old City in the great capital of Cuba. Its church possesses one of the most beautiful façades in all Latin America, dating back more than 300 years, and is graced with a lovely interior as well. Alongside the church is Cristo Park with its grove of gorgeous tropical trees, the flamboyants.

"Things go very well with us," explained Father John J. McKniff of the American Augustinians, "if you'll take the pains to understand what we mean when we say this. We carry the handicap here of a bad past. The clergy have long been too few and here in Cuba many churchmen are accused of having stood with Spain and fought against independence. Until 1920 a church-going man was ridiculed in Cuba and condemned as unpatriotic."

"Have things changed any?" I asked.

"Very much so. Today a substantial number of people of every class in Cuba, but particularly among the poor have recaptured an affection for their religion."

"What class of people have you in El Cristo Parish?"

"Of the 15,000 parishioners, two-thirds are poor and the remainder are lower or upper middle class except for a handful of wealthy. The great majority are poor; as the days pass take note of how they live."

My immediate observation as we moved about was the heartiness and joviality of the street people. Havana has less of the desperate poverty found elsewhere. The distinctive form of cheap lodging in Cuba is the *solar,* a hollow square of single-room apartments around a patio. The multistoried variety is called the neighborhood house, the *casa de vecindad.*

"The ramshackle structures are being torn down but not without protests from the proprietors," explained Father McKniff. "They lose money on the deal. A single room in a *solar,* with no facilities expected, brings $25 a month. The modern apartment, which is much more expensive to build and far more space-consuming, brings only $85 to $90. Hence many owners hold out for the old."

We entered a spectacularly constructed neighborhood house where most of the thirty families who lived behind the three-storied porches that lined three sides of the patio seemed to be leaning over the rail. Young and old waved down to the Padre while everybody in the well-filled courtyard had a friendly word. Evidently some housewives found it better to cook in the yard. "Take a peep here!" one woman called gaily and showed us her delicious-looking and savory-smelling stew of meat, potatoes and beans.

"There are blocks and blocks of these fine folk living in neighborhood houses," observed Father McKniff.

"What about their religious life?" I asked.

"In their own way they've always had a great deal of religion. Most have had no priests so they've practiced at home. Among them, all-night vigils with prayer for the dead were and still are common. These are called *velorios,* home devotions that are often badly dosed with superstitions and sometimes with abuses. We estimate that even today 10,000 *velorios* a year are conducted in homes of the parish. But we are getting the folk back to Sunday worship. Over 25 per cent of the parish, some 4,000 people, now come to Mass."

"Are private functions on the decline?"

"No, not at all. The people love home devotion. I find a few moments every evening to join one or other of the neighborhood groups that meet in homes or in the patio of a neighborhood house. There will be forty or fifty at these gatherings to recite the rosary."

"How much charity for one's neighbor do you find in the parish?"

"A surprisingly great deal. I think the finest example is our school, entirely a product of parish zeal."

"What is special about it?" I asked.

"The fact that a substantial portion of the cost of construction and all of the teaching is supplied by the people of the parish. A group of dedicated women led by Imelda Rivero gets the credit for bringing into being this second parochial school in all Cuba. The first belongs to the Dominican parish at Vedado. Imelda ranked high in her college graduation class and normally would have gotten a job as a government teacher. She undertook instead to make a modest beginning for the parish school. From the start she established perfect discipline and won the confidence of the parents. Teaching Sisters were out of the question for us but as the school grew other women teachers in the parish took posts at great financial sacrifice. Today we have twelve classrooms headed by lay teachers living on substandard salaries out of devotion to this enterprise. Government authorities offered Imelda a major educational post at a handsome salary. I told her to take it. She broke down and cried. 'I'd rather die than leave these children,' she answered."

In each classroom every child has a uniform and shoes. "Some $2,000 a year goes into clothing to permit the youngsters to come to school," Father McKniff explained.

For North Americans who are tempted to feel that they hold a monopoly on generosity it is interesting to know that modestly fixed middle class people are the sinews of El Cristo school. Jesus Pernas, owner of the Saturnia department store in the parish, inquired one day how the poor were able to go to school at El Cristo. As a result he began contributing $75 a month and his encouragement of his employees brought an additional $50 a month. Thus from this one local source the desire to join sacrifice with sacrifice brought $1,500 a year.

But the grade school is not all that El Cristo offers in education.

Maria Dolores Espina, another young teacher in the parish, became interested in building up a night school. She is a gregarious spirit, a maker of warm friends, a winner of confidence, an inspirer to fine ideals. Today she heads a staff of twenty-five Havana teachers each of whom gives three nights a week of precious time gratis for the operation of the El Cristo school for adults in which 400 members of the parish are enrolled.

At nine o'clock one evening I went to the social hall of the El Cristo Young Christian Workers. Games, chats and a little music were in progress, and two young fellows were on a ladder finishing a paint job. In a cubby off the hall an older boy was conducting an instruction class.

"Good evening, Padre," said a young man with a bright smile, "I am Orlando Martinez. Welcome to our quarters."

"Orlando is the president of El Cristo Y.C.W.," explained Father McKniff. "Thanks to him our section has been labeled the best in Cuba. And thanks to him hundreds of young fellows in the parish are living Christian lives both in their factories and with their families."

There are more examples of commendably strong religious life in Middle America than is commonly recognized. One such center hidden away in a quiet corner of Puerto Rico is the Redemptorist parish of Cagues, outside San Juan. It counts 73,000 people, 40,000 in the urban area and 33,000 in the *campo*. Seven to ten American Redemptorists are constantly on duty and supply eighteen Masses a Sunday, ten in the city and eight in the country. An estimated 30 per cent of those in a position to attend Sunday worship do so. Of the 15,000 children of school age a thousand are being trained in the parish schools.

"Perhaps our people show up best in their Legion of Mary work," noted Father McGrone, the pastor. "It has been organized now for twenty years and we have eleven units of about twenty members each. Their principal activity for the past several years has been house to house visitation. We can credit these good people with reducing greatly the number of carelessly entered unions without church marriages."

"Nocturnal adoration of the Blessed Sacrament in this parish is also outstanding," explained Father Gildea who was my companion on my visit. "Exposition takes place at six every Friday morning and townsfolk make visits during the day. There is a Holy Hour at 7:30 Friday evening and then teams of adorers, including many groups of men, pray in turn through the night until six o'clock on Saturday morning."

Throughout Middle America there is widespread evidence of the popularity of worship of Christ in the Blessed Sacrament. The Papal Delegate to Mexico cited the very beautiful example of a village of 200 Tarahumara Indians in northern Mexico who team up to mount perpetual guard before the Blessed Sacrament in their church throughout the year.

Most extraordinary in this line in recent years was the outpouring of 60,000 men to receive Holy Communion at the Men's Mass at midnight during the Second National Eucharistic Congress at San José in the little country of Costa Rica in 1955.

From early morning on Wednesday men began gathering in crowds at the San José churches in order to go to confession. As late afternoon approached it became evident that the ordinary facilities established for confession were completely inadequate. Hence some very extraordinary ones had to be resorted to. Makeshift confessionals were set up in neighborhood factories, in schools, at the airport and in the San José Central Park. Along several principal avenues automobiles and jeeps were made to serve. Visiting bishops and archbishops as well as all available priests were employed as confessors. As the hour of Mass approached and men faced the prospect of not being shriven, any priest who appeared was literally mobbed.

The ceremony proved to be the greatest spiritual event in the history of Costa Rica. "This San Jose Men's Mass is much more significant than it may appear," commented a prelate who attended, "and this for two reasons. First, it emphasizes the strong and growing accent on worship of Christ in the Eucharist in Latin America as distinct from widespread veneration of the saints during days when priests were practically unavailable. Secondly, the congress reveals the strong trend among the men back to the active practice of their faith."

I took the occasion of my visit to Costa Rica's congress to ride out from San José to celebrated Turrialba. Turrialba is the seat of the Inter-American Institute of Agricultural Sciences, a special agency of the Organization of American States. The Institute possesses a sightly central building for research and administration and 2,500 acres of crop and cattle land for experimentation.

My companion on the road to Turrialba was Bishop Perres Hernandez, Auxiliary Bishop of Bogotá, a very pleasant person whose deep devotion to the rural people of his homeland is illustrative of another factor in the Middle American scene on which I wish to comment.

"I've come to Turrialba to look for a cow," explained the Bishop. "The small farmer of the country area in which I am interested needs dairy products from an animal that will not cost too much to keep, that will stay healthy in the uplands, that can be used for meat and meat products when the farmer wants to slaughter it for such purposes. Hence, my dear Padre, I'm searching for a cow—my kingdom for a cow!"

At Turrialba I watched the Bishop searching for his cow. He saw the carefully raised Jersey and Guernsey stock in the experimental herds. He saw also the handsome specimens of the new Santa Gertrudis stock from Texas. The Bishop carefully gathered information on cattle to report to his people back home.

"Your Excellency," I remarked at one point in our conversation. "It is wonderful to find you so engrossed in these day to day needs of your people."

"Padre," His Excellency replied, "it's a way of doing that is in the air today everywhere in Latin America, in my country quite as here in Middle America. We are all concerned with what makes people stronger, healthier, better fed, better schooled, better prepared to live life wisely, better able to be faithful to their religion. Anyone genuinely interested in man as man knows that a people that is broken by social wrongs and weaknesses can't properly worship its God."

It is the whole man that thoughtful people are trying to help in Latin America today. So often I found examples of the priest who respected the technician but, as well, of the technician who respected the role that the man of the Church must play if a fuller, richer life is to belong to the people of Latin America.

Dr. Justo Morales, the Director of Economics and Welfare at Turrialba, demonstrated how from a purely practical angle he as a technician recognized these related roles. He drove us through the countryside surrounding the experimental station, a district comprising some twenty-five communities.

"These people here are probably the most surveyed people on the globe," the Doctor remarked. "Happily they enter into the inquiries with gusto, so well have they been sold on the idea of helping others."

"What do you think you've established by your inquiries?" I asked.

"I think we've determined that the key idea that must grow in every community is the recognition by its guides and leaders that the community already contains within itself much of the abilities and resources whereby it may improve itself provided the local leadership is able to galvanize this latent power into action."

"Who do you regard as the guides and leaders in a community?"

"They are the teacher, the priest, the county agent, the agricultural extension agent, the community officials, the citizens with the influence or the knack for stimulating the people to better community work. They are the persons both foreign and native to the community who can whip up the local will to live better."

"What should be the role of the priest, Your Excellency," I asked Bishop Perres Hernandez, "in a typical community such as we are considering?"

"I tell my priest," he replied, "that he should not presume that he is automatically the community leader. He should take his place in the socio-economic program as one who has an intelligent knowledge of it but whose role is to encourage others. His role is to guard the Christian principles involved. He should constantly be stirring his people but he should take the village leadership only after being chosen by the community members when they can't agree on a layman from among themselves."

Morales and all others who have the full life of the *campesino* at heart deprecate any unbalanced emphasis on one or other phase of the socio-economic program such as cooperatives alone. "The school program counts," Morales notes, "the agricultural extension agent, the organizer of cooperatives, the social worker, the health officer. The spiritual and moral principles, then, that are represented by the priest should impregnate it all."

By force of circumstances many priests interest themselves in this socio-economic program. "I worked for nine years in my parish," explained Padre Pastor Escalante of Tixkokob in Yucatan, "I built up the life of devotion, I organized my sodalities, I provided a very popular sports center with an illuminated court for night basketball. I trained a dramatic club that's so successful that we are invited every year to perform in Merida. But all to no avail. I could not stifle the conviction that kept gnawing me that to perform properly my religious duties I could not justifiably avoid the socio-economic problems of my people. 'They will be more Christian,' I found myself repeating, 'if their living conditions can be a little more human.'

"The people earn a bare 25 pesos a week here. They have land, but very poor soil, poor poultry, poor diet of tortillas and chile. I determined on a quiet, modest program of domestic activities for the individual home that would aim primarily to strengthen the Christian family."

The dilemma of this excellent Mexican priest is typical. He is city bred, one of eight brothers in a good family of Merida. He is strong and hefty, with clear eyes and a thoughtful face that bespeak quiet good judgment. He abhorred the prospect of creating a furore by engaging in any unusual activity and dreaded entering a field of which he had no knowledge. But the irrefutable logic of the facts added up to a demand for action.

"I read a great many books and sought technical advice," Padre Escalante explained. "I tried to make myself a specialist in the socio-economic program. Then I began instructing my people in simple ways to better themselves. Latest step is the purchase of a thousand day-old chicks from the United States."

We arrived at Tixkokob a few days after the chicks. Padre Escalante had distributed 20 chicks each to fifty families in the parish who had been previously instructed on exactly how they were to feed them, the temperature at which they must keep the improvised incubators in which the chicks were placed. Various medicines were distributed as recommended by the Heifer Project with instructions for using these as well. A team of ladies in the parish was specially trained to be the inspectors.

"Let's go out and see how things are going with the chicks," proposed the good man, a gleam of excitement in his eye.

Our first stop was at the home of a henequen worker whose wife

Melinda was the new owner of 20 chicks. José, the husband, a big bruiser of a man, opened the door.

"Welcome, Padre," he cried in a loud voice. "I suppose you've come to see how the lady is handling the animals. Well, a queer procedure it all is."

"Welcome, Padre," added Melinda who appeared at this point. "José says he's raised chicks all his life and he never heard of such strange rules as we have."

"What have you done about the rules, Melinda?" the Padre asked quietly.

"Oh, I've followed them to the letter, Padre, I would never disobey a thing you say, Padre, even if José thinks it's all wrong."

"Thank you, Melinda. These rules, José, are very unusual for us here, I know, but this poultry is new for this part of the world. We hope that by being very careful with them we can raise a type, José, that will give us much more meat per animal and more eggs. Be patient with us and our queer ways."

"Of course, of course, Padre," assured José. "We all trust you, Padre, I'm sure you will give us something that will be very helpful."

"Thank you for your vote of confidence, José. I hope that I may be deserving of it."

At the next home two little urchins pulled open the door when Padre knocked and they and two others behind them all screamed with delight when they saw the priest.

"Padre, Padre, Padre!" they cried. "Mama, Padre's here!"

"It's good you came, Padre," said one little girl of seven. "Mama has been awful bad, Padre. You gave us all a big box of beautiful chicks and now mama refuses to let us touch a single one."

"Yes, Padre, she won't even let us look in through the door at them," said another.

"She won't even let us feed them Padre," added a third.

"Thank God you are here, Padre," exclaimed the mother of the excited brood at this juncture as she approached with a big smile on her face and extended her hand. "I had begun to despair of my life, let alone of saving the poor dear chicks. My children are in open rebellion, Padre."

"Now, children dear," exclaimed the bewildered priest, "please don't blame mama for those terrible rules about the chicks. You must blame me."

"Oh, no, no, no. We won't blame you for anything, Padre. We won't blame you."

When, many minutes later, we were on our way again I made my comment to Padre Escalante.

"One thing is quite clear, Padre Escalante: if these people young and old didn't believe implicitly in you you'd have small chance of saving your chicks."

"They are wonderful people."

"How do they pay you for them?" I inquired.

"I have asked them for all the Monday eggs. Nobody in Yucatan works on Monday and, I've explained, neither should the hens. If they do and lay any eggs, I've requested these for the parish. We'll sell them to pay for the next project."

"What will that be?"

"I think we'll start a hammock cooperative."

"A hammock cooperative?"

"Yes. The hemp is a local product and enough to weave a hammock costs five pesos, which the cooperative would supply. Two people can weave a hammock in three or four hours of leisure time. Finished hammocks will be sold by the cooperative to dealers for 10 to 12 pesos apiece."

Disarmingly simple though the thinking of this country priest in Yucatan seems to be, it has a profound potential for Middle America and all Latin America.

"Different men say it in different ways," explained one of the officers at Turrialba, "but all arrive at one great conclusion, namely, that it is the small farmer in the back country and the modest family man of the urban community who must be reached and must be helped to find the way to obtain an income above bare subsistence. Thus quite without knowing it each individual farmer will contribute to the strength of his nation and to the entire Latin American world."

It is fascinating to discover the priests, Brothers and Sisters who in one way or another have entered into this pattern of construction in Middle America.

In 1941 Father John Peter Sullivan of the New England Jesuits got together fourteen young Jamaican clerks and every Tuesday evening for a year he drilled them in the principles of cooperatives and of the Christian social outlook that is necessary as sound basis for cooperatives. With this little group he began a credit cooperative, each member depositing threepence (now four cents) a week into the treasury. Each was free then to borrow up to a British pound as a family loan. He was to pay ten per cent of it back each month with one per cent interest. From this start the Sodality Credit Unions of Jamaica came into being. Today their family loans run into tens of thousands of dollars yearly and their benefits have contributed substantially to the well-being of the Jamaicans they serve.

Out at Seaford Town on the island of Jamaica Father Kempel in 1940 organized fifteen men to market 50 dozen eggs. He had rough going at the start but two years later he had eighty farmers organized in a marketing cooperative selling a thousand dozen eggs a week at a price which allowed a tidy profit for both the merchant and the farmer (previously squeezed out of any reasonable return). Today this first successful marketing cooperative in Jamaica has grown into other enterprises that contribute to the well being of the family folk of Seaford Town.

Then there were the fishermen. Father Sullivan sent three of his Jamaican clerks among them and after patient labor they launched a successful marketing cooperative for these coast people, badly harassed by the middle men who refused them a decent return on their catch. "These clerks were Jamaicans," Father Sullivan explained, "they knew their people well. They had the cooperative vision and felt they were building men and women. This is the pattern by which we lick poverty. And, too, by which we build spiritual quality. Put something substantial in the stomach and, in the ordinary course of events, the prayer on the lips and in the heart will follow."

Mother Mary Alicia and Mother Mary Adele, two remarkable Belgians of the Canonesses of St. Augustine, work among the townsfolk of Roseau on the dreamland island of Dominica whose 60,000 inhabitants belong to the new West Indies Federation.

"Tourists love Dominica," explains Mother Adele, "and they write home about the mountain waterfalls, the deep blue of the Caribbean. But we work behind the scenes, see the broken homes, the hunger, malnutrition, diseases, immorality. The homes are narrow huts. The wages are far below living standards and, despite that, are often squandered. The only way to give our people a better existence is to lift them to a higher economic standard.

"In 1951 Mother Alicia and I, in our rounds as social workers, decided to help these careless, carefree people organize a credit union. We were only women, it is true, but the very fact that we were women in religious garb with no conceivable interest in what they did with their money except to see them use it better made it easy for us to get the men into line and prompt them to save their shillings in the credit union treasury. Today there are twelve credit unions here with a total membership of 3,000."

So outstanding was the work of these two religious that the British authorities secured a study fellowship for Mother Alicia from the United Nations Technical Assistance Agency.

"Our credit unions have had success beyond our fondest expectations," states Mother Alicia. "Men and women of Dominica are generously giving their time and talents for the sheer love of helping the small people of the island to work out a better way of living. We have two aims: first, to make the individual man and woman more efficient through education; secondly, to improve their lot through group action.

"All over the island where credit unions are operating, weekly study groups are organized to train possible leaders in adult education. For instance, the Roseau Credit Union held three discussion evenings weekly for six months at which thirty to forty persons were present. The likely leaders were thus mobilized to organize neighborhood circles of twelve members each to make them better members and increase their savings."

Mother Adele and Mother Alicia have given special attention to making the women better homemakers. "We began the Social League of Catholic Mothers in 1950 with twenty members," Mother Alicia explains. "Now it has five branches on the island with 450 members. We gave the women a goal—'Each community a better place to live in.'

"The League members wanted to learn more about home management, food, clothing, housing. We hit upon reciprocal teaching as an interesting and inexpensive method. For instance, Lily Jones cooks wonderful dishes of fried fish. We got her to give lessons to the others. Matilda Evans does beautiful sewing. She felt very important conducting sewing classes for her neighbors. Then we gave classes in first aid, in prenatal care and in bringing up the baby. We instituted a course of ten lessons for young married couples. Miss Horne, a government nutrition expert, gave two short courses to leaders so that they could pass on nutrition ideas to others."

"Do you feel, Mother," I asked Mother Alicia, "that you've done something for these people that will accomplish lasting good?"

"We think so. Poverty and social injustice are what we have to be afraid of in Dominica as breeders of Communism. We think we are succeeding in giving these people the idea of meeting together to solve their problems through the credit union groups and, among the women, through their League. Even for problems bigger than they can handle themselves they now have a method for meeting and deciding to appeal to the government authorities. As one man puts it, 'We don't feel so helpless now.' "

During my stay in the Dominican Republic, a much larger land than the tiny island with the similar name, Father Harvey Steele of the Scarboro Foreign Missions of Canada drove me from the capital, Trujillo, north to the Royal Valley in the heart of the Cibau. High up on the Santo Cerro we were treated to a superb view of the glorious valley country, rich and green, carpeted with the red flowering amapola tree. The National Shrine of the Sacred Heart tops the mount and an obliging religious showed us the plaque in the floor of the edifice that marks the spot where Christopher Columbus erected a cross over the new-found land of Hispaniola.

"Our valley has been blessed to this day," commented the nun. "We have a rich black loam for a topsoil that in places is five meters deep (16 feet). Our people are simple and unlettered but wonderfully good. We say we have the blackest soil and the whitest souls in the Caribbean."

But the most interesting phenomenon in the Cibau, I would judge, is its cooperatives. And the creator of the cooperatives of the Cibau was my escort, Father Harvey Steele.

"Through this valley from Moca to Santiago," explained Father Harvey as we drove, "we'll find a credit union every five miles. The parish of Macoris has 20 of them."

"How many units have you now in the Dominican Republic?" I asked.

"Our Federation of Cooperatives has presently almost 150 units with over 15,000 members. Some 80 per cent of these are here in the Cibau. The farmers here are simple men who until the law decreed otherwise went without shoes. Now they often come to church carrying their shoes in their hands, ready to put them on if the policeman catches them barefoot. They enjoy a modest prosperity in the valley but traditionally they are terrific gamblers. Now the cooperatives have them saving."

"How much do they save?"

"The goal we set for them is $10 a year. Many don't reach this level but on the other hand one union has reached an average of $58 per member for the year and five other unions averaged between $35 and $45 per member for the year."

"They must take the idea seriously."

"Very seriously. Our experience here corresponds to that of all similar efforts in this part of the world, namely, that for success the cooperative movement has to be something much more than a savings plan. It has to represent a movement with training behind it and with sound moral principles which influence the rank and file."

"Just how do those ideas apply here?" I asked.

"When I began a few years ago I soon heard that the men were saying, 'The Padre doesn't know us; he doesn't know that most of us are not men who keep their word. He's going to fail.' I determined to be sure I didn't fail. I insisted on a half hour's teaching a week for the men for months before I'd let them begin activities. Then I made it a rule that within a year after membership they had to straighten out their marriage if it wasn't in order and they had to go to church on Sunday. The plan worked. There's real enthusiasm and high regard for the cooperatives here today."

"Is it going to last?"

"I think so. The best little piece of evidence in this direction happened to me the other day. I asked a twelve-year-old boy in one of these towns what he wanted to be when he grew up. 'I want to be the president of the cooperative,' he replied. To him the most respected man in town was the man who held that office."

While we were in the city of Santiago we attended the monthly meeting of the Altagracia cooperative and I had my chance to meet one of these presidents. He was Manuel Saulio.

"Manuel," confided Father Steele as the meeting was coming to order, "runs a little factory in town which employs fifteen persons. Since getting into the cooperative movement Manuel has a half hour class in religious instruction on company time at the beginning of each day. He has spent over $400 in the past several years buying shoes for men from the country so that they can come to church and regularize their marriages. He is one of the most respected men in the area."

No priest has any role in the operation of the parish cooperatives; the men must conduct everything themselves. Father Steele gave me a running commentary on men and affairs as the meeting moved along.

"Do you see that young fellow at the end of the second row? That is Francisco Martinis. He is 37 years old. He is an example of what is happening around here. He is a warehouse worker earning $40 a month, a moderately good wage in these parts. He has a good wife and six kids who love him very much but he was providing for them very badly. He used to drink hard and gamble recklessly every weekend. Manuel persuaded him to join the cooperative."

"Francisco experienced a real conversion of life. He was caught up with a passion to keep a good home such as Manuel described at the meetings. He stopped drinking and gambling. He made a deposit every week. He was the first man in the co-op to hold a loan book, the first to pay back the loan, the first to buy a share in the consumers co-op that the Altagracia credit union established. Today his wife can dress neatly, keeps a wonderful home for him quite as Francisco had dreamed of having, and the youngsters are clean and well fed. He's an exceptional example but there are many more like him here in the Dominican Republic."

I took a new look at this priest by my side. The recollection came to me of the statue of Saint Maria Euphrasia in the Good Shepherd Reformatory of San José in Costa Rica, printed below which was Maria Euphrasia's motto handed down as a legacy to her daughters, "A soul is worth more than a world." Father Harvey Steele as well as many another missionary in Middle America is living by Maria Euphrasia's standards.

But more stirring than the missionaries, from whom we have a right to expect a top performance, is the constant discovery of ardor and love and generosity in lowly folk from whom we are ready to expect nothing because God, we mistakenly suppose, has given them so little.

In Concepcion in interior Panama, Father John Cusack of the Vincentians and I stopped at a gas station and a little fellow filled our tank. Father Cusack had a bag of beautiful Boquete oranges and gave one to the boy.

"Oh, thank you, Padre," the youngster smiled and immediately pushed the fruit into his pocket. "I'll bring it home tonight to my little sister. She'll be so happy."

Father Cusack gave him a second one for himself.

"This happens often with me," he remarked as we drove away. "I'm constantly bumping into young people who'll tuck away a candy bar for their little brother or display other beautiful evidences of affectionate attention. I've been converted to the belief that these folk of Central America are a people of fine sensibilities. Knock on any door, enter any home no matter how lowly, and you're almost bound to find someone inside with a touch of Heaven-sent nobility."

Chapter 2

The Mayan without His Priest

I RECALL a Sunday evening ride over country roads between Peto and Merida in the Yucatan Peninsula. Each time we left the empty highways and passed through a town, wraith-like visions in white were caught out of the black night and focused in the beam of our auto lights. These were Mayan men and women strolling in their Sunday best.

Over a thousand years before the birth of Christ, about the time that Homer was giving the Greeks his Iliad and Odyssey, a people called the Mayans migrated to Central America and established themselves in the country embracing the Yucatan Peninsula in southern Mexico and great portions of Guatemala. By the fifth and sixth centuries when the German invaders from the north were overrunning the Roman Empire, Mayan civilization was at its brilliant best in a region within the confines of present-day Guatemala. By the seventh century this era of greatness declined but Mayan leaders with their skills and vision moved their center north to the Yucatan Peninsula. Shortly the so-called New Empire flourished gloriously.

As in Homer's Greece, the city-state was the Mayan unit of political organization. These cities evidently counted as many as 30,000 inhabitants, with the lavish homes of the wealthy built of stone. Mayan craftsmen were skilled in fashioning jewelry of silver, gold and bronze and Mayan weavers created fine fabrics and embroidered them expertly. Mayan scholars were in some fields, for example, in mathematics and astronomy, more advanced than our ancestors in contemporary Europe. Some of their buildings and remnants of their sculpture are dispersed over the terrain of today's Yucatan and Guatemala, to stir our imaginings on this lost past. Unfortunately their written records, destroyed by the early Spanish clergy, no longer exist. They had "books" of skin and paper-like substances and a combination of ideographs and phonetic characters for their written language. The Mayan civilization, along with the Aztec and Inca, ranks among the greatest of the Western Hemisphere.

Destruction of the records was part of the lusty onslaught on the Mayan form of worship. The Mayan recognized God the Creator as supreme but, as in so many religions throughout the world, the day to day religious life was concerned with propitiating a multiplicity of minor deities whose power to do harm was the primary consideration.

Today there is quite complete separation between the descendants of the Mayans of the Old Empire in Guatemala and those of the New Empire in Yucatan. Yucatan is practically speaking an island, a low stony country protruding into the Gulf of Mexico, inaccessible except by boat or airplane. Its one big port is Progreso, near Merida. More than half of the population possesses more than fifty per cent Mayan blood. Most of the inhabitants are concentrated in the northwest where Yucatan's only important crop, henequen, is grown and the fiber sold to the rope manufacturers of the world. The predominantly Spanish population prevails in this area. Then comes a sector stronger in Mayans where maize is grown. The dry bush turns to rain forest as we move southeast. The population thins out as the forest deepens and in the separate political division known as Quintana Roo only two groups of humans are found, the chicle extractors, who live by supplying the wants of the world's chewing gum addicts, and segments of politically unregenerate Mayan Indian rebels who pass their lives in the rain forest.

These Mayans, as well as larger bodies of the race living in Guatemala, are among the most unusual of the inhabitants of Middle America. They are Christian but with qualifications. Since the early 1940s two teams of Maryknoll Missioners, totaling some 60 priests and Brothers and with Maryknoll Sisters as collaborators, have been working in Yucatan and Guatemala, a portion of them serving the population of Spanish origin and many among the Mayan as a major object of their labors.

In Yucatan, there are plenty of Mayans today who have no revolt in their hearts and who view impatiently the rebellious elements among their confreres. The majority consider themselves loyal citizens of Yucatan. They are endeared to their elliptical houses, their distinctive garb, their language which is used by a substantial proportion of the people on the peninsula. No one calls them Indians. They are respected citizens because their disposition and their habits are very attractive. For one thing, they bathe daily as against less accepted habits in this regard in other parts of Mexico. In each Mayan home is a cedar chest in which carefully washed and ironed clothing is stored.

"When is a Mayan a Yucatecan?" I asked Father Vincent Mallon of the Maryknollers.

"Everybody accepts a Mayan as a Yucatecan," replied Father Mallon, "so long as he doesn't make solemn profession of being an Indian. In this latter case his state of mind is held to represent a revolt against current Yucatecan culture and a reversion to pagan superstitions."

East on the peninsula in Quintana Roo still lives today the unreconciled element of the Mayan population. For four centuries there have been uprisings and one of the major rebellions, called the War of the Castes, occurred in the nineteenth century.

In the dead of the night of July 30, 1847, a body of Mayan Indians swept into the village of Tepich and consummated a horrible slaughter of all the whites there. Thus the so-called War of the Castes was launched. Its immediate cause was a series of shameful wrongs done the Indians but the more remote cause was the abiding longing in the Mayans for independence, never stamped out by the Spaniards.

After a number of exchanges with government troops the Indians retreated to the Quintana Roo bush and rain forest.

"Interestingly enough," Father Robert E. Lee, Maryknoller from Brooklyn, explained to me, "despite their hostility toward their conquerors the Mayans did not abandon Christianity. At this time they had been long neglected and had no knowledge of Christian teachings but they clung to the fragments they recalled of Christianity. They selected tribesmen to serve as priests and one individual, a native of Peto, José Maria Barrera, took over as chief priest. He taught his confreres to adapt certain Catholic practices such as baptism, marriage, and the Mass.

"A ceremony was evolved at which round tortillas and corn gruel were offered before the cross, the tortillas representing the Body of Our Lord and the gruel the Blood. The name *oxdia,* a Mayan adaptation of the Spanish word *hostia,* was given to these tortillas. The recitation of the novena of the Holy Cross, of the Rosary in Spanish and of the litany of the Blessed Virgin in Latin accompanied the ceremony. In imitation of Holy Communion all present partook of the tortillas and corn gruel."

"What is the story," I asked Father Lee, "of the so-called talking cross of these Indians?"

"The talking cross was a fraud that the chief prayer leader Barrera foisted on the Mayans with the aid of a ventriloquist named Miguel Nahuat. From this cross emanated the mandates for the carrying on of the war. When this 'divine' oracle dictated this new Mass rite what Indian could resist?"

Peace with the Mayan *sublevados* was technically established by the government in 1904 but many continued to maintain their political independence. They paid no taxes, accepted no vote and only recently have accepted government schools.

The first Maryknoll missionaries went among these Mayans of the bush in 1943. In January 1946 I visited the two pioneers in Carrillo Puerto, a village in the heart of the forest, Fathers John McGuire and Robert Lee. At the time the pair were getting acquainted with the extraordinary doings of some five thousand twentieth century rebels against the sixteenth century white invaders of their land.

"We are the first priests among these people in over a century," Father Lee explained. "The prayer leaders as well as the Indian rank and file receive us readily and it can be safely expected that they will accept the re-education which we shall undertake to give them."

"Do they still carry on their makeshift rites?"

"Yes," replied Father McGuire, "Padre Sebastian Peniche from Merida and I journeyed recently by horse to Xmaben (Shmaben) and the Indians enacted the corn-gruel Mass for us."

"They have no intention of relinquishing their rituals immediately," observed Father Lee. "Last Ash Wednesday Father McGuire rode to Chancah, their shrine village some ten miles from here, to confer the ashes on those studying the catechism. Imagine his surprise when the Indians came out to meet him with black smudges on their foreheads. The prayer leader, Norberto Ye, had beaten Father to the draw!"

"In the village of Dzulah, one of our catechists, Victor Alcocer, witnessed the Indian blessing of the new fire on Holy Saturday," explained Father McGuire. "All the hearth fires in the huts had been extinguished at midnight of Good Friday. A large group of men gathered before dawn in front of the chapel and took turns rotating a stick between the palms of their hands until one of them created a spark and ignited a pile of wood shavings. A candle was lighted from this fire and brought into the chapel where the prayer leader began his orations. Then each man brought fire from the chapel to his hearth and rekindled the fire there that would be conserved until next Good Friday."

"Meanwhile shotguns were discharged throughout the village," added Father Lee. "This was the Mayan version of the jubilant church bells at the Gloria of the Easter Vigil Mass."

"There's a certain beauty to all this crude improvisation," I remarked.

"That is the case with the native marriage here," Father Lee noted. "The prayer leader takes a lighted candle from the bride and another from the groom and presses the wax of the two into one. Then he blows out the united flames, thus enacting the ritual text 'until death do ye part.' Then he makes three signs of the cross over the couple and implores them to love, help and be faithful to each other."

Getting these rebels back to the Church represents the good work of Mayan catechists from northwest Yucatan. A very able and zealous Mayan woman, Ernestine Jimenez, after living for months among the tribal Indians persuaded the chief of the Shcacal (Ish-cah-cal) subtribe, Concepcion Cituk, to have his marriage blessed and to return to receiving the sacraments. Doctor Sylvanus Morley, author of the key work on the Mayans, who recently passed away, remarked to Father Lee one day that Concepcion had approached him in the forest years ago and asked him to get the Mayans guns to fight the government. The canker of discontent dies hard.

However, the average Mayan is not warlike. There are intelligent, upstanding, educated types like Pedro Kim, manager of the henequen estate of Señor Joaquin Peon. Then there are the simple laborers of the inarticulate rank and file. In Peto one Sunday morning Father Ed Koechel brought me to talk to a group of four Mayan *milperos,* as the operators of a *milpa,* or small farm, are called. They were Pedro, Juan, José and Santiago.

Following the practice around Peto, which is in the maize-growing area, these four men come into the city each weekend and at daybreak Monday morning walk four hours and more back to their fields.

"How large are their *milpas?*" I asked Father Koechel.

"They say that each works from 100 to 150 mecates, which is from 10 to 15 acres apiece. Even with a good corn crop they have to take on extra work to make ends meet. This means periods of labor each year in a sugar mill, a lumber colony, or in carpentry around town."

"How many children have they?"

The discussion on this point was a protracted one but finally Father Koechel had the figures. "The four men have had a total of 33 children," he reported, "but 20 of the 33 are already dead. José, the eldest, has had 12 children but eight have died."

José was a shy, sweet old man. He looked at me with gentle, watery eyes and in a wistful voice made a remark to me in Mayan.

"What did he say?" I asked Father Ed.

"He said life is surely a struggle."

In Father Donald Hessler's church in Bacalar, on the edge of the rain forest in southeast Yucatan near the Mayan refuge, Ade Bethune has sketched a representation of Christ and the Worker and placed beneath it the text in Spanish of Isaiah 1:18. The Spanish *Venid y entendamonos* is a more beautiful rendering of this text than the English, for the Spanish touches more deftly poor mankind's tormented heart—"Come and let us have an understanding." These Yucatecan *milperos* have learned from life to appreciate a kindly Master who addresses them with such words.

The largest concentration of Mayans in present-day Guatemala is in the mountain province of Huehuetenango (Way′-way-tay-nan′-go). The province counts 150,000 Indians and 50,000 *ladinos,* as the modern-living portion of the population is called. Thus 75 per cent of the inhabitants are Indian. Doctor Recinos in his careful study of the province tells us that less than 7,000 children go to school; 85 per cent of the population is illiterate; less than 12,000 of the 200,000 inhabitants wear shoes though 30,000 others use sandals or other foot coverings.[1]

Down in Guatemala City, Juan Rozales, editor of the Catholic weekly, impressed upon me the low estate of the tribal Indian in Guatemala.

"In the main stream of Guatemala," explained Juan, "there are three classes: first, the rich, who are a money aristocracy and not one of blood; secondly, the middle class which is large and in which a distinction is made between upper and lower middle based on education and culture; thirdly, the lower class, many of whose members rate as the shoeless ones.

"The Indian does not figure in this classification at all. He is non-caste. Since Indians are listed in the population, this means that of our three million and a quarter population a bare million and a half is ladino and more than a million and a half are not popularly regarded as an accepted component of Guatemalan society."

"How does an Indian enter Guatemalan society?"

"A few Indians abandon their people, put on Western clothes and shoes, enter the money economy. Usually they are coolly received by the ladinos and their own disown them for their move. Their children, however, are quickly accepted if the family meets with economic success."

"Are the Indians a body of discontents?"

"As a body, no. Only a small minority expresses dissatisfaction with their place in Guatemalan life. Yet the majority of Indians retain a strong dislike for the ladino as a person. For the most part they are a meek people, accepting their lot in silence."

Occasionally, as in Yucatan, the Indian talks back. The last violent uprising of the Indians against the ladinos took place in 1898 in Soloma in Huehuetenango Province when twenty ladinos were massacred.

Guatemala follows the pattern of most of the countries of the Middle American mainland in that it possesses a central mountain mass with lowlands on each of the waterfronts. Its Pacific coastal plain is less than 30 miles deep and its Caribbean lowlands are a scantily inhabited wilderness. The great bulk of the inhabitants live in the colorful uplands with their electric-blue skies and foaming milk-white clouds, their bright flowers and birds and butterflies.

Hardly a country in Latin America, then, can match the colorful variety of costumes and fabrics of the Guatemalan Indian world. Each community has its distinctive *huipil,* or blouse, made with unique textiles, weaving methods, natural dyes and tribal technique. Every community has its own costume and some are exquisite. An old crone sitting by the road selling fruit may be wearing a garment that would make a museum piece and giddy farm girls will display lovely color combinations that would be the envy of a Park Avenue fashion artist.

Antigua, Guatemala's capital of early Spanish days, and the lake region between Guatemala City and Quezeltenango are the popular tourist areas of the country. We leave these behind and give a passing wave to Chichicastenango which while Mayan has been invaded so heavily by the curious that life there has lost some of its normalcy. On we go to the city of Huehuetenango, a gracious provincial town whose population is heavily ladino. In its neighborhood is Chiantla with its shrine to Our Lady of Candelaria. As a Central American shrine it is second only for popular devotion to the Black Christ of Esquipulas of southern Guatemala.

A number of villages in the neighborhood of the new route of the Panamerican Highway count strong groups of ladinos. Such is San Pedro Necta that Father John Lenahan and I visited on horseback. We mounted a steep trail and soon were within a stand of pine that created the pleasant freshness of the temperate zone, yet was thin enough so that we could look through the trees to the grandeur of the peaks about us. At this isolated village in the coffee country, both ladinos and Indians came to greet us but San Pedro Necta is predominantly a sphere of the ladino.

This mountain journey prompts me to mention the excellent job that was done by UNICEF to get 110 barrels of dried milk, 250 pounds to the container, up to the Indians of the Cuchumatanes. All the transportation was handled by Indian porters. I saw the eight Indians struggling up the cliff-like path to San Pedro Necta, the huge container handled by poles and rope harness. Four Indian porters carried each of the containers destined for the other mountain centers. For months the local Indian appointees carefully distributed the milk to mothers and children.

With Father John Lenahan I rode into the classic Mayan country which lies in the Cuchumatanes Mountains beyond the *cumbre* at Tojquia (Toh-kee-a). Traditionally this marked the end of the vehicle road. In 1945 during my first visit we took horses at Tojquia and from then on could move only by horse or on foot. By 1955 a jeep road had been constructed to Soloma and a few spots beyond. For generations and centuries this area has been isolated from the world. The merchant, the traveler, hesitates to penetrate this realm where tradition has it that the outsider is not wanted.

Language likewise represents a barrier. Four derivatives of Mayan are spoken—Mam, Aguacateca, Chuj and Jacalteca. Spanish is not liked even by those who know it. However, language creates no barrier among the Indians themselves. They keep to their tribe so far as marriage is concerned, but in commerce they mingle freely and are passably enterprising. This aptness for trade may eventually prove the open sesame to the outside world once some roads are built. Economically the province is rated very low but there is a great potential in coffee growing. There are also lead mines, and cattle can be raised.

"As I see it," explained Father Paul Sommer, one of the Maryknoll pioneers here, "the school is the principal road to improvement of these people. It must be a cultural venture and not merely a matter of a little instruction."

"How do the people take to schools?" I asked.

"When I opened our school in Jacaltenango the parents were quite unenthusiastic despite the fact that they represent the most alert tribe in the mountains. I gathered only forty children. But then I campaigned among the fathers and mothers. 'You owe it to your youngsters to teach them a little Spanish,' I explained. 'You should prepare them for more than you had yourself.' The idea caught on. Today the school has almost 500 pupils."

"How do the young people themselves feel about it?"

"Our main hope lies in the young people. In the village of San Andres, which is near Jacaltenango, the elders opposed a school. The young men protested. 'Why should we in San Andres drag behind while the people in Jacaltenango go ahead?' they asked. 'Why do we have to continue forever shuffling along behind our fathers burning copal?' At last the elders relented."

"The copal refers to following the ceremonies of the *costumbre,* does it not?" I asked.

"Yes," replied Father Sommer. "The slow awakening of a desire among the young for more from life than their fathers had includes the wish to grow away from burning copal. But the fact remains that the throwback to Mayan religious practices in Guatemala known as the *costumbre* is still quite widespread."

"Is it correct to say that the early missionaries failed?"

"No, not at all. The early missionaries, who in this section were the Mercedarians, followed the good traditions of the Church. While they were remolding the spiritual culture of the people from the Mayan practices to Christianity they avoided creating a vacuum by destroying the old before they had introduced the new. All would have gone well if the clergy had been numerous enough for a long enough time and if a steady social advancement had been possible. But the missionary supply was cut off and on the heels of neglect came a partial retrogression. The people clung to the village church and to many Christian ways but the dead past came to life again. The *costumbre* today is a remake of the Mayan rites of pre-Spanish days."

"What has ten years of renewed Catholic Church life through the return of the missionaries done to the Indians here?" I asked Father Sommer.

"In the first place, there has been an enormous change in a social and human way. Everywhere in these mountains the Indian has the feeling that the Church once again is interested in him as a loving mother, ready to guide him in his problems and stand beside him in sorrow and adversity.

"As to the practice of their religion, there has been an enormous change. In the way of worship, I recall at Jacaltenango being satisfied with thirty-five Communions on our first Christmas Day there. Today a thousand Indians go to Communion every Sunday and several thousand attend Divine Worship. Practically no Indians were married ten years ago. Now in Jacaltenango it is regarded as a shameful thing not to enter into marriage in the established fashion with a ceremony in the church. At Ixtahuacan (Ish′-tah-wa-kan) there wasn't a confession during the first six months after the priest's arrival; today there are five hundred confessions a week. Today hardly an Indian dies in these parts before the priest is called to his bedside to help him meet his God and to administer the Last Rites. For religious instruction, two thousand laymen, principally Indians, have been enlisted in the 'Each one teach five' program that currently has such a vogue here in Guatemala."

"How do you explain the persistence of the *costumbre?*"

"First of all, let's make it clear that attachment to the *costumbre* is diminishing steadily. But generations of habit make the Indian slow to change."

"Where can I see the rites in practice?"

"I suggest that you visit one of our new stations, Santa Eulalia, where the first Maryknoller in permanent residence, Father Joe Halpin, has been stationed less than a year."

Father John Lenahan and I mounted by jeep the impossible road to Santa Eulalia. On the way up, Sisters Anna Marie and Helen Peter of the Maryknoll Sisters, both experienced horsewomen, passed us on their mounts as they came down. Both of them are teachers at the Maryknoll Sisters College in Guatemala City but had been loaned for two weeks to organize catechetical classes here among the mountain women.

The town of Santa Eulalia is magnificently poised over 8,000 feet above sea level on a summit which shows it off dramatically to the entire area. At the church we found two other Maryknoll Sisters, Sisters Thomas Marie and Cabrini, participating in the training program. Santa Eulalia by the census has 1,086 houses, all occupied by Indians except for thirty which are held by ladino officials and traders. In the town and surrounding *aldeas* are found 8,500 Indians. The church is large though not particularly beautiful.

"The big thing here is the *costumbre,*" began Father Halpin, who knew nothing of my conversation with Father Sommer. "After a year, a good fourth of the people of the town have renounced the practices and the remaining three-fourths continue them in varying degrees. Let me show you what goes on."

We stepped into the church by a side door. There, scattered about the edifice were some fifty women and a few men, all chanting audibly and thus creating the effect of a chorus of voices but each praying separately. All were in an attitude of prayer. Each held a candle in his or her hand and, understandably, was dripping the candle grease on the floor, already badly stained. Some of the devotees were up front near the statue of Santa Eulalia, patron of the town. Some were far in the rear of the church facing the door and thus with their backs to the altar. Still others were grouped in larger or smaller numbers about the remainder of the church's statues.

"How do you who live closely to all this explain what is going on?" I asked Father Halpin.

"Father Sommer and others who have specialized in this *costumbre,*" Father Halpin replied, "are best able to supply the answers. Today is Ahau, the big Mayan feast of the dead which occurs every twenty days. All here, however, are not praying in the same way. The group up front is praying to the patron saint of the pueblo. Those at the rear door pray to the spirit of the cross empaneled in the door. Those at the various statues have still another approach. The theme of Mayan prayer is propitiatory, begging the spirits of the dead not to harm the living."

"These women don't seem to be praying on their knees," I noted.

"No, they are sitting on their heels. Note also that the man when he prays goes on the left knee, not the right."

"There seems to be no burning of incense on the church floor here," I commented.

"No, we have succeeded in eliminating this practice. Every Maryknoller who takes charge of a parish like this begins the slow and delicate process of leading the people away from their assumed rights to use the Christian edifice for practices of Mayan origin.

"The people in the absence of the priest have used the church for a combination of Catholic worship, which they have never sought to abolish, and Mayan practices that have come down to them from bygone days. My first duty on coming here was to make friends with everybody and establish myself firmly as the proper Christian representative.

"Then I undertook the long process of correcting the abuses. For a start I persuaded the people not to burn copal, which is their incense, on the sanctuary floor and not to enter the sanctuary with lighted candles. In other places such as Soloma and Jacaltenango this was done without irritation by laying new tile in the sanctuary and putting in a communion rail.

"After another period of time I persuaded the people not to burn copal in the body of the church. The final step will be to do away with the practices of the *costumbre* on the church steps. I haven't yet tackled this. Come out on the steps and I'll show you."

Out on the church steps and in the plaza were still more people engaged in prayer. Quite as at the well known tourist church of Chichicastenango, men and women had kindled small charcoal fires on the stone and in these fires were dropping copal as incense.

"These people," Father Halpin explained, "are performing acts of private devotion quite as are the people in the church. In addition to this, however, there is the local village organization of the devotees, an organization found in the other towns and villages of the area. This organization has chosen an official representative for public prayer who has the Spanish title of *alcalde rezador,* the village prayer minister.

"Note now the oven-like construction at the foot of the church steps that is freshly white-washed. On its top is a cross with its vertical and horizontal beams of equal length. This is the Mayan, not the Christian, cross. At this construction the *alcalde rezador* comes at regular intervals for official prayer, performs his public devotion and burns incense."

"The *costumbre,* then, represents not mere individual devotion but an organized cult," I remarked.

"That's right. For various Christian feasts throughout the year this organization during the years when there were no priests here conducted ceremonies. Now, even though the priest has come back, this organization tends to continue to function and it is not wise to seek to disband it too brusquely. For instance, for Good Friday the leaders asked to hold their own procession. I gave them permission but explained that they had to be out of the church by three o'clock for the official Good Friday ceremony which would be the Stations of the Cross."

"I admire all the kindly prudence that this policy of gentle persuasion represents," I commented. "It is evident what a huge task all of you face rebuilding the long neglected Catholic life."

Father Halpin brought me through the busy neighborhood about the church. It was market day and there was plenty of noise and activity.

"Señora Maria, meet this Padre who is visiting us," Father Halpin called to a woman with a child who crossed the plaza. Maria was a doughty countrywoman who gave us a generous smile, exchanged a pleasant word and passed on.

"Maria is a good instance of our problems of reconstructing a damaged faith," explained Father Halpin. "When I first arrived she brought me her child for baptism. I asked her if she was married. 'No, Padre,' she replied quite unhesitatingly. 'How many children have you, Maria?' I asked. 'Four,' she replied. 'And I suppose they are all by different men, Maria,' I ventured. 'Yes, that's right, Padre. But I want you to know I am a good woman, Padre. I have never stolen from anybody in my life and I never treat anybody unfairly.' The ladies in my parish home in St. Louis would have a hard time catching Maria's point of view but I dare say the Lord understands her handicaps."

Back that evening with Father Sommer, I found him very interested in my experience.

"The Santa Eulalia women praying to the spirit of the cross in the church door represent one of our major problems among the Mayans," he commented. "The Mayans of old probably employed a more or less square cross. This was for them a symbol representing the four points of the compass. The Christian cross has the elongated vertical. A square cross is still often found in Mayan homes and along the roadside. In our program of renewal we must disabuse the family people of their superstition regarding every cross, namely, that each has a spirit within it which the devotee must propitiate and that leaves it only when the cross crumples from rot."

"How important is the feast of Ahau which the Mayans celebrate today?" I asked.

"Ahau is a feast given much importance in the established calendar of worship. This calendar directs Mayan society quite as our calendar directs us. The Mayan month has 20 days and this is divided into four periods equivalent to our week but of five days each. Every fifth day is an ora day, the Mayan day of prayer."

"The ora day, then," I noted, "is like our Sabbath Day."

"Yes, with this important qualification, namely, that Mayanism is polytheistic. It has four principal gods and each of these is worshiped in one of the four weeks of the month. These are the so-called year-bearer gods. Each in turn is believed to carry the earth on his shoulders for a year by means of the local Indian forehead strap, the mecapál. Each time an earthquake occurs the people feel that the year-bearer is weakening and thus stumbling under the weight of his burden. Hence they hasten with offerings to give him strength to walk aright. This year the year would be carried by the god Ben and thus among Mayans he would be in special honor this year. The other three year-bearer gods are Lambat, Chinax and Watan."

"What special observance takes place on the Mayan equivalent of our Sunday?" I asked.

"There is an official act of public worship, a ceremony regarded by the Mayans to be as important as our Mass. The *alcalde rezador* of whom Father Halpin spoke took care of this."

"If I understand you, then, the *costumbre* includes official acts of worship after the Mayan pattern," I said.

"Yes, that's right. For some generations the *alcalde rezador* in Santa Eulalia and other communities has lighted his charcoal and burned his copal (incense) every five days as an act of official worship at the official praying stand outside the Catholic church in each of these towns of the Cuchumatanes Mountains."

"Rather bizarre for a reputedly Catholic country," I commented.

We had moonlight in the mountains that night and I stole a moment to leave the Padres and walk with my thoughts out among the peaks. I recalled another evening when I witnessed the candumble at Bahia in Brazil. On that distressing occasion I observed the syncretism that brought together religious rites to West African gods and Catholic practices in a country of South America. Now here in Central America was another syncretism of ancient Mayan practices and Catholic devotions. Both were the product of hungry but misled spirits adrift because priestly guides are lacking in Christian Latin America. The scientist tells us that nature abhors a vacuum. So, it seems quite evident, does the heart of man. If you deprive him of the God-sent worship of his Creator he will contrive a worship of his own.

Chapter 3

The Red Blood of Leadership

MISS GREEN ENCOUNTERED Elza Torre in the classroom corridor of one of the American colleges in Rio de Janeiro. It was in the 1930s.

"Elza, I'd like to say a word to you some time when it's convenient."

"Why not now, Miss Green?" Elza replied.

"Good! Elza, I don't mean to flatter you but I've been watching you. You're a born leader. I'd love to see you become a Protestant with us."

"Oh, I couldn't," Elza cried, quite spontaneously, "I'm a Catholic."

"Indeed! Then I'm sorry I spoke to you. I hadn't noticed you practicing any religion."

Elza distractedly went to her room and sat down at her desk. She felt quite mortified. She was a daughter of the Ambassador of Mexico to Brazil. Miss Green was right, she admitted to herself, she had not been practicing her religion. She had not gone to Mass since coming to Rio. Her father was a declared anticlerical and certainly was not inclined to encourage her to keep up her duties.

Next Sunday Elza went to Mass. "Miss Green has gotten me back to my faith," she murmured to herself as she entered the long-unfrequented church.

Elza's father's next assignment was to the United States and Elza entered the College of Mount St. Vincent in New York. Then in 1937 her father was named Governor of Yucatan and took up residence in a spacious home in Merida, his city of origin. The day Elza returned home she met her aunt, a positive-minded socialite, very busy in the life of Merida and Yucatan.

"Elza, you must join the Yucatan Catholic Action," the aunt declared.

"I haven't the least idea what it's all about," replied Elza.

"You'll find out," answered the aunt. "We're going to make you president of the young women's section."

Evidently the aunt had the same opinion of Elza's capacities as had Miss Green. But Elza was quite dismayed after the first Catholic Action meeting and told her aunt so.

"You got me into this," she said. "Now you've got to save me from making a perfect fool of myself."

"That I will," said the aunt, and for twenty minutes after dinner each day for three months the older lady instructed the young girl. Elza became a dynamic leader of the movement and for the twenty years that have intervened since her homecoming she has done yeoman work for her religion in Yucatan.

"I've gotten a thrill out of every minute of it," Elza told me when I talked with her in Merida. "But after watching our young college graduates for twenty years, first my own generation and then those who followed, I am puzzled to find so many who seem to miss the need to work for the big ideas of life. Not only here in Yucatan but all over Latin America we have a tremendous unharnessed potential of fine young people for worthwhile accomplishment. Why does it seem so hard to get them harnessed?"

Elza's comment is of course a commonplace, the observation of so many who have worked for a period with the Latin American public and who, while appreciating the many who show spirit, become aware of the tremendous possibilities latent in the large numbers who have not yet been set afire for achievement.

Always interesting are the many fine projects that are gaining results in leadership. One of the best in the university world of Middle America is the Agrupacion Catolica Universitaria (Catholic Groupment of University Students) of Havana. The elite created by this select organization makes itself felt throughout Cuba. Germinally this is the Jesuit Sodality of Mary for university students, founded in 1931 by Padre Felipe Rey de Castro, S.J., at the University of Havana.

The quarters of this organization, handy to the impressive buildings of the university in the heart of Havana, are the last word in modernity. Adjacent to the entrance is a large patio restaurant fresh with tropical foliage that creates the atmosphere of a Florida hotel. Here the members chat at breakfast after the Sunday Mass and Communion. Upstairs are boarding quarters for seventy and in the building are libraries and several specially air-conditioned study rooms, a chapel handy to the entrance for easy visits, a Bureau of Information and Catholic Promotion for the groupment's literature campaign, an indoor lunchroom and discussion chambers. This Havana ACU hostel is a model for the world.

One of the secrets of success of the ACU is the rigorousness of the entrance requirements. There is a long routine of application, a postulancy and nine months of aspirancy. Then comes the big day of the year, the solemn act of consecration of the new members on the Feast of the Immaculate Conception. Today more than 500 are on the roles, a major source of supply being the B.A. students from Jesuit colleges throughout Cuba doing graduate work at the University of Havana. Of the 500 members almost 300 are professional men in Cuba today—82 doctors, 104 lawyers, 94 engineers, 40 priests.

"This body of men possesses a splendid spirit and makes a strong impact on Cuban life," explained Father Edward McCarthy of the American Augustinians who operate the Catholic University of Villanova in Havana. "Some 15 to 20 of our professors at Villanova are ACU men from the University of Havana."

Alberto Guzman, an alert young man, was our guide through the hostel. Reserved and modest though he was it was evident that Alberto was proud of his connection with the groupment.

"Do you have objectives besides the main one of living your careers as representative Catholics?" I asked.

"Yes, the ACU has a well-worked-out service program in which many take part. In the barrio of Las Yaguas, one of the poorest in Havana we operate a dispensary in which 20 ACU doctors and four dentists take turns at the work. They maintain as well a school for 300 children in Las Yaguas conducted by teaching Sisters."

"You supply also the personnel for the San Lorenzo clinic founded by our Padre Spirali," noted Father McCarthy.

"Yes," agreed Alberto. "There are other medical and charitable projects as well. But we think that some of our best work is being done in developing here in Cuba a new order of ideas."

"To what do you refer?" I asked.

"For instance, there is our collaboration with Bishop Alberto Martin of Matanzas in setting up a model parish that could revolutionize Catholic life in all Latin America. As you are aware, our parishes in Cuba and elsewhere are not maintained by the weekly alms of the faithful as in the United States. Instead, there has been from Spanish times a system of allowances from the government which gives everybody the impression that the Church is supported by the state and that gifts by individuals are mere superfluous acts of piety. As a matter of fact, almost everywhere today the allotments from the state where they still exist at all are merely nominal and are more a hindrance than a help to good church life.

"Secondly, personal support for the priest, ordinarily quite meager, has long been furnished by a series of offerings known as stole fees that are paid in connection with the administration of the sacraments. This has been still more poisonous in its effects and persons like Bishop Martin are keenly aware of this.

"Recently the Bishop made an arrangement with the ACU to conduct a survey in one of his communities as to the influence of these forms of support on Catholic life. Many of the poor and uneducated who were approached pulled no punches in making known to our investigators, all of them laymen, that they had the utmost disdain for what they regarded as traffic in the sacraments. Some saw the priest not at all as a zealous man interested in their good but as a petty merchant urging them to accept his stock in trade, the sacraments, for the fees that would accrue to him.

"Our members feel that as laymen they can do what the priests themselves would find it difficult to do, namely, work systematically among the families of Bishop Martin's new model parish and train them to support the Church by free-will offerings. The traditional stole fees have been abolished. If the idea succeeds it can lead to a complete change of attitude toward religion, particularly among the rank and file."

"I find," Father McCarthy remarked to me after we had departed, "that these men of the ACU possess the most precious ingredient needed by the Church in Cuba, a sense of leadership among the laity. Father Spirali, who was the initiator of the great idea of a Catholic University for Cuba and who inspired the assumption of the work by the American Augustinians, had this goal of lay leadership very much in mind. He was not merely interested in education but strongly interested in Cuba as well, and shrewdly calculated that a Catholic university was the key instrument to serve this end."

Villanova in Havana is a vigorous reality today. Father Spirali in 1946 won the backing of several Cuban families of means and in 1950 the Cuban Congress voted a formal recognition of this first private university in the nation and approved of its right to give degrees. Today it has a thousand students and provides courses in fourteen disciplines. It has five substantial buildings and a beautiful chapel. The school is conveniently placed for day students in a suburb of Havana and carries only one great handicap, the high cost of the land in its neighborhood. University property for the moment is limited to twenty-five acres because the contiguous acreage is priced currently at $7 per square meter.

"We are serving all classes of the country," explained Father McCarthy. "Currently 30 per cent of our students are from among the wealthy, 60 per cent are middle class, and 10 per cent come from the poorer class."

"What kind of a faculty have you?" I asked.

"The faculty is one of our finest assets," Father McCarthy replied. "It numbers approximately a hundred, of whom more than a dozen are women. We have important specialists among the Augustinians from the United States and a number of the Cubans are not only top-flight professors but outstanding Catholics as well. The Dean of Engineering is Manuel Suarez Carreño, a man with a family of twelve children whose business has suffered through his assumption of this post. But for him it is a spiritual dedication. You must meet him."

We walked through the busy corridors and found Professor Suarez in his office, a quiet, unpretentious man.

"I hear you are educating some very fine engineers, Professor Suarez," I remarked.

"Father, I hope that is true," he replied, "but the subject involves a point in my philosophy that has become a matter of honor with me. I tell my young men that I am not interested merely in making them good engineers. They must be, I insist, distinguished leaders in Cuban life as well, impregnated with Catholic ideals."

"There are others of similar stamp among the staff here," Father

McCarthy noted as we continued through the buildings. "The Director of Psychology, Jose I. Lasaga, is one of those who belongs to the ACU, and is very apostolic. The Dean of Law, Marino Perez Durán, is outstanding. I see Dr. Gonzales del Valle approaching us. He is a professor of law. I'll present him to you."

The introductions over, Father McCarthy remarked, "Dr. Gonzales is the organizer of a novel institution in the university, an annual retreat for the faculty."

"Do many participate, Doctor?" I asked.

"The first year we had twenty in attendance; at our latest exercises the figure had jumped to seventy. For some of the men it took great courage to join us the first time. But the very act of openly declaring their position on religion in this fashion has given them a sense of strength that has changed their whole outlook on life."

The most interesting person at Villanova in Havana is Father Lawrence Spirali, the spark of this Augustinian enterprise. He is an Italian mountaineer from the Abruzzi, short, pudgy, direct, volatile.

"When I came as an immigrant to the United States," he explained as we sat at dinner one evening, "I was already twenty years old. I didn't have a penny so I took a job cleaning the streets in Philadelphia. I resolved to get an education and then determined to become an Augustinian priest. This whole island is my life and all the people, particularly the poor people, and that means the vast majority, are my love. If we educate the more capable people in the right way they will do the right thing, I am sure, for the lowly and the backward."

Another enterprise that provides us with the full flavor of the drama of building leadership in Middle America is the unusual story of the next-to-miraculous growth of the Catholic University of Puerto Rico. Here in charmingly unorthodox fashion we witness the burgeoning of a poor man's university in which the poor men themselves have played a substantial role in the accomplishment.

One morning I took a plane out of San Juan, Puerto Rico's capital, for the 25-minute flight to the island's second city, Ponce, a thriving provincial town of some 200,000. I had the good fortune to find myself sitting beside Señorita Aurea Cintron, member of a San Juan family who was brought up in New York and who secured her B.A. at the University of Marquette. She was a professor of English on the

Catholic University faculty, returning to school after a visit with friends.

"Who is doing the work of building up the university?" I asked Aurea.

"Everybody!" She replied quite spontaneously. "The students, we of the lay faculty, the Sisters, the priests, as well as Puerto Rican families, many of them without great means, are all involved in one way or another. It is quite extraordinary. Everybody knows that there's not a penny to spare and everybody is so carried away with enthusiasm for this university for the plain folk of Puerto Rico growing up out here in the middle of the sugar-cane fields that nobody considers time or trouble when it's a question of lending a hand."

When I encountered Sister Francis Xavier, the Dean of the College of Women, I told her of Aurea's words.

"That is typical of the spirit that we are able to count on here," she observed.

"Is it really a poor man's university?" I asked.

"Yes, quite literally so. Of the 2,500 on the roles, 10 per cent of the students are from families of means, 30 per cent come from homes in moderate circumstances and 60 per cent are from among the poor. Our fees are very low. Bishop McManus has instructed us to charge approximately $5 per credit hour while the average charge for the country as a whole is $15 per credit hour. And this in face of the fact that there is no endowment or other sources of operating income."

"When you speak of students from among the poor do you mean the *real* poor?" I persisted.

"Yes, I mean the *real* poor," Sister replied with feeling. "I mean boys like Gaspar Valedon. He is taking a science course in order to become a doctor. Gaspard gets up at 3 A.M. to milk the cows and do the farm chores. Then he walks an hour and a half to catch a bus for a half hour's ride to school. After his day of classes he takes the bus again, walks that hour and a half again and does the farm chores before getting to bed.

"There are families with girls like Sofia Martinez whom her mother brought here to enroll for the nursing course. The mother asked the fee and then counted it out in one dollar bills. 'I have been saving these up for five years for Sofia,' she exclaimed happily.

"One girl, Gabriela Colomo, finished her teacher training course and had no money to feed herself or to transport herself to and from the practice school where she was required to teach a year without salary. The driver of a privately owned bus along the route offered to carry her to school each day and home again free and the head teacher at the school loaned her money to buy herself food until she got her salaried assignment. I assure you, there are some wonderful sacrifices made in this neighborhood in the common hunger of these simple people to better themselves and to see others bettered."

I found Ponce's Catholic University very good to look at. Broad lawns of green grass garnished with shrubbery and tidy walks lined with hedges separate the simple two-story buildings built of reinforced concrete, pleasingly designed in tropical architecture. There are eight buildings today with a total of some 130,000 square feet of floor space, valued at a million and a quarter dollars. Another million dollars' worth of construction is planned. A university chapel is now in operation, which serves also as the neighborhood parish church. The latest building to be erected is the Maria Aguayo Law Center.

The current faculty numbers sixty priests and religious teachers from twelve different religious communities plus seventy lay faculty members. Most the religious faculty comes from the United States while most of the lay members are Puerto Rican. Father William F. Ferree of the Marianists of Dayton, Ohio, was University Rector when I paid my visit, but on his call to Rome in 1957 Father Thomas A. Stanley of the Marianists took his place. Cardinal Spellman has supplied the current Vice Rector, Father Ivan D. Illich, from among the clergy who work for the Puerto Ricans in New York.

"Our greatest hidden resource is our splendid faculty," commented Father Ferree. "All its religious members are contributed by their communities and during the early years many of the lay members worked for but a fraction of their proper salaries. Now for the good of the university we are aiming to pay the standard remunerations of above-average educational institutions in the United States.

"But the services rendered by the faculty are far beyond their established tasks. Their voluntary collaboration in all branches of our operation including the work of promoting the university is unique. The student body, then, is unbelievably loyal and generous in giving us their time and cooperation. After seven or eight years we have had no need of replacements of furniture and equipment which other institutions and laboratories tell us they must renew every two or three years. This all-round helpfulness explains why we can function on an annual operating budget of $400,000. Our great financial concern is to find benefactors for capital investments in buildings."

"How did Bishop McManus get the courage to launch this huge enterprise?" I asked Sister Francis Xavier, who is one of the project's early pioneers.

"He felt almost literally pushed into it," she replied. "For twenty-five years the Redemptorists and other clergy of the island had been building an extensive system of Catholic primary and secondary schools but there was an almost complete absence of Catholic higher education. Further, the Bishop's neighborhood of Ponce, which represents the south-central and southeastern parts of the island, were completely devoid of higher educational facilities of any kind. The Bishop saw plainly that here was a logical spot for a Catholic institution.

"However, when the Bishop visited Brooklyn in the late 1940s he was turned down by all the major religious communities specializing in education that he approached and his situation was desperate. Then came his fateful conversation with Mother Charles Edward, head of the Sisters of St. Joseph of Brentwood. He spoke so eloquently of the need that he completely won Mother to the enterprise and Mother in turn spoke so convincingly to him of the possibility of using for a university some of the trained personnel among the religious Sisters conducting colleges in the United States that the university became a reality by the time the Bishop left Brentwood that day.

"In August 1948 three Sisters of Brentwood from the College for Women in Brooklyn, two Dominican Sisters of Amityville, Long Island, and two Sisters from the Dominicans of Adrian, Michigan, opened the College for Women of the future university. Two priests had a part in the project but this was one of the rare occasions in history when religious women played the dominant role in launching a Catholic university. The Sisters' communities in the enterprise rose to eight and the Sisters to thirty-five. Mother Charles Edward's distinctive contribution was administrative specialists, including three trained and degreed librarians who very early built up a relatively small but technically satisfactory library that won the admiration of the accreditation authorities, who were understandably cool toward this university launched on a shoestring. Suffice it to say that within five years accreditation was secured."

"What did you use for buildings?" I asked.

"For the start we used makeshift structures in Ponce. Then friends of the Bishop, the Ferree family of Ponce, gave him ninety-two acres of sugar-cane fields and what was at the time a colossal gift of $200,000. Father Hammon of the Redemptorists initiated the work in the sugar-cane fields. Other friends came forward and thus we have what we have today."

An unusual instance of the growth of local political as well as socio-economic leadership presents itself in the little country of British Honduras, a land counting only some 75,000 inhabitants but so distinctly nation-minded that it has refused to enter the West Indies Federation which has recently come into being.

Gene Koppock, a tall blond pilot from Vancouver, Washington, carried me in his Cessna over the sultry swamp country from Chetumal, Mexico's southernmost port, to Belize, British Honduras' capital. Outside Belize on an 80-acre site stands St. John's College. The St. Louis Jesuits have nurtured the faith in British Honduras for over sixty years. With St. John's as the spark, they have helped the colony fight ignorance and poverty. British Honduras is on Main Street so far as Caribbean hurricane traffic is concerned, for hurricanes nose-dive here with uneasy frequency. In 1931 one made a direct hit on Belize and St. John's and brought death to eleven Jesuits and twenty-two students. Another in 1942 laid waste fifty-seven of the churches, schools and residences in the colony.

"We have forgotten the past and live in a new day," explained Father Raskowsky, the rector of St. John's, as we examined the eight new hurricane-proof, ferro-concrete buildings which house the 400 students. "These young fellows don't spend much time bemoaning the handicaps of their country. There's an element among them who look at the prospects of British Honduras in the bright hope of morning. They are working hard for self-government and for economic well-being from the development of their country's resources."

Later in the day at the cathedral rectory I met George Price, Philip Goldson and other young men and mentioned these words.

"Father Raskowsky and his professors at St. John's put the spark in us that set us going," remarked George Price. "Back in 1948 we told Father our desire to make something of British Honduras and asked him to help us prepare. He opened a Sunday morning study club for St. John's alumni on the social teachings of the Church and a group of fifteen of us participated. This was the start."

"Did you have political ideas in mind at the time or were you more concerned with a better livelihood?" I asked.

"We wanted both," answered Philip Goldson. "Father Marion Ganey and others had started the cooperative movement and we already saw how much we could do to improve ourselves economically. But we felt we should also get into politics."

"George Price was the leading politician in the group," explained one of the others in the circle. "He became one of the founders of the People's United Party, the PUP. Nicholas Pollard, another in the group, became secretary of the General Workers' Union. Some of us felt Nick as labor leader was a little too violent and thus gave ground to the charge that we were leftist. This was never our intention."

"The secret of our success was consistent hard work on the Battlefield," asserted George Price. "The Battlefield, Father, is the open square near the Government Offices in the center of town. We had our pitch there under a lamp-post and almost nightly for years we gathered there and harangued the crowd. I have a special affection for that little spot under the lamp-post where the pitch stood since it is there that we hammered out our plans to do something worthwhile."

"How did matters develop?" I asked.

"In the election campaign of 1954," Price answered, "PUP put up its list of candidates and won a majority for the first time. We captured eight of the fifteen places in the Legislative Assembly. We had no religious issues in mind and Anglicans and Methodists were as important in PUP as Catholics but because of the special preparation of St. John's men, six of the eight assemblymen were Catholic. As a consequence of the elections, four out of ten of the Government Cabinet were PUP men."

"And probably as a consequence of our years of haranguing," said another in the group, "in 1954 three of our PUP leaders, Leigh Richardson, Philip Goldson and Herman Jex, were in the committee that went to London to discuss the granting of greater political power to the citizens of British Honduras. They brought home some important concessions."

"What do you think of these young men and their efforts?" I asked Bishop Hickey, the kindly and venerable father to both priests and people in British Honduras.

"I am proud of all that they have done to show the spirit of Christian leadership in public affairs that every young man of Christian ideals should exhibit," he replied. "They may make mistakes and they should be forgiven if they do. However, they carry a great responsibility; they cannot be excused if they prove dishonest or disloyal to each other, if they prove selfish despite their Christian training."

Over 2,000 priests, Brothers and Sisters from the United States labor in Middle America and a substantial number engaged in secondary education speak of the hopeful signs in the new generation that point toward a greater sense of leadership.

Mother Raphael of the strikingly beautiful Merici Academy in Havana, where Ursulines from the United States collaborate with their Latin American Sisters in operating this splendid institution with more than 500 students, had an interesting comment for me. I asked her if the young ladies of the school showed much generosity and enterprise.

"My off-hand answer would be no," she answered. "Our girls during their years in school are beautifully docile, lovable, hungry to know what we think is the right thing to do, yet so often they give us the impression that they lack any great discipline of their wills, any sense of responsibility.

"But then they leave us and shortly they are married. They come back to us on one or another occasion and time and time again we are surprised at what we see in them that we had not noticed before. They have matured. Casually they will speak of situations that arise within their families or in their social circle and they will say, 'As a Merici girl I realized that I could not fail to take hold and show some leadership,' or, 'The group wanted something done and said that with my training under the Madres I'd have to take charge, so I did.'

"They often display commendable enterprise. Elena Aiscobe de Hernandez recently treated with the mayor of Havana for facilities to set up a relief center and dispensary in a poor section of Havana for Merici charitable work. Yveles Molinet de Bosch of Santiago has organized a center for Merici charities in that city. Her husband, a graduate of the Jesuits at Belem and an ACU member, has organized an ACU groupment in Santiago. As I think it over I must admit that I see a growing sense of leadership among our graduates and among the younger set in Cuba in general."

The Sisters of Mercy conduct St. Catherine's College in Belize and have an attractive new building by the harbor, fanned continuously by soft breezes from the Caribbean. It is a school where simplicity is in the air and where one would not look for dreams of derring-do. One of the Sisters told me, however, of a conversation she had with one of the young girls which reveals the thoughts that are abroad.

The girl's uncle is very active among the alumni of St. John's College who have shown enterprise in British Honduras. Speaking one day with the Sister the young girl remarked, "When I grow up I hope to do something worthwhile to change the world."

"What's that you say?" asked the Sister.

"Well, that's what my uncle's trying to do, you know. He doesn't talk about it but one day he told me that once when he was in New Orleans he stopped to look at the books in a bookshop window and he saw one entitled, *You Can Change the World.* He went into the shop and bought the book. It was by a priest named Father Keller and he had to pay three dollars for it but he says it was worth all he paid for it because ever since it has been his inspiration in all that he tries to do. And maybe I can be like my uncle."

While in Mexico City I was a guest of the priests and students of Mexico's brand new mission society, founded by Bishop Escalante, which now possesses a handsome new seminary housing more than a hundred candidates preparing to follow in the footsteps of the society's first missionary contingent that is at work in Asia.

One afternoon I visited an acquaintance of mine, a gentleman who lives in the heart of the city.

"Where are you staying?" he asked me after we had exchanged greetings.

"I am visiting the Missionaries of Guadalupe," I replied, "the Mexican society which has sent its first band of three priests to Japan."

"Splendid! These men should be a symbol to us people of Mexico, to all Latin Americans. Latin America, despite its own needs, must be known throughout the earth as a continent that has the habit of giving a helping hand to its neighbor peoples all over the world. With this reputation Latin America will be truly self-respecting; it will be truly great."

For North Americans, the secret to cordial relations with our Latin American neighbors lies in the recognition that every land in Latin America possesses a people proud of its integrity, jealous of its world esteem, earnest in its aspirations to be a good world neighbor.

Individual friends keep the flame of friendship burning by gracious words and the constant exchange of heart-warming courtesies. So it should be among nations, between our North American homeland and the countries to the south. If we fail in these amenities, friendship will cool.

FOOTNOTES

SECTION ONE Brazil, the Colossus

Chapter 2

1. Fernando de Azevedo, *Brazilian Culture,* Macmillan, 1950, p. 145.
2. *Ibid.,* p. 153.

Chapter 4

1. Azevedo, *op. cit.,* p. 33.
2. Charles Wagley, *ed., Race and Class in Rural Brazil,* UNESCO, 1952, p. 28.
3. Azevedo, *op. cit.,* p. 147.
4. Melville J. Herskovits, *Life in a Haitian Valley,* Knopf, 1937, p. 55.
5. Edison Carneiro, *Candomblés da Bahia,* Bahia, 1948.
6. Herskovits, *op. cit.,* p. 147.

Chapter 6

1. Willard Price, *The Amazing Amazon,* Heinemann, London, 1952.
2. *Ibid.,* p. 9.
3. Preston E. James, *Latin America,* Odyssey, 1950, p. 492.

Other references:

Charles Wagley, *Amazon Town,* A study of man in the tropics. Macmillan, 1953.

Josue de Castro, *The Geography of Hunger,* Little, Brown, Boston, 1952.
p. Avencio Villarejo O.S.A., *Asi es la Selva,* Sanmarti, Lima, 1953.
Alain Gheerbrant, *Journey to the Far Amazon,* Simon and Schuster, 1954.

SECTION TWO Lands of the South

Chapter 1

1. John F. Bannon, S.J., and Peter M. Dunne, S.J., *Latin America, an Historical Survey,* Bruce, 1950, p. 193.
2. Quoted in Leturia, *La Emancipacion Hispanoamericana,* p. 7.
3. Bannon and Dunne, *op. cit.,* p. 460.

Other references:

William J. Coleman, M.M. *The First Apostolic Delegation in Rio de Janeiro and its Influence in Spanish America,* Catholic University Press, Washington, D.C., 1950.

Charles Edward Chapman, *Hispanic America, Colonial and Republican,* Macmillan, 1947.

Donald E. Worcestor and Wendell G. Schaeffer, *The Growth and Culture of Latin America,* Oxford University Press, New York, 1956.

Chapter 2

1. Bannon and Dunne, *op. cit.,* p. 568.

Chapter 3

1. James, *op. cit.,* p. 257.
2. Bannon and Dunne, *op. cit.,* p. 586.
3. Bannon and Dunne, *op. cit.,* p. 590.

Other references:

Harris Gaylord Warren, *Paraguay, an Informal History,* University of Oklahoma, 1949.

William E. Barrett, *Woman on Horseback.* The story of Francisco Lopez and Elisa Lynch, Doubleday, 1952.

Chapter 4

1. James, *op. cit.,* p. 241.
2. Rutgers University Press, 1957, pp. 177-210.
3. Alejandro Magnet, *El Padre Hurtado,* Editorial del Pacifico, Santiago, 1954, p. 40.

SECTION THREE World of the Andes

Chapter 3

1. "The Scotsman," Edinburgh, Dec. 24, 1956.
2. Victor W. von Hagen, *Highway of the Sun,* Little, Brown, 1955, p. 59.
3. John and Mary Collier, "An Experiment in Applied Anthropology," *Scientific American,* January, 1957.

Chapter 5

1. Alexander, *Communism in Latin America,* Rutgers University Press, 1957, p. 70.

SECTION FOUR The Rise of Protestantism

Chapter 1

1. Searle Bates, *Religious Liberty, an Inquiry,* New York, 1945.
2. Data appear in *Occasional Bulletin,* May 6, 1958, published by the Missionary Research Library, New York City.

Chapter 2

1. Azevedo, *op. cit.,* p. 156.
2. Elizabeth Elliot, *Through Gates of Splendor,* Harper, 1957.

SECTION FIVE Vignettes of Middle America

Chapter 2

1. Adrian Recinos, *Monografia del Departamento de Huehuetenango,* Ministerio de Educacion Publica, Guatemala, 1954, p. 222.

Other references:

Robert Redfield, *The Folk Culture of Yucatan,* University of Chicago, 1941.

Encuesta Nacional sobre Sentimiento Religioso del Pueblo de Cuba, Agrupación Catolica Universitaria, Havana, 1954.

Lesley Byrd Simpson, *Many Mexicos,* University of California, 1952.

Appendix 1

CATHOLIC STATISTICS FOR LATIN AMERICA 1957

Compiled by William J. Gibbons, S.J.
From official figures as published in the Annuario Pontificio, Vatican City, 1958*

* William J. Gibbons, S.J. and Research Associates, *Basic Ecclesiastical Statistics for Latin America 1958,* World Horizon Reports, Maryknoll Publications 1958. Detailed data for every diocese in Latin America will be found in this study.

Catholic Statistics for Latin America 1957

TABLE I — AREA AND POPULATION

SOUTH AMERICA

Countries	Area (Square Miles)	Total population	Population density	Catholic popu-lation	Catholics per priest	Catholics per parish
(1)	(2)	(3)	(4)	(5)	(6)	(7)
1—Argentina	1,085,542	22,146,000	20.4	20,117,000	3,795	14,957
2—Bolivia	410,343	3,256,000	7.9	3,087,000	4,553	8,434
3—Brazil	3,580,476	60,080,000	16.8	56,190,000	6,122	14,916
4—Chile	297,153	6,495,000	21.9	5,845,000	2,660	9,598
5—Colombia	457,499	13,150,000	28.7	12,942,000	3,574	9,993
6—Ecuador	118,174	3,803,000	32.2	3,584,000	3,027	7,560
7—Paraguay	162,776	1,690,000	10.4	1,612,000	5,217	10,891
8—Peru	549,537	9,294,000	16.9	8,545,000	5,107	9,569
9—Uruguay	72,407	2,687,000	37.1	2,407,000	3,636	15,732
10—Venezuela	355,763	5,900,000	16.6	5,736,000	5,396	11,336
11—Guianas	172,689	769,000	4.5	139,000	1,132	3,095
Totals	7,262,359	129,269,000	17.7	120,203,000	4,625	12,520

CENTRAL AMERICA AND MEXICO

Countries	Area (Square Miles)	Total population	Population density	Catholic popu-lation	Catholics per priest	Catholics per parish
(1)	(2)	(3)	(4)	(5)	(6)	(7)
12—Costa Rica	18,354	992,000	54.1	943,000	4,140	10,140
13—El Salvador	14,820	2,206,000	148.8	2,182,000	8,100	16,050
14—Guatemala	41,249	3,186,000	77.2	3,094,000	11,290	16,460
15—Honduras	48,162	1,426,000	29.6	1,403,000	9,900	18,250
16—Brit. Honduras	8,844	84,000	9.4	50,000	1,750	4,990
17—Nicaragua	54,335	1,068,000	19.6	1,013,000	4,840	10,550
18—Panama	36,901	895,000	24.2	679,000	6,780	8,590
19—Mexico	780,035	28,252,000	36.2	27,223,000	4,530	13,630
Totals	1,002,700	38,095,000	38.0	36,584,000	5,030	13,670

CARIBBEAN ISLANDS

Countries	Area (Square Miles)	Total population	Population density	Catholic popu-lation	Catholics per priest	Catholics per parish
(1)	(2)	(3)	(4)	(5)	(6)	(7)
20—Cuba	45,036	6,166,000	136.9	5,620,000	8,145	26,500
21—Dominican Republic	18,635	2,309,000	123.9	2,290,000	8,420	21,200
22—Haiti	11,957	3,404,000	284.7	2,378,000	5,380	15,150
23—Bahama Is.	4,466	85,000	19.0	15,000	500	840
24—Jamaica	4,449	1,581,000	365.2	102,000	1,275	12,098
25—Trinidad, Dominica Grenada	3,252	1,125,000	345.9	504,000	2,650	5,550
26—Curacao	376	187,000	495.6	128,000	1,960	4,250
27—Guadalupe, Martinique	1,076	555,000	515.8	550,000	2,570	6,470
28—Puerto Rico	(3,434)	2,353,000	685.0	2,200,000	5,800	19,150
Totals	92,681	17,764,000	191.7	13,785,000	5,860	16,700
Grand Totals	8,357,740*	185,136,000**		170,572,000	4,790	13,020

* Figure in chart is of circumscriptions as in Annuario Pontificio; by United Nations and government data, total area is 7,913,623 square miles.

** Figure in chart is total of data in Annuario Pontificio; by United Nations and government data, total is 191,055,000.

TABLE II – PERSONNEL

SOUTH AMERICA

Country	Cardinals	Arch-bishops	Bishops	Total priests	Diocesan priests	Religious priests	Seminarians	Sisters
(1)	(2)	(3)	(4)	(5)	(6)	(7)	(8)	(9)
1–Argentina	2	9	36	5,301	2,368	2,850	632	13,692
2–Bolivia	—	2	17	678	241	437	53	877
3–Brazil	3	23	126	9,179	3,830	5,220	1,261	24,659
4–Chile	1	3	18	2,197	816	1,381	187	4,349
5–Colombia	1	6	39	3,621	2,079	1,542	1,019	11,814
6–Ecuador	1	3	10	1,184	546	638	160	2,429
7–Paraguay	—	1	7	309	145	164	55	390
8–Peru	—	4	22	1,673	735	938	210	1,609
9–Uruguay	—	1	4	662	198	464	59	1,842
10–Venezuela	—	2	18	1,063	405	542	92	2,204
11–Guianas	—	—	3	123	9	114	2	374
Totals	8	54	300	25,990	11,372	14,290	3,730	64,239

CENTRAL AMERICA AND MEXICO

Countries	Cardinals	Arch-bishops	Bishops	Total priests	Diocesan priests	Religious priests	Seminarians	Sisters
(1)	(2)	(3)	(4)	(5)	(6)	(7)	(8)	(9)
12—Costa Rica		1	2	228	120	108	45	437
13—El Salvador		1	5	269	132	137	53	438
14—Guatemala		1	7	274	86	176	27	241
15—Honduras		1	4	142	55	87	20	145
16—Br. Honduras		—	—	29	3	36	3	108
17—Nicaragua		1	5	209	92	117	19	303
18—Panama		1	2	100	41	59	21	160
19—Mexico		9	34	6,020	4,518	1,367	1,990	18,560
Total		15	59	7,271	5,047	2,077	2,178	20,392

CARIBBEAN ISLANDS

Countries	Cardinals	Arch-bishops	Bishops	Total priests	Diocesan priests	Religious priests	Seminarians	Sisters
(1)	(2)	(3)	(4)	(5)	(6)	(7)	(8)	(9)
20—Cuba	1	2	5	690	223	467	73	2,408
21—Dominican Republic	—	2	3	272	77	195	46	655
22—Haiti	—	1	5	442	266	176	43	593
23—Bahama Is.	—	—	1	30	9	21	6	53
24—Jamaica	—	—	1	80	5	75	18	212
25—Trinidad, Dominica & Grenada Is.	—	1	3	190	14	176	15	288
26—Curacao	—	—	1	65	3	62	—	325
27—Guadalupe & Martinique	—	—	2	214	87	127	23	385
28—Puerto Rico	—	—	2	369	81	288	31	847
Totals	1	6	23	2,352	765	1,587	255	5,766
Grand Totals	9	75	382	35,613	17,184	17,954	6,163	90,397

Statistics of Religious Brothers in Latin America are not available.

Table III — Religious Institutions

SOUTH AMERICA

Countries	Parishes	Churches	Schools	Male Students	Female Students	Total Students	Charitable Insti-tutions	Insti-tutional Residents
(1)	(2)	(3)	(4)	(5)	(6)	(7)	(8)	(9)
1—Argentina	1,345	4,489	998	54,063	192,593	246,656	577	74,676
2—Bolivia	366	1,765	337	12,416	13,370	25,996	36	4,078
3—Brazil	3,767	25,308	3,206	226,861	349,243	609,449	1,290	290,523
4—Chile	609	2,589	912	108,304	104,396	212,700	256	17,562
5—Colombia	1,295	2,817	4,272	136,702	211,402	355,099	768	237,673
6—Ecuador	474	1,521	465	41,725	53,846	98,927	155	14,940
7—Paraguay	148	414	121	10,735	11,039	23,274	41	3,154
8—Peru	893	4,656	324	36,393	54,990	95,885	94	18,092
9—Uruguay	153	435	207	23,441	31,589	55,030	44	16,859
10—Venezuela	506	1,073	272	23,082	34,247	57,329	117	9,959
11—Guianas	45	140	279	18,392	20,811	39,203	34	1,143
Totals	9,601	45,207	11,393	692,114	1,077,526	1,819,548	3,412	688,659

CENTRAL AMERICA AND MEXICO

Countries	Parishes	Churches	Schools	Male Students	Female Students	Total Students	Charitable Institutions	Institutional Residents
(1)	(2)	(3)	(4)	(5)	(6)	(7)	(8)	(9)
12—Costa Rica	93	576	46	3,119	4,404	7,523	22	3,716
13—El Salvador	136	654	82	7,597	11,698	19,495	24	4,158
14—Guatemala	188	1,174	72	5,130	9,200	14,330	10	20,000
15—Honduras	77	626	35	1,415	1,525	5,316	10	2,660
16—Br. Honduras	10	123	84	—	—	11,825	—	—
17—Nicaragua	96	352	74	7,857	8,798	16,655	19	2,083
18—Panama	79	193	26	4,442	5,066	9,508	8	506
19—Mexico	1,998	13,671	2,022	189,930	259,081	450,711	324	29,972
Totals	2,677	17,369	2,441	219,490	299,772	535,363	417	63,095

CARIBBEAN ISLANDS

Countries	Parishes	Churches	Schools	Male Students	Female Students	Total Students	Charitable Insti-tutions	Insti-tutional Residents
(1)	(2)	(3)	(4)	(5)	(6)	(7)	(8)	(9)
20—Cuba	212	799	339	28,066	33,004	61,070	81	97,355
21—Dominican Republic	108	624	61	5,996	9,424	15,420	24	4,081
22—Haiti	157	920	513	31,757	23,380	55,137	36	2,040
23—Bahama Is.	18	47	34	1,672	1,664	3,336	5	300
24—Jamaica	9	79	169	8,996	9,749	18,745	9	922
25—Trinidad, Dominica & Grenada Is.	91	230	260	32,947	32,528	84,996	9	910
26—Curacao	30	33	133	17,860	16,978	34,838	12	1,451
27—Guadalupe & Martinique	85	119	17	2,263	2,546	4,809	10	720
28—Puerto Rico	115	465	84	—	—	34,446	22	541
Totals	825	3,316	1,610	129,557	129,273	312,797	208	108,320
Grand Totals	13,103	65,892	15,444	1,041,161	1,506,571	2,667,708	4,037	860,074

Appendix 2

U.S. CATHOLIC MISSIONARIES IN LATIN AMERICA, JANUARY 1, 1958

SUMMARY

	South America	Middle America	West Indies	Total
Priests & Brothers	492	276	364	1132
Sisters	312	99	558	969
Lay Missionaries	3	17	6	26
Totals	807	392	928	2127

One third of the U.S. Catholic missionary personnel serving overseas is at work in Latin America. On January 1, 1958 there were 6,120 U.S. priests, Brothers, Sisters and lay missionaries overseas and of these 2,127 were stationed in South America, Middle America and the West Indies. In 1940 the same area was served by 489 U.S. missionaries.

The following country-by-country statistics, listed according to the religious institute supplying the personnel, is published through the courtesy of the Mission Secretariat, Washington, D.C.

The term Middle America as employed in the text of the book includes all of the political divisions between the United States and South America. In Appendix 2 the term Middle America includes only the mainland countries while the term West Indies is employed to cover the island world.

Most of the sending societies supplying personnel have more than one province in the United States. In the tables, the name of the city appearing after the name of the institute indicates the provincial seat of multi-province institutes or the institute motherhouse.

SOUTH AMERICA

ARGENTINA

Institutes of Men

Columban Fathers (S.S.C.) .... St. Columbans, Nebr.	1
Marian Fathers (M.I.C.) .... Chicago, Ill.	4
Passionists (C.P.) .... Union City, N.J.	2
Redemptorists (C.SS.R.) .... New York, N.Y.	1
Salesians (S.D.B.) .... New Rochelle, N.Y.	1
Total	9

Institutes of Women

Christian Charity Sisters .... Wilmette, Ill.	1
Notre Dame School Sisters .... Milwaukee, Wis.	1
St. Casimir Sisters .... Chicago, Ill.	5
Total	7

Summary for Argentina

Institutes of Men	9
Institutes of Women	7
Total	16

BOLIVIA

Institutes of Men

Dominicans (O.P.) .... Chicago, Ill.	6
Franciscans (O.F.M.) .... New York, N.Y.	15

Franciscans (O.F.M.) Oakland, Calif.	1
Franciscans (O.F.M.) St. Louis, Mo.	1
Maryknoll Fathers Maryknoll, N.Y.	68
Diocesan Clergy Chicago, Ill.	1
Diocesan Clergy La Crosse, Wis.	1
Diocesan Clergy St. Louis, Mo.	5
Total	98

Institutes of Women

Charity of St. Vincent de Paul Emmitsburg, Md.	9
Maryknoll Sisters Maryknoll, N.Y.	39
Total	48

Summary for Bolivia

Institutes of Men	98
Institutes of Women	48
Total	146

BRAZIL

Institutes of Men

Franciscans (O.F.M.) New York, N.Y.	41
Franciscans (O.F.M.) St. Louis, Mo.	28
Franciscans (O.F.M. Conv.) Syracuse, N.Y.	22
Franciscans (T.O.R.) Loretta, Pa.	3

Holy Cross Brothers (C.S.C.) Austin, Texas	6
Holy Cross Brothers (C.S.C.) Eastern Vice Province	1
Holy Cross Brothers (C.S.C.) South Bend, Ind.	2
Oblates of Mary Immaculate (O.M.I.) Washington, D.C.	18
Redemptorists (C.SS.R.) New York, N.Y.	59
Redemptorists (C.SS.R.) Oakland, Calif.	1
Redemptorists (C.SS.R.) St. Louis, Mo.	36
Total	217

Institutes of Women

Bernadine Sisters Villanova, Pa.	39
Felician Sisters Lodi, N.J.	3
Franciscan Sisters Pittsburgh, Pa.	6
Franciscan Sisters Third Order Regular Alleghany, N.Y.	8
Holy Cross Sisters Notre Dame, Ind.	9
Notre Dame School Sisters Milwaukee, Wis.	1
Precious Blood Sister Adorers Wichita, Kan.	8
Sacred Heart Society Albany, N.Y.	2
Sacred Heart of Mary Religious (R.S.H.M.) Tarrytown, N.Y.	1
Ursuline Nuns (Roman Union) Waterville, Me.	2
Total	79

Lay Missioners

Grail, The 2
Grailville, Loveland, Ohio

Summary for Brazil

Institutes of Men 217
Institutes of Women 79
Lay Missioners 2

Total 298

BRITISH GUIANA

Institutes of Women

Mercy of the Union Sisters 18
Washington, D.C.
Ursuline Nuns (Roman Union) 3
Kirkwood, Mo.
Ursuline Nuns (Roman Union) 2
New York, N.Y.
Ursuline Nuns (Roman Union) 1
Waterville, Me.

Total 24

CHILE

Institutes of Men

Carmelite Fathers (O. Carm.) 4
Chicago, Ill.
Divine Word Missionaries (S.V.D.) 4
Techny, Ill.
Holy Cross Fathers (C.S.C.) 13
South Bend, Ind.
Maryknoll Fathers (M.M.) 42
Maryknoll, N.Y.
Oblates of Mary Immaculate (O.M.I.) 1
Lowell, Mass.
Precious Blood Fathers (C.PP.S.) 20
Dayton, Ohio

Total 82

Institutes of Women

Christian Charity Sisters	2
Mendham, N.J.	
Christian Charity Sisters	2
Wilmette, Ill.	
Immaculate Heart of Mary Sister Servants ..	18
West Chester, Pa.	
Maryknoll Sisters	17
Maryknoll, N.Y.	
Sacred Heart Society (R.S.C.J.)	1
St. Louis, Mo.	
Total	40

Summary for Chile

Institutes of Men	82
Institutes of Women	40
Total	122

COLOMBIA

Institutes of Men

Maryknoll Fathers (M.M.)	1
Maryknoll, N.Y.	
Salvatorians (S.D.S.)	1
Milwaukee, Wis.	
Total	2

Institutes of Women

Daughters of Wisdom	2
Ozone Park, N.Y.	
Sacred Heart Society (R.S.C.J.)	1
St. Louis, Mo.	
Sacred Heart of Mary Religious (R.S.H.M.)	16
Tarrytown, N.Y.	
Salvatorian Sisters (S.D.S.)	2
Milwaukee, Wis.	
Servants of Mary	5
Kansas City, Kan.	
Total	26

Summary for Colombia

Institutes of Men	2
Institutes of Women	26
Total	28

ECUADOR

Institutes of Men

Salesians (S.D.B.) 1
New Rochelle, N.Y.

PARAGUAY

Institutes of Men

Redemptorists (C.SS.R.) 5
New York, N.Y.

PERU

Institutes of Men

Carmelite Fathers (O. Carm.) 4
Chicago, Ill.
Marianists (S.M.) 28
Kirkwood, Mo.
Maryknoll Fathers (M.M.) 43
Maryknoll, N.Y.
Salesians (S.D.B.) 1
New Rochelle, N.Y.
Diocesan Clergy 1
Milwaukee, Wis.
Diocesan Clergy 2
Portland, Ore.

Total 77

Institutes of Women

Franciscan Missionaries of Mary (F.M.M.) .. 2
New York, N.Y.
Immaculate Heart of Mary Sister Servants .. 38
West Chester, Pa.

Maryknoll Sisters 14
Maryknoll, N.Y.
Precious Blood Sisters 3
O'Fallon, Mo.
Sacred Heart Society (R.S.C.J.) 1
St. Louis, Mo.

Total 58

Summary for Peru

Institutes of Men 77
Institutes of Women 58

Total 135

URUGUAY

Institutes of Men

Salesians (S.D.B.) 1
New Rochelle, N.Y.

VENEZUELA

Institutes of Women

Medical Mission Sisters 25
Philadelphia, Pa.
Ursuline Nuns (Roman Union) 5
New York, N.Y.

Total 30

Lay Missioners

Not attached to any group 1

Summary for South America

Institutes of Men 492
Institutes of Women 312
Lay Missioners 3

Total 807

MIDDLE AMERICA

BRITISH HONDURAS

Institutes of Men

Jesuits (S.J.)	4
Chicago and Detroit	
Jesuits (S.J.)	12
Milwaukee, Wis.	
Jesuits (S.J.)	34
St. Louis, Mo.	
Total	50

Institutes of Women

Holy Family Sisters	3
New Orleans, La.	
Mercy of the Union Sisters	12
Washington, D.C.	
Total	15

Summary for British Honduras

Institutes of Men	50
Institutes of Women	15
Total	65

CANAL ZONE

Institutes of Men

Vincentians (C.M.)	14
Philadelphia, Pa.	

Institutes of Women

Franciscans	7
Amarillo, Texas	
Maryknoll Sisters	15
Maryknoll, N.Y.	
Total	22

Summary for Canal Zone

Institutes of Men	14
Institutes of Women	22
Total	36

COSTA RICA

Institutes of Men

Franciscans (O.F.M. Conv.) 25
Syracuse, N.Y.

Institutes of Women

Franciscan School Sisters 7
Milwaukee, Wis.

Summary for Costa Rica

Institutes of Men	25
Institutes of Women	7
Total	32

EL SALVADOR

Institutes of Men

Franciscans (O.F.M.) 3
New York, N.Y.
Salesians (S.D.B.) 1
New Rochelle, N.Y.

Total 4

GUATEMALA

Institutes of Men

Franciscans (O.F.M.) 8
New York, N.Y.
Maryknoll Fathers (M.M.) 33
Maryknoll, N.Y.

Total 41

Institutes of Women

Maryknoll Sisters 9
Maryknoll, N.Y.

Lay Missioners

Not attached to any group 1

Summary for Guatemala

Institutes of Men 41
Institutes of Women 9
Lay Missioners 1

Total 51

HONDURAS

Institutes of Men

Franciscans (O.F.M.) 23
New York, N.Y.
Jesuits (S.J.) 2
Milwaukee, Wis.
Jesuits (S.J.) 12
St. Louis, Mo.

Total 37

Institutes of Women

Franciscan School Sisters 5
Milwaukee, Wis.
Notre Dame School Sisters 4
St. Louis, Mo.

Total 9

Summary for Honduras

Institutes of Men 37
Institutes of Women 9

Total 46

MEXICO

Institutes of Men

Assumptionist Fathers (A.A.) New York, N.Y.	1
Benedictine Fathers (O.S.B.) Collegeville, Minn.	8
Maryknoll Fathers (M.M.) Maryknoll, N.Y.	25
Oblates of Mary Immaculate (O.M.I.) San Antonio, Texas	8
Oblates of Mary Immaculate (O.M.I.) Attached to non-U.S. Province	1
Passionists (C.P.) Union City, N.J.	2
Total	45

Institutes of Women

Maryknoll Sisters Maryknoll, N.Y.	9
Sacred Heart Religious (R.S.H.M.) Tarrytown, N.Y.	2
Sacred Heart Society Albany, N.Y.	1
Ursuline Nuns (Roman Union) New York, N.Y.	2
Total	14

Lay Missioners

AID Paterson, N.J.	4
Grail, The Grailville, Loveland, Ohio	1
Not attached to any group	11
Total	16

Summary for Mexico

Institutes of Men	45
Institutes of Women	14
Lay Missioners	16
Total	75

NICARAGUA

Institutes of Men

Capuchins (O.F.M. Cap.) Detroit, Mich.	19
Capuchins (O.F.M. Cap.) Providence, R.I.	8
Christian Brothers (F.S.C.) Beltsville, Md.	2
Christian Brothers (F.S.C.) Glencoe, Mo.	2
Christian Brothers (F.S.C.) Lafayette, La.	4
Christian Brothers (F.S.C.) New York and New England	4
Total	39

Institutes of Women

Carmelite Sisters Wauwatosa, Wis.	4
Maryknoll Sisters Maryknoll, N.Y.	8
St. Agnes Sisters Fond du Lac, Wis.	5
Total	17

Summary for Nicaragua

Institutes of Men	39
Institutes of Women	17
Total	56

PANAMA

Institutes of Men

Claretian Missionaries (C.M.F.) 1
Chicago, Ill.
Claretian Missionaries (C.M.F.) 2
Los Angeles, Calif.
Vincentians (C.M.) 18
Philadelphia, Pa.

Total 21

Institutes of Women

Franciscan Sisters 2
Amarillo, Texas
Maryknoll Sisters 3
Maryknoll, N.Y.
Servants of Mary 1
Kansas City, Mo.

Total 6

Summary for Panama

Institutes of Men 21
Institutes of Women 6

Total 27

Summary for Middle America

Institutes of Men 276
Institutes of Women 99
Lay Missioners 17

Total 392

WEST INDIES

BAHAMA ISLANDS

Institutes of Men

Benedictine Fathers (O.S.B.) 23
Collegeville, Minn.

Institutes of Women

Charity of St. Vincent de Paul 25
New York, N.Y.
Dominican Sisters 5
Adrian, Mich.

Total 30

Lay Missioners

Not attached to any group 2

Summary for Bahama Islands

Institutes of Men 23
Institutes of Women 30
Lay Missioners 2

Total 55

BARBADOS

Institutes of Women

Ursuline Nuns (Roman Union) 1
Kirkwood, Mo.

CUBA

Institutes of Men

Augustinian Fathers (O.S.A.) .... 1[illegible]
Villanova, Pa.

Institutes of Women

Dominican Sisters St. Catherine de Ricci ... 24
Albany, N.Y.
Most Blessed Trinity Missionary Servants .. 4
Philadelphia, Pa.
Providence Oblate Sisters 1
Baltimore, Md.
Ursuline Nuns (Roman Union) 1
New York, N.Y.

Total 30

Summary for Cuba

Institutes of Men	12
Institutes of Women	30
Total	42

DOMINICAN REPUBLIC

Institutes of Men

Recollect Augustinian Fathers (O.R.S.A.) Omaha, Nebr.	4
Redemptorists (C.SS.R.) New York, N.Y.	10
Salesians (S.D.B.) New Rochelle, N.Y.	1
Scheut Fathers (C.I.C.M.) Arlington, Va.	1
Total	16

Institutes of Women

Dominican Sisters (O.P.) Adrian, Mich.	20

Summary for Dominican Republic

Institutes of Men	16
Institutes of Women	20
Total	36

HAITI

Institutes of Men

Oblates of Mary Immaculate (O.M.I.) Lowell, Mass.	26
Salesians (S.D.B.) New Rochelle, N.Y.	1
Total	27

Institutes of Women

Daughters of Wisdom Ozone Park, N.Y.	3
Holy Cross and Seven Dolors Sisters Manchester, N.H.	2
St. Anne Sisters (S.S.A.) Marlboro, Mass.	2
Total	7

Summary for Haiti

Institutes of Men	27
Institutes of Women	7
Total	34

JAMAICA

Institutes of Men

Jesuits (S.J.) Baltimore, Md.	2
Jesuits (S.J.) Boston, Mass.	71
Jesuits (S.J.) New York, N.Y.	1
Passionists (C.P.) Union City, N.J.	10
Total	84

Institutes of Women

Dominicans St. Dominic of Blauvelt Blauvelt, N.Y.	10
Franciscan Third Order Sisters Alleghany, N.Y.	21
Marist Missionary Sisters Framingham Centre, Mass.	8
Mercy of the Union Sisters Washington, D.C.	11
Total	50

Lay Missioners

AID 2
Paterson, N.J.
Not attached to any group 2

Total 4

Summary for Jamaica

Institutes of Men 84
Institutes of Women 50
Lay Missioners 4

Total 138

LEEWARD ISLANDS

Institutes of Men

Irish Christian Brothers (F.S.C.H.) 7
New Rochelle, N.Y.

Institutes of Women

Canonesses of St. Augustine 9
New York, N.Y.

Summary for Leeward Islands

Institutes of Men 7
Institutes of Women 9

Total 16

PUERTO RICO

Institutes of Men

Benedictines (O.S.B.) 11
Collegeville, Minn.
Capuchins (O.F.M. Cap.) 30
Pittsburgh, Pa.
Franciscans (O.F.M.) 5
New York, N.Y.
Holy Ghost Fathers (C.S.Sp.) 30
Washington, D.C.

Marianists (S.M.)	29
Dayton, Ohio	
Mercy Fathers (S.P.M.)	2
Brooklyn, N.Y.	
Redemptorists (C.SS.R.)	69
New York, N.Y.	
Trinitarians (M.S.SS.T.)	3
Silver Springs, Md.	
Diocesan Clergy	1
Bridgeport, Conn.	
Diocesan Clergy	1
Hartford, Conn.	
Diocesan Clergy	3
New York, N.Y.	
Diocesan Clergy	2
Philadelphia, Pa.	
Total	186

Institutes of Women

Benedictine Sisters of Pontical Jurisdiction	5
St. Joseph, Minn.	
Charity of St. Vincent de Paul	19
Normandy, Mo.	
Divine Providence Sisters	18
Allison Park, Pa.	
Dominicans St. Catherine of Sienna	14
St. Catherine, Ky.	
Dominican Sisters	24
Adrian, Mich.	
Dominican Sisters	80
Amityville, N.Y.	
Franciscan Sisters	6
Glen Riddle, Pa.	
Franciscan Sisters	25
Pittsburgh, Pa.	
Holy Family of Nazareth Sisters	11
Philadelphia, Pa.	
Mercy Sisters	29
Pittsburgh, Pa.	

Mission Helpers of the Sacred Heart 7
Towson, Md.
Most Blessed Trinity Missionary Servants .. 34
Philadelphia, Pa.
Notre Dame School Sisters 56
Wilton, Conn.
Sacred Heart Society 1
Albany, N.Y.
St. Joseph Sisters 56
Brentwood, N.Y.

Total 385

Summary for Puerto Rico

Institutes of Men 186
Institutes of Women 385

Total 571

TRINIDAD

Institutes of Women

Carmelites, Corpus Christi (O. Carm.) 3
Middletown, N.Y.

VIRGIN ISLANDS

Institutes of Men

Redemptorists (C.SS.R.) 9
New York, N.Y.

Institutes of Women

Canonesses of St. Augustine 12
New York, N.Y.
Charity of St. Elizabeth Sisters 11
Convent, N.J.

Total 23

Summary for Virgin Islands

Institutes of Men	9
Institutes of Women	23
Total	32

Summary for West Indies

Institutes of Men	364
Institutes of Women	558
Lay Missioners	6
Total	928

Appendix 3

PROTESTANTS IN LATIN AMERICA, 1957

As compiled by Dr. Frank W. Price, Missionary Research Library, New York City

I South America

Argentina	364,000
Bolivia	29,000
Brazil	1,776,000
Chile	370,000
Colombia	46,000
Ecuador	5,000
Paraguay	23,000
Peru	73,000
Uruguay	10,000
Venezuela	18,000
South America Total	2,714,000

II Middle America

Costa Rica	11,000
Cuba	216,000
Dominican Republic	23,000
El Salvador	29,000
Guatemala	143,000
Haiti	313,000
Honduras	22,000
Mexico	911,000
Nicaragua	38,000

Panama	48,000
Puerto Rico	147,000
West Indies Federation	
Jamaica	654,000
Trinidad	222,000
Other islands	311,000
Middle America Total	3,088,000

III Colonial Latin America

Bahamas and Virgins	57,000
Bermuda	19,000
British Honduras	27,000
Falklands	1,500
Guianas, Fr. & Neth., Antilles	225,000
Colonial Total	329,500
Latin America Total	6,131,500

GLOSSARY OF LATIN AMERICAN TERMS FOUND IN THE TEXT

Aldea — Subdivision of a civil community. In early colonial days the term used to describe a settlement where Indians were instructed in the faith and trained to Christian living. See also *Doctrina* and *Reduction*. Today an aldea is a small village.

Alcalde rezador — Leading prayer minister, a Spanish term taken over by Mayan practicants of the *costumbre* (q.v.) Guatemala.

Altiplano — High plateau country, usually above 10,000 feet. Term often includes entire area with its mountain ranges.

Anaconda — A huge constrictor snake 20 to 40 feet long, held in great dread in lowland tropical America.

APRA — Alianza Popular Revolucionaria Americana (American Popular Revolutionary Alliance), a strong political party in Peru.

Arroyo — Inlet of a river, sometimes fed by a stream.

ASICH — Acción Sindical y Economica Chilena, a Catholic labor and socio-economic movement in Chile.

Auxiliar inmediato — Term designating local aid, or monitor, or leader of a class of the Radio Schools of Sutatenza, Colombia.

Bandeirantes — Name in Brazil for the pioneer explorers among the Paulistas of the Sao Paulo region who opened up the plains country, subduing or pushing back the Indians. Modern Brazilian term for boy scouts.

Barraca — A hamlet or plantation center.

Barracone — Cheap lodging house of one-room apartments built along a corridor with toilet and water spigot at corridor's end.

Branco — A white person in Brazil.

Brete — Brazilian for a device employed for gripping cattle and holding them motionless for branding or castrating.

Buenas tardes — "Good afternoon" or "Good evening."

Caboclo — A person of American Indian physical type in Brazil. See also *Indio.*

Cafeçita — Strong concentrate of coffee served in a demi-tasse; Brazilian.

Campesino — Field worker; hence a general term for a plantation or rural laborer.

Campo — Literally, field; by extension, countryside or country.

Candomble (Kan-dóm-blay) — A folk ceremony compounded by African slaves representing a mixture of West African animistic rites and Catholic devotions. It now prevails in the Bahia area, Brazil. Sometimes Indian and African gods are combined in a caboclo candomble. There is a relationship between candomble in Brazil and voodoo in Haiti.

Capataz — The foreman of a working crew or plantation community in Spanish-language countries.

Capitaz — Foreman on landed estates in Brazil.

Casa grande — The owner's home on a Latin American estate.

Carioca — Nickname for a resident of Rio de Janeiro.

Casa de vecindad — Multi-storied cheap lodging house with one-room apartments around patio on ground floor and off interior porches on other floors.

Charque — Term in Brazil for semi-cured beef which thus preserved can be stored for months.

Costumbre (kos-toom-bray) — Mayan religious practices in Guatemala. See Chapter, "The Mayan without His Priest."

Conquista espiritual — Mission work. Literally, "Spiritual conquest." Arrangement by the Spanish government with a religious community (e.g., Jesuits in Paraguay Reductions), granting them civil as well as spiritual authority for the building of a complete Christian society.

Consultorio — Medical clinic which serves as out-station for social medical work.

Conventillo	Simple residence consisting of rows of small rooms for emigrant hacienda workers without families.
CREFAL	Regional Center for Fundamental Education in Latin America. (Centro Regional de Educacion Fundamental America Latina)
Creole	Person of European blood born in Latin America, as distinct from the Peninsular, a person of European blood born in Spain or Portugal.
Cruzeiro	The basic unit of coinage in Brazil.
Cumbre	Mountain pass.
Doctrina	Community organization resembling modern closed catechumenate in which Indians new in the faith were instructed and trained to Christian living. See also *Aldea* and *Reduction.*
Estancia	Large ranch or landed estate. Term prevalent in Argentina. See *Fazenda, Fundo, Hacienda.*
Estanciero	Owner of an estancia; refers principally to Argentina. See *Fazendeiro, Hacendado, Patrón.*
Estrada	The rubber-tree route through the jungle for a normal day's collection of sap by the seringhero.
Favela	A squatter settlement in Brazil, particularly in Rio de Janeiro.
Fazenda	Portuguese for hacienda, a large landed estate devoted to cattle raising or agriculture. Term prevalent in Brazil. See *Hacienda, Estancia, Fundo.*
Fazendeiro	Owner of a fazenda. See also *Estanciero, Hacendado, Patrón.*
Fervorino	A sermon notable for its warm appeal based on religious sentiment rather than on doctrinal content.
Friary	Residence or convent of members of religious communities known as friars.
Fundo	Plantation for general farming, cattle raising or wine producing. Term prevalent in Chile. See also *Fazenda, Hacienda, Estancia.*

Gaucho	Term for cowboy distinctive of Plate River country. Argentina, Uruguay and southern provinces of Brazil. Gauchos developed distinctive culture still figuring in Argentine literature and music.
Giro	The circuit or route followed by the missionary in his periodic journeys through rural areas.
Hacendado	Owner of a hacienda or large landed estate. See *Fazendeiro, Estanciero, Patrón.*
Hacienda	Large landed estate. See *Fazenda, Estancia, Fundo.*
Homem de cor	(man of color) Designation for an individual Negro in Brazil. See Negro.
Indio	The tribal Indian of the interior of Brazil. Not accepted in Brazil as term for evolved Indian. See *Caboclo.*
Inquilino	Tenant worker on cattle-raising or wine producing plantations in Chile.
Jangada	Small seagoing raft of peeled logs held together by pegs, with centerboard, sail and steering oar, originated by Tupi Indians along Brazilian coast.
Llameador	The miner who puts the match to the explosion powder.
Ladino	Term in Guatemala for a non-Indian member of the population other than pure white.
Latifundismo	The social problem created by the prevalence of large landed estates.
Latifundista	Owner of a large landed property.
Mato Grosso	Literally, "Great Forest," a province of western Brazil possessing forest areas but also large expanses of open savannah country.
Milpa	Corn patch or small farm, Yucatan.
Milpero	An operator of a *milpa,* a small farm in Yucatan.
Mulatto	Person of mixed Negro and white blood
Negro	Used in Brazil to designate the Negro race; not accepted as term for individual. See *Homem de cor.*

Pantanal	Portuguese for flood plain. Designation for numerous lowland areas in Mato Grosso and neighboring provinces, Brazil.
Patrón	Owner of a hacienda or other enterprise; popularly, one's "boss."
Patronato	The sum of the Holy See's grants and concessions to the new republics in Latin America. See *Real Patronato.*
Paulista	Historically, a resident in Sao Paulo area of Brazil, hardy Portuguese with heavy strain of Indian blood, celebrated as an enterprising pioneer and slave trader. Today, a citizen of the city or province of Sao Paulo.
Peninsular	Person of European blood born in Spain or Portugal as distinct from a Creole, one of European blood born in Latin America.
Peón	A peasant worker on a landed estate. Term prevalent in Mexico.
Porteño	Person who lives in Buenos Aires, Argentina.
Pucarara	A snake of the rattler family but without a rattle, thick-bodied and six to seven feet long, among the deadliest for its poison in tropical America.
Real Patronato	Literally the "royal patronage," a term for the Holy See's grants and concessions to the Spanish Crown for the government of the Church in Latin America.
Reduction	An Indian community under the direction of a missionary group in which wandering tribes have been "reduced" to settled life and are under training in Christian living. See Paraguay Reductions (index).
Retiro	Section of a cattle range in Brazil.
Rezador	A lay reciter of prayers in Brazil; a species of neighborhood catechist.
Roto	Low income worker in Chilean urban areas; also a "displaced" person or sometimes a tramp.
Santo (often santito)	Literally saint. Term in Spanish and Portuguese countries for holy card.
Seringhero	Spanish for collector of wild rubber from jungle trees.

Seringueiro	Portuguese for wild rubber collector.
Sertao	The undeveloped back country of interior Brazil, usually poorly watered, used for sustenance farming and raising cattle.
Solar	Cheap lodging built as a hollow square with single-room apartments around a patio. (Cuba).
Sublevado	Revolutionary or rebel.
Tigre	The popular name for the jaguar or puma in wilder areas of Latin America.

Index